Children's
Emotions and Moods
Developmental Theory and Measurement

Children's
Emotions and Moods

Developmental Theory and Measurement

WITHDRAWI

Michael Lewis
and
Linda Michalson

University of Medicine and Dentistry
Rutgers Medical School
New Brunswick, New Jersey

Plenum Press • New York and London

Library of Congress Cataloging in Publication Data

Lewis, Michael, 1937 Jan. 10–
  Children's emotions and moods.

  Bibliography: p.
  Includes index.
  1. Emotions in children. 2. Emotions in children—Testing. I. Michalson, Linda. II. Ti-
tle. [DNLM: 1. Emotions—In infancy and childhood. WS 105.5.E5 L675c]
BT723.E6L48 1983   155.4.'12   83-2456
ISBN 0-306-41209-8

For Benjamin and Felicia
Through loving,
you have taught me to observe more closely
the smiles of joy and the tears of sorrow.

M. L.

For D.

L. M.

Preface

No one would deny the proposition that in order to understand human behavior and development, one must understand "feelings." The interest in emotions is enduring. Yet, within the discipline of psychology, the study of feelings and emotions has been somewhat less than respectable, a stepchild to the fields of cognitive science and psycholinguistics. Perusal of the language acquisition literature reveals a greater concern among psychologists for the acquisition of prepositions than for terms that convey feelings. Without question, issues related to emotion, its development, and its measurement have been neglected in the research literature until quite recently.

From a developmental perspective, Piaget and his followers have articulated a complex theory of transition and change in intellectual behavior. Nearly a century ago, Freud proposed an elaborate theory of personality development in which some aspects of emotional growth were considered. We await the construction of a comprehensive theory of emotional development. Recognizing such a need, we set out over a decade ago to solve what seemed to be a relatively simple problem: By observing young children, could one successfully classify children in terms of individual differences on emotional dimensions such as happiness, fear, and anger?

The task appeared easy. One could send graduate students into a preschool and ask them to observe children for several days, after which they would rank the children in terms of differences on various emotional dimensions. Not surprisingly, graduate students found that the task was reasonable, one that they could successfully perform. The students achieved high observer reliability, and their rankings of the children seemed to correspond to simple behavioral checklists. This outcome suggested to us that it was feasible to rank children on dimensions other than cognitive differences. No longer did investigators have to be limited to evaluating children, teachers, or programs solely in terms of intellectual variables.

Our work in developing a formal assessment instrument that could be used in a systematic way to measure individual differences in children on emotional dimensions was at first slow. We lacked a theory of emotional development to point the way. It became obvious that our task involved more than measuring children's behaviors that we thought reflected emotional differences. We needed a theoretical structure on which to hang our behavioral observations and to provide insight into how the particular behaviors fit into the larger scheme.

In 1978 Lewis and Rosenblum proposed the idea of viewing emotion in terms of a structural analysis. This analysis divided emotion into components and permitted the study of each component individually. Until this time, the study of emotional development was largely restricted to the study of a single component. Some investigators studied the development of emotional expressions (e.g., smiling), some studied the development of emotional states (e.g., physiological changes), and others studied the development of emotional experiences (e.g., the subjective feelings of emotion). These different approaches to the study of emotion can best be organized into a coherent frame of reference through a structural analysis of emotion. Our work proceeded more rapidly as we began to recognize the ways in which simple observations of children's behaviors might fit into the larger scheme of emotional development.

The present volume is the culmination of our efforts to outline a theory of emotional development and to construct an assessment instrument for measuring children's emotions. Two major themes are reflected in the volume. The first, a theoretical account of emotion and emotional development, is the focus of Chapters 1 through 7. The second, the measurement of individual differences, is the focus of Chapters 8 through 12.

As we have made our journey, the field itself, as is often the case, has recognized the importance of this topic. Thus, along the way, many new and exciting findings have appeared, and we have had the opportunity to use many of them in formulating our thoughts. The Foundation of Child Development, under the direction of Orville Brim, supported a Social Science Research Council Committee on Social-Emotional Development. Michael Lewis had the privilege of serving on this committee and of hearing some of the major issues in the study of emotion addressed.

We have moved toward the writing of this volume in stages. In 1978, *The Development of Affect* (edited by M. Lewis and L. Rosenblum) and, in 1979, *Social Cognition and the Acquisition of Self* (by

M. Lewis and J. Brooks-Gunn) laid the groundwork for the theory proposed in the current volume. Finally, *The Socialization of Emotion* (edited by M. Lewis and C. Saarni, in press) will present additional data on some of the aspects of the developmental theory proposed here.

We view the current volume as one step toward the articulation of a comprehensive theory of emotional development. Before this can happen, several steps are necessary. First, psychologists must reify emotional development much as they have cognitive development. This must occur despite the errors involved in reification. The hope is that through reification, the study of emotional development may be legitimized.

Second, emotion must be recognized as being a complex phenomenon that requires a structural analysis. By reducing emotion to components of a manageable size and scope, psychologists can begin to understand emotion and to articulate models of its development. It would be foolish to regard cognitive development as a single entity. Thus, the study of cognitive development is reduced to the study of its components, including memory, perception, and language. The same approach needs to be taken in studying emotional development.

Third, measurement systems must be devised in order that the study of emotion may proceed from a sound empirical basis. This is not to imply that empirical tools alone are sufficient for understanding emotion. Emotions are, after all, private acts. As such, active participation by the subject is necessary for understanding the phenomenon. Perhaps we will witness eventually the rise of a behavioral phenomenology.

It has been in the measurement of emotion that the most serious advances in the study of emotion have been made. Most investigators, however, have focused on the measurement of a single component, emotional expression, and on specific features, primarily the face. Facial measurement systems are highly sophisticated and require hours of precise analysis of changes in the facial musculature. A broader measurement system, one that will permit the study of emotion under more naturalistic conditions, is necessary. Moreover, such a measurement system should advance the study of individual differences in emotion, a topic of great importance.

All three issues are considered in this volume. It is our wish that with its publication, we will have moved one step closer to a better understanding of the development of children's emotions and moods.

MICHAEL LEWIS
LINDA MICHALSON

Princeton, New Jersey

Acknowledgments

We would like to express our appreciation to the people who provided assistance and support in conducting the research reported in this volume and in preparing the manuscript. Susan Painter helped collect and code the data; Jim Rosso and Donna Hiromura prepared the illustrations. Donald Rock, Al Rogers, Larry Stricker, and John Jaskir provided statistical expertise in the data analysis phase of the research. A very special thank you goes to Laura Van Horn and Joanne Branham, who organized and typed many drafts of these chapters.

Sections of Chapter 3 will appear in *Emotion, Cognition, and Behavior*, edited by C. E. Izard, J. Kagan, and R. B. Zajonc (New York: Cambridge University Press, in press). Portions of Chapter 5 appear in "From Emotional State to Emotional Expression" by Michael Lewis and Linda Michalson. This paper was presented at the Symposium on Human Development from the Perspective of Person and Environment Interactions, University of Stockholm, Stockholm, Sweden, June 1982, and will appear in *Personality Development as Person-Environment Interaction*, edited by D. Magnusson and V. L. Allen (New York: Academic Press, in press). Portions of Chapters 6 and 7 appear in a chapter by Michael Lewis and Linda Michalson, "The Socialization of Emotions," in T. Field and A. Fogel (Eds.), *Emotion and Early Interaction* (Hillsdale, N.J.: Erlbaum, 1982). Portions of Chapter 8 appear in a chapter by Michael Lewis and Linda Michalson, "The Measurement of Emotional State" in C. E. Izard (Ed.), *Measuring Emotions in Infants and Children* (New York: Cambridge University Press, 1982). The data reported in Chapters 9 through 12 were collected as part of Linda Michalson's doctoral dissertation at the New School for Social Research.

Support for the research was generously provided by grants from the U.S. Office of Child Development and from the Carnegie Corporation. We are very grateful to Barbara Finberg of the Carnegie Corporation for supporting the final year of data collection. The writing of the manuscript was funded in part by a grant from the Foundation of Child Development. Orville Brim deserves special acknowledgment for his continued faith in the value of our effort and for his belief that emotions and emotional development constitute an important aspect of human life.

Finally, our deepest appreciation goes to the children and day-care centers who participated in our study. In order to preserve the anonymity they requested, we will not thank them by name, but without their cooperation we could not have accomplished our research aims.

Contents

1

Why Study Emotion?

This is a volume about emotions, moods, and their development. We will spend considerable time in Chapter 2 defining terms, but for the time being, let us consider "feelings" to be those activities that are often distinguished from "thinking." Emotions are a subset of feelings, and moods are the enduring aspects of emotions. In attempts to apply categorical labels to human behaviors, labels such as *cognitive, affective,* and *emotional* are often more confusing than clarifying. Thus, while we try in this chapter to set the stage for the study of emotion and mood, the terms *emotion* and *affect* may be used interchangeably.

We will not avoid the topic of cognition or the role it plays with emotions in affecting the course of development. Rather, if we are at all successful, we will have argued convincingly that both feeling and thinking are the natural contents of private acts experienced by every individual. Cognition and emotion should not be regarded as separate and independent acts, however, but as interactive components in a rich structure of internal events. Cognition and emotion are interwoven, like individual themes of a fugue. The development of these private acts, along with the development of social behavior, is the basic concern of caregivers and children in the opening years of life.

The set of specific problems that constitute the focus of this volume grew out of a series of observations of infants and young children. The nature of these issues can best be captured by referring back to these observations. Our discussion, then, begins with two examples of the phenomenon that we have attempted to understand and measure.

Rosie, a house guest for several days, is speaking about her host's two children. She remarks that the two children are quite different: the first appears to be sociable, smiles often, always stays near adults, and has much to say to them. Rosie states, "I am surprised at how friendly and interested your daughter Ellen is in meeting new people. Your son is so shy and seems to be afraid. Paul never smiles and seems to avoid me. Why, Paul never even looks at me!"

The second example takes place in a day-care center. The particular classroom being observed contains sixteen 18- to 24-month-old children:

Betty K., a student at the local college, has just finished spending one week observing the children in the room. During a staff discussion with three teachers, she observes, "Tommy is not like the other children—he's so clever and competent. He plays by himself for hours, and when he really gets into something he doesn't give up! His cousin Terence, on the other hand, is always angry, hits other children, doesn't listen to or obey me, and kicks objects around on the floor. I wonder what's going on in their home?" The teachers do not know, but they agree with Betty K. that these children certainly are not alike.

What is one to make of the house guest's comments or the student teacher's observations? Our analysis revealed that at least three aspects of the observers' remarks warrant further consideration. First, both Rosie and Betty K. are talking about *emotional* rather than cognitive behavior. While Betty K. makes reference to Tommy's cleverness, a term usually reserved for a cognitive description, her intention is to focus on what she sees as Tommy's competence, his feelings of control and self-esteem. Rosie, on the other hand, is clearly talking about feelings. In general, the observed differences in the children have centered on their feelings or emotions.

As will be discussed in more detail later, the interpretation of emotional behavior (indeed, of any behavior) is usually predicated on a behavior-by-situation analysis. For example, Rosie noticed particular behaviors, such as facial expressions including smiling and gaze aversion and postural activities, that occurred in response to particular events, such as unfamiliar situations and people. Although studying the children in a nursery-school setting rather than in a home, Betty K. also embedded her observations in a behavior-by-situation analysis. Tommy's notable behaviors were solitary play in a structured play situation and perseverance under frustration, while Terence's salient actions included hitting, kicking, and disobedience in a variety of settings that involved many people. In both examples, the focal behaviors were restricted in two senses. First, they were associated with feelings rather than cognitions. Second, the observations were anchored to specific situations or sets of situations.

The second point to be made from the examples is that both Rosie and Betty K. seemed to be talking about emotional behavior that was enduring. Their observations pertained to behaviors that occurred in particular situations from which an emotional state was inferred. However, rather than talking about the momentary occurrence of a single emotional state, the observers referred to characteristics of the children that might apply across many different situations. While Rosie's observations were restricted to a small set of different situations in the home of a friend, Betty K.'s observations of children in day care gave her an opportunity to watch children in a large number of diverse situations. It was in that context that Terence's aggressive nature became obvious, since the same general type of behavior (e.g., hitting, kicking, and disobeying) was seen in multiple situations.

The remarks of both Rosie and Betty K., therefore, alluded to enduring attributes of the children rather than to transient emotional states. Such observations, which attribute to individuals consistent and long-term rather than momentary emotional states, might be regarded as observations of moods or, as others have labeled them, personality characteristics. The distinction is between a single observation, such as "Terence hit a child who tried to take away his toy," and a general observation, such as "Terence will probably hit any child who tries to take away his toy."

There are two ways to regard this tendency to react in a consistent manner to many situations. On the one hand, it may be the result of a predisposition to feel a certain way in response to a class of similar events. Or it may be a function of a preexisting state that is relatively independent of the present class of events. In other words, the distinction is between "he is easily made angry" and "he is always angry." It is the difference between (1) a trait-by-situation interaction and (2) a trait.

The issues associated with each position are discussed later. For now, let us just say that most studies of feelings and emotions have focused on the elicitation of one emotion or a set of emotions in response to a highly defined single situation. Little attention has been given to individual differences in emotional expression, and even less attention has been paid to the enduring aspects of emotional behavior across diverse situations, the phenomenon we call *mood*. Both topics are of central concern to this volume. The problem of how to measure individual differences in emotions and moods has been the primary focus of our research.

The third point that emerges from the examples stresses *individual differences* in the children. Rosie's observations of two siblings and Betty K.'s observations of the nursery school class make us aware of more than the manner in which different children express emotions in particular contexts. Rather, our interest is drawn to differences in the amount or degree of particular emotions expressed by different children over time. In the examples, what is important are individual differences in the amount of sociability expressed by the siblings and differences in the degrees of competence and anger exhibited by the nursery-school children. Whatever set of situations observers use, it is apparent that they draw conclusions about the emotions or moods of other persons from their observations of behaviors in context. Moreover, they typically have little difficulty in describing differences in the children they are asked to observe based on differences in the levels of emotion displayed. For instance, when given the task of ranking a small group of children on happiness, anger, sociability, or fear, students, even at the undergraduate level, show a rather high degree of consistency in their ratings. When these students are asked about their judgments, they often cite key emotional behaviors that they have observed either across a wide variety of situations or over time. For example, hitting, yelling, and kicking are some of the behaviors that indicate anger, whereas a behavior that indicates sociability might be the amount of time a child spends in proximity to another person. (Since this behavior may also reflect fear, one must consider both the nature of the situation in which it is expressed and concurrent behaviors.) In short, this consistency among student observers indicates not only that the task is reasonable (they understand what we want them to do), but also that there is some general agreement among people in terms of their ability to rate individual children based on differences in children's levels of emotional reactions.

In discussing these examples, we have not addressed several issues important to the study of emotion. For instance, missing from the discussion of individual differences is the critical issue of age differences. Clearly, age differences in the experience or expression of emotions can be attributed to many factors, including differences in (1) the capacity of events to elicit a particular emotion; (2) the physical abilities of children to express an emotion through a particular behavior; and (3) the degree of cognitive sophistication available to produce and experience the emotion. For example, a mother who puts on glasses or a wig may elicit crying in younger children (indicative of wariness or fear) but laughter in older ones. Here, the difference in the emotional reaction is probably not due to a difference in the children's physical abilities to produce the expression (younger children do laugh and certainly older children cry) but is a function of the capacity of the situation to evoke the same emotion across age. In other words, this particular event may produce apprehension in younger children, but it does not have the same disturbing effect on older children. Perhaps because of a more developed cognitive system, older children are likely to respond with laughter and delight to the same event that causes younger children to cry.

Finally, some differences in the experience of certain emotions may depend entirely on cognitive maturity. For example, one would not expect young infants to experience guilt or shame, since both of these emotions require the recognition that one's own behavior violates a standard; the perception of the violation cannot occur until the standard is learned or created. Although facial *expressions* resembling guilt or shame have been observed in young infants (Izard, 1979b; Izard, Huebner, Risser, McGinnes, & Dougherty, 1980; Pannabecker, Emde, Johnson, Stenberg, & Davis, 1980), it is unlikely that these expressions are linked to or reflect emotional *experiences* of guilt or shame until the prerequisite cognitive schemata have developed (see Chapter 5).

Nor did we discuss in our opening examples the difference between emotional and cognitive states. In the examples, feeling and thinking activities tended to be separated into two mutually exclusive domains. As was indicated earlier, however, the distinction between emotional and cognitive behaviors does not reflect an insensitivity to the connections between them but is intended to force us to focus our attention on the emotional instead of the cognitive quality of the behavior. In fact, research has shown that emotional expressions, especially facial expressions, are often good indicators of specific cognitive attainments (Charlesworth, 1969; Ramsay & Campos, 1978). For instance, in her analysis of the responses that Piaget used to characterize an infant's cognitive structures, Haviland (1976) showed us that Piaget himself relied on behaviors that reflect emotions such as interest, surprise, and joy:

> Lucienne sees Piaget at the extreme left of her visual field and smiles vaguely; she then looks away but constantly returns to the place in which she sees him and dwells on it. If the infant had merely turned her head with a vacant gaze and no facial mobility, Piaget probably would have found it difficult to say that she recognized him or was "bringing to himself [sic] the image of his [sic] desires." (p. 360)

In short, looking at or attending to was insufficient evidence for Piaget that Lucienne recognized her father. What was required was a facial expression of recognition that included looking plus something else. This "something else" appeared to be interest and pleasure, expressions that are more emotional than a mere "vacant stare."

Surprise or astonishment is another emotional variable often used to assess cognitive ability. For instance, Charlesworth (1969) used surprise at the disappearance of an object to judge the infant's understanding of object permanence. Piaget also used surprise:

> When Jacqueline is watching Piaget's watch, he drops it; it falls too fast for Jacqueline to follow the trajectory, or so Piaget suggests, so that she does not follow the movement and then she "looks at [Piaget's] empty hand with surprise" (p. 16). Here, it is the surprise that indicates to Piaget that the child thought she had control over the watch and was surprised when it disappeared without any behavior change on her part. (Haviland, 1976, p. 361)

In a similar fashion, the emotions of curiosity and anger can be used to measure understanding or knowledge, and examples are to be found throughout Piaget's descriptions of his experiments with his children (Piaget, 1954). It should be clear from these illustrations that the inferences drawn about children's intellectual ability are closely tied to the observations of classes of their behavior that include motor and emotional aspects. Without either set of behaviors, it would be more difficult to deduce which mental structures are available to a young child, especially during the prelinguistic stage of development.

The reciprocal roles of cognition in emotion and emotion in cognition are topics of recent interest (Lazarus, 1982; Lewis, Sullivan, & Michalson, in press; Zajonc, 1980) and will reappear in Chapters 3 through 7. The need to perceive similarities and differences, to make comparisons, and to have a plan are all cognitive activities that are part of any emotional sequence. Whether their role is chiefly in the elicitation of feelings, in which case an emotional state is dependent on but not necessarily made up of a cognition, or in the perception or evaluation of one's own or another's feeling, or even in the essence of the emotional state itself remains open to question.

The measurement of emotional behavior is another issue that we have passed over rather quickly. Since the end of the nineteenth century, scientists have measured emotions primarily in terms of either facial or physiological changes. In certain circumstances, phenomenology, the subjective report of personal experiences, has also been a source of data on emotions. In our examples, we intentionally avoided mentioning the physiological aspects of emotions, since the everyday experiences of individuals do not afford an opportunity to observe many physiological responses to environmental events. Changes in facial behaviors, on the other hand, are widely used in daily interactions to recognize emotional states of others, as are changes in vocal, postural, and locomotive activities. In the everyday expressions of emotions, these categories receive the most attention (Argyle, 1975).

We have not fully addressed these issues because we chose to emphasize the emotional aspects of behavior, their enduring quality, and the notion of individual differences in the intensity of their expression. However, no satisfactory theory of emotional development or measurement system can avoid such topics. Consequently, each of these themes is discussed in later chapters.

Our observations have suggested that people share a common core of experience and knowledge about emotions and moods. It therefore seemed that a systematic investigation of individual differences in enduring emotional states, an investigation conducted outside the experimental laboratory, would be a reasonable task. The various stages and consequences of such an investigation are described in this volume, the focus of which is the articulation of a theory of emotional development and the construction and testing of an instrument with the ability to measure individual differences in children's emotional states or moods.

Why Not Study Cognition?

Why have we chosen to study and measure the emotions of children rather than their cognitive abilities? Since the 1930s, the study of emotion and emotional development has been relatively stagnant, until quite recently, when there has been a renewal of interest and research in this area. In examining some of the more prominent child psychology textbooks (Carmichael, 1946, 1954; Jersild, 1933; Murchison, 1933; Mussen, 1970; Mussen, Conger, & Kagan, 1979; Osofsky, 1979), one finds that the page allotment to emotional topics is and always has been rather sparse.

A topical analysis of the differences in page allocations in various textbooks is presented in Table 1. The particular text and its year of publication are followed by the total number of volume pages. The remaining columns contain the number and percentage of pages devoted to various topics, including emotional, personality, social, perceptual-cognitive, motor-biological, and methodological issues. Such distinctions among areas are not easy to make. This difficulty is partly due to the interrelatedness of topics as well as to the fact that some chapters are arbitrarily identified as nonemotional. For example, attachment and dependency discussions are categorized as emotional, but father–infant and peer interaction chapters are included in the social category. We made this distinction when we felt that the focus of the work or the attention of the author was less on emotional issues and more on the social relationships involved. In addition, psycho-

Table 1. Topical Analysis of Child Psychology Textbooks: Breakdown of Topics by Number and Percentage of Pages

Text	Total pages	Emotional	Personality	Social	Perceptual-cognitive	Motor-biological	Methods, etc.
Jersild (1933)	447	66 (15%)	63 (14%)	42 (9%)	178 (40%)	49 (11%)	49 (11%)
Murchison (2nd ed.) (1933)	926	42 (4%)	149 (16%)	43 (5%)	265 (29%)	335 (36%)	92 (10%)
Carmichael (1946)	1,000	39 (4%)	92 (9%)	0 (0%)	359 (36%)	328 (33%)	182 (18%)
Carmichael (2nd ed.) (1954)	1,216	87 (7%)	110 (9%)	63 (5%)	447 (37%)	323 (27%)	186 (15%)
Mussen (1970)	2,282	188 (8%)	164 (7%)	368 (16%)	850 (37%)	656 (29%)	56 (3%)
Osofsky (1979)	918	93 (10%)	10 (1%)	117 (13%)	153 (17%)	322 (35%)	223 (24%)
Mussen et al. (5th ed.) (1979)	555	39 (7%)	52 (9%)	147 (27%)	133 (24%)	106 (19%)	78 (14%)

pathology chapters were not included in the emotional category if their focus was more on applied clinical than on emotional themes.

Recognizing the somewhat arbitrary nature of the classification system, one can still see that there have been few changes over the last 50 years in the percentage of pages devoted to emotional topics. For instance, in the 1930s Murchison (1933) and Jersild (1933) devoted between 4% and 15% of their pages to emotional topics while in the 1970s Osofsky (1979), Mussen (1970), and Mussen et al. (1979) devoted 10%, 8%, and 7%, respectively. Compared with the coverage of perceptual-cognitive topics, the space devoted to emotional topics is meager. Furthermore, this lack of balance between emotional and perceptual-cognitive discussions is apparent across time and applies to each of the volumes surveyed. Although the selection of textbooks is neither exhaustive nor random, this survey underscores the relatively minor role given to emotional topics in the past.

Even within the discussions of emotion, the scope of coverage is limited in terms of the kinds of emotions discussed. When one examines the same sample of textbooks, it becomes obvious that more emphasis is given to negative emotions than to positive emotions (see Table 2). There is more written on sorrow, gloom, and sadness than on laughter and humor and more on jealousy than on sympathy. Without question, the most lengthy discussions have concentrated on fear, anger, and aggression. In every textbook surveyed, one or more of these feelings were allotted the largest number of pages.

Although we have quantified our survey of child psychology textbooks, one would need only to glance at the shelves in any psychology library to discover that of the books written about emotions, the vast majority are on aggression and hostility. Other topics represented, in descending order of frequency, include anxiety, shyness, fear, bereavement and grief, jealousy, laughter and humor, loneliness, and love. Even the number of words in the English language referring to negative emotions is significantly greater than the number of words referring to positive emotions, even though among nonemotional concepts, positive terms outnumber negative ones (Averill, 1980).

More recently, however, issues related to positive emotions have occupied an increasing number of pages in child psychology textbooks. For example, in the volumes edited by Osofsky (1979) and Mussen (1970), attachment topics are given either the most or the second most number of pages compared with other feeling states. And while jealousy receives more attention than sympathy, the recent work on empathy and role taking may alter this balance (Hoffman, 1978; Masangkay, McCluskey, McIntyre, Sims-Knight, Vaughn, & Flavell, 1974).

Table 2. Emotions Discussed in Child Psychology Textbooks (Number of Pages)

Text	Fear, wariness, anxiety	Sorrow, gloom, sadness, depression	Anger, rage, aggression, hostility	Jealousy	Attachment, dependency	Love, affection	Pleasure, joy, laughter, humor	Sympathy	Sex, sensuality
Jersild (1933)	25	4	6	6	—	1	5	—	—
Murchison (2nd ed.) (1933)	2	1	3	1	—	—	2	—	—
Carmichael (1946)	8	—	5	2	—	3	3	1	2
Carmichael (2nd ed.) (1954)	21	—	10	2	—	9	4	2	2
Mussen (1970)	—	—	102	—	86	—	—	—	—
Osofsky (1979)	3	—	2	—	5	—	3	—	—
Mussen et al. (5th ed) (1979)	9	4	5	—	9	—	—	—	—

These data do not tell the entire story, however. Significant contributions to emotion theory have been made in the past two decades by investigators such as Tomkins (1962, 1963), Ekman (Ekman, Friesen, & Ellsworth, 1972); Lewis (Lewis & Brooks, 1978; Lewis & Brooks-Gunn, 1979; Lewis & Michalson, 1982a,b,c); Izard (1971, 1977); Plutchik (1970, 1980a,b); Arnold (1960); Sroufe (1979b); and Emde (Emde, Gaensbauer, & Harmon, 1976). Nevertheless, issues related to cognitive theory and cognitive development continue to permeate the *zeitgeist* and capture the interests of most scientists.

This concern with cognition as the most important aspect of development also manifests itself in measures of individual differences in development. Almost all of the current measures of children's developmental status are based on cognitive variables (Lewis, 1976). These measures are used not only to assess children but also to plan treatment programs and to evaluate intervention outcomes. Thus, not only do scientists tend to study cognition at the expense of other aspects of human behavior, but public policy and decision-making actions are determined by this activity as well. Although it has been shown repeatedly that all cultural activities, including scientific pursuits, are influenced by and influence the *zeitgeist* (Kuhn, 1970), it is still somewhat surprising that individual differences in cognitive ability remain the most important determinant of social policy. It is particularly surprising when social policy pertains to infants and young children, since most existing measures of cognitive ability designed for children during the first years of life are generally not very reliable or valid (Lewis & Fox, 1980). Given the force of a prevailing *zeitgeist*, however, it is small wonder that few useful measures of individual differences other than cognitive ones have been developed or used to assess children's development, to initiate intervention programs, or to evaluate outcomes.

Why did such a role for cognition emerge and remain dominant? Zigler and Trickett (1978) suggested that the use of the IQ as a measure in the evaluation of childhood intervention programs became popular because standard IQ tests are well-developed instruments that are easily administered and that relate to other behaviors of theoretical and practical significance. A more detailed analysis of this problem is too far removed from our present concerns to be covered here, although the problem must be addressed eventually inasmuch as the development of a new assessment instrument must compete in the public arena with existing cognitive instruments.

The success of our venture may be judged more by current cultural values than by its worth from a scientific point of view. Anderson and

Messick (1974) were among the first to issue an appeal to broaden the definition of competence to include more than cognitive components. More recently, social competence rather than IQ has been cited by Zigler and Trickett (1978) as a more important source of individual differences and a more powerful influence on public policy:

> Social competence, rather than IQ, should be employed as the major measure of the success of intervention programs such as Head Start. (p. 793) Social competence must reflect the success of the human being in meeting societal expectancies. . . . These measures of social competence should reflect something about the self-actualization or personal development of the human being. (p. 795)

Greenspan (1980), as well, suggested that the critical aspects of competence might be temperament, character, and social awareness, each of which involves factors similar or related to emotional processes. Finally, Scarr (1981) has proposed that the term *intellectual competence* be used in assessing children's school abilities. Her notion of intellectual competence includes the cognitive, motivational, and social aspects of what Zigler (1979) called "social competence." The motivational and adjustment aspects of such an assessment clearly overlap with the affective domain.

From a scientific point of view, there is relatively little reason to base public policy decisions, intervention strategies, and assessment procedures on cognitive rather than social or emotional bases. Thus, whether we agree on the particular measure of competence—be it IQ, cognitive level, or educational achievement; motivational and emotional variables; or even physical health—the need to broaden our measurement interests to include various aspects of children's abilities is vital.

While we cannot pretend to know the cause of the preoccupation with cognition, it appears that deep-seated in our child-rearing system is a belief that intellectual development in children is highly related to and may even ensure their success as adults. When parents are questioned about what they want for their children, four major goals usually emerge. Parents, regardless of the children's age, typically want their children to be happy, healthy, successful, and intelligent. Notice that the goals include physical health, career success, and happiness, as well as wisdom. These categories are not unlike those mentioned by Zigler (1979) under the rubric of social competence.

Underlying these four goals is the general premise that being smart (having highly developed intellectual skills) will ultimately lead to the other goals. In other words, most of us subscribe to the argument that cognitive abilities (usually in the form of academic achievement or IQ) are directly related to the acquisition of wealth, happiness, and physical health, as well as to the absence of psychopathology.

Although the data do not support this model (McClelland, 1973), it has become and remains a predominant theme in social policy. For example, one of the early assumptions of the Head Start program was that if we make children smarter, we will make them happier and more successful and will at the same time eliminate problems of social disorganization such as juvenile delinquency, truancy, alcoholism, and drug abuse (Hellmuth, 1968). Zigler himself has now challenged this premise: "Stated most simply, we believe that one can obtain a very high IQ score and still not behave admirably in the real world that exists beyond the confines of the psychologist's testing room" (Zigler & Trickett, 1978, p. 791).

Empirical evidence suggests that cognitive variables, such as grades in school and academic ability, are not good predictors of future success:

> It seems so self-evident to educators that those who do well in their classes *must* go on to do better in life that they systematically have disregarded evidence to the contrary that has been accumulating for some time. In the early 1950s, a committee of the Social Science Research Council . . . looked into the matter and concluded that while grade level attained seemed related to future measures of success in life, performance within grade was related only slightly. In other words, being a high school or college graduate gave one a credential that opened up certain high level jobs, but the poorer students in high school or college did as well in life as the top students. (McClelland, 1973, p. 2)

This finding seems to be true for jobs ranging from factory worker, bank teller, or air traffic controller (Berg, 1970) to scientific researcher (Taylor, Smith, & Ghiselin, 1963). Jencks (1972) noted that while a person's occupation may be related to the amount of education received (insofar as educational background enables one to enter the occupation initially), when the effects of education are statistically controlled, the relationship between childhood IQ and later occupation all but disappears. Aptitude test scores seem to be no better at predicting later success than are school grades or IQ:

> Thorndike and Hagen (1959), for instance, obtained 12,000 correlations between aptitude test scores and various measures of later occupational success on over 10,000 respondents and concluded that the number of significant correlations did not exceed what would be expected by chance . . . Holland and Richards (1965) and Elton and Shevel (1969) have shown that no consistent relationships exist between scholastic aptitude scores in college students and their *actual accomplishments* in social leadership, the arts, science, music, writing, and speech and drama. (McClelland, 1973, p. 3)

In studies showing that scores on general intelligence tests correlate with proficiency across jobs (e.g., Ghiselli, 1966), the effects of social-class background or of personal credentials are seldom taken into account. It is fairly well established that social-class background is related to getting higher scores on ability tests (Nuttall & Fozard, 1970), as well as to having the right personal credentials for success. Consequently, the relationship between aptitude or intelligence and job success is likely to be illusory, a product of their joint association with social class.

Intelligence measures, then, do not seem to predict successful job performance very well. They also bear little relationship to later earnings (Duncan, Featherman, & Duncan, 1972; Jencks, 1972). Likewise, within a given occupation, academic credentials do not have much effect on income, although such credentials, as was pointed out earlier, may be related to the occupation entered. Family background seems to be more related to income levels than either IQ scores or academic variables (Jencks, 1972).

If cognitive and intellectual measures do not predict a person's later career success or wealth with much accuracy, what about happiness and health? If we make children smarter, will they be healthier and happier, if not wealthier and wiser? Does intellectual ability promote better adjustment to life as is often claimed? In independent studies, Jensen (1972) and Kohlberg, LaCrosse, and Ricks (1970) examined longitudinal data from a sample of gifted individuals and concluded that the gifted experience more occupational, marital, and social success than nongifted individuals and have lower incidences of alcoholism and homosexuality. However, the data were based on Terman and Oden's (1947) study, in which no attempt was made to equate for the opportunity to achieve success. The gifted subjects came from socioeconomic backgrounds superior to those of the nongifted subjects. Again, a failure to take into account social class and all that it entails—educational advantages, job contacts, and occupational credentials—may result in spuriously high correlations between intelligence and success. Finally, satisfaction with one's job does not appear to be related to educational attainment (Jencks, 1972), nor is there evidence that intelligence is related to less neuroticism (McClelland, 1973).

Given the disappointing showing of cognitive measures in explaining career success, job earnings, or satisfaction with life, one might want to consider altering the path assumptions. Perhaps life's outcomes are more influenced by "happiness" than by cognitive skills. If Zigler is correct that self-actualization or personal development may be a more important source of individual differences, then emotional and motivational variables may be the causal factors in a successful and intellectually rewarding life. Jencks (1972) has found that noncognitive attributes seem to play a larger role than cognitive skills in determining career success or failure. In particular, whether the subject stayed in school was found to predict later income as well as test scores did and to predict occupational status better than test scores did.

Although there are few data on the subject, there is some reason to believe that emotional variables also play an important role in children's early intellectual development. For example, "personality traits" may be more predictive of later cognitive growth than earlier measures of cognitive difference. In a study of the predictive value of both earlier IQ scores and the degree of pleasure or happiness the child showed in taking the test, Birns and Golden (1972) found that the happiness rating was far more predictive of later IQ scores than was the earlier IQ measure. There is also evidence that early differences in emotional response predict later adaptation and competence. In particular, positive affect during play at 18 months has been shown to predict competence in a peer group at 3 1/2 years of age (Waters, Wippman & Sroufe, 1979). Positive affect and enthusiasm at 24 months seem to be related to measures of adaptation at 5 years (Arend, Gove, & Sroufe, 1979). Finally, Scarr (1981) has reported that being cooperative, attentive, less active, socially responsive, and well adjusted at 2 years of age is as predictive of higher IQ scores at 4 years as having a higher IQ score at 2 is predictive of being well-motivated to learn at 4.

The argument is also apparent in the work on attachment and exploration as it relates to the role of emotions in affecting intellectual development. Attachment can be viewed as an emotional or affectional tie between two people, in most cases between child and parent. It can also be viewed in its functional role, namely, that of providing a secure base from which children can explore their environment (Ainsworth & Bell, 1970). Given children's need (indeed, the need of all organisms) for exploration and novelty *as well as* the concurrent need for predictability and familiarity, attachment is conceptualized as the mechanism for providing the affective capacity for this duality of experience (Sroufe, 1979a). Through the establishment of reciprocal and responsive interactions and the emergence of a sense of self, children are able to establish relationships that, among other things, provide them with a secure base from which to explore their environment (Lewis & Brooks-Gunn, 1979). The underlying feeling state associated with attachment relationships is one of love and security. From this feeling state, infants are able to develop a variety of other competencies, including the abilities to explore, to relate to peers, and to maintain ego resiliency (Arend *et al.*, 1979). Ainsworth and her colleagues (Ainsworth, Blehar, Waters, & Wall, 1978) have also argued convincingly for the interface between this feeling state and children's commerce with the environment, a commerce that includes emotional as well as cognitive components.

Whereas attachment and the relationship of attachment to cognition have received some attention in the research literature, the feeling states of competence and efficacy and their relationship to performance have received more attention. White (1975, 1978; White & Watts, 1973), Lewis (Lewis & Goldberg, 1969b), and Seligman (1975) have argued that feelings of competence and power and the reciprocal feeling of learned helplessness are important determinants of other skills and capacities often considered cognitive in nature. For example, infants who receive more contingent responses to their actions (presumably, infants who feel more competent) have more efficient exploration skills (Lewis & Goldberg, 1969b). These infants show faster habituation to redundant information than do infants who feel less competent.

Even more striking are the results from a recent study in our laboratory in which children 10–24 weeks of age were placed in two groups (Lewis, Sullivan, & Brooks-Gunn, 1983). In one group, infants' arm-pulling behavior resulted in the appearance of a picture. The second group served as a yoked control that received the same amount of stimulation but had no control over the appearance of a picture. It was hypothesized that control of the environment—that is, feelings of efficacy—would produce alterations in the infants' emotional state. Specifically, we predicted that competent infants would be more likely to show positive affect (smiling) and to stay awake and alert longer than powerless infants. Indeed, the results suggested that the infants able to control their environment were likely to stay awake longer and were less likely to cry than the infants who were equally stimulated but who were not in control of the stimulus.

A further example of the role of emotions in promoting success comes from research on the effects of anxiety on intellectual performance and educational achievement. The relationship between this feeling state and performance is not linear. Large and small amounts of anxiety may seriously affect cognitive as well as motor performance, whereas moderate amounts of anxiety may be facilitating (Sarason, 1980).

There is an accumulating body of evidence showing that emotions can affect physical health as well (Cherry, 1980). For example, there appears to be a direct link between a person's feelings and the body's immunological system. Negative emotions especially, such as anger and anxiety, may lower a crucial biological threshold and increase the risk of infection. Furthermore, manipulation of emotional states by means of biofeedback or medication may diminish physical pain and enhance one's general sense of well-being, as well as prevent sickness (Benson, 1975).

Other medical research suggests that personality traits may contribute to the development of heart disease and cancer. Much publicity has been devoted to the link between heart disease and the "Type A" personality, characterized by behaviors such as irritation, impatience, frustration, and anger (Friedman & Rosenman, 1974; Glass, 1977). The link between personality and cancer is somewhat more tenuous. There is some evidence that cancer patients who appear to be "model adults" (conscientious and dutiful) have experienced a disturbed childhood, filled with loneliness and hurt. Their stoicism as adults, in fact, hides a basic despair, and within a short time after a spouse dies or a job is lost, the first symptoms of cancer may appear (LeShan, 1977). Findings from a study of cancer in identical twins suggests that the twin who died of leukemia was the one who had experienced an emotional upheaval. Additional evidence of a link between emotions and cancer comes from a longitudinal study of more than a thousand graduates of Johns Hopkins University in which the subjects who developed major cancers were reported to be low-key, nonaggressive people, not close to their parents.

Not only is it possible that negative emotions, such as grief or anger, may contribute to heart disease and cancer, but positive emotions may actually prevent or cure physical illness (LeShan, 1980). In a personal account about the effects of a progressive and painful illness of the connective tissues, Cousins (1979) reported that 10 minutes of laughter (in response to Marx Brothers' movies) relieved his pain. Given about 1 in 500 chances of recovery, 16 years later Cousins reported that through laughter and humor, he was without pain and able to engage in sports.

A longitudinal study of 100 Harvard students showed that of those students judged to have the best mental health during college, only 2 had become seriously ill or died by the age of 53. Nearly half of those considered less well adjusted had fallen ill or died by their early 50s (Vaillant, 1977). Similarly, a longitudinal study of medical school graduates found evidence that only a quarter of the subjects judged to be either calm and stable or lively and flexible had endured a heart attack or cancer, compared to over three-quarters of a group of moody, irritable persons (Cherry, 1980). It seems, then, that both negative and positive emotions play a role in physical health. A word of caution is in order, however. It must be recognized that the role of emotions in physical health is likely to be modified by temperamental and environmental factors.

⋙⋙⋙⋙⋙⋙

In this discussion, we have tended to treat feelings and cognitive states as if they represent different domains that can be isolated from one another. We prefer a unified model, however, defined by the assumption that the competencies associated with these domains are all aspects of the same unified development of the individual (Lewis & Cherry, 1977; Lewis et al., in press). Investigators should be oriented to discovering the common bases for behavior that make possible what some observers call *separate capacities*. The implications of a unified model include the understanding that these competencies are all aspects of individual development. Thus, this model does not limit the phenomena to be explained to behavior that the scientist categorizes as either cognitive or emotional.

A second feature of the model is the emphasis on the holistic nature of human behavior. While we may choose to focus on one aspect, we must at the same time recognize the limited nature of our study. Thus, the model implies that causal chains of behavior may move from cognitive, emotional, or other domains back through an individual before resurfacing as new capacities, since these behaviors originate within the individual and not within any separate domain. Finally, this model presupposes an interdisciplinary perspective that includes biological, cultural, and psychological orientations.

In concluding the discussion, we view the scientist's search for developmental principles as being not unlike that of the blind men in the well-known Indian fable: Several blind men, it will be recalled, wanted to know what an elephant is, and each decided to make his own investigation. Each man happened to touch a different part of the elephant, and thus, each had a different perception of the animal. Each thought he knew the true nature of the elephant; and although each was, in part, correct, all were wrong because the elephant is more than those separate aspects. Scientists approach the study of individual development in a similar fashion, studying linguistic, cognitive, social, emotional, and physical development separately. None of these exists by itself, nor does each entirely explain individual development.

In this chapter, we have argued that in order to understand development, scientists must move away from the preoccupation with cognitive variables and redirect their attention to emotional development. We challenged the assumption that by increasing the cognitive abilities of children we are ensuring their later success and happiness in life. Instead, we cited studies showing that cognitive variables such as grades in school, IQ, and achievement test results do not predict occupational status, earnings, job satisfaction, or life adjustments. Indeed, there is some evidence that "emotional" variables, such as feelings of security, of pleasure in doing a task, or of competence, may have a more powerful influence on children's development. While the effort to determine which is more important, cognition or emotion, may be futile, we must, nevertheless, broaden our perspective of development, placing more emphasis on emotional behavior and development than in the past.

In order to study children's emotions, it is necessary that we have a working theory of development as well as an assessment instrument for measuring emotional development. The construction of the instrument was the goal of our research. To date, most investigators of children's emotions have selected one emotion for study and have measured it in an experimental laboratory under highly controlled and highly artificial conditions. While laboratory studies are clearly important, they do not reveal how children respond in more natural circumstances.

Even though in the past few years researchers have returned to the study of emotion, this area of inquiry is still plagued by the difficulties of measuring emotions in infants and young children. Despite the relatively large number of standardized instruments available for assessing cognitive development, emotional measures are scarce. The existing scales are usually restricted to measures of a single emotion or are appropriate for use only with older children. Tests for infants are generally used to gather descriptive data regarding the age of appearance of particular skills or behaviors. The few instruments that do include emotional variables tend to rely on subjective rating techniques to assess either general emotional tone (i.e., positive or negative affect) or general social adjustment. In addition, rather narrow measures of single emotional states have been taken in laboratory situations. While such studies may provide interesting data on children's emotions, the usefulness of laboratory experiments in understanding development in real-life settings has been repeatedly questioned (Riegel & Meacham, 1976). Unfortunately, much of contemporary developmental psychology can be described as "the science of the strange behavior of children in strange situations with strange adults for the briefest possible period of time" (Bronfenbrenner, 1977, p. 513).

What we set out to do was to devise an instrument that could be used to measure children's emotions in natural environments. To be maximally useful, this instrument had to be able to measure more than one emotion. If we could assess more than one emotion, we could then study the interaction among emotions as well as individual differences in children on the basis of their emotional profiles.

As we pointed out earlier, it is clear that in everyday life, people generally have little difficulty when asked to identify children's emotions or to describe differences between children on the basis of emotional behaviors. Would we be able to accomplish the same thing with a more systematic measurement system? If we were successful, such a measurement instrument could be helpful in designing and evaluating intervention programs for children and, at a higher level, in planning public policy related to children's welfare. Thus, our initial task was to determine if we could construct a measurement instrument with the ability (1) to measure a variety of emotional states rather than one; (2) to measure these states in settings related to the everyday activities of children; (3) to tap individual differences in children's emotional states; and (4) to generate an emotional profile for each child. Moreover, such an instrument should be capable of measuring emotions in children across the first three years of life.

The present volume outlines our efforts to accomplish these goals in the following way. In this chapter, we emphasized the importance of the study of emotion. In Chapter 2, we examine what emotion is and how it may differ from affect, mood, and personality characteristics. Chapter 3 describes different approaches to the study of emotion as well as specific theories. Issues pertaining to the structure and development of emotion are examined in Chapter 4, and a specific theory of emotional development is described in Chapter 5. The role of socialization in emotional development is the focus of Chapters 6 and 7. In Chapter 8, we raise problems intrinsic in measuring emotion and address the question of how one can infer in other people what are essentially "private acts." The actual construction of the measurement scales is detailed in Chapter 9, and tests of its reliability and validity are described in Chapters 10 and 11. Chapter 12 concludes the volume with a detailed analysis of how to use the scales to generate individual profiles of emotional states. The case histories of four children are reviewed for the purpose of illustration. The Scales of Socioemotional Development and coding sheets are contained in the appendixes.

2

Emotion: An Overview

Having argued that the study of emotional development is important to understanding children's overall development, we shall now attempt to define more precisely what we mean by the term *emotion* and how this term might differ from other terms, such as *affect, mood, temperament,* and *personality*. This undertaking is not easy even though some attention has already been given to this topic (Arnold, 1960; Izard & Buechler, 1979; Plutchik, 1980a). Even these reviews may leave the reader somewhat confused since one of the most difficult tasks in the study of emotion and emotional development is that of definition. If one were to ask, "What is emotion?", one would find the answer both hard to come by and idiosyncratic. In Table 3, 28 different definitions of emotion are presented (from Plutchik, 1980a). Clearly, emotion is not easily defined, and there is no agreement about what it might be. For at least 80 years, psychologists have struggled to define emotion and to find a place for it in behavior theory (Strongman, 1978). This problem continues into the 1980s.

While everyday experience confirms the existence of emotions (i.e., we feel, we know we feel, and we know what we feel), and while people can generally identify different kinds of emotions (e.g., joy feels different from anger), a survey of the literature reveals that attempts to define emotion frequently give way to elaborate systems of taxonomy in which the classification of different types of emotion becomes the primary task. The questions asked turn from what emotion is to how many emotions there are, which emotions are fundamental, and what relationships exist among specific emotions and between emotion and cognition.

The lack of agreement about what constitutes an emotion seems to have been a major hindrance in the study of emotion and emotional development. In some sense, this lack of definition has made investi-

Table 3. Definitions of Emotion Found in the Psychological and Psychiatric Literature[a]

"My theory . . . is that the bodily changes follow directly the perception of the exciting fact, and that our feeling of the same changes as they occur *is* the emotion" (William James, 1884).

"Ideas are cathexes—ultimately of memory traces—while affects and emotions correspond with processes of discharge, the final expression of which is perceived as feeling" (Sigmund Freud, 1915).

"The emotional excitation of specific quality that is the affective aspect of the operation of any one of the principal instincts may be called a primary emotion" (William McDougall, 1921).

"An emotion is an hereditary 'pattern-reaction' involving profound changes of the bodily mechanism as a whole, but particularly of the visceral and glandular systems" (John B. Watson, 1924).

"An emotion may thus be provisionally defined as a somatic readjustment which is instinctively aroused by a stimulating situation and which in turn promotes a more effective adaptive response to that situation" (Harvey A. Carr, 1929).

"For the theory that emotional experiences arise from changes in effector organs is substituted the idea that they are produced by unusual and powerful influences emerging from the region of the thalamus and affecting various systems of cortical neurones" (Walter B. Cannon, 1928).

"The peculiar quality of the emotion is added to simple sensation when the thalamic processes are roused (Walter B. Cannon, 1929).

"Emotion is not primarily a kind of response at all but rather a state of strength comparable in many respects with a drive" (B. F. Skinner, 1938).

"Emotion is an acute disturbance of the individual as a whole, psychological in origin, involving behavior, conscious experience, and visceral functioning" (Paul T. Young, 1943).

"Affects are originally archaic discharge syndromes that supplant voluntary actions under certain exciting conditions" (Otto Fenichel, 1946).

"Basically, emotion is an expressive plasmatic motion. . . . These two basic directions of biophysical plasma current [from the center toward the periphery, or vice versa] correspond to the two basic affects of the psychic apparatus, pleasure and anxiety" (Wilhelm Reich, 1949).

"Feeling, in the sense of affect, arises from involuntary motor attitude, maintained as readiness or wish, and held in leash pending the lifting of whatever form of interfering mechanism, or functional barrier, is holding up the action" (Nina Bull, 1951).

"The common idioms 'in love,' 'in fear,' 'in anger,' suggest a definition of an emotion as a conceptual state, in which the special response is a function of circumstances in the history of the individual" (B. F. Skinner, 1953).

---

[a] From *Emotion: A psychoevolutionary synthesis* by R. Plutchik, New York: Harper & Row, 1980, pp. 81–83. Copyright © 1980 by R. Plutchik. Reprinted by permission of Harper & Row.

"We define an emotion . . . as a particular state of strength or weakness in one or more responses induced by any one of a class of operations. We may make as many distinctions as we wish between separate emotion" (B. F. Skinner, 1953).

"Emotion is activity and reactivity of the tissues and organs innervated by the autonomic nervous system. It may involve, but does not necessarily involve, skeletal muscular response or mental activity" (M. A. Wenger, F. N. Jones, & M. H. Jones, 1956).

"Emotion can be both organizing (making adaptation to the environment more effective) and disorganizing, both energizing and debilitating, both sought after and avoided" (Donald O. Hebb, 1958).

"We define 'emotion' broadly as: 1) episodes or sequences of overt and incipient somatic adjustment, 2) often loosely patterned and variable, 3) usually with concurrent exciting sensory effects, perhaps also perceptual attitudes characterizable as desirable or undesirable, pleasant or unpleasant, 4) related to the intensity effects or perceptual meaning of a stimulus, 5) synergic with organic changes of A- (approach) or W- (withdrawal) types" (Theodore C. Schneirla, 1959).

"Emotion is the felt tendency toward anything intuitively appraised as good (beneficial), or away from anything intuitively appraised as bad (harmful). This attraction or aversion is accompanied by a pattern of physiological changes organized toward approach or withdrawal. The patterns differ for different emotions" (Magda Arnold, 1960).

"An emotion may be defined as a patterned bodily reaction of either destruction, reproduction, incorporation, orientation, protection, reintegration, rejection, or exploration, or some combination of these, which is brought about by a stimulus" (Robert Plutchik, 1962).

"Emotional feelings guide our behavior with respect to the two basic life principles of self-preservation and the preservation of the species" (Paul MacLean, 1963).

"Emotions [are] the result of neural dispositions or attitudes that regulate input when action is temporarily suspended" (Karl H. Pribram, 1967b).

"Emotion [is] the association between certain widespread changes in ongoing operant behaviors and the presentation or removal of reinforcers" (J. R. Millenson, 1967).

"Emotion is the preparatory signal that prepares the organism for emergency behavior. . . . The goal of this behavior is to restore the organism to safety" (Sandor Rado, 1969).

"Emotions are phases of an individual's intuitive appraisals either of his own organismic states and urges to act or of the succession of environmental situations in which he finds himself. . . . At the same time, because they are usually accompanied by distinctive facial expressions, bodily postures, and incipient movements, they usually provide valuable information to his companions" (John Bowlby, 1969).

"Emotion is a complex process that has neurophysiological, motor-expressive, and phenomenological aspects" (Carroll Izard, 1972).

(continued)

Table 3 *(Continued)*

"An affect is a sensation of pleasure, unpleasure, or both, plus the ideas, both conscious and unconscious, associated with that sensation" (Charles Brenner, 1974).

"Emotion [is] a complex disturbance that includes three main components: subjective affect, physiological changes related to species-specific forms of mobilization for adaptive action, and action impulses having both instrumental and expressive qualities" (Richard S. Lazarus, 1975).

"Any particular species of emotion (anger, esteem, wonder, etc.) may be characterized by its own particular structure and described by specifying its situation, its transformations (instructions and bodily expression) and its function" (Joseph De Rivera, 1977).

---

gations of the phenomenon suspect and even invalid. However, this predicament (i.e., the inability to define the object of study) should not prevent one from studying issues pertaining to emotion, since definitional issues are often problematic in the history of science. The focus should be on the phenomena themselves, rather than on definition (Kagan, 1978). Having agreed that certain phenomena may represent a class of events uniquely different from another, one can then pursue investigations without necessarily having a definition.

Ekman *et al.* (1972) have noted that in most studies of emotion, the behavior investigated is thought to be emotional primarily because observers are able to reach some agreement in using the lay vocabulary of emotion terms to describe the behavior. Moreover, in their own investigation, they include any article that the author *says* is about emotion: "When we use the word 'emotion,' in many cases the discussion will apply equally to the various aspects of the terms, and therefore there will be no need to specify one" (p. 13). In other words, if investigators can agree that a particular event, such as the approach of a stranger, produces a consistent set of responses in 8-month-old infants, such as movement toward the mother, crying or gaze aversion, and heart-rate acceleration, then whether they call this coherence between situation and response *fear* or the *inability to assimilate a discrepant event* becomes relatively unimportant.

Some investigators have gone so far as to conclude that since emotion cannot be well defined, the phenomenon does not exist. Duffy's view of emotion is one of the most extreme. For Duffy (1934, 1941, 1962), it is essentially meaningless to try to study emotion at all, because emotion "has no distinguishing characteristics." Emotional behaviors are not different in kind from other behaviors, since all behaviors follow the same principles. Instead, Duffy replaces the term *emotion* with *arousal*. Yet, this is also a hypothetical construct with little empirical support for its validity as a unitary concept. Difficult to define and awkward to measure, arousal does not account for all varieties of emotional behavior; a necessary condition for emotion to occur may be an aroused organism, but arousal need not imply emotion. Physiological changes similar to those occurring during emotion may be seen in hard physical exercise unrelated to any emotional experience.

Others besides Duffy have challenged the notion of emotion or have defined it in terms of neurophysiological arousal (e.g., Bindra, 1968, 1969; Leeper, 1948, 1970; Lindsley, 1950, 1951, 1957, 1970). For instance, since there is no one thing to which emotion can be meaningfully and unequivocally said to refer, Lazarus (1966, 1968; Lazarus, Averill, & Opton, 1970) called it a "response syndrome." In this view, the overall pattern of relationships among causes, symptoms, and courses allows one to use the word *emotion* descriptively and allows the possibility of classification. Lazarus also suggested that although concepts of emotion are important in the description and classification of behavior, they are not necessarily of much use in its explanation.

In contrast, the study of cognitive psychology or intellectual behavior does not demand the definitional necessity that investigators seem to impose on the study of emotion. Indeed, a lack of definition of the terms *cognition, intellectual behavior,* and *IQ* has not impeded inquiry into this area. For example, *IQ* has been defined as that which can be measured by an IQ test (Kamin, 1974). Definitions of *cognition* are evolutionary-adaptive (Wilson, 1975), physiological, or behavioral (Kagan, 1978) in the same way that definitions of *emotion* are (see Chapter 3).

In the study of thinking, psychologists have come to appreciate (although not resolve) the distinction between *competence* (some underlying structure or ability) and *performance* (some measurable manifestation of that competence). In biology, scientists distinguish between genotype and phenotype, again separating an underlying structure from its manifestation. Psychologists must recognize this independence in the emotional domain as well. In the definition of emotion that we shall propose, this distinction is realized by separating emotion into various components, such as emotional expression (which can be observed directly) versus emotional state and experience (which are internal activities of the organism).

Although taxonomy is the lowest form of epistemology, it provides at least a structural foundation from which to proceed. The reliance simply on taxonomical distinctions as an explanatory device, however, independent of a search for sets of coherences, would be in error. Even if one focuses on coherences between situations and behaviors, leaving aside taxonomical or definitional issues, one must still distinguish between sets of events regarded as *emotional* from those better labeled *cognitive*. Why is one set of coherences considered an emotion and not a cognition? For example, attention is usually considered more a cognitive process than an emotional one. But why is this event, attention, different from more emotional events, such as fear, anger, or joy? These questions suggest that some phenomena are more obviously categorized as cognitive (e.g., memory and problem solving), although they may contain emotional aspects as well (Bower, 1981). Some coherences are clearly emotional (e.g., happiness, anger, or fear). Between these two categories is a category that consists of coherences not easily categorized as either cognitive or emotional (e.g., curiosity and interest). Such questions return us to issues of categorization and taxonomical systems.

What Is Emotion?

When we speak of emotion, we mean to talk about a complex set of behaviors that occur around an equally complex set of situations or stimulus events. The observation of certain features of that coherence can be labeled *emotional*. Examples of what these may be and how they can be measured will occupy much of the discussion. Since emotional events are a continuous part of all human activities, a definition of emotion independent of other aspects of human behavior, such as cognition, is not readily available. Although some cognitive events may elicit emotional *states*, no emotional *experience* is without some cognitive processing (see Chapters 4 and 5).

In a discussion of the development of fear Lewis (1980) enumerated five different types of fear. Although the examples that follow focus on the emotion fear, the issues depicted pertain to emotions in general. In examples of these types of fear, the term *fear* appears best to describe the emotional component of the child's response, although alternative terms such as *anxious* or *wary* might be used. Whatever the label, all imply that the child exhibits a unique yet specific set of behaviors from which one can infer a specific emotional state. Fear, like all emotions, is a highly complex phenomenon involving an understanding of the child's behavior, the situation in which the behavior occurs, and the attribution that the caregiver and society give to that coherence of behaviors and situations.

Example 1

A 2-year-old child and his mother sit in the pediatrician's office. It is their turn to see the doctor. As they enter the room, the child stares at the doctor and his white coat, screams, turns away, and clutches his mother's leg.

The first example appears to be a case of learned fear. The child has previously experienced an unpleasant action, the agent of which was the doctor. For example, the child may have received an injection and, by his behavior, may have indicated that he was hurt. Now, two months later, the child, capable of utilizing past experiences, behaves differently as a consequence of this ability. Specifically, the child remembers or associates the previous noxious event with the current situation. The doctor and the white coat (the salient stimulus dimension) are associated with the injection and the feeling of pain; the child responds with fear. Later, the child may remember and associate pain with the words "going to the doctor." Or the child may not remember or associate the events until he experiences an event that triggers the memory, such as the doctor's office, the doctor's face, the doctor's white coat, or the needle itself. In any case, the child's reaction to the present situation is affected by a past event. Such fearful behavior may generalize to other situations that have similar dimensions. For example, the child may react fearfully to any new office, to any strange male, or to anyone wearing white coats.

This example derives from Watson's (1924) theory of emotion, which is based on a conditioning model of three innate emotions: rage–anger, happiness, and fear. This model has been found inadequate by others, however. For example, Valentine (1930) showed that there are many not easily defined or classified stimuli that also evoke fear. Hebb (1946) also challenged the conditioning model, citing evidence of phenomena, such as the appearance of mutilated and unresponsive bodies, that evoke "spontaneous fear." Nevertheless, although not all fears (or all emotions in general) are learned, some fears and emotions appear to be. In these cases, the expression of a unique set of responses to a particular situation requires some cognitive activity, including recognition (discrimination), association, and recall. The cognitive activity may itself be inferred from the emotional response, as was discussed in Chapter 1.

Example 2

A 1-month-old infant is lying in her crib looking at the mobile above it. Suddenly a loud bang sounds behind the crib; someone has dropped a pile of dishes. The infant startles, her blood pressure and heart rate increase, and she throws out her limbs and starts to cry.

In this example, the young organism experiences an intense, sudden, and unexpected change in the level of energy reaching her sensory systems. Without question, stimulus events characterized by these three elements seem to be capable of eliciting fear. This is true not only for young and immature infants but for children and adults as well. Thus, it is reasonable to recognize a class of events that produce unlearned fear. It should not be surprising that the human nervous system is designed to respond to some stimuli as noxious. Fear may be part of the response to a noxious event, that aspect that protects organisms by enabling them to avoid (or to try to avoid) similar situations in the future. The innate biological prewiring of specific classes of responses to specific stimulus events may not involve much (if any) cognitive activity, except insofar as the perception of the event is a cognitive activity itself. An example of the interplay between cognition and biological disposition is provided in the next example.

Example 3

A 2-year-old child is riding her tricycle with her mother as she walks through the park. A stranger walks over to the little girl, says "Hello" to the mother, and asks the child if she likes to ride her tricycle. The mother smiles and returns the greeting, while the child freezes, stops pedaling, turns toward the mother, frowns, and starts to whine.

This phenomenon has most commonly been called *stranger fear* or *stranger anxiety*. In this situation, the child is afraid of new people but shows positive behaviors to familiar people. The development of this fear (sometimes called *wariness*) usually occurs after the first eight months of life. Before this age, children generally exhibit positive behaviors in all social experiences. Thus, at an earlier age, this stranger, who now elicits fear, may have evoked affiliative behaviors, such as smiling.

Stranger fear has been considered by some a maturationally determined, biologically derived response, the function of which is to limit the number of people to whom infants can become attached (Schaffer & Emerson, 1964; Scott, 1963). Alternatively, it has been considered a manifestation of children's cognitive ability to compare various novel social events, such as strange people, with an internal representation of their caregiver (Schaffer, 1974). Even when the elicited emotion is viewed as the consequence of a cognitive task (i.e., the comparison of representations of familiar others with the stranger), the cause of the fear state seems to be related to its social significance. Thus, stranger fear has been considered an index of infants' primary relationship with significant others (i.e., infants' attachment to their primary caregiver), since it represents a discriminably different response to various adults (Ainsworth et al., 1978).

Example 4

An 8-month-old infant is sitting in his mother's bedroom. In the bathroom, his mother is dressing for the evening and has put on her new long-haired wig. As she steps into the bedroom, the infant stares at her intensely for a moment and suddenly begins to cry.

In this example, a cognitive process seems to result in an emotional response. The child has formed a schema of his mother. This schema involves the integration of the stimulus properties of this person, including the visual, auditory, and olfactory properties. The schema is highly complex, and because the child has already achieved the cognitive milestones of object and person permanence, an important and radical change may produce an emotional response. This sudden and unexpected change may elicit interest and arousal. The child orients and tries to make sense of this alteration in a familiar stimulus array. If the child cannot easily assimilate this transformation or accommodate the old schema to this new event, fear may result as a consequence of a violation of expectancy (Berlyne, 1960; Hebb, 1946; Kagan, 1974).

Although cognition is involved, the way in which cognition produces the emotional state is still unexplained. The connection between cognition and emotion in some cases may be prewired, and the inability to assimilate an event automatically causes fear. In other cases, the connection between a cognition and an emotion may be learned, and the inability to assimilate an event is perceived by the child as loss of control. Loss of control may be associated with painful events; thus, the fear state arises from a painful association.

Example 5

A 2-year-old child is playing in a sandbox in the park. Her mother is standing close by. As the child glances up from the sandbox, she sees her mother walking away. She begins to call "Mommy, Mommy," and starts running toward her mother with arms outstretched.

In the final example, adaptive functions are shown to be intimately connected to emotional states. This situation involves the child's fear of losing her mother. It is clear that (among primates at least) the loss of the primary caregiver increases the probability of the child's death.

It is extremely important, therefore, for infants to participate in the regulation and control of the interaction between themselves and their mother (Lewis & Rosenblum, 1974a). In particular, infants may help to regulate the physical distance from the mother. This regulation, which is performed by both members of the dyad, involves a wide variety of behaviors. Initially, because of the infant's helplessness, the mother may be the most active regulator within the dyad, but she is by no means the only one. Through crying, eye contact, and smiling, infants also regulate this distance. As infants mature and are able to move away from the mother as well as to follow her, they become increasingly capable of assuming a larger role in the regulation of the distance from the mother. Thus, in this example, the child is shown attempting both to move toward the mother and to get her to return.

Fear states resulting from the loss of primary caregivers appear to be adaptive because they are biologically useful. The eliciting of emotional states through an adaptive function may reflect the action of innate releasing mechanisms. The connection between adaptive functions and emotions has been recognized by others (Izard, 1979a; Plutchik, 1962, 1980b; Tomkins, 1962). Alternatively, it may reflect a learning process and the interplay between a cognitive and an emotional state. For example, the loss or distancing of the mother may have been associated in the past with painful events or with loss of control.

Although the above examples focus on fear, they pertain to different classes of emotions in general. Since emotions involve a complex set of coherences between behaviors and situations, any definition of emotion must capture this complexity. Whatever the ultimate definition, the roles of adaptive, biologically significant structures as well as cognitive structures must be recognized if we are to understand emotional behavior. Emotions are the result of a multitude of biological imperatives, situational constraints, and socialization practices. Only by recognizing their complex interplay can emotional development be fully understood.

A Working Definition of Emotion

Even this brief overview makes clear that it is extremely difficult to produce a satisfactory definition of *emotion*. Rather than trying to define *emotion*, we prefer to represent emotion in terms of a structural analysis in which the components of emotion are specified rather than explained. In such an analysis, emotions consist of five major components that together constitute *emotion*. These five components are labeled *elicitors*, *receptors*, *states*, *expressions*, and *experiences* (Lewis & Rosenblum, 1978a). Although others have also noted that a complete definition of emotion must take into account the experience (conscious, subjective feeling), the neurophysiological state, and the expression of emotion (e.g., Izard, 1977), no attention has been given to an analysis of each component, to its role in the total structure that we call *emotion*, and to its developmental course. In Chapters 4 and 5, these five aspects and their developmental features are discussed in detail. For now, the following definitions should suffice.

Emotional elicitors are situations or stimulus events that trigger an organism's emotional receptors. These stimuli may be either internal or external, and the capacity of these elicitors to evoke responses may be either innate or learned.

Emotional receptors are relatively specific loci or pathways in the central nervous system that mediate changes in the physiological and/ or cognitive state of the organism. The process through which these receptors attain their emotional function and the type of events that trigger their activity may be genetically encoded or acquired through experience.

Emotional states are the particular constellations of changes in somatic and/or neuronal activity that accompany the activation of emotional receptors. *Changes in* is the critical aspect of this definition. Emotional states are largely specific, transient, patterned alterations in ongoing levels of physiological activity. The issues related to the specific, transient, and patterned nature of emotional states have important consequences for the discussion of moods and are addressed later in this chapter.

Emotional expressions are the potentially observable surface features of changes in face, body, voice, and activity level that accompany emotional states. The constituent elements and their patterning, as well as the regularity with which they are associated with particular emotional states, may be either learned or innate.

Finally, *emotional experiences* are an individual's conscious or unconscious perception, interpretation, and evaluation of his or her emotional state and expression. This cognitive process is influenced by a range of prior social experiences in which the nature of the eliciting stimuli and the appropriateness of particular expressions have, in part, been articulated and defined for the individual by others.

Emotion versus Affect

One of the taxonomical distinctions often drawn in the literature is between emotion and affect. Webster's Third New International Dictionary (1976) defines *emotion* as "a physiological departure from homeostasis that is subjectively experienced in strong feeling ... and manifests itself in neuromusculature, respiratory, cardiovascular, hormonal, and other bodily changes preparatory to overt acts which may or may not be performed." *Affect* is defined as "the conscious subjective aspect of an emotion considered apart from bodily changes." From these definitions, we can see for the layperson, *emotion* corresponds to what we call *emotional state* and *affect* corresponds to *emotional experience*.

Izard (1977), on the other hand, views *affects* not as the experiential component of emotion but in terms of a broader set of events that includes both emotions and drives. *Drives* are defined as physiological needs, such as hunger, thirst, elimination, pain avoidance, and sex. In this scheme, emotions are a subset of affects. Whereas drives derive from the internal needs of the organism and are usually goal-directed and persist until satisfied, emotions arise out of an adaptive necessity of the organism's interaction with the external environment. Such distinctions, while perhaps useful from a theoretical perspective, have little heuristic value. In the subsequent discussion of emotional development, the distinction between emotional elicitors, receptors, states, expressions, and experience is regarded as more important than a distinction between emotion and affect.

Primary versus Secondary or Derived Emotions

The notion of primary and secondary or derived emotions is intimately connected to developmental issues. From either a biological or a learning position, the notion of primary or "fundamental" emotions implies that certain emotional states precede others in a developmental sequence. Secondary or derived emotional states emerge subsequent to the earlier primary set.

In many models of emotional development, the position is taken that the earliest emotional states that exist in the organism are the general states of pleasure and distress (Bridges, 1932; Lewis & Brooks, 1978; Sroufe, 1979b). A second set of emotional states is differentiated from these general states. Of some interest is the nature of these early differentiated states. Plutchik (1962) suggested that through an analysis of adaptive behavior, one can determine what these primary emotions might be related to. Eight basic patterns of adaptive behavior are identified that are thought to represent the basic dimensions of all emotional behavior: incorporation–affiliation, rejection, destruction, protection, reproduction, reintegration, orientation, and exploration. These adaptive functions are translated into a subjective or introspective language that employs the words that people generally use to describe their feeling states: acceptance–trust, disgust–loathing, anger–rage, fear–terror, joy–ecstasy, sadness–grief, surprise–astonishment, and expectancy –anticipation. The two terms provided for each emotion reflect an intensity or arousal dimension associated with feeling states.

In contrast to the eight emotions postulated by Plutchik, other investigators have identified and defined empirically 10 fundamental emotions: interest–excitement, joy, surprise–startle, distress–anguish, anger, disgust–revulsion, contempt–scorn, fear, shame, and guilt (Darwin, 1872; Ekman et al., 1972; Izard, 1971, 1977; Tomkins, 1962, 1963). Each of these emotions is also thought to have an adaptive function. They are labeled *fundamental* because each is assumed to have a specific and innately determined neural substrate, a characteristic neuromuscular expression, and a distinct subjective quality (Izard, 1977). Of the 10 emotions, 9 have been observed in the facial expressions of infants within the first year of life (Izard et al., 1980).

Since it is reasonable to assume that some emotional states precede others, one might be willing to talk about these emotional states as primary. In the most general case, the emotional states of distress and pleasure are primary, and all other emotional states are somehow "derived" from these. However, caution should be taken, since the appearance of one emotional state prior to another does not necessarily imply that the second is derived from the first, only that the second emerges at a later point in time. Thus, although signs of fear may appear before shame, shame may succeed fear only because the cognitive mechanisms for shame develop later. Alternatively, it may be that the neural "program" for one emotional state may develop later than another. For example, the sexual state may mature later than the state of joy.

When a secondary emotion is comprised of two emotions, we may assume that the secondary or derived emotion is related to and dependent on the more fundamental emotions. Plutchik (1980a), for one, considered many such combinations in trying to describe emotion mixtures. For example, he suggested that joy plus acceptance equals love and friendliness, fear plus surprise equals alarm and awe, and joy plus fear equals guilt. Plutchik's analogy is that of the color wheel, in which primary emotions are similar to primary colors and subsequent emotions are compared to hues derived from mixtures of these primary colors.

The issue of emotion mixtures is of considerable importance and will be returned to later in this chapter as well as in Chapter 7. There is some question about whether emotions can be characterized as single-state occurrences. The emotional life of the human organism is so highly complex and fluid that the existence, let alone the demonstration, of a pure and single emotional state is unlikely. From a phenomenological point of view, when people are asked how they feel in response to a particular elicitor, they report a complex set of emotions rather than a single one. For example, Schwartz and Weinberger (1980) presented a group of college students a questionnaire that consisted of descriptions of emotional situations, such as "You have just graduated from Yale." They then asked the subjects to imagine the situation and to rate which and how much of each of six emotions they felt. The emotions to be rated, by means of a simple 1-to-5 scale, included happiness, sadness, anger, fear, depression, and anxiety. In this particular example, mean ratings were 4.09 for happiness, 2.74 for sadness, 1.38 for anger, 2.57 for fear, 2.36 for depression, and 3.40 for anxiety (G. Schwartz, personal communication, 1979). Thus, these subjects did not limit their reports of emotional experiences to a single emotion; when given the opportunity, they demonstrated that their experience consisted of many emotions, often competing ones.

In an analysis of the sequence of emotional states, one emotion may precede another for at least four reasons. Figure 1 presents a 2 × 2 matrix depicting four possible sequences. The salient dimensions in this analysis are (1) whether, in a sequence of emotions, the emergence of emotions later in time is independent of or dependent on the development of earlier emotions and (2) whether the emergence of later emotions is a function of maturation or learning. For the sake of convenience, the sequence of only two emotions is considered, although a more elaborate analysis could be conceived by considering the development of additional states in (1) the same fashion as the first two; (2) a new fashion; or (3) some combination.

In Case A (dependent–maturation) Emotion 2 is dependent on Emotion 1, and this dependence is related to maturation. The emergence

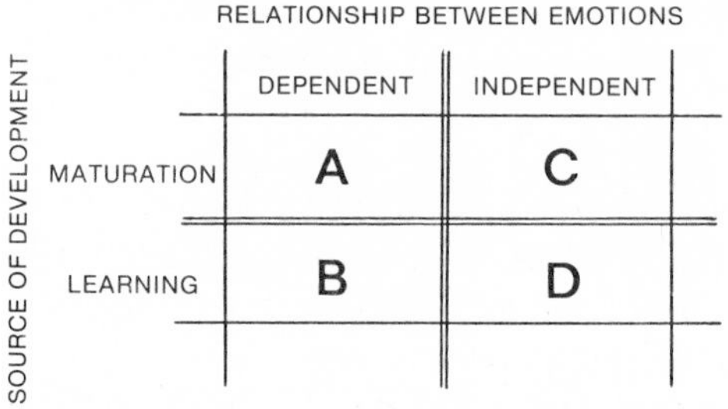

Figure 1. Possible sequences of emotional states.

of Emotion 1 activates the mechanisms necessary for Emotion 2, thereby enabling the second emotion to occur.

In Case B (dependent–learning), Emotion 2 is dependent on Emotion 1, but this dependence is based on the acquisition of cognitive structures rather than maturation. These structures occur as a result of Emotion 1 and lead directly to Emotion 2. Alternatively, the cognitive development of the second emotion may be related to a cognitive achievement associated with the first. Thus, the two emotional states are related, but they are related through the cognitions.

In Case C (independent–maturation) Emotion 2 is independent of Emotion 1 and emerges at a later point in time. The reasons for its later occurrence are related to its dependence on neuromaturational processes and their timing. Thus, although Emotion 2 always comes after Emotion 1, their relationship is not one of dependence.

Likewise, in Case D (independent–learning) Emotion 2 always follows Emotion 1. The cause of the sequence is the later development of cognitive structures that underlie Emotion 2 but which are not dependent on the cognitive underpinnings of Emotion 1.

In all four cases, the second emotional state is distinct from the first. In an alternative view of this sequence, the second emotion may be more directly related to the first. For example, the second emotional state may be an auxiliary of the first with additional emotional components as yet undefined. Still, the second emotion can be categorized as belonging (1) to a class of either independent or dependent states and (2) to a class related to either maturational unfolding or learned states. A complete picture of emotional development probably involves all possible cases. Also to be considered is the possibility of "families" of sequences with one "family" of emotional states following one sequence and other "families," other sequences.

Emotion, Mood, and Personality

If one could scan the emotional life of children, one might see a continuous stream of emotions, each related to a set of particular elicitors, to a preceding emotional state, and to the temperamental disposition of the individual child. One might also see that these vary in their sequential patterns and duration. Psychologists tend to study emotions in isolation because of the nature of the observational procedures, the measurement systems, and the experimental paradigms. Thus, psychologists may present a particular elicitor and usually for a brief period of time watch the subject's response. For example, the physiological response of the subject to a frightening elicitor may be measured. In this type of study, emotional responses (and by inference, emotional states and experiences) are seen as transient, that is, as having a specific onset and a brief duration.

In addition, the most careful measurement systems employed (e.g., Ekman & Friesen, 1978; Izard, 1979b) require a limited amount of observation time. During that time period, a particular emotional state is inferred through the analysis of facial musculature changes. Thus, emotions are measured as isolated events with fast rise times and are seen as unrelated to preceding emotional states and to the overall status of the subject. Even though mixtures of emotions in facial expressions may be coded, the emotions are still measured separately. Such experimental and measurement methods are not compatible with the view of emotional states and experiences as a chain of events. Theories derived from such studies consequently may be limited by a failure to recognize that emotional states and experiences, measured by emotional responses, exist in a continuous flow and influence one another.

If one imagines emotional life as a continuous chain of states and experiences, three factors can be identified that may be related to this sequence: (1) the nature of the elicitors, both the internal and the external events to which emotional life is related; (2) the contextual relationship of an emotional state to preceding and subsequent states; and (3) the characteristics of the subject.

1. *Elicitors.* The specific nature of the elicitor clearly affects the emotional state. Certain elicitors are much more likely to elicit some emotions than others. For instance, loss of support or falling will almost always elicit distress or fear in individuals at all ages.* Little more needs to be said here, since much will be said later about the relationship between elicitors and emotional states.

2. *Contexts.* Emotional states do not occur as single events, yet the effect of an emotional state on subsequent states has received relatively little attention. For example, an emotional state of joy preceded by an emotional state of sadness is likely to have different characteristics than a state of joy preceded by a state of fear or preceded by another state of joy (Moore, in press). Thus, an elicitor may produce a modified state as a function of a previous state, may produce a different state, or may produce a combination of states. A joy elicitor after a joy state might

---

* Although these elicitors are usually associated with distress, some adults seem to find excitement or enjoyment in similar situations, such as riding on a roller coaster. We would say that the roller coaster does elicit a state of fear, but the subject interprets that state as enjoyable.

lead to an elated state, a joy elicitor after sadness might produce guilt, and a joy elicitor after fear might produce relief.

3. *Subject characteristics.* A third influence on the nature of an emotional state in response to a particular elicitor is the characteristics of the subject. Here, the issues of temperament, personality, and previous experience play a role. It is likely that for some people emotional states and experiences are more intense and more lasting than for other people, regardless of the nature of the elicitor or of the preceding emotional state. The sources of such individual differences reside in a set of factors related to the disposition of the organism. Such dispositional factors may include arousal level, drug usage, or biological differences related to temperament. Consider, for example, the temperamental dimension of soothability. Children who are less able to be soothed are likely to be more subject to longer and more intense negative emotional states.

Nine temperamental characteristics have been articulated by Thomas, Chess, Birch, Hertzig, and Korn (1963): rhythmicity, mood, activity, adaptability, distractability, persistence, threshold, intensity, and approach. These dimensions, characteristics of the nervous system, influence the emotional life of children by intensifying particular emotional states as well as by affecting the sequential flow of these states. An example of the effect of temperament on emotional state is that a "difficult" baby (i.e., one not easily soothed) is less likely to exhibit pleasant emotional states and is more likely to exhibit negative ones. Even pleasant states may soon turn to discomfort or distress if the pleasant state is prolonged past a certain point.

In a recent study, children's temperament was shown to interact with the nature of the mothers' message in their response to a stranger (Feinman & Lewis, in press). The mothers' message (neutral or friendly toward the stranger) had little effect on "difficult" children's fear responses. In contrast, the mothers' message was shown to modify the fear responses of "easy" children. In this study, temperament was shown to play a role in modulating emotions through the mediation of cognitive information.

Personality may also play a role in modifying an elicitor through its effect on the perception and interpretation of the elicitor (Beck, 1971). Thus, a happy elicitor for one type of personality may be a negative elicitor for another. In our discussion of the socialization of emotion (Chapters 6 and 7), we present data showing the same imagined elicitor (e.g., a child's graduation from school) produces different emotional states for different people, which may be a function of the personality of the subject.

Finally, previous experience may play a role in the effect of an elicitor inasmuch as certain elicitors take on different meanings, depending on the past experience of an individual. Thus, for one child, a visit to the pediatrician's office may be characterized by pain. The thought of going to the doctor for that child will produce fear, whereas for a child who has never experienced such pain, the elicitor "visiting the doctor" will not produce fear.

For each of these three factors—temperament, personality, and previous experience—the subject's idiosyncratic experience, rather than the nature of the elicitor or its place in the chain of events, may be responsible for the particular emotional state and experience that is observed.

Emotion and Mood

Returning to the scanning machine, one might see that some emotional states and experiences are not transient events. In the sequence of emotions, some states (on some occasions) may last longer than others. We use the term mood to reflect those emotions that are not transient. An emotion may not be transient for several reasons. One is related to the nature of the elicitor. For instance, the success in choosing a stock that rises rapidly in value and results in a great monetary return for the investor constitutes an elicitor of joy and may have a more lasting effect than an elicitor of finding a lost dime or quarter. Some events are also sadder than others. For example, children may feel sad because the store is closed and they cannot buy any ice cream. In this situation, they are likely to feel sad for only a short period of time. People may also feel sad when their dog is run over by a car. In this case, the sadness may persist for a much longer period of time.

It seems reasonable to imagine that sustained emotional states and experiences (i.e., moods) can be caused by the nature of the elicitor. Mood is the term we would use to reflect those emotional states and experiences that have a relatively long duration. Compared with transient emotional states, moods are more likely to influence subsequent behavior and to color the way people perceive and interpret the world (Bower, 1981). It is not difficult to imagine events that are more powerful than others. Some elicitors are so powerful that by their very nature, they elicit long-term emotional states. Such events are usually labeled traumatic. In fact, traumatic events are, by definition, single events that have potentially long-term influences on emotional states (Freud, 1920).

The preceding emotional state of the child may also have an important influence on the duration of the following events. Exactly what sequences facilitate, inhibit, or alter subsequent states is unclear, since little work on state sequences has been undertaken. It may be the case that if children experience a sad event after having experienced a previously sad event, the sadness will endure longer. Thus, if a child's dog dies after his best friend goes on vacation, the sadness felt over both of these events occurring sequentially is likely to produce a different quality or intensity of sadness than if the two events were separated by a long time interval. Many examples of the combined effects of sequential emotions can be imagined. A sad elicitor following a frustration is likely to result in a longer period of sadness than the isolated occurrence of the sad elicitor. Repeated elicitation of excitation may lead to displeasure. Also, an amusing event that occurs after a frightening event is often not amusing. In all of these examples, the emotional state may be prolonged, enhanced, or altered by the events preceding it. These examples underscore the interdependence and flow notion of emotional states and experiences. They bear on the issue of mood by pointing out that the emotional life of organisms is not a series of short and narrowly defined temporal events.

While both the nature of the elicitor and preceding events play roles in the duration of an emotional state (i.e., a mood), the most likely cause of moods is related to the characteristics of the subject. The temperament and personality structures of children are the factors most likely to affect the duration of any particular state. As was pointed out, children's temperament should play an important role in moods. The data on easy and difficult babies (Brazelton, 1969; Thomas & Chess, 1977; Thomas, Chess, & Birch, 1968) indicate clearly that there are important individual differences in soothability, rhythmicity, regularity, and adaptability, which play an important role in children's moods. For example, children who are not easily soothed are more likely to exhibit distress moods than easily soothed children, who might experience transient states of distress but who are easily comforted and do not continue to be distressed.

The personality structure of the individual may also contribute to moods. Although it is true that some specific and powerful elicitors are likely to produce a particular mood (e.g., sadness as a consequence of the death of one's dog), the elicitor cannot continue to be effective unless the individual is willing and able to "re-present" it internally. That is, the dog's death cannot continue to serve as an elicitor of sadness unless the person is able and willing to re-present the departed dog as the elicitor for the continuing state. In other words, external elicitors may be of relatively short duration, but what the person does with these elicitors affects mood. In most cases, the external elicitor disappears and individuals themselves must re-present that elicitor internally if the elicitor is to have its continuing effect. Although some external elicitors are probably by nature more apt to be re-presented (e.g., death), the degree of re-presentation might well be a function of the person's personality. In the case of traumatic events, however, it may not be the individual's personality that re-presents the event; it may be the power of the stimulus itself, however that stimulus may be specified.

In the preceding discussion, the distinction between emotion and mood has been made on the basis of the duration of a particular emotional state or experience. Although not easily defined with regard to how long, the long-term existence of an emotional state or experience is labeled *mood*. Others might regard mood as differing from emotion in terms not only of duration but also of intensity. In such definitions, moods not only last longer but are also less intense than emotional states or experiences. Whether such a distinction in terms of intensity is warranted remains to be empirically determined. Certainly, there are moods that by their nature are quite intense. Depressed individuals may suffer from an emotional state of long duration, and in light of their behavioral repertoire (e.g., suicide attempts), the intensity of the emotion appears quite marked. It may be that intensity adheres to Helson's (1964) adaptation theory, so that sadness preceding happiness seems more intense than sadness following sadness. However, the degree of the absolute intensity of sadness in the two conditions may not differ. It is not clear how one would go about studying whether they, in fact, do differ.

In the research literature on moods, *moods* are generally defined as "states of emotional or affective arousal of varying, but not permanent, duration" (Wessman, 1979). Moods are usually seen as milder than emotions and of longer duration. Moreover, unlike emotional states, they frequently seem not to be related to specific eliciting situations. Moods have also been described as predispositions to respond in certain ways and to experience certain kinds of feelings. The research literature on moods contains little information about their development.

Nowlis (1965, 1970) has conducted some of the major research on moods. To assess changes in subjects' feelings as a consequence of drug ingestion, Nowlis and his colleagues developed a Mood Adjective Checklist for subjects' self-reports of how strongly they experienced various feelings. Twelve empirically based mood factors are consistently found in studies using this checklist: aggression, anxiety, surgency, elation, concentration, fatigue, vigor, social affection, sadness, skepticism, egotism, and nonchalance.

In Cattell's (1965, 1966, 1973) studies on mood 9 "state dimensions" are usually obtained. These dimensions have been designated: anxiety, extraversion–introversion, depression–elation, regression, high arousal–low activation, fatigue–energy, effort, stress, and guilt.

Finally, in a longitudinal study of college students, mood measures have been shown to be related to personality characteristics (Wessman, 1979; Wessman & Ricks, 1966). There appear to be a number of personality differences between people who are characterized by a happy mood and those characterized by a depressed mood and between people who are stable and those who are variable in mood. For example, variability in mood seems to be related to low degrees of denial and repression.

Developmental Perspective

We have suggested that the role of temperament is important in the development of mood. If one envisions temperament as a modulator of particular emotional states and experiences, enhancing the duration of some and affecting the sequential chain, then it is possible to think of emotional states and experiences as being influenced by infants' temperament and thus as affecting mood.

Child A and Child B, having equal amounts of a distressed state, may differ in the acquisition of distress moods as a function of temperamental differences. Child A, a difficult child, is more likely to experience distress moods than Child B, an easy child. In addition, temperament may affect the state directly by controlling what state the child is likely to have. For example, Child A and Child B, both aroused, are presented with a potentially positive elicitor. Child A, with a difficult temperament, may respond to the positive elicitor with distress, whereas Child B may respond with excitement and delight. Such examples implicate temperament as an important factor in affecting both emotional states and moods. Unfortunately, too little work has been conducted from a developmental perspective to examine the relationships among emotional state, temperament, and mood.

Another factor that may affect infants' and young children's moods may be the nature of their social experience. Recall that certain elicitors or sequences of elicitors are more likely than others to affect the duration of state. Infants and children who are subjected to a continuous stream of unpleasant elicitors are more likely to have prolonged and continuous distress states and distress moods. The socialization practices of parents toward their young children, especially in terms of alleviating and producing certain emotional states and experiences, have been viewed as the primary cause of long-lasting emotional states or moods.

The study of the socialization of emotion—in particular, the response of parents to their infant's emotional states—is a recent undertaking. Yet, data exist that support the view that socialization may have a significant influence on subsequent emotional states, experiences, and moods. Bell and Ainsworth (1972), for example, have shown that parental responsivity to an infant's distress in the first quarter of the first year of the infant's life results in less distress (i.e., crying) and more communicative behavior in the last quarter of the first year. Although these data have been questioned (Gewirtz & Boyd, 1977a,b), the general thesis—that the socialization of emotional states may affect subsequent moods—is fundamental to Bell and Ainsworth's argument.

Likewise, Lewis and Goldberg (1969b) have shown that the general responsivity level of the socializing agent is particularly effective in enhancing a "generalized expectancy," which includes measures of mood changes, such as increased interest in the environment, alterations in states of readiness to respond (arousal), and increased positive states ("affective motivation"). In contrast to these positive socialization effects is the state of "learned helplessness," in which lack of responsivity may result in general dispositions (moods) to feel helpless and depressed (Seligman, 1975). Thus, from a developmental perspective, transient emotional states may lead to moods through the characteristics of the subject (particularly temperament) as well as the nature of the socializing experience.

Emotion and Personality

One aspect of the durational characteristics of states is the fact that some states are more characteristic of individuals than others. That is, some individuals are more likely to exhibit certain states across a variety of eliciting conditions. The distinction between frequency and duration is the distinction between personality and mood. The following example characterizes this aspect of repeated occurrence of emotional states and experiences that we are referring to.

Two graduate students in developmental psychology were given the assignment of observing three children in a nearby preschool program. On two days a week for four successive weeks, the students observed the three children for two hours. Their observations included coding the children's activities, whom they played with, and their predominant facial expressions over successive 15-second intervals. The following summaries are based on 16 hours of observation of each child.

B was observed almost always to be in the company of other children and to play a variety of games. His predominant facial expression was smiling. B appeared to be happy and sociable.

G, on the other hand, was seen part of the time to be playing alone, although most often she was in the company of another child. G tended to play with few toys, and G's play was characterized by throwing things about rather than by sharing. G's facial expression was one of sadness and anger. G was characterized by the graduate students as a rather angry child who was often found fighting with peers and resisting the teacher's requests.

L played alone. Her play was usually low-keyed and quiet. She was often seen with her head lowered and on several occasions was observed on her teacher's lap crying. The students described L as sad and afraid.

These three children can be characterized in emotional terms. In fact, if one took any single observation and was asked on the basis of that observation to predict the child's response to another child (a particular elicitor), one would predict that B would show a happy, sociable response, G an angry response, and L a sad response. Thus, single observations can be used to predict future emotional responses of a particular child.

That these children showed a *consistency* in their emotional responses to a particular or a general set of elicitors over repeated observations suggests that the emotional states being observed were not only associated with the elicitor but idiosyncratic to the particular child. The consistency and the idiosyncratic nature of the response (i.e., individual differences to the same elicitor) indicate that some feature of the children's disposition was being tapped. Therefore, the ongoing emotional state can be considered a personality characteristic. That is, it occurs frequently and can be used to characterize the child rather than the eliciting event. Consistent and predominant emotional states appear to be what is meant by the term *personality characteristic* (Pervin, 1980).

We choose to distinguish between mood and personality characteristics on the following basis. Mood can be characterized by the long duration of a particular emotional state. A personality characteristic can be characterized by the frequent occurrence of an emotional state, often independent of the eliciting event. The distinction between mood and personality characteristics may reside in the distinction between duration and frequency. Both are comprised of emotional states or experiences. Thus, a person who responds with an emotional state of sadness consistently across elicitors that do not necessarily produce sad states in others can be said to have a personality characteristic of depression. The person who maintains this sadness over a long period of time can be said to be in a sad or depressed mood.

Enduring and idiosyncratic moods are the equivalent of personality characteristics. We believe that the duration of emotional states defines moods, and that the repeated occurrence of moods characterizes personality. Yet each can remain independent of the other. Moods, as we have indicated, affect emotional states. Likewise, personality can influence both by affecting the nature of the elicitor and/or the nature of the response. In the case of elicitors, a personality characteristic may cause the occurrence of the same elicitor and thus, through the chain of elicitor→ receptor → state → experience, produce a consistent emotional response. For example, children may repeatedly ask for their teachers' attention in situations in which their attention cannot be given. The children's behavior thus produces an elicitor of rejection. Personality structure can also operate on the interpretation of particular elicitors. For example, when the teacher does respond, the child may interpret the response as inadequate and still feel rejected.

Beck (1976), Seligman (1975), Schachter and Singer (1962), and others have tended to think of depression as a person's interpretation of events so as to seem random and beyond her or his control. For these investigators, the cognitive interpretation results in the depression. However, what they failed to address is how personality structures lead to such cognitive assessments. That the structures are idiosyncratic and recurrent over a variety of situations suggests that there may be some personality characteristics involved.

The notion of a connection between emotion and personality is not new. Personality traits may be interpreted as mixtures of basic emotions or as composed of repeated, mixed emotional states. A *personality trait* is "simply a tendency or disposition to react to interpersonal situations with consistent emotional reactions" (Plutchik, 1980a, p. 173). Personality judgments are based on repeated evidence of certain types of emotional reactions. Although there is virtually no empirical evidence regarding the development of personality, it has been suggested that personality traits develop from the mixing of emotions through persisting situations (Plutchik, 1980a). In other words, children's characteristic ways of responding to situations that repeat themselves frequently over time become, as it were, their personality.

The research in this area is usually designed to identify the emotional components of adult personality. Typically, judges are asked to decide which primary emotions comprise each personality trait, and factor-analytic techniques are applied to determine the relationship among personality traits. Different traits may contain the same components comprised of differing intensities, or they may have additional components. Plutchik (1980a,b) has identified 8 primary emotional dimensions that he believes permit the synthesis of all the emotions and interpersonal personality traits recognized in our language. Cattell (1946) earlier analyzed the ratings of subjects on 171 traits by cluster analysis and identified 35 clusters that comprise the "standard reduced personality sphere."

Finally, recent data from G. Schwartz's laboratory (personal communication, 1979) suggest that personality variables may affect the way in which emotional responses are patterned. For instance, the emotions of happiness, sadness, anger, and fear were differentiated in terms of facial electromyographic (EMG) patterns only for subjects who scored neither exceptionally high nor exceptionally low on a depression scale (i.e., the "normal" subjects). In other words, there appears to be a greater association between the subjective experience of emotion and the emotional response patterning for normal subjects than for highly depressed or "low-normal" subjects. Furthermore, the association between facial EMG and self-reports of positive emotions were greater for normal subjects, whereas for the negative emotions, the association was greater for the depressed and low-normal groups. Such studies still beg the question of how personality structures themselves come into being or what comprises them. If we view personality structure as a mixture or patterning of emotions, then it makes little sense to say that a pattern of emotions (i.e., personality) leads to a patterning of emotional responses.

Developmental Perspective

From a developmental point of view we have already addressed the issue of how emotional states or experiences may develop into moods. Both the subject's characteristics (temperament) and the nature of the elicitors (including the socialization experience) seem to be primary factors affecting the individual's mood. While temperament certainly plays an important role, we suggest that emotional states and experiences are largely determined by the social world of the young child (see Chapters 5, 6, and 7). This view provides for a system whereby early emotional states and experiences are both facilitated and interpreted for children by their caregiver. These early emotional states and experiences must in some way themselves become the context or structure for the development of later states. For example, if children very early on are subjected to fear-inducing events, they will experience much fear. This experience, in turn, will increase the likelihood of being afraid and, in turn, should cause them to feel fear more readily under low fear-eliciting conditions. The same could be said for emotions other than fear. Thus, the early experiences that produce negative emotional states may create structures that are likely in themselves to lead to further negative states. The fact is that these emotional experiences tend to become feedback systems that reinforce themselves. These early experiences are the material for both moods and personality, which, in turn, affect the subsequent duration and frequency of other emotional states and experiences.

We have suggested that both moods and emotional states can be viewed as reflecting personality structure to the degree that they are idiosyncratic and occur with some regularity, often independent of the elicitor. Thus, the development of personality as well as the development of mood has to do with the regular occurrence of emotional states and experiences. That these emotional states, experiences, and moods are ultimately affected by personality structure suggests that from a developmental perspective, this system must be considered in terms of a feedback mechanism. Given that we are reluctant to attribute personality to very young organisms, it seems likely to be the case that this feedback system activates itself around emotional states and temperament. This belief is reasonable in light of the similarity between temperamental variables and later personality characteristics. Although there are few empirical studies to support this claim, temperamentally difficult infants may develop personalities quite different from easy babies (Thomas & Chess, 1977; Thomas, Chess, & Birch, 1970). If this is the case, then individual characteristics such as temperament may provide the mediating conditions for connecting emotional states and personality structures. The predicament of how one can have idiosyncratic and repeated emotional states to a variety of elicitors without a personality structure to mediate that consistency can be addressed by postulating temperament as the intermediary structure. Thus, temperament controls the regularity of emotional states in response to different elicitors until such time as a personality structure emerges from these states to act as an organizer of the states themselves.

This process is depicted in Figure 2. Here elicitors (I) modulated by temperament (T) lead to emotional states (S_{1x} or S_{2x}). These states have certain features, including duration and frequency. The patternings of the set of states (S_{1x} or S_{2x}) lead to or are themselves personality structures. The subsequent development of personality structures, in turn, serves to modulate the elicitors in place of or in addition to the

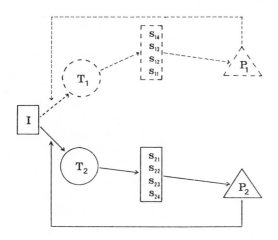

Figure 2. The relationship between temperament (T), emotional state (S), and personality (P) as a function of the elicitor (I).

original temperament (T_1 or T_2). This sequence is developmental in nature.

In Figure 2, the same elicitor (I) is shown to have a different effect on two subjects, depending on their temperament. In one subject, an easy temperament (T_1) produces (depending on the elicitor) a set of states (S_{1x}) that is quite different from the set for the second child, who has a difficult temperament (T_2). For the second child, the states (S_{2x}) contribute to a personality structure (P_2) that is different from the personality structure of the first child (P_1). These two personality structures, in turn, feed back into and affect the subjects' responses to the elicitor. For example, an intense game for the easy child might lead to a set of positive emotional states, which may produce a nonfearful personality structure. This same arousing game for the difficult child would lead to a set of distress states, which, in turn, might produce a fearful personality structure. The personality structures of these two children will result in different responses to the same game.

Individual Differences in Emotion

In the preceding chapter, we addressed the issue of why we chose to study individual differences in emotion rather than in cognition or intelligence, as others have done so frequently. In our discussion, we focused on the fact that individual differences and their role in the individual's well-being throughout the life cycle must be more than differences in cognition. Few systematic attempts at measuring individual differences in emotion have been undertaken.

In considering individual differences in emotions, one can focus on several aspects. One can focus on the transient emotional states and experiences of individuals. However, transient emotional states and experiences are most often related to the elicitor that produces them and to their position in the chain of emotional states or experiences. In order to measure individual differences in emotion, and in order to study the development of individual differences, one must consider emotional states and experiences that are not transient, and that do not depend primarily on eliciting conditions. Such a demand immediately turns our attention to individual differences in emotional states and experiences that are enduring. As we have tried to indicate, an investigation of enduring emotional states and experiences necessitates the study of mood. In studying mood, we may be looking at the growth of personality and individual differences in personality structure. Such a conclusion appears logical in light of the foregoing analysis.

Rather than approaching the study of personality and mood in the more traditional way, we will seek in subsequent chapters to focus attention on individual differences in emotional states and experiences. That such an inquiry simultaneously addresses the issues of mood and early personality structure is fortuitous and exciting.

3

Approaches to the Study of Emotion

A complete review of theories of emotion is a major undertaking well beyond the scope of this volume, and overviews of the field have been provided elsewhere (Gardiner, Gardiner, & Beebe-Center, 1970; Plutchik, 1980a; Plutchik & Kellerman, 1980; Strongman, 1978). Rather, in this chapter we shall examine three approaches to the study of emotion that have heuristic value. These approaches are the physiological, the cognitive, and the motivational approaches. Each approach is discussed in terms of theories that illustrate it. No attempt is made to include every relevant theory, however.

Most of the theories included in this chapter are not concerned with developmental issues. The supporting evidence for these theories comes from studies in which the experimental paradigms are suitable only for organisms capable of verbal and/or written reports. The theories generated from such data, while at times touching on developmental issues, are not themselves developmental. Yet issues pertaining to development are highly relevant to discussions of emotion theory. For example, any theoretical approach distinguishing between levels of emotion (i.e., between primary and secondary, or derived, emotions) is by definition developmental. Even if secondary emotions are defined as mixtures and not necessarily derivatives of primary emotions, a developmental component is still required—if only because secondary emotions emerge later than primary ones. Issues pertaining to emotional expression and its socialization require a developmental perspective. Even theories that profess the universality of emotional expressions and states and the necessary correspondence between them must account for individual differences in the expression of particular emotional states. Such differences are likely to be a function of socialization and therefore are developmental in nature.

Cognitive theories of emotion involve developmental issues as well. Following the seminal work of Piaget, investigators have argued that mature cognitive activity is the consequence of a series of profound transformations of cognitive structures. These transformations take place during the first 12 years or so of life. If, as cognitive-affective theorists maintain, there is an intimate connection between cognition and emotion, then the impact of cognitive development requires that one consider its consequences in the emotional life of children.

The focus of this chapter is primarily on the three approaches to the study of emotion; the major developmental issues and theories are discussed in the next four chapters. First, however, we put the study of emotion in a broader perspective by considering its philosophical roots.

Philosophical Inquiries into Emotion

Questions about the nature of emotion and its effects are not exclusive to contemporary psychology. Since the time of Aristotle, philosophers have speculated about the nature of emotion, where it comes from, what its effects on the organism are, and how one emotion can be distinguished from another (Diamond, 1974; Reeves, 1958). Two philosophical theories in particular have influenced contemporary emotion theory. Aristotle, in the fourth century B.C., is generally considered the first person to think systematically or extensively on the topic of emotion. In the seventeenth century Descartes proposed a dualistic theory that appeared again in later discussions on emotion.

For Aristotle, emotion, or "passion," was an experience involving the activity of both the mind and the body. According to his "rationalist, common sense doctrine of emotion," the emotional process is activated when an organism perceives an object either real or imagined as good or bad with regard to that organism's well-being. This perception of the object as having the potential for producing pleasure or pain arouses in the organism a desire about or tendency toward that object. This desire is manifest both as a feeling (attraction or repulsion) and as physical activity (bodily changes and facial expressions) and may result in overt action either to satisfy or resist the desire.

Thus, Aristotle identified four features that contribute to emotion: (1) an object or emotional stimulus; (2) a perception and a cognitive evaluation of the stimulus as good or bad; (3) a resulting feeling of pleasure or pain with respect to that object (physiological state); and (4) a pursuit or avoidance of the object (behavioral expression). Some or all of these components are critical to contemporary definitions of emotion.

Centuries after Aristotle, Descartes proposed a theory of emotion based on a contrast of passion with reason. In Cartesian theory, emotion is defined as the excitation of the soul caused and maintained by the movement of animal spirits. The emotional process begins, according to Descartes, when an object is perceived and its image is projected to the pineal gland (a structure near the top of the brain where the "soul" was believed to exercise its functions). The association of past experiences with the object affects the image and arouses "animal spirits" (a liquid substance believed to regulate the body). The arousal of animal spirits excites the pineal gland. This process is experienced by the soul as emotion. At the same time, some of the animal spirits flow into the nerves, resulting in visceral changes and overt behavior. The viscera send the animal spirits back to the brain, which reinforces and strengthens the passion.

There are several problems with this theory, the most obvious of which is the notion of animal spirits, a notion that was discredited later with the discovery of the circulation of the blood. A second problem is not unique to Descartes's theory but pertains to any theory that depends on the association of past experience with the stimulus to elicit the emotional response. The problem here is explaining how an object can initially arouse an emotion, before any associations are formed. Finally, there is seemingly no provision made for the termination of the emotional process once the animal spirits are activated.

In contrast to Aristotle's earlier view of emotion as an active tendency in relation to an object that is experienced psychologically and physiologically, Descartes conceptualized emotion as the consequence of a passive soul stirred by bodily upset caused by an image of an object forming an impression in the brain. Although the idea that the soul interacts with the body by means of the pineal gland is an extremely mechanistic explanation of emotion, the notion that emotional activity originates in a brain structure was an important contribution to emotion theory as well as a particular solution to the mind–body problem.

Finally, for Aristotle, emotion provided a motivation for the organism to act, while for Descartes, emotion was a disorganizing experience. The Cartesian theory of emotion probably has had a less obvious impact on contemporary theories of emotion, although the conception of emotion as having a disorganizing, chaotic, and interfering effect on behavior reappears in many psychological theories of emotion (Strongman, 1978).

Other philosophers, both before and after Descartes, have speculated on the nature of emotion, but for the most part, they have had little significant influence on contemporary theories. One exception is worth mentioning, however, and that is the humoral theories of emotion that originated in the Galenic medicine of the Middle Ages. Humors were theorized to be bodily secretions that produce temperamental differences in emotional reactivity. Humoral theory is currently represented in contemporary endocrine research (Pribram, 1980). Historically, humoral theories were replaced by physiological and neurological theories in the late nineteenth and early twentieth centuries. About two centuries after Descartes, the first psychological theory of emotion was formulated by William James.

The Physiological Approach

The search for the origins of emotions and arguments about the mechanisms underlying emotion and their location characterize the physiological approach to emotion theory. Of the three approaches discussed in this chapter, the physiological approach has generated the longest and most vigorous research effort. Partly as a result of early definitions of emotion that assigned a large role to somatic and/or visceral changes in the production of emotion, much of this research has been devoted to specifying and trying to locate the physiological correlates of emotion (Black, 1970; Buck, 1976). Such efforts have met with varying success, in part because the laboratory techniques necessary for conducting such research are not yet sufficiently refined. Investigators have also tended to oversimplify what is an extremely complex phenomenon. As a consequence, many physiological theories are speculative, built on small pieces of data around particular points.

One way to approach this discussion is from the point of view of the five components of emotion that were enumerated in the previous chapter. Recall that emotional *elicitors* are either internal or external stimuli that activate emotional *receptors* located in as-yet-unspecified areas of the organism. The activation of these receptors produces an *emotional state* in the organism. This state is likely to be reflected in overt behavioral *expressions* of the emotion. The organism's interpretation and evaluation of these expressions, as well as its perception of the internal state, constitute the subjective *experience* of the emotion.

This conceptualization provides a framework for discussions of the physiology of emotion. Three issues in particular lie at the heart of physiological discussions. The first concerns whether emotions originate in central or peripheral structures of the body; this is a discussion of receptors. The second involves the issue of whether specific responses or patterns of responses are associated with particular emotions or whether instead a general arousal is at the core of emotion; this is a discussion of states. A third discussion addresses the question of whether emotions are the physiological responses *per se* or whether they are bodily changes *as perceived by the organism*. In other words, do emotions represent nothing more than the underpinnings of a set of cognitive processes? This discussion takes place at the level of emotional experience.

Emotional Elicitors and the Physiological Approach

Physiological theories are not overly concerned about specifying the nature of the elicitor. Noxious stimuli, used to elicit fear in laboratory experiments involving animals, usually consist of electrical shock. Mild electrical shocks are also used to elicit fear and anxiety in human subjects. In a study designed to look at differential patterns of physiological response between fear and anger in human subjects, Ax (1953) used electric shock as a fear elicitor and verbal abuse of the subject by a laboratory assistant as an anger elicitor. Positive emotions, in contrast, are studied by implanting electrodes within the brain of the animal in "pleasure centers" (Olds, 1955; Olds & Fobes, 1981). Finally, a diffuse state of general physiological arousal has been elicited by injections of epinephrine (Schachter, 1964).

Emotional Receptors and the Physiological Approach

Receptors are the organismic sites that are activated by emotional elicitors. Two major sites have been implicated in the origin of emotion: the peripheral and the central nervous systems.

Peripheral Theories

Peripheral theories of emotion are characterized by an emphasis on the role of the sensory organs and muscles in emotion as they are controlled by the autonomic nervous system (ANS). This approach was launched by James (1884, 1890) late in the nineteenth century. Basically, James turned Aristotle's doctrine of emotion upside down by suggesting that a physiological event (visceral or somatic) occurs prior to the felt experience of emotion. Emotion, as defined by James, is the perception of these peripheral changes as they occur. Emotion originates in the periphery and is relayed to the brain, where it becomes the conscious experience. James's theory led investigators on a search to identify the nature of the peripheral changes that are critical to the felt experience of emotion.

A similar theory was proposed by Carl Lange (1885/1922), although Lange viewed changes in the vascular system as being more essential to emotion than changes in the viscera or soma. Lange, unlike James, defined emotion solely in terms of peripheral responses, in this case circulatory reactions: the perception of the physiological change was not necessary to the emotion. Wenger (1950) later elaborated on Lange's ideas, declaring that emotion is the visceral action elicited by the ANS. It may involve, but does not necessarily involve, bodily changes or mental activity (Wenger, Jones, & Jones, 1956). All subjective feelings associated with emotion are ignored, and emotion is equated solely with visceral response.

Peripheral theories of emotion can be criticized on a number of counts, many of which Cannon (1927) used to attack James's theory. Cannon enumerated five problems that apply to all peripheral theories. First, he noted that emotional behavior is not impaired when the viscera are separated from the central nervous system (CNS) of animals. However, the fact that animals continue to exhibit emotional behavior in the absence of visceral sensation does not necessarily mean that the emotional experience has not been affected. Research on humans suggests that patients with spinal cord injuries report a decrease in their subjective emotional experience after the injury, and some report acting emotionally without any corresponding feeling (Buck, 1976).

Second, Cannon noted that the diffuse visceral changes associated with emotional states are also found in nonemotional states, such as physical exertion, fever, or exposure to heat and cold. Subsequent research has also failed to locate different patterns of physiological responses for different emotional states (Lacey, Kagan, Lacey, & Moss, 1963). The possibility still exists, however, that changes in muscular responses, in conjunction with visceral changes, underlie emotional differentiation.

Third, Cannon pointed out that the viscera are relatively insensitive structures. This observation does not prove that the viscera are incapable of contributing to emotional experience.

Fourth, Cannon suggested that visceral changes are too slow to be the source of emotion. It has been shown that both emotional experience and emotional expression can occur after the presentation of an emotional stimulus in an interval of time too short for feedback from peripheral visceral structures to occur (Newman, Perkins, & Wheeler, 1930).

Cannon's fifth point was that the artificial induction of visceral changes known to occur in specific emotions does not produce the emotion, a point confirmed by subsequent research (Schachter, 1964).

Although the importance of peripheral mechanisms as a component of emotion continues to be demonstrated (Black, 1970; Fehr & Stern, 1970), most research finds them to be no more than a vague reflection of general arousal. They may be necessary but do not seem to be sufficient for the occurrence of emotion. The issue of even their necessity to the expression of emotion is raised in clinical studies. One must conclude on the basis of such studies that although visceral feedback normally plays an important role in emotional processes, it is neither necessary nor sufficient for all kinds of experience or behavior.

Central Theories

Central theories of emotion are physiological theories that locate the origins of emotion in the CNS. Central theories generate hypotheses concerning the CNS in combination with the ANS. In peripheral theories, to repeat, the bodily changes accompanying or causing emotion are located in the viscera or soma and are under the control of the ANS. The neurological tradition is concerned more with the relationship between emotions and brain structures and activities. The focus of many of the central theories is on identifying the particular brain structure(s) producing emotion.

The first psychological theory to suggest that emotions are produced by a brain mechanism was that of Cannon (1927, 1931). On the basis of a series of experiments with cats in which different parts of the brain were removed, Cannon (1929) demonstrated that visceral activity alone does not account for emotional expression. Cannon's research drew attention to the importance of subcortical structures to emotion. He believed that the thalamus, in particular, was the source of emotion, that the experience of emotion depends on neural impulses relayed from the thalamus to the cortex, and that the expression of emotion depends on neural impulses sent from the thalamus to various motor centers of the body.

About the same time, Bard's (1928) research suggested that the hypothalamus was the critical structure in emotional reactions. Later research has confirmed the fact that both the thalamus and the hypothalamus are involved in emotion to some extent (Pribram, 1980). There is little evidence, however, that emotion is produced within either the thalamus or the hypothalamus or that it is experienced and expressed when these structures are released from inhibition.

After Cannon, the locus of emotion was extended to the limbic forebrain. Papez (1937) proposed that the emotional mechanism is not located in any one specific center of the brain but instead is mediated by several cortical structures. According to his theory, sensory impulses from the periphery travel to the thalamus, where they split into three different pathways or "streams of excitation" on their way to the cortex. The "stream of movement" leads to structures of the forebrain, where the movement patterns are coordinated; the "stream of perceiving" leads to the lateral parts of the cerebral cortex responsible for thought processes; and the "stream of feeling" leads from the hippocampus through the fornix to the mammillary body (part of the hypothalamus), the anterior thalamic nucleus, and the gyrus cinguli.

Whereas emotional expression was thought to depend on the hypothalamus, the cortex was believed to be necessary for the mediation of the subjective emotional experience. Although some of this theory is based on empirical data showing that cortical structures (for example, the hippocampus) as well as subcortical structures are involved in emotion, there is no evidence that the hypothetical neural circuit delineated by Papez is specific to emotion.

MacLean (1949, 1954, 1970) also believed the limbic system to be responsible for the integration of emotional experience, but he suggested that the "effector mechanism" was probably the hypothalamus, which connects the periphery to the cortex and gives sensory impulses their emotional tone. MacLean made no attempt to trace the cortical pathways underlying emotion. Rather, he speculated that all limbic-system structures are involved in emotion in some way and that no specific mechanisms are responsible for particular emotional patterns.

The complexity of the neural circuitry was underscored by Delgado (1960, 1964, 1966) after a long series of investigations into the brain mechanisms underlying emotion. Delgado recognized that it is possible for single behaviors to be involved in various emotional as well as nonemotional expressions and that the same emotion can be produced by electrically stimulating *different* brain locations.

Based on experiments involving the electrical stimulation of different areas of the brain, Delgado divided the brain into three parts. The first division consists of that part of the brain in which no emotional effects are produced by electrical stimulation. The second division involves locations where electrical stimulation produces only emotional behavior and no subjective experience. The third area includes structures that, when electrically stimulated, produce both emotional behavior and emotional experience. Parenthetically, such a demonstration lends support to our structural analysis of emotion into state, expression, and experience.

All of the evidence provided by these theories, as well as others, has been integrated into Pribram's (1967a,b, 1970, 1980) theory of emotion. For Pribram, the entire brain is involved in the regulation of feeling; yet, at the same time, each part of the brain plays a very specific role in the totality. Emotions are activated by neural processes when an incongruity exists between some stimulus input and the organism's "plans." That is, emotions occur when an unexpected environmental event creates an incongruity for the organism between past experiences and the current input; this incongruity causes an alerting or a habituating reaction on the part of the organism, which, in turn, sets in motion various brain processes that attempt to "control" the input into the sense organs. Pribram's research represents an attempt to delineate the biological underpinnings of the resulting feelings.

Two dimensions of feelings are important in Pribram's theory. First, feelings have a "protocritic" dimension that is related to the intensity (or quantity) of the stimulus event. Second, feelings have an "epicritic" dimension, which is related to the qualitative aspects of the stimulus and the cognitive dimension (labeling) of feeling states. The biological roots of the first dimension are thought to involve three sets of control systems. First, there are "neurochemical control systems" that establish relatively enduring states by means of homeostatic regulations. Hormones secreted in different concentrations probably account for differences in reactivity and thus differences in emotional disposition and temperament. The chemical characteristics of each state are as yet incompletely specified (Pribram, 1971, 1977; Stein, 1978). A second system, the "neuroelectrical control system," interfaces with the neurochemical control system to regulate the stability and changes of these states. This system is responsible for feelings and expressions of arousal and activation. In this system, unlike the first, control is exercised by way of neural circuitry rather than chemical regulation. A third control system is responsible for coordinating the arousal and activation generated by the second system. The third system underlies feelings and expressions of effort and comfort.

The peripheral mechanisms proposed by earlier investigators are not directly responsible for the feelings the organism experiences, in Pribram's (1980) view, although such mechanisms may be involved in the brain regulations of state:

> They are involved in the registration in memory of changes, so that the organism can habituate to them. Thus they are the components of which stable neural (core-brain) representations of bodily states are put together.

> Changes in these core-brain states, not in the somatic inputs per se, appear
> to be related to the experiencing of the protocritic dimension of emotion
> and emotional feelings. (pp. 262–263)

The essence of emotion in Pribram's theory of emotion is the regulation of changes in stable states, core-brain states, and body states.

> Brief episodic mild changes in stability are experienced as arousing and
> interesting (novel); more severe disruptions are painful and frightening.
> When control is exercised to contain such changes, it is experienced as
> effortful; when little control is needed, behavior is automatic and the ex-
> perience is one of comfort. (pp. 263–264)

The processing of this protocritic dimension, as we have been discussing, takes place in the core-brain systems of the brain stem and the limbic forebrain. The cortex contributes to the experience of emotions in a more complex fashion that is not well specified. Evidence reviewed by Pribram (1980) suggests that a cortical contribution by way of input to core-brain structures is responsible for the epicritic (cognitive) dimension of feeling states.

Arnold (1950, 1960, 1970) must be mentioned in any discussion of physiological theories of emotion, although her theory is more cognitive than physiological in both its orientation and its later influence on the field. Arnold assumed that the identification of the brain structures and physiological pathways mediating between the perception of a stimulus event and the emotion felt and expressed can be attained through an analysis of the cognitive-phenomenological aspects of emotion. The goal is to trace the neural pathways that mediate the psychological processes experienced in emotion. The specific psychological experiences that must be accounted for neurologically include (1) the cognitive appraisal of the sensory experience; (2) recall and affective memory; (3) the imagination of what is to come; and (4) the action tendency (which is the "felt emotion").

The evidence Arnold reviewed led her to conclude that the limbic system mediates the experience of liking or disliking (i.e., controls cognitive appraisal), that the hippocampus is responsible for the recall of past experiences and action impulses, and that the cerebellum amplifies the action pattern and organizes action for the whole body. This organized pattern of impulses from the cerebellum is related to the ventral thalamus and the frontal lobe. Relays from the frontal lobe as well as from the hypothalamus go to the premotor cortex, which is assumed to mediate the subjective experience of the action impulse. The physiological component of Arnold's theory is speculative and has little empirical support.

Although Hebb's (1949) theory has been associated with notions of cognitive incongruity and its effect on emotion, his contribution to physiological theories of emotion is a neurological explanation of emotion without reference to consciousness. According to Hebb, emotion is a neural process that is inferred from and causes emotional behavior. Central to Hebb's theory is the notion that emotional upset is a cortical disorganization of phase sequences. A phase sequence is a series of cell assemblies; a *cell assembly* is defined as

> a diffuse structure comprising cells in the cortex and diencephalon (and also, perhaps, in the basal ganglia of the cerebrum), capable of acting briefly as a closed system, delivering facilitation to other such systems and usually having a special motor facilitation. (Hebb, 1949, p. xix)

Phase sequences are experienced in the form of perceptions, thoughts, images, concepts, etc. Unpleasant emotions are the result of disruptions in phase sequences, while pleasant emotions are the result of developing phase sequences.

Later, Hebb (1958) recognized that the idea of the disruption of assembly action from physiological and anatomical postulates is not justified physiologically. Rather than concentrating on individual assemblies, Hebb began to focus on the arousal system; overfacilitation from the arousal system is involved in the disorganization of phase sequences. Emotional disturbance is the result of a conflict between phase sequences, a lack of sensory input for phase sequences, or even metabolic changes. Even in its revised form, Hebb's theory still suffers from broadly defined concepts that lack empirical support.

✖✖✖✖✖✖✖✖✖✖

The search for the mechanisms of emotion and arguments for their location either within or between the peripheral and the central nervous systems is an important enterprise. The failure to find a unique relationship between discrete emotions and peripheral changes under the control of the ANS led investigators to examine other, more central mechanisms. Even today, there are theorists who view emotion in terms of muscular changes, particularly in the face (e.g., Tomkins, 1962). Whether it is productive to restrict the notion of bodily change to one system or another cannot be answered.

The continuing quest for the locus of emotion raises a critical issue: Are the physiological changes that investigators believe accompany emotional states and experiences located in a single system or in multiple systems? From the 1930s on, there has been general agreement that multiple brain centers are involved in emotion. Yet, although the entire brain is involved, each part may still play a specific role in the emotional process. Clearly, an organismic approach requires that the total organism be considered. Thus, it will be necessary to look both at the coordination of multiple systems and at select patterns within single systems in order to describe emotion through physiological changes.

Physiological investigators continue their search for the locus of emotion. With advances in technology as well as new discoveries in pharmacological research, this approach is likely to become less speculative in the future. Pribram (1980) has already foreshadowed the direction that this new research will take. The risk, however, is that many of the broader issues involved in the study of emotion, especially those related to its phenomenological aspect, will be overlooked in highly mechanistic and reductionistic discussions of emotion.

Emotional States and the Physiological Approach

An emotional state is the particular constellation of changes in the physiological activity that accompanies the activation of emotional receptors (whether located in the periphery or the CNS). Such states are unrelated to the organism's perception of the physiological changes. The issue of concern in the physiological approach with respect to states involves whether specific responses or patterns of responses are associated with particular emotions or whether a general arousal state is the primary factor.

Recall that in the strong version of peripheral theories, emotion is equated with visceral activity of the ANS (e.g., Wenger et al., 1956). It may, but does not necessarily, involve mental activity. Thus, for Wenger, emotion is not a mental experience nor the result of the perception of a bodily state as James postulated; rather, it is the bodily state itself. Conceptualized in this fashion, all organisms, including newborn babies and nonhuman primates, have emotions and are always in some emotional state because autonomic activity is continuous. Even the state of homeostasis is a state of emotion, and emotions may change from this state.

Concomitant with this idea is the notion that unique patterns of visceral activity exist for specific emotions and are the basis of emotional differentiation. James also believed that different emotions have unique patterns of visceral or somatic changes. Differences in emotions from this point of view, then, are defined by differences in ANS or somatic patterns and not by differences in subjective experiences. Although evidence supporting this proposition is scant (Ax, 1953; Wolf & Wolff, 1947), theorists who still subscribe to it believe that with the development of more sophisticated measurement techniques, it is only a matter of time before many of the physiological changes will be identified.

Because of the problems in conceptualizing emotion solely in terms of peripheral activity, including the difficulty of distinguishing emotional from nonemotional states and distinguishing one emotional state from another, investigators, as we have already said, tried to locate the relevant physiological changes in the CNS, rather than in the peripheral mechanisms of the ANS, and to describe emotion in terms of neural circuits and structures. Although theoretically it should be possible to distinguish among specific emotional states on the basis of differences in neural circuitry or the functioning of different structures, most brain theories do not address this issue in any major way.

In contrast to theories that postulate specific physiological states for specific emotions are state theories. State is an important area of investigation since research has failed to demonstrate any relationship between unique bodily changes and emotional states. What has been shown is that in response to certain emotional elicitors, organisms show changes in bodily function *even though these changes do not correspond to particular emotional states.* As a consequence of such findings, a more general bodily change is postulated. Thus, emotional elicitors do produce bodily changes, although they do not appear to be specific to the particular elicitor any more than they are specific to the particular emotional state.

How, then, can specific emotional states or experiences be related to a general arousal system? Since motion or its absence is often used as one of the criteria defining the arousal continuum, one might talk about agitation and distress on the high end of the continuum and depression on the low end. However, the most widely viewed relationship between arousal and emotion is one that posits a cognitive connection among specific emotional elicitors, general arousal, and specific emotional states or experiences. Such theories, which are discussed in detail later, argue that specific emotional elicitors are related to specific emotional states or experiences through a combination of general arousal followed by an interpretation of that arousal (e.g., Mandler, 1975; Schachter & Singer, 1962).

Theories relating specific emotional states to general arousal that do not involve a cognitive explanation must meet the challenge of how specific emotional states are derived from a general arousal state. The postulation of specific kinds of hedonic tone in association with general arousal—together with the postulation of specific kinds of durational or directional behavior, such as moving toward or moving away—might be one method of solving this problem (Ricciuti & Poresky, 1972; Schlosberg, 1954; Young, 1961). Or by considering the total behavioral repertoire of the organism, and not merely the physiological response pattern, one might find that the patterning of various responses around general arousal, even though not varying in intensity, provides the specificity necessary for the elicitation of specific states.

Lindsley's (1951, 1970) activation theory of emotion is an attempt to establish empirical relationships between emotional behavior and arousal, measured by EEG patterns. Lindsley found the brain-stem reticular formation to be ultimately responsible for both emotional excitement (arousal) and EEG activation, although the hypothalamus also plays a role. It is the activating system of the hypothalamus that sends impulses to the thalamus and the cortex that produces the experience of emotion and that sends impulses to the periphery for the expression of emotion. Lindsley suggested that since emotion is always accompanied by intense EEG activation, emotion represents the extreme of neural excitation. Accordingly, Lindsley's theory is restricted to explaining only extreme emotions and not intermediate emotions or mixed states.

Lindsley's theory is an example of a theory that employs only one dimension in accounting for emotional states. By assuming that all activity is arranged along one continuum, ranging from apathy to intense excitement, there is no means for making qualitative distinctions among emotions. Nor is there a way to distinguish emotion from effort, which also produces EEG activation. Although there is evidence that the brain stem reticular formation is active in emotion, there is no indication that it actually generates emotion instead of merely relaying neural excitation.

Although his major focus is on the motivational properties of emotion, Tomkins (1981) also uses the concept of affective arousal in his theory. Affective arousal allows human beings to meet every contingency in their environment. The neural correlate of affective arousal, for Tomkins, is the density of stimulation, that is, the frequency of neural firing per unit of time. Differences in activation are a function of three variations in the density of neural firing: stimulation increase, stimulation decrease, and stimulation level:

> Any stimulation with a relatively sudden onset and a steep increase in the rate of neural firing will innately activate a startle response. . . . If the rate

of neural firing increases less rapidly, fear is activated, and if still less rapidly, then interest is activated. (p. 317)

※※※※※※※※※※※

Physiological discussions frequently take place at the level of emotional state. The major concern is with depicting or describing the nature of the state: Are there specific responses or patterns of responses that are unique to particular emotional states, or is there only a general arousal state common to all emotions to which some other component or dimension must be added in order to distinguish different emotions? One of the major research issues in discussions of state concerns the existence of a coordination or patterning of different responses within a particular system or across systems. There is some information suggesting that the expectation of co-occurrences of response may be inappropriate. For instance, various responses within a system such as the ANS are unlikely to co-occur around either emotional states or cognitive activities (e.g., Lacey et al., 1963). In measurements of blood pressure, heart rate, skin resistance, and other ANS responses, little or no co-occurrence of different responses is found within the ANS. Studies have also failed to show any co-occurrence of different aspects within a single autonomic response, such as peak magnitude of heart rate deceleration, latency to peak magnitude, and heart rate variability (Lewis, Dodd, & Harwitz, 1969). Such findings support a notion of "desynchronization."

What is needed in order to understand the relationship between emotional states and bodily changes may, in fact, be a much more complex analysis of patterning. Since research has been relatively unsuccessful in showing any relationship between bodily changes across or within a system and particular emotional states, in order to maintain that such a relationship does, in fact, exist (and we have no reason to believe that it does not), it may be necessary to look at patterns of responses. This investigation will require not only more complex measurement systems but more complex recordings of various responses. The availability of microcomputers for such purposes opens up the possibility of such analyses.

One of the most promising discoveries in the field has been reported by Schwartz and his colleagues (Schwartz, Fair, Greenberg, Friedman, & Klerman, 1974; Schwartz, Fair, Salt, Mandel, & Klerman, 1976a,b). These investigators have identified specific patterns of facial muscle activity for several different emotions. By asking people to imagine happy, sad, and angry situations, Schwartz found that each of these subjective experiences was accompanied by a unique pattern of muscular electrical signals. In fact, through electrodes measuring the electrical output of four muscles located near the forehead, eyebrows, mouth, and jaw, Schwartz claimed that he could judge what people felt even when their facial expressions revealed nothing (Schwartz, Ahern, & Brown, 1979; Schwartz, Brown, & Ahern, 1980).

Emotional Expression and the Physiological Approach

Generally, in the study of the physiology of emotion, investigators are not primarily concerned with emotional expressions except as they contribute to an understanding of the physiological correlates of emotion. The independent variable in such studies is usually physiological, although the resultant changes in behavior may be of some interest. Two types of behavioral measures are commonly taken. More frequently, direct behavioral descriptions of typical emotional responses are made, usually in animals. Behavioral measures of emotionality may include resistance to handling, vocalization, startle and flight, urination, and defecation (e.g., Brady & Nauta, 1953). Such behaviors may be made in response to CNS stimulation (either electrical or chemical) or ablation.

Studies of the effects on emotionality of CNS stimulation or ablation have not in general contributed significantly to the physiological literature, since it is difficult to determine the precise location or extent of either a lesion or a stimulation. The picture is further complicated by large individual differences in behavioral reactions and evidence of mass action in the brain, as well as equipotentiality among different areas of the brain. All that can really be said is that certain areas of the CNS appear to be involved in emotion, but no specific mechanisms have been found that mediate particular emotional patterns.

In the first type of study, emotional behavior is measured directly. The second type of behavioral measure sometimes used in the study of the physiology of emotion is derived from techniques designed to study conditioned emotional responding (CER) and active and passive avoidance. The CER procedure measures behavior indirectly, in terms of ongoing operant behavior. Active avoidance involves making a fear-motivated response to avoid an aversive stimulus, while passive avoidance involves learning to avoid an aversive stimulus by not making a response. Studies using this technique have been reviewed in much detail by Strongman (1978).

Emotional Experience and the Physiological Approach

Emotional experience is the result of the organism's perception, interpretation, and evaluation of its internal physiological state and overt behavioral expressions. Several physiological theories have made use of this component in trying to explain the process of emotion. In these theories, emotion is not equated with the physiological response *per se* or even with specific patterns of physiological responses, although these may be important components of the theory. Rather, emotion is thought to be the *perception* of the bodily changes as a result of an "exciting event" (James, 1884, 1890) or the cognitive evaluation of the situation in which a general physiological arousal is produced (e.g., Schachter & Singer, 1962; Schachter, 1964).

In the first case, there is an implicit assumption that unique patterns of physiological change accompany specific emotions and that it is the perception of these different patterns that is responsible for the differentiation of the subjective experiences of emotion. In the second case, the organism's response is only that of general physiological arousal; it is both the perception of this arousal state and an interpretation and cognitive evaluation of the environmental circumstances leading up to the arousal that produce the unique emotional experience.

><><><><><><><><

Most physiological theories are speculative and are built around data gathered on nonhuman subjects. The generalizability of such findings to human subjects is problematic. The conclusion that one draws from such studies is that many structures of the brain are involved in producing emotion, as are many neurochemical reactions, which have only begun to be studied. Even were one able to explain the physiological substrates of emotion, however, one would still be required to explain the subjective, phenomenological experience involved.

The Cognitive Approach

Many physiological theories of emotion cannot explain why we respond emotionally to some stimuli and not to others, nor are they able to account for individual differences in discrete emotional responses. To do so requires the addition of a cognitive dimension to the account of emotion. Although a case could be made that cognitive and emotional events are distinct, the questions asked in any discussion of emotion must raise the broadest considerations, namely, what is the role of cognition in emotion?

Some believe that emotions are nothing but interpretive cognitive actions and arousal (e.g., Mandler, 1975, 1980; Royce & Diamond, 1980; Schachter & Singer, 1962). Although theories such as these make it quite clear that no special status should be awarded to "interpretive cognitive action," they must be explained and appear to have a higher status than "emotion," which is often considered a mixture of arousal and interpretation.

Cognition can play a role in the emotional life of the organism in many ways. Some of these are more direct than others. It is illuminating to examine the various ways in which cognition plays a role in order to clarify the already-known aspects of the role of cognition in emotion and to suggest new ones. An integrative framework for this discussion is again provided by our structural analysis of emotion.

Emotional Elicitors and the Cognitive Approach

We start with elicitors as the first element in the emotional sequence. However, the emotional life of the organism is one of continual flow, in which an emotional state or experience must be placed in the context of an ongoing sequence and thus related to past emotional states and experiences as well as to the individual characteristics of the organism. Keeping this in mind, let us start by looking at the role of cognition at the level of elicitors, realizing that any discussion of elicitors must take the preceding state into account.

Elicitors may be of two types. First, there are elicitors that act directly on a sensory system and seemingly require little or no cognitive processing. An example of such an elicitor is a loud noise. Stimuli that are intense and have fast rise times seem to act on the organism as emotional elicitors without cognitive interpretation. Of course, perception occurs at a sensory level, but this involves sensation without interpretation. In addition to certain auditory stimuli, certain stimulus dimensions in the visual modality (e.g., brightness, black–white contrast, and curvature) also seem to require little cognitive processing. Such stimuli may have a one-to-one correspondence with receptors, and all that is required for their processing is an alert organism.

A second class of elicitors includes those that require some form of cognitive processing. Such events have their effect to the degree that they pass through some information-processing system. Stimulus properties such as novelty or familiarity, for example, must be processed in order to produce an emotional effect. In the visual field, a repeated presentation of the same event leads to lack of interest or boredom, as measured by reduced attending (in both fixation and heart rate responses). The observation that an event was originally considered interesting but now is no longer so suggests an important role for some form of cognitive activity. Schema acquisition, recognition, and recall have been postulated as the cognitive processes responsible for the effectiveness of the stimulus in producing some type of emotional response (Lewis & Goldberg, 1969a; Schaffer, 1974).

Another way in which cognition and elicitors may interface is through past associations and learning. For instance, past associations of one stimulus with either a noxious or a pleasant outcome are cognitions that will affect the individual's subsequent emotional response to the stimulus. Memories and associations constitute the cognitive link between events that may have had no emotional consequence and those that have. Watson and Rayner (1920) laid the groundwork for research on conditioned emotional responses by demonstrating that a rat associated with a sudden, loud noise could cause fear in a child who once had shown only approach behaviors to the rat. This fear (expressed through crying and moving away) was long-lasting and generalized to similar animals and objects. In this example, the role of cognition in giving meaning to elicitors is considered in terms of the immediate and automatic associational value acquired by certain stimulus events that appear to occur so rapidly that associational links rather than interpretative mechanisms seem to be employed.

Cognitive processes may play another, more direct role in the actual creation of emotional states and experiences through the interpretation of the elicitor. Theories that depend on the proposition that emotional states are created through certain cognitive activities can be categorized into two types: appraisal theories and discrepancy theories. Both focus on the quality of the elicitor.

Appraisal Theories

Appraisal theories are based on the hypothesis that a cognitive appraisal of a stimulus situation produces an emotional response. For example, Arnold's (1960, 1970) theory of emotion, although containing both neurophysiological and cognitive elements, has as its central construct the cognitive act of appraisal. Appraisal is defined as the immediate, automatic evaluation of anything encountered as either good (i.e., beneficial to one's well-being) or bad (i.e., harmful to one's well-being). This appraisal results in a tendency to approach what is evaluated as "good" and to avoid what is "bad." What is not judged as either "good" or "bad" is ignored.

The basis of most appraisals is memory. A new object evokes a memory of the emotion associated with past experiences with similar objects. Imagination may also play a role in the emotional process to the degree that before people act, they may try to imagine whether the consequences of that action will be good or bad, beneficial or harmful. Both the appraisal of the conditions and the possibility of action determine the nature of the emotional tendency (e.g., fear or courage). If conscious judgment and deliberate decision warrant, the tendency results in overt action. In this particular appraisal theory, then, emotion is a felt tendency with respect to an object or event that arises when the object or event is appraised as either good or bad. The appraisal is a function of both memory (objective as well as affective) and imagination and culminates in a plan of action for coping with the situation.

Another example of an appraisal theory is provided by Lazarus (Lazarus et al., 1970; Lazarus, Kanner, & Folkman, 1980; Lazarus, Coyne, & Folkman, 1982). In this theory also, emotions are believed to originate in particular kinds of cognitive appraisals. Basic to the theory is the view that organisms are constantly in the process of appraising and reappraising all stimuli with regard to their personal relevance and whether the organism can cope with them. Such appraisals lead to certain kinds of activities (physiological, cognitive, and behavioral) in an attempt to cope with the appraised situation. Appraisals can be either benign or threatening. Benign appraisals result in an automatic emotionless adaptation to a situation, reappraisal if additional information warrants, or positive emotional states. Threatening appraisals, on the other hand, lead either to direct action in an attempt to remove the threat or, when no direct action is possible, to benign reappraisal. As the organism continues to appraise and reappraise objects and events, fluctuations in emotion are observed.

Here are two examples of appraisal theories. Arnold's theory is essentially a reformulation of Aristotle's doctrine of emotion. Since Arnold's major concern was with speculating about the neural pathways that mediate between the initial appraisal and the subsequent action of the organism, she has not given much consideration to the nature of elicitors likely to produce favorable or unfavorable appraisals. Nor has she addressed the issue of why some objects are evaluated and others are not. How these evaluations are made and whether the resulting action tendency is a consequence of the physiological state or of the cognitive evaluation are questions not answered.

In contrast, Lazarus's research efforts have been aimed primarily at investigating the determinants of appraisal rather than its physiological substrates. Lazarus has provided some evidence that the degree of the emotional response depends on whether the cognitive appraisal is benign or threating and that certain physiological responses are related to cognitive attempts at coping with stress. Most of Lazarus's work is based on the effects of highly stressful stimuli. Consequently, Lazarus's theory is more relevant to strong negative emotions, especially fear.

Discrepancy Theories

In a second type of theory that involves cognitive processing at the level of the elicitor, emotions are regarded as the product of certain discrepancies between external events and internal representations or schemata. Incongruity presupposes differentiation, since the schema of a familiar referent must exist in the organism's mind and also must be utilized for the recognition of the discrepancy to occur. Hebb (1946, 1949) was the first to relate incongruity to emotion by demonstrating that fear is evoked by events highly discrepant from previous experience. For example, the detached head of a monkey shown to other monkeys produces extreme fear, Hebb reasoned, because of its incongruity.

Berlyne (1960) suggested that the unfamiliar or the novel event may evoke fear or pleasure, contingent on the conditions. Pleasure is evoked when the stimulus is novel or curious "to the right degree" (Berlyne, 1970). Learning in general takes place through conflict or disequilibrium; if the organism lacks information about a stimulus event, uncertainty is generated. To reduce the uncertainty, the organism may actively explore the event. Berlyne's concept of conflict reduction is perhaps a better explanation of general exploration than of other emotional responses.

More recently, Kagan (1974, 1978) has embraced the incongruity hypothesis. He has also suggested that an unexpected or a discrepant event can produce emotion. The organism's first response to a discrepancy or an unexpected change in the physical parameters of a stimulus event is characterized by an inhibition of motor activity and decreased heart rate. This state is not fear; rather, it is viewed as a "special state" with different outcomes depending on the cognitive processes that follow (Kagan, 1974). For example, if the event is easily assimilated into a cognitive schema, the organism will return to baseline levels of response. A special cognitive competence, thought to emerge between 7 and 9 months of age in Western infants, has been hypothesized as playing a major role in the child's emotional reaction to discrepant events. This competence has been described both as the "activation of hypotheses" (Kagan, 1974) and as the ability to perform simultaneous comparisons (Schaffer, 1974).

The incongruity hypothesis is basically a *post hoc* explanation of fear (Lewis & Brooks, 1974). It is difficult to determine on an *ad hoc* basis the similarity or congruity of a series of events. As a result, prediction of fear response is nearly impossible. Moreover, the infant may have different categories for comparing internal schemata and external events; thus, depending on what schema is used as the referent, different orders of similarity may be generated. For example, an infant might order the mother, a male cousin, and a strange adult female differently: If familial relationship is the comparison, mother and cousin would be judged to be similar, whereas if gender is the comparison, mother and strange adult female would be judged to be similar. Therefore, the comparison figure and the infant's strategy must be taken into account.

Another inadequacy of the incongruity hypothesis is pointed up by the failure of the familiar to elicit boredom or withdrawal consistently. The approach of the mother elicits a very high positive affect. Affect preferences based on familiarity may be salient to the infant. There can be no question that infants enjoy and show positive affect to familiar events, the mother being the best example.

Other problems occur when the incongruity hypothesis is evoked. How does incongruity theory explain why approach often is necessary to elicit both positive and negative responses? Also, the capacity of infants to develop specific aversions to individuals (Bronson, 1972) may be better explained by previous experience than by discrepancy. Infants may be afraid of a baby-sitter because in their past experience, the sitter's arrival has meant that the parent is leaving. This conditioned fear may have nothing to do with incongruity; rather, it may have to do with the infants' past experiences. In general, infants may be able to evoke internal representations of past experiences that were painful or frightening and to associate them with current events. Interestingly, since the current event has an internal representation, it would have to be considered familiar rather than novel. In this case, a familiar event would elicit fear.

In a paper on the acquisition and violation of expectancy, Lewis and Goldberg (1969a) suggested that the chief function of violation of expectancy (or discrepancy) is to alert the organism. The result is a general arousal. In Lewis and Goldberg's (1969a) research, arousal was measured by observing the surprise expressions on 3- to 4-year-old children's faces. Of 14 instances of surprise, 13 occurred in response to a violation of expectation. The specific affective behavior (smiling) occurred afterwards. Thus, the chief function of violation of expectancy or discrepancy seemed to be to arouse the organism. The specific affective behaviors depended on the context of the violation and the nature of the other cognitions that the infant utilized at that point.

Thus, for example, a mother's putting on a mask may be a violation of expectancy for infants and may produce alerting. Whether the infants laugh or cry depends on the context and the infants' specific cognitions. For example, the infants may cry if the mask is put on when the mother is expected to read a bedtime story but may laugh when it is put on during play. In both cases, the infants perceive the discrepancy. In the former case, it produces fear because they understand it not to be related to bedtime, and in the latter, it produces delight because they understand it to be related to play. Thus, the discrepancy of the mask has only an arousing effect; other factors determine its emotional tone. Gunnar (1980; Gunnar-Vongnechten, 1978), for example, showed that the movement of an unfamiliar toy frightened infants when they had no control over its movement. The frightening toy was changed into a pleasant toy by allowing the infants to control its actions. This result suggests that the properties of the object are arousing, whereas properties associated with the individual (e.g., the extent to which the individual can control the event) determine the hedonic quality of the response. A more complete description of the relationship between cognition and emotion requires a less linear conceptualization of the relationship. We have tried to compare the cognitive-emotional relationship with a musical fugue in an attempt to convey the nonlinear nature of the relationship (Lewis, Sullivan, & Michalson, in press).

A somewhat different version of discrepancy theory has been presented by Siminov (1970). In this model, emotion is defined as the consequence of the organism's "need" for information with respect to reaching a goal, multiplied by the difference between "necessary information" and "available information." Information is viewed as the possibility of reaching a goal because of a particular communication. Siminov perceived the human organism as continually striving to attain the behavioral and physiological tranquility of satisfied needs. Too little and too much information vis-à-vis the attainment of this goal results in negative and positive emotions, respectively. In the case of negative emotions, a lack of information prevents the organism from organizing itself appropriately; in this case, the nervous mechanism is activated in a way that leads to negative emotional states. Positive emotions, in contrast, result from a surplus of information over and above what is necessary for the satisfaction of needs. Specific emotions, from this viewpoint, can then be classified in terms of (1) the strength of the need; (2) the extent of the informational deficiency or redundancy; and (3) the specificity of the action aimed at satisfying the need.

Although discrepancy theorists argue that the emotional state *per se* is produced by particular cognitive processes (as do the appraisal theorists), exactly how cognitive or information processing leads to an emotional state or experience is not clarified. One possibility is that cognitive activities may be prewired into the nervous system and that, when activated by certain elicitors, they "release" particular emotional states. Such a position is evolutionary-adaptive in perspective; exactly how an evolutionary necessity relates to emotional states is difficult to determine, however. For such theorists, cognitive actions and information-processing behaviors could themselves be considered elicitors of subsequent emotional states. From this point of view, the failure to assimilate an event, the violation of an expectancy, or even the approach of a stranger constitute cognitive elicitors of emotional states through their action on some as-yet-undefined receptors.

On the other hand, one could argue that these events are events that in the past have been connected or associated with negative outcomes. In that case, these events might produce emotions through their associational connections as described previously. In these ways—either through learning or through prewired connections and interpretive acts— cognitive processes might produce emotion.

Emotional Receptors and the Cognitive Approach

Receptors are assumed to be located in the autonomic, somatic, and/or central nervous systems. When activated, they produce an emotional state. There is little role for cognitive functions at the level of emotional receptors. Indeed, a discussion of emotional receptors focuses on nervous system structures and physiological concepts rather than on cognitive structures and concepts.

Emotional States and the Cognitive Approach

Emotional states, like receptors, have generally been defined in terms of bodily processes rather than cognitive processes. As we have seen, physiological theories of emotion have regarded emotional states in two different ways: either as specific changes occurring in the autonomic, central, or somatic nervous systems or as general physiological arousal varying in degree. From both points of view, the role of cognition appears to be minimal. Even past experiences may affect such states only to the degree that the changes they induce might be more or less intense, depending on the physiological rather than the cognitive status of the organism. One possible role of cognition here is the use of cognitive processes to block the emotional state from awareness.

Emotional Expression and the Cognitive Approach

The role of cognition in emotion is most relevant at the level of emotional expression. Emotional expressions have been viewed as a feature or a direct consequence of an emotional state (Darwin, 1872; Ekman et al., 1972; Izard, 1971, 1977; Tomkins, 1962, 1963) or as the consequence of an emotional state interfaced with learning experiences (Lewis & Brooks-Gunn, 1979; Lewis & Michalson, 1982c). The first position maintains that fixed neuromuscular connections exist between internal state changes and facial expressions as well as select postural and vocal expressions. These natural, biologically linked connections are hypothesized to exist on the basis of the reported universality of facial expressions across vastly different cultures (Ekman, 1972, 1973a). If, in fact, facial, postural, and vocal behaviors are universal and iso-morphic with emotional states, the need to postulate a cognitive role associated with emotional expressions becomes superfluous.

Research based on the idea that there is a direct link between facial expressions and emotional experience (i.e., the facial feedback hypoth-esis) has been critically reviewed by Buck (1980). Yet, there is some evidence that assuming different emotional expressions may influence the quality of one's emotional experience. For example, Laird (1974) showed slides of children playing versus slides of Ku Klux Klan mem-bers to adults while asking them either to draw the corners of the mouth back and up (i.e. smile) or to bring their eyebrows down and together and to contract the jaws (i.e., frown). He found that his subjects felt happier looking at the slides when "smiling" and angrier when "frown-ing." The effect of the slide condition on the emotion experienced was as much as seven times larger than the effect of the expression, however. In studies such as this one, the results may be subject to experimenter bias. That is, the subjects may conclude that a particular emotion is desired by the experimenter even though the experimenter does not ask them to assume specific expressions but tells them, instead, which facial muscles to contract. Thus, the responses that subjects give may be more the consequence of social expectations than of facial feedback (Buck, 1980).

An alternative theory of emotion, in contrast to more biologically oriented theories, uses the notion of socialization to imply that expressive behavior may not have a one-to-one correspondence with internal physiological states of the organism (Lewis & Michalson, 1982a). This lack of concordance may be due to a variety of factors that are discussed in Chapters 5, 6, and 7. On reflection, it should be obvious that although facial expressions might be biologically connected to internal states, how and when to express emotional states are rules learned through socialization experiences. It is easily demonstrated that people often express emotions incongruent with internal emotional states, perhaps because of common knowledge that the expression of a particular emotion is inappropriate (such as expressing anger toward one's boss) or because of a refusal to acknowledge or recognize (either consciously or unconsciously) a particular state that one is in (for example, denying anger when insulted).

There are many reasons that emotional expressions and emotional states may not be isomorphic. In all cases, the need to postulate some form of learning is evident, a need that suggests a role for cognitive processes in the expression of emotion. Because of the influence of socialization on emotional expressions, some theorists (e.g., Izard, 1978) have argued that "purer" (i.e., biologically based) emotional expressions can be observed better during the early part of the life cycle, prior to socialization altering their expression. Consequently, such theorists have focused their attention on emotional expressions in infancy, arguing that infants could not possibly have learned these rules (e.g., Izard & Buechler, 1979). However, Brooks-Gunn and Lewis (1982) have demonstrated that mothers' responsivity to their infant's emotional expressions is already differentiated by the time the infants are 3 months old. If reinforcement principles are applied, the fact that mothers are less likely to reinforce fretting and crying than smiling suggests that socialization practices probably exert differential impacts on emotional expressions from the beginning of life. Such problems require a developmental theory to explain the relationship of state and expression (see Chapter 5).

Emotional Experience and the Cognitive Approach

Emotional experience constitutes that component of emotion that by its very nature requires cognitive processing. By definition, emotional experience is a cognitive activity whereby the organism, reflecting on its emotional state or expression or on the eliciting condition and the responses of other people, comes to interpret, evaluate, and infer emotional experiences (i.e., those conditions most characterized by statements such as "I am sad" or "I am afraid"). The nature of different emotional experiences is the focal point for most inquiries into the role of cognition in emotion.

Cognitive processes can enter into emotional experience in at least two ways: (1) in the perception of unique physiological changes within one's own body or (2) in the cognitive interpretation and evaluation of a general arousal state. The first role of cognition is illustrated in James's (1884, 1890) theory of emotion. According to James, it is the *perception* of the bodily changes as they occur that constitutes the emotion: seeing oneself cry makes one sad, trembling makes one angry, and smiling makes one happy. The basis of emotional differentiation is the occurrence and perception of different patterns of bodily changes unique to particular emotional states. All that is cognitively required on the part of the organism is the perception of internal physiological changes in state.

Tomkins (1962, 1963, 1970) also believed that differences in emotional experiences originate in differential patterns of bodily response (primarily facial) and that a minimal amount of cognitive processing is involved, beyond the perception or registration of such changes:

> Affects are sets of muscles, vascular and glandular responses located in the face and also widely distributed through the body, which generate sensory feedback which is inherently either "acceptable" or "unacceptable." These organized sets of responses are triggered at subcortical centers where specific "programs" for each distinct affect are stored. These programs are innately endowed and have been genetically inherited. They are capable, when activated, of simultaneously capturing such widely distributed organs as the face, the heart, and the endocrines and imposing on them a specific pattern of correlated responses. One does not learn to be afraid or to cry or to be startled, any more than one learns to feel pain or to gasp for air. (Tomkins, 1970, pp. 105–106)

The sensation of these responses is the experience of the emotion. Although Tomkins recognized the role of responses occurring in parts of the body other than the face, his primary focus has been on changes in facial musculature. James, on the other hand, envisioned the involvement of a much broader variety of bodily responses in emotional experience.

The second way that cognition enters into emotional experience is in the interpretation and evaluation of a general arousal state. This role is illustrated in the theory of Schachter and Singer (1962; Schachter, 1964). For Schachter and Singer, the physiological substrate of emotion consists of general physiological arousal rather than specific patterns of physiological changes. Since this general arousal state is common to all emotions, the organism cannot make distinctions in emotional experience based solely on differences in internal physiological cues. Rather, some cognitive interpretation and evaluation of the arousal are necessary. This "cognitive context" is provided by external cues. From knowledge of the situation in which the arousal occurs, including the social behavior of other people, the individual creates, as it were, the emotional experience.

The work of Schachter and his colleagues laid the foundation for Mandler's (1975, 1980) theory of emotion. In this theory, cognition seems to play a dual role in emotion, first as an elicitor of an emotional state, then as an interpretive-evaluative act. For Mandler, the interruption of ongoing thought or behavior, a discrepancy or a conflict, produces a general autonomic arousal, which is responsible only for the intensity of the emotional experience. The specific quality of the emotion depends on the accompanying evaluation of the internal state and the environment.

Although ANS reactions produce emotional experiences only in conjunction with cognitive evaluations, which are usually previously acquired or assigned, cognitive evaluations and judgments may occur in the absence of ANS activity. Thus, one can talk about being happy or sad without the accompanying state of happiness or sadness. For example, patients with spinal cord lesions (and thus without physical sensation) reported that they experienced "a cognitive kind of emotion" in the absence of any physiological state (Buck, 1980). In Mandler's theory, there are also instances where "pure" cognitive activity can generate ANS activity and produce a full-blown emotional reaction through the retrieval of the appropriate context.

Whether emotion involves a specific physiological state or a general state such as arousal, the interpretation of that state may provide emotions with their particular phenomenological quality. For theories in which general arousal constitutes the internal emotional state, specific emotional experiences are facilitated either by the subject's interpretation of, knowledge about, or direct observations of the situation in which arousal takes place. This facilitation can occur either through the observation of the expressions of others in the situation or through knowledge of what emotional state is "appropriate" to that particular situation (e.g., we know that we should feel sad at funerals and not when someone wins a lottery). For theories in which specific physiological changes define different emotions, the interpretation of that state may rely less on external events and more on specific somatic, visceral, or neural responses. For instance, making a face distinctive to a specific emotion may generate the corresponding emotional experience (Laird, 1974), presumably because the subject has produced a set of unique responses related only to that specific emotion.

Although cognitive theories stress the need to consider the role of appraisal as well as the roles of the physiological and situational cues that play a part in emotion, more work is needed in detailing the particular cognitive processes that affect various emotional responses and in specifying their antecedent conditions. However, there can be no doubt that the perception of the stimulus and the evaluation of it with respect to its personal significance are contributing factors to at least some emotions.

The role of cognition in emotional experience implies a particular cognitive structure that is often taken for granted, but that, from a developmental perspective, must be considered. Specifically, the interpretive-cognitive structure that underlies emotional experience is the self. While more detailed attention will be paid to the development of the self and its role in emotional experience later (Chapter 4), we should note at this point that in order to have an emotional experience (which we presume takes the linguistic form "I am happy"), it is necessary not only to be able to reflect on the nature of the elicitor, the bodily response, and the context of this response but also to have some knowledge about the self.

There are two aspects of the self that have received considerable attention (Lewis & Brooks-Gunn, 1979). The first, the subjective or existential self, refers to knowledge that the self is different from others. This cognitive distinction appears to have its origins in the early months of life and has been considered one of the early conservation achievements. The second aspect is the objective or categorical self. The categorical self refers to specific features of the self that have a longer developmental history. Such features include physical characteristics that change over age, gender characteristics that remain invariant, role characteristics, and state characteristics.

The emergence of the cognitive structure that we call the self appears to be necessary in order for an emotional experience to occur. Since an emotional experience involves a reflection on the self, it implies that the individual can make distinctions between the self and others. When an emotional state is elicited, the individual must be able to recognize that set of bodily changes as its own. Developmental failure, as a consequence of biological insult or mental illness, may affect an individual's ability to differentiate the self from others. In this event, the individual's emotional experience may be expected to be radically upset not only through the disruption of the various cognitive processes described previously but also as a consequence of the inability to make the self–other distinction.

Emotional experience and cognition should also be considered in terms of socialization effects. The interface between knowing and meaning—and even the processing of information—may be related to cultural and socialization factors. Certainly at the level of interpreting behavior, socialization and cultural differences must play an important role. While the process that connects an elicitor, a receptor, a state, and an expression may be invariant across cultures, the particular meaning assigned to such a sequence (and thus the experiential component of the sequence) may be quite different. For example, a woman in a white gown may elicit a positive emotion in our culture since we interpret that elicitor to mean marriage. Yet the same elicitor in another culture may be experienced as sad since white is the color of mourning and may reflect the loss of a beloved object. In this example, the process, whether it is cognitive or affective, is the same, but the eliciting event produces different emotions solely as a consequence of the interpretation of the elicitor.

Similar socialization processes may be at work at the level of experience. Although Schachter and Singer's (1962) theory considers interpretation a function of the social milieu in which the cognitive appraisal occurs, we can imagine instances in which the same emotional state has a history of differential response on the part of others and therefore the emotional experience may be different. That is, two different elicitors may produce similar undifferentiated emotional states in young organisms; through socialization, these emotional states become differentiated. Such a theory of emotional development is outlined in more detail in Chapters 5 and 6.

The Motivational Approach

The evolutionary notion that emotions are derived from biological necessity is essentially the argument that emotions are drives or motives. To say that an organism is hungry is to imply that the feeling of hunger will result in particular behaviors. Thus, a feeling state is similar to a drive. One of the major philosophical issues in Western thought concerns the relationship between action and thought: knowing does not necessarily provide the reason for doing. In psychology, drive is a hypothetical construct postulated as the cause of behavior.

The discussion of drives as activators has a long history in American psychology. One school addresses drives as innate action patterns. The classic example of these innate patterns is the farm animal that eats rusty farm equipment when it is iron-deficient. In general, eating when one is hungry implies an innate action pattern associated in some one-to-one relationship with a particular drive state. Alternatively, it can be postulated that drives are associated with behaviors through learning and experience. As a consequence, certain action patterns are realized over others: those action patterns that are preferred are those that satisfy the drive. Theorists subscribing to such views think of learning in terms of drive reduction. They believe that the patterns of action most associated with the satisfaction of drives are the most likely to be learned.

Whether there are innate action patterns associated with particular drives or whether action patterns are learned through drive reduction (or some other mechanism), the concept of drive serves in some sense to explain action. Yet, the exact mechanisms by which drives lead to action are not well articulated. Thus, the issues of drive, desire, or thought and their relationship to action are not well understood.

Motive means something that causes a person to act. Thus, a motive, like a drive, is a concept used to explain action. Implied in the notion of human motives is an intention or a will that underlies the action. Theories that view emotions as motives that impel action can be divided into two classes: (1) those that view emotion as a consequence of an action pattern and therefore as reinforcing that pattern and (2) those that view emotion as producing an action pattern based on the evolutionary history of the species.

Emotion as the Consequence of Action

The view that emotion is the consequence of action is related to the issue of hedonism. Central to the hedonic tradition is the belief that people act in such ways as produce pleasure and avoid pain. The emotional consequences of an action are regarded as the primary cause of that action: actions that are likely to result in pleasure or to reduce pain will be taken; actions that are likely to lead to pain will not be taken.

This view of emotion as motivating action through the emotional consequence associated with the action appears reasonable. For example, students study for examinations because it feels good to pass and it feels bad to fail. Adults work hard in order to enjoy the profits of their labor at a later date. It should be noted that according to this view, behavior is motivated by the possibility of its emotional consequence. Even though the emotional experience occurs after the action, it is believed that the reinforcement value of this experience serves to produce the same set of behaviors again so that one will experience pleasure or avoid pain.

We do not mean to suggest, however, that emotions must always follow the chain of behaviors. In fact, "delay of gratification" is a primary socialization goal in industrial societies. Both the length and the complexity of the behavioral chain culminating in reward may be increased through socialization. For example, a hungry infant usually experiences only a short delay between crying and being fed, in contrast to a 4-year-old, who may have to wait several hours for dinner.

According to the psychoanalytic viewpoint as well as some recent theoretical writings on delay of gratification and impulse control (Mischel, 1974), the increased delay and increased behavioral repertoire in an action sequence are factors that generate important cognitive structures. Here is an example in which the delay of an emotion creates cognitive structures. Cognitive structures are produced by such delays through processes labeled "secondary thought" (Freud, 1960) or "elaborated thought" (e.g., Hartmann, 1958; Mischel, 1974). The delay of immediate consequences forces the organism to develop circuitous cognitive pathways. For instance, if the organism cannot eat immediately when it is hungry, then it may imagine itself eating in order to feel good.

If emotions are thought of as motives in this way, then emotions, especially feeling good (pleasure) and feeling bad (pain), become reinforcers in a particular action chain. In many cases, these hedonic reinforcers seem to be unlearned. For example, it is unlikely that the good feeling produced by eating when hungry is learned. Rather, eating feels good because of an innate biological connection between food in some part of the digestive tract and relief from hunger. On the other hand, some emotional reinforcers seem, at least at first glance, to be learned. There is no intrinsic reason that it should feel good to get an "A" on a French examination. The issue, however, becomes more complex when one moves from the particular event, such as doing well on a test, to its more general form, such as being competent. It may be the case that being successful in anything (depending on the cultural definition of success) is rewarding, that is, produces a positive hedonic state. In this event, the developmental issue pertains only to specifying which particular actions will be associated with positive or negative states.

Are there any emotional reinforcers that are learned? On reflection one may be faced with the predicament of arguing that all behavioral patterns are by definition biologically related to hedonic reinforcers. Thus, for example, in response to the argument that masochism is the result of certain learning experiences in which pleasure is obtained through receiving pain, it may be that in each of us there is a destructive aspect that derives pleasure from pain. Although such a view seems farfetched, it is not unlike that of Freud's idea of death instinct.

The argument that a positive hedonic tone can be attached to the broadest of human activities, including the satisfaction of basic biological needs, as well as the need for competence, power, and control, suggests that the function of culture may be to specify those particular action patterns associated with hedonic tone (i.e., an experiential factor). The predicament of attributing a learning aspect to hedonic tone is illustrated in cultures that value certain action patterns seemingly not associated with pleasure. For example, if competence is associated with a positive hedonic tone, why is it that some cultures seek to reduce independence mastery? One answer might be that it is mastery to suppress a wish for mastery. Other examples can be found in the realm of human experience called *altruism*. By definition, one is altruistic to the degree that one is willing to sacrifice those actions that lead to a positive hedonic tone. The positive hedonic tone then becomes associated, for example, not with sitting down when tired, but with giving up your seat to an older person. In a certain sense, it is not unreasonable to argue that "being good feels good." Such a structure may be part of human experience. However, which actions are considered "good" is almost totally a function of personal upbringing and cultural values.

From the viewpoint of emotions as motivational reinforcers, one might argue that the function of the cultural milieu is to create unique action patterns. To the degree that the subject both learns action patterns and remembers them, emotional consequences can be potent generators of behavior. We are still confronted by the problem of what causes behavior to occur in the first place. Here, the learning process is particularly important, and learning reinforcement theories may apply. The particular action patterns of a culture that lead to positive hedonic consequences may be acquired either through single-trial learning or through the slow construction of an association between action patterns and emotion. This latter position is certainly consistent with what is known about social learning and would seem to explain in part why people act as they do.

Emotion as the Antecedent of Action

In our discussion so far, we have focused on emotion as the consequence of behavior. There is, however, a strong position that views emotion not as the product of action but as its antecedent. This view of emotion is usually associated with biological explanations of emotion. Two categories of theory represent this viewpoint: evolutionary theory and traditional psychoanalytic theory.

Evolutionary Theories

Darwin (1872), the source of the evolutionary tradition in the study of emotion, argued that the process of evolution applies not only to anatomical structures but to intellectual and expressive behaviors as well. Emotional expressions, he believed, have a functional significance in the lives of animals: they act as signals and prepare the organism for action, and they also communicate to others what action is about to be taken, thereby increasing the organism's chances of survival. Although Darwin believed that most emotional expressions are innate, he felt that once they have occurred they are subject to voluntary control and can be used as a means of communication through either conscious expression or inhibition of the emotional behavior.

Emotions, according to Darwin, are by their nature associated with action patterns necessary for survival. For example, the sight of a predator elicits fear in the organism, the action pattern of which is to flee. Or a baby's cry elicits nurturance in the mother and a concomitant behavioral repertoire of nursing, holding, or retrieving the infant. Viewed in this way, emotion is both a state of the organism and a response that is basic to survival. In all cases of positive and negative emotions, the emotional elicitor produces specific action patterns as part of the emotion.

Several theories also take an evolutionary stance (e.g., Izard, 1977; 1979a; Plutchik, 1980a,b; Tomkins, 1962, 1981). In these theories, the affective system is viewed as the primary motivational system of the organism and as part of the genetic endowment of infants. Certain emotional expressions are present in neonates that facilitate their survival by attracting attention and motivating the caregiving behaviors and social exchanges that are crucial to healthy development. These early expressions include the distress cry, the smile, interest, startle, and disgust (Izard, 1978). Although not necessarily evident at birth, nine innate (primary) emotions are thought to comprise this affective-motivational system. These emotions are interest, enjoyment, surprise, fear, anger, distress, shame, contempt, and disgust (Izard, 1977). These emotions can be observed as discriminable sets of muscular and glandular responses located in the face and distributed in the body that generate sensory feedback to the organism. These emotions have adaptive value, since they are connected to action patterns necessary for survival.

Some detailed attempt has been made to connect specific affects with specific biological needs. Plutchik (1980a), for example, enumerated eight adaptive patterns of behavior that are the functional basis for all emotions: incorporation, rejection, destruction, protection, reproduction, reintegration, orientation, and exploration. These basic adaptive patterns are the functional basis for all emotions recognized in humans and animals. Eight emotions accompany the functional patterns: acceptance, disgust, anger, fear, joy, sadness, surprise, and expectancy. Although the specific behaviors that accompany these patterns may vary across different species, their survival function is common to all species.

Bowlby's (1969, 1973) theory of emotion draws on evolutionary as well as psychoanalytic principles. He defines emotions as

> phases of an individual's intuitive appraisals either of his own organismic states and urges to act or of the succession of environmental situations in which he finds himself. . . . At the same time, because they are usually accompanied by distinctive facial expressions, bodily postures, and incipient movements, they usually provide valuable information to his companion. (Bowlby, 1969)

The influence of cognitive theory can be seen in Bowlby's notion of the appraising process, which may or may not be conscious. Emotions begin as an appraisal. This appraising process continues to monitor not only the environmental event but the bodily changes and ongoing activities as well. The evolutionary perspective is best seen in two aspects involved in the appraisal process: (1) the need to compare a stimulus with some sort of standard and (2) the need to select certain behaviors in preference to others. The standards of comparison are those likely to promote species survival. When the appraisal puts the input into categories that

> potentially signal activation of one or another of the behavior systems that mediate instinctive behavior, . . . the subject is likely to experience emotion—alarm, anxiety, anger, hunger, lust, distress, guilt, or some other comparable feeling depending on which behavior system is activated. (Bowlby, 1969)

Thus, emotion is directly connected to instinctive behavior. The organism's cognitive appraisal of a situation with respect to an internal standard that is innate to the species presumably activates one of several emotional behavioral systems, which are also innate. The particular emotional system of interest to Bowlby is attachment.

It is important to understand that the theories just discussed have a strong bioevolutionary slant. By defining emotions in part as action patterns, theorists avoid the dualism between knowing, thinking, and feeling on the one hand and action on the other. In other words, feelings or emotions have an action component built into them. The task for the theorist, then, is to connect cognition or knowing with feeling in order to connect knowing with action.

Psychoanalytic Theories

The psychoanlaytic theory of affect is also based on a concept of biological instincts or drives (Rapaport, 1953, 1960). At one point in his career, Freud postulated two classes of instincts—sexual instincts and ego instincts—that he believed influenced all human behavior by regulating the direction and the nature of action. The ego drives included hunger, thirst, and aggression, as well as impulses to control others, to wield power, to attack, and to flee from danger. Later, Freud identified these instincts as life instincts and postulated a new category—death instincts—that included the aggressive drives.

The source of each hypothesized instinct was thought to be a biological, internal process, and the aim of each instinct was discharge and pleasure. The object of the drive depended on experience and learning.

Basically, the affects, for Freud, were primarily a form of energy that required some kind of direct or indirect expression. The assumption was that the expression of an affect could undergo various displacements and transformations. If the affect was inhibited or repressed because of learning and experience, its energy would be expressed indirectly in the form of neurotic defense mechanisms, such as phobias, obsessions, or compulsive rituals. Thus, conscious, subjective feelings were only one type of evidence of a person's emotions. Dreams, free associations, slips of the tongue, postures, facial expressions, and voice quality reflected a person's repressed emotions.

The psychoanalytic view of emotions assumes that (1) an unconscious process occurs between the perception of the stimulus evoking the emotion and the physiological or visceral (autonomic) change; (2) the peripheral autonomic change and the feeling of the emotion are both discharge processes of the same drive source of energy; and (3) all emotions are mixed expressions of conflicts. Both the feeling of the emotion and the bodily change result from an unconscious evaluation.

Emotion as a Motive to Learn

In the consideration of emotions as a motive to learn, emotions assume certain drive or motivational characteristics inasmuch as they precede behavior. In this discussion, two pieces of evidence are relevant. First, Zajonc (1980), studying adult subjects in a dichotic listening task, found that they could not discriminate between a familiar and a novel auditory signal when asked which they had heard before. Yet, they were able to state a preference for the more familiar event. Second, 10-week-old infants were observed in a contingent learning task in our own laboratory (Lewis, Sullivan, & Brooks-Gunn, 1983). The data showed that although the youngest infants showed little evidence of learning, these same infants exhibited state and affect changes when compared with a control group that received an amount of stimulation that was equal but that was not contingent on their behavior. The contingent group of infants were able to stay awake and alert longer than the control group.

How is one to view the results of these two studies? In both cases, little learning could be demonstrated. What about the affective changes? The adults showed clear emotional preferences for the familiar event, while the infants who received contingent stimulation stayed awake longer and smiled more. Both examples may be instances of an emotional state producing cognitive behavior, in some sense being responsible for the resulting cognitive achievement by maintaining and propelling the organism through its interactions with the environment. In both cases, one could not argue that the organism was not engaged in some cognitive activity, since both perception and learning can take place below threshold level (i.e., below criteria). Nevertheless, affective changes may have provided the motivation necessary to enable the subjects ultimately to reach criteria. Particularly in the case of infants, a lack of learning does not imply the absence of hypothesis generating or testing, which may be facilitated by the energizing effect of the emotional state.

Everyday examples of the influence of emotion on cognition or learning are available. Events may arouse us and cause behavioral changes in us that result in cognitive activity and altered structures. Even the negative arousal assumed to be associated with unassimilated events may have powerful motivating properties that cause organisms to "work harder" in order to understand.

Emotional states may precede action to the degree that the emotional state serves as a motive to act. Such motives to act can be derived either from the intrinsic nature of the stimulus or from qualities of the organism. For instance, stimuli may be so interesting that organisms are compelled to find out more. Alternatively, the motive may be in the nature of the organism. In Amsel's notion of frustration effect, for example, frustration may lead to increased vigor in performance (Ryan & Watson, 1968).

Emotions may also motivate action through the history of outcomes. Thus, if the organism acts in a certain way that leads to a positive experience, the results of that positive experience may serve as a motive to repeat that action. It is interesting to note here that motives interface with cognitions: a motive to act in a similar way implies the existence of cognitive mechanisms for retaining and utilizing past information.

Emotions as Markers and as Instigators

Within the motivational approach to the study of emotion, we have considered emotions as motives to act or think in certain ways. Emotions can also be thought of as markers or as instigators of certain thought patterns (Lewis, Sullivan, & Michalson, in press).

Much attention has been focused on the roles of "hot" versus "cold" cognitions (see Zajonc, 1980). The general assumption underlying this issue is that many cognitive processes have different levels of efficiency or different outcomes depending on whether the cognitive processes are "marked" or tagged with a specific emotional tone. Markers may have two effects.

First, cognitive processes marked with emotional tags might be more efficient than those not marked. For example, the retrieval of past events from short-term and long-term memory may be facilitated by emotional markers (Norman & Rumelhart, 1975). Information may enter memory not only as a function of the content or sequence of the material but also as a function of the nature of the emotional tag. Clearly, the schema of a person in a white laboratory coat is more likely to be remembered if it is associated with fear than if it is not marked with any emotion.

Second, markers may be associated with the emotional content of events as those events are affected by the emotional state of the individual. There is evidence that emotions have a powerful influence on cognitive processes such as recall, fantasies, and social perception. Bower (1981), for example, found that adults recalled more events when the events were affectively congruent with their mood during recall. Therefore, the view of emotions as markers refers not only to the emotional tag attached to the cognitive event but also to the emotional state of the individual as the individual interacts with the cognitive event.

The view of emotions as instigators, in contrast, is centered on the issue of whether certain feelings can actually cause people to think in particular ways. In this view, the relationship between thought and emotion may be regarded in the same way as the relationship between other action patterns and specific emotions. Emotions may not only elicit, in some biological way, certain action patterns (Plutchik, 1980a,b), but, in fact, emotions may be responsible for specific thought patterns. Imagine, for instance, that you hear one of two different messages: (1) your cousin was hit by a car, or (2) your cousin won the state lottery. Different emotions will be elicited depending on which message you were given. These different emotions are likely to create different moods, which will influence your subsequent thoughts even though such thoughts may be unrelated to the original message (Moore, in press).

With the exception of the view of emotions as motives, relatively little empirical work has been conducted within the motivational approach. The paucity of theory and information in this area may be the consequence of the Western view of motivation in which human behavior is regarded as the product of a rational mind. The bias inherent in the research literature is more apparent when one considers that many non-Western cultures stress the primacy of feelings over thought. In these cultures, the motivational approach might have greater intuitive appeal.

The Cognitive-Emotional Fugue

A great deal of theoretical work in the study of emotion has centered specifically on the relationship between emotion and cognition. Currently, two opposing models are used to characterize the relationship between these domains. In the first model, emotion is viewed as the consequence of certain cognitive processes (Lazarus, 1982). Although recognizing that a certain level of cognitive development is necessary for the expression of some emotions (e.g., guilt), many investigators argue that early in development, information processing precedes the emotional response (Kagan, 1974). For example, the failure to assimilate an event is thought to produce wariness or fear in infants, whereas mastery is thought to result in pleasure or enjoyment.

A second model of the relationship between emotion and cognition views emotional responses as preceding cognitive processing (Zajonc, 1980). According to this model, emotion is a motive or drive with an action-producing or maintenance function. The independent nature of emotion is recognized; emotions are considered to be events that do not require cognitive processes for their occurrence.

In previous sections, we discussed issues and theories associated with the model in which cognition precedes emotion (e.g., appraisal and discrepancy theories), as well as issues associated with the model in which emotion precedes cognition (the motivational approach). Because both models fail to capture the complexity of the process, we

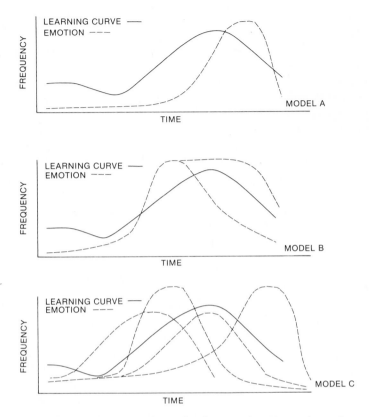

Figure 3. Models of the relationship between learning and emotion.

have developed a third model, based on the metaphor of a musical fugue (Lewis *et al.*, in press). We have labeled this section "The Cognitive-Emotional Fugue" to suggest that this third model may better represent the relationship between emotion and cognition than either of the two traditional models. In this model, the cognitive-emotional relationship is depicted as a complex interplay of processes, similar to the themes of a fugue, which are often lost and reappear (Hofstadter, 1980).

The empirical evidence for this model comes from a study of contingency learning in which both facial expressions of infants and the learning of an armpull response were measured. In the experimental task, infants had to learn that a single motor response (an armpull) resulted in a favorable outcome (the onset of an audiovisual event). Learning was indexed by changes in armpull rate. The hypothesized relationship between emotion (measured by facial expressions) and learning (measured by changes in armpull rate) is presented in Figure 3 in terms of the three models. In Model A, emotions associated with learning are hypothesized to peak only after the infant has learned the contingency relationship. In Model B, emotions are hypothesized to peak before the infant actually learns the contingency, possibly as the result of prewired mechanisms, such as interest. In this model, emotions may (1) decline before learning or (2) remain high until the infant ceases to respond. In Model C, emotions are hypothesized to occur throughout the learning process. Whereas positive emotional expressions (e.g., smiling and vocalizing) may be the consequence of learning and mastery (i.e., "It feels good!"), they also may be a necessary prerequisite for learning (i.e., "I cannot learn unless all is well"). In Model C, the separation of emotion into a number of constituents is essential for considering the interplay between emotion and cognition.

The Many Faces of Learning

The subjects in our experiment were five 24-week-old infants (three boys and two girls). The infants sat in an apparatus that delivered a three-second presentation of a color slide of a smiling infant accompanied by a recording of the "Sesame Street" theme song. An armpull response triggered stimulus onset.

The learning curves generated by the armpull responses of these subjects were well-differentiated. The points of learning identified for each curve were (1) baseline, or one minute of nonreinforcement when armpulling did not produce a consequence; (2) the first minute of the session after the infant's initial encounter with the consequence; (3) one minute prior to response acceleration, the point at which responses exceeded and remained above baseline; (4) the first minute of acceleration; (5) one minute prior to peak response rate; (6) the first minute at peak rate; (7) one minute prior to sustained decline in response; (8) the first minute of decline; and (9) the final minute of the session.

In addition to recording armpulls, we videotaped the infants' facial expressions throughout the course of the experiment. Facial movements were later coded using the Maximally Discriminative Facial Movement Coding System (Izard, 1979b). In addition, vocalizations and fret cries were coded, as were head or gaze aversion and lower lip, thumb, or hand sucking. Although not emotional expressions *per se*, oral behaviors may be motivated by stress or boredom and may thus serve a comforting or self-stimulating function.

The data are presented in Figures 4, 5, and 6 in terms of the mean

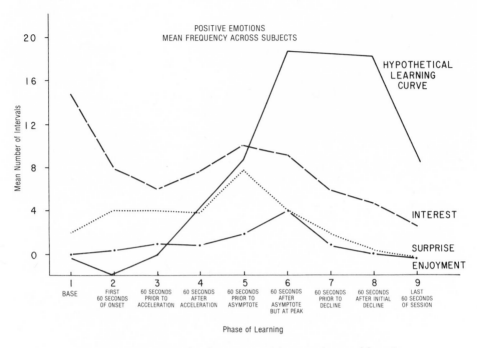

Figure 4. The relationship between positive emotions and learning.

number of three-second intervals during which particular expressions occurred as a function of the point of learning. The following picture emerges when these data are considered in terms of the metaphor of a fugue comprised of two themes, cognition and emotion: The infant is placed in a new situation and the fugue begins. Surprise is present and interest is high. The experiment starts; reinforcement is delivered for an armpull response. The infant sees that something new is happening; surprise and fear increase, interest decreases. The infant's activity level also drops, and armpulling declines below baseline. This dip in responding may reflect the infant's awareness: "Something is happening. What is going on?" The increase in fear may reflect the infant's lack of information about and lack of control over the new event.

The decline in activity serves to diminish the reinforcement. A new response causes reinforcement to reoccur. During this phase (the end of orientation and the beginning of acceleration), the infant begins to recognize the relationship between action and outcome. Fear decreases and interest begins to rise. During the acquisition phase, interest and surprise continue to grow as fear declines. The infant is quite alert

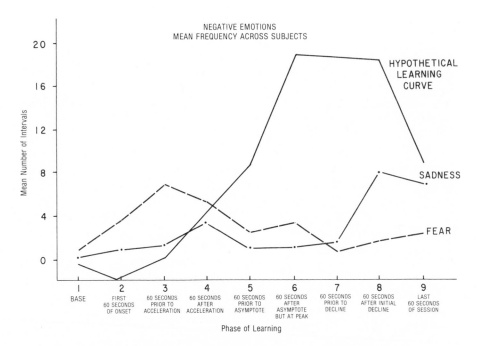

Figure 5. The relationship between negative emotions and learning.

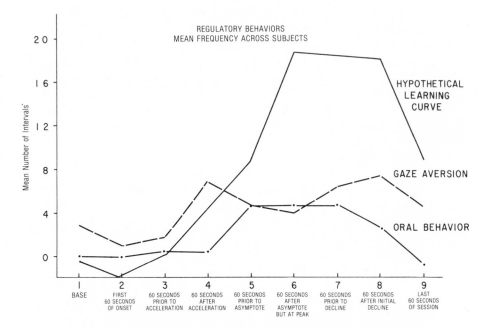

Figure 6. The relationship between self-regulatory behaviors and learning.

and it now becomes necessary to modulate this arousal state. Self-regulatory behaviors (gaze aversion and oral activity) are used for this purpose and are exhibited at relatively high levels.

Learning is achieved by the asymptotic phase, when enjoyment peaks. Fear is low and self-regulatory activity is high. Following the solution of the problem, armpulling declines in conjunction with many of the emotional expressions. This decline may reflect a general drop in arousal and interest. With the decline in arousal, the infant no longer needs self-regulatory behaviors. Cognitive solution brings enjoyment, a decline in arousal, and a decline in self-regulatory activity.

During the postasymptotic phase, sadness appears. This expression may be associated with fatigue or boredom, although it is not accompanied by an increase in self-regulatory responses as one might expect. Thus, the observed increase in sadness after learning may be associated with a "postsolution recoil." Although the infant's sadness is probably not the equivalent of adult sadness, its expression may have a parallel in older children who appear unhappy when an enjoyable activity comes to an end.

If the cognitive-emotional process is viewed in terms of well-defined temporal bouts, each of which has a definite beginning and end, then one would expect to observe a decline in all responses at the end of the experiment. The fact that sadness increased after learning, however, suggests that the termination of the experiment may constitute an artificial event imposed on the ongoing flow of emotional and cognitive behaviors. One might imagine that the emotion of sadness is the first note in the next sequence of the cognitive-emotional fugue. It is possible that the "posttask blues" are an important factor in motivating and reorienting the individual to new tasks.

The results of this study are relevant to the three models described earlier in the following ways. First, the results underscore the need to distinguish between different emotions and their relationships to cognition. Discussions of global emotional states (i.e., positive or negative emotions) obscure interesting and significant aspects of the dynamic interplay between emotional and cognitive behaviors. Second, it is clear that some emotions occur before the cognitive solution to a problem (i.e., learning) and that other emotions occur later. The particular emotions observed seem to interface with the learning process rather than either producing it or being produced by it. Emotions may provide the setting for each learning phase and may be the consequence of that learning.

In short, the data indicate that simple linear models of the relationship between cognition and emotion are inadequate. The relationship between these domains is quite complex, is continuous, and is more finely tuned than is usually depicted by traditional models. In conceptualizing the relationship between emotion and cognition, neither process should be described as causing the other. Rather, the best model is of two processes continually and progressively chasing each other, weaving their separate strands of behavior into a single composition not unlike that of a musical fugue.

✗✗✗✗✗✗✗✗✗✗✗✗

What has emerged from this review of three approaches to the study of emotion is that there is no one theory that is comprehensive enough to account for all the phenomena associated with emotion and that is also well supported by empirical data. Each theory has something to contribute to the field as a whole: unique ideas, new combinations of ideas, or novel observations and experimental evidence.

The physiological approach is noted for attempting to delineate the physiological substrates of emotion and for stressing the importance of the viscera and the subcortical and cortical brain structures in emotion. The cognitive approach is concerned with the importance of perception, interpretation, and evaluation in determining the effect of the elicitor, the emotional expression, and/or the emotional state and experience. The role of cognition in interpreting both internal and external cues has been detailed. The motivational approach concentrates mainly on the function of emotion in the ongoing life of the organism. Emotion is seen as having a motivating effect on action as a reinforcing consequence of particular actions, as the instigator of certain actions, as markers, and as motives to learn. In any complete theory of emotion, the contributions from all three approaches must be recognized. The example of the blind Indians describing the elephant comes to mind (see Chapter 1). Given the vast body of information and theoretical speculation that constitutes the study of emotion, a focus on the individual limbs of the beast must be viewed as a failure of perspective.

4

The Structure of Emotion: The Development of Five Components

This and the next three chapters are devoted to the topic of emotional development. Although emotional development takes place over the life of the organism, the discussion in these chapters is restricted to the opening phase of life. The changes in emotional development that take place during the later years are not discussed nor is development during other critical periods, such as adolescence. We have limited ourselves in this way in the expectation that although a careful analysis might reveal changes at other periods of life, the processes underlying these changes—the biological and social forces that provide the impetus for development and produce individual differences—are constant across developmental periods. Thus, although society may allow the aged, but not preadolescents, to express sorrow by crying, the processes underlying these changes in the nature of emotional expression have their roots in the early socialization experiences of children. While important differences in emotional development may be found at various points in the life cycle, an understanding of the rules governing development in the early stages should help to clarify later changes. Indeed, close scrutiny may reveal these to be changes in content rather than in process.

In order to talk about developmental issues involved in the study of emotion, it is necessary first to analyze emotion into its various components: (1) elicitors, (2) receptors, (3) states, (4) expressions, and (5) experiences. Although others have made some distinction among several of these components, no one has discussed all five in any detail. A separate discussion of each is necessary for understanding the developmental processes underlying emotion as well as for the study of individual differences in emotion. In this chapter, then, each component is defined, and the developmental issues associated with each are considered. The possible roles of cognition in interaction with each of these components are discussed as well. In the study of emotion, the developmental issues associated with the connections among these components are as important as the developmental issues associated with each individual component. These issues are discussed in the next chapter. Chapters 6 and 7 focus on developmental issues from the point of view of socialization.

Emotional Elicitors

Definition of Elicitors

In order for an emotion to occur, a stimulus event—the *emotional elicitor*—must trigger a change in the internal, physiological state of the organism. This event may be either an external or an internal stimulus. External elicitors may be nonsocial (e.g., loud noises) or social (e.g., separation from a loved one). Internal elicitors may range from changes in specific physiological states (e.g., a drop in blood sugar level) to complex cognitive activities (e.g., problem solving). Since it is obviously much harder to identify and manipulate an internal elicitor than an external one, most research deals with external stimuli, with attempts to determine precisely which features of the elicitor activate the emotion.

A major problem in defining an emotional elicitor is that not all stimuli that produce a physiological change in the individual can be categorized as emotional elicitors. For instance, a blast of Arctic air may cause a drop in body temperature and elicit shivering, but one is reluctant to classify this occurrence as an emotional event. Consequently, the definition of an emotional elicitor tends to be somewhat circular, inasmuch as an elicitor is defined in terms of the consequences it produces. Since feeling cold is not considered an emotion, the blast of Arctic air is not regarded as an emotional elicitor.

Development of Elicitors

What are the developmental issues associated with elicitors? First, there are classes of elicitors with little developmental history. A loud and sudden noise causes startling and possibly fear in organisms throughout their life. The sight of food, once associated with the relief of hunger, almost always serves as a positive elicitor if an organism is hungry. Thus, it is possible to imagine a class of events, either biologically determined or learned in the very beginning of life, that will consistently produce an emotional state.

Even for this class of automatic elicitors, however, the developmental experiences of organisms may be such as to inhibit or restrict the elicitor from operating in its natural way. That is, the elicitor, if it could be measured, remains constant in its effect, but other aspects necessary for the organism to realize its effect may interfere. Exactly how or where in the emotional process this interference occurs is not known. It might occur as a consequence of perceptual defense mechanisms and the resultant failure to perceive the elicitor. Or the effect of an elicitor may be modified by the deactivation of an emotional receptor and the resulting inhibition of the emotional state. For example, pain receptors can be deactivated by competing stimuli (e.g., loud music during dental surgery) or by drugs that inhibit receptor function at the CNS level. Finally, an elicitor may be rendered ineffective through a failure on the part of the organism to experience the emotional state. The failure to experience the emotional state might be the result of (1) a reinterpretation of the state; (2) competitive learning (e.g., in anorexia, food and eating are associated with negative outcomes); or (3) some unconscious motivation that prohibits the experience of the particular emotion elicited by the stimulus event. In these examples, an elicitor acts on the organism in a nondevelopmental fashion, and the failure of the organism to experience the same feelings over time is due to the imposition of other factors. In other words, the elicitor–response structure may remain constant but is overridden by other processes. This is the basic distinction between change and development: in the former, the structure remains but is subsumed by another process, while in the latter, the structure changes.

In the class of elicitors with a developmental course, the structure that supports the elicitor–response connection undergoes change. Within this class are elicitors that are biologically connected to a response, as well as elicitors that are connected to a response through learned associations. For example, infants' fear of strangers may be biologically programmed; over time, stranger fear may decline because the biological structure supporting the elicitor–response connection has broken down or has been altered through experience. Learned associations between elicitors and responses may also be subject to developmental change because new structures are formed or old ones are extinguished. For instance, the formation of new structures can be predicated on cognitive changes. The data from numerous sources suggest that important cognitive factors play a role in mediating the effects of classes of events in the elicitation of fear (Campos & Stenberg, 1981; Feinman & Lewis, in press; Lewis, 1980; Schaffer, 1974). Implicated in this research are several important cognitive processes and capacities, the development of which is critical for the elicitation of fear states and experiences. Their developmental course appears to parallel that of fear, especially fear elicited by strangers and fear elicited by the loss of the mother.

Several of these cognitive processes are considered here, and more could probably be added to the list. These capacities are regarded as critical and serve as examples of the role that cognitive development might play in mediating the development of fear elicitors. First, memory, both recognition and recall, must play an important role in the elicitation of fear. Children must be able to recognize and associate past events that were noxious. For example, the white coats of doctors may become associated with pain and thus acquire the capacity to elicit fear. Recall, a more difficult cognitive skill, is also necessary for past experience to have an effect. How can children experience fear and distress when their mother is absent if they cannot recall her? Schaffer (1974) discussed the processes that mediate infants' fear of the strange. Among these is the ability to compare stimuli simultaneously.

In terms of cognitive expectancy, violation *per se* does not seem to be a fear elicitor. In fact, violation of expectancy may be arousing, and the particular emotion produced may depend on whether the organism can assimilate and control the event (Kagan, 1974; Lewis & Goldberg, 1969a). Here, too, the role of cognition and the effects of past experiences have not been fully appreciated. Violation of expectancy, or novelty, may elicit arousal. The inability to assimilate the novel event can elicit distress. Why these responses result in fear is unclear, however. It is possible that fear results as a consequence of children's inability to control the impinging events. That is, the inability to assimilate the event is upsetting and results in fear *to the degree that the event cannot be controlled.* If it can be controlled, it may be upsetting but will not produce fear (Gunnar, 1980; Gunnar-Vongnechten, 1978).

Tracing the developmental course of elicitors is more difficult when the critical dimensions of particular elicitors are analyzed. It may be the case that the ability of certain elicitors to produce an emotional response diminishes over time but that the class of which they are members continues to be effective. In other words, concentrating on the general features of elicitors rather than their specific content may be a more profitable enterprise. For example, the specific elicitor, separation from the mother, shows a developmental course (Weinraub & Lewis, 1977). Children typically exhibit little fear of separation until the last quarter of the first year. Fear peaks at around 18 months of age and then falls off around 24 months. However, the more general class of elicitors, fear of uncontrollable events, may always elicit fear. It is not the running away from a novel object that produces fear; rather, it is the inability to get away from, to avoid, or to control the object that produces the fear state. Fear may be produced by lack of control, if lack of control in the past has been associated with noxious events. This proposition is supported by research finding that 1-year-old infants are not afraid of an unusual toy when they can control it but are fearful when they cannot (Gunnar, 1980; Gunnar-Vongnechten, 1978). The effect produced by manipulating infants' ability to control a stimulus confirms the importance of loss of control in the elicitation of fear.

These examples demonstrate how developmental processes may influence the effect of an elicitor on the response. An emotional elicitor may or may not have a developmental course, depending on the way in which the stimulus itself is defined. Definitions that are too specific result in developmental theories based on changes in structure over time. In fact, age changes in the effects of certain elicitors may reflect not changes in the elicitor–response structure but merely changes in the ability of highly specific elicitors to produce an emotion. The extent to which the elicitor is defined very narrowly may be the extent to which it is possible to talk about the developmental course of elicitors. When elicitors are considered as a broad class, there may be little developmental change. What appears to be a developmental change in the effect of an elicitor may actually be a function of how the elicitor is defined.

Emotional Receptors

Emotional receptors may be either (1) relatively specific loci or pathways in the CNS that mediate between elicitors and particular states or (2) nonspecific general systems related to arousal and through arousal to particular states. Information about emotional receptors is scarce. Whether these receptors can even be located is open to question. The discussion of the developmental history of receptors, therefore, is speculative.

Definition of Specific Receptors

Specific receptors are select cells or neural structures located in the CNS. Their function is to detect and respond to certain classes of events. For example, an innate releasing mechanism (IRM) is thought to be an innate neural mechanism that operates as a specific receptor in response to highly specific environmental stimuli. When activated by a particular stimulus event (the "releaser"), the IRM responds through the release of instinctive behavioral patterns that presumably increase the organisms's chances of survival (Hess, 1970). For instance, the quality of "babyishness" is considered a releaser of the mothering response in human beings, with more mothering being elicited by greater babyishness (Hess, 1967). It has been argued that the schema of the human face constitutes an innate releaser of the smiling response in babies (Spitz & Wolf, 1946; Wolff, 1963). Bowlby (1957) hypothesized that smiling behavior increases the infant's chances of survival, since it makes the infant more appealing to the mother. The apparently unconscious perception of the pupil size of other people during interpersonal contact can also act as a releaser, triggering an increase in pupil size in an observer (Hess, 1965; Simms, 1967; Stass & Willis, 1967). Ethological studies have also demonstrated that certain behaviors in one organism can release certain responses in the organism perceiving these behaviors. These responses may elicit additional behaviors in the original partner of the interacting pair.

What these specific emotional receptors are like or where they may be located is still to be discovered, although research on anger and rage, as well as on pleasure (self-stimulation), implicates the hypothalamus. Studies have shown that the electrical stimulation of certain areas of the hypothalamus elicit a full-blown rage reaction, including attack (Akert, 1961; Hess, 1954, 1957). While stimulation of the middle portion of the hypothalamus may produce rage, stimulation of the anterior hypothalamus produces fear ("flight behavior"), and stimulation of the posterior portion generates curiosity and alertness. The most critical region of the brain for self-pleasure stimulation seems to be the lateral hypothalamus (Olds, 1962). The effects of hypothalamic lesions on emotional behavior have confirmed, for the most part, the results of these stimulation experiments (Bard, 1928; Wheatley, 1944).

Findings based on electrical stimulation and brain lesion techniques suggest the existence of specific brain centers for different emotions. The findings are controversial, however (Strongman, 1978). Such studies usually are concerned only with emotional behavior and do not address the subjective experience of emotion. Furthermore, although the hypothalamus has been shown to play a critical role in emotional behavior, its activity interacts in complex and unknown ways with other areas of the brain, particularly structures and regions of the limbic system. Ethical problems involved in human experimentation have limited the study of the brain centers of emotion in humans. Because the precise functions of and interconnections among various parts of the nervous system differ from species to species, it is difficult to generalize the findings on physiological substrates of emotion from animals to humans.

Individual differences in behavioral reactions complicate the issue even more, as does the fact that the effects of particular lesions may not be immediately apparent or may appear only under certain conditions. As a consequence of the evidence of some equipotentiality among various areas of the brain and the development of pharmacological techniques that make possible the investigation of the neurochemical regulation of emotions, the search for specific receptor sites is giving way to the search for neurochemical pathways that traverse areas of the brain. The levels of neurochemicals or the ratios between the levels of two or more neurochemicals along these pathways may be more important than specific receptor sites in the emotional process.

One neurological model that supports the notion of specific emotional receptors derives from research on the responses of specific visual cortex cells to specific stimuli. Theories of specific cells in perception suggest that there are specific neurons devoted to detecting highly specific events. Microelectrode studies conducted by Hubel and Wiesel (1962, 1968) have identified cells in the visual cortex of the cat that are activated only when a bar of light is presented at a certain angle. Different cells respond to different angles. Other cells respond only to movement through the visual field and movement only in a single direction. Some cells are so highly specialized that they are activated only by a line in a particular orientation and of a specific length and width. Other cells in the visual cortex respond to patterns such as curves and angles. In monkeys, some cells may be so finely tuned that they respond only to specific shapes and objects (Gross, Rocha-Miranda, & Bender, 1972).

In the field of affect, Tomkins (1981) has promoted the idea of affect receptors and has speculated on the role they might play. For Tomkins (1980) "organized sets of responses are triggered at subcortical centers where specific 'programs' for each distinct affect are stored" (p. 142). The activation of these centers is thought to be innate. That is, there are certain classes of events that automatically trigger these centers. Since the role of learning is not emphasized, it is uncertain whether new receptors develop. Tomkins (1980) suggested that the skin is the primary receptor for a set of important affects (perhaps all) and that the facial skin may "lead and command widespread autonomic changes" throughout the body. In other words, the skin contains the affect receptors. If this is the case (and there is little evidence that it is), then stimuli could elicit emotional behavior through the mediation of the face. According to Tomkins's analysis, the face, rather than showing the response produced by an affect center somewhere in the CNS, is itself the receptor.

Development of Specific Receptors

Little attention has been paid to developmental issues pertaining to specific receptors. In general, these receptors are thought to be in place at birth and to be biologically determined and genetic in origin. Speaking about the programs of these receptors and the consequences of their elicitation, Tomkins (1980) stated that these programs are "innately endowed and have been genetically inherited" (p. 142). Thus, there may be little reason to postulate a developmental course in the maturation of specific receptors. If Tomkins is correct, they exist at birth and are influenced by neither development nor culture.

Yet, the developmental course of an IRM is such that it may become increasingly selective toward releasers during the course of the organism's life (Hess, 1970). This increased selectivity may be due either to a narrowing of the range of effective eliciting stimuli through the elimination of individual stimuli (e.g., in the cases of the habituation to specific releasers or the strong negative conditioning of aversive stimuli) or to the selection and strengthening of a few releasers from a large range of potential releasers (e.g., the social imprinting of presocial bird species; Lorenz, 1965). Thus, the human face becomes more effective as an elicitor of the smiling response in babies, and at the same time, smiling becomes increasingly selective as a function of age (Ahrens, cited in Hess, 1970). The notion of increasing selectivity as a consequence of the experience of the individual would appear to apply generally across IRMs.

Although there is little information on this topic, it is possible to imagine the development of specific neurological centers. There is no reason to assume that all centers exist at or soon after birth and develop at the same time or rate. In this case, two distinct courses of development can be hypothesized, one biological and the other culturally interactive. In the first, neurological development might proceed independent of experience. Thus, although all centers are not present at the same time, the unfolding of each may take place almost exclusively within a biological time-frame. In the second, the neurophysiological development of these centers might interact with either social or subsequent biological experiences. For example, if a young organism is under great stress or exposed to much fear, this experience may interact with a developing "fear center" and produce changes in that center. The dimensions affected by experience might include ease of elicitation or rate of impulse discharge. The development of a fear center might also be affected by an abnormal discharge of biochemical agents. Thus, the secretion of too much epinephrine may modify the center.

Much of the early research on emotion was predicated on the notion of specific brain receptors that produce specific responses. However, the data failed to confirm the notion of specificity. When a particular elicitor was presented to subjects, psychophysiological measures failed to show any distinct patterns corresponding to discrete emotions. While Ax (1953) reported some evidence of physiological differentiation between anger and fear, other research has failed to uncover any autonomic response patterns that correlate with particular emotional response (e.g., Lacey & Lacey, 1958). Much of the work in this area suggests that a generalized psychophysiological response may be common to all emotion-producing stimuli (Strongman, 1978). Thus, emotional elicitors may produce emotional responses through the mediation of a *general* receptor system. This system, usually studied in terms of arousal mechanisms, is considered in the next section.

In view of the sparse evidence of differentiated response patterning in distinct emotions, little can be said other than that the viscera are probably necessary to the emotional process. Is this an accurate assessment of reality or the consequence of inadequate conceptualization and/or measurement? Had other response measures been looked at in these experiments, would different outcomes have resulted? For example, if facial responses had been considered valid measures of emotion, then fear, anger, and passion stimuli might have produced specific patterned responses. This finding would support the notion of a one-to-one correspondence between elicitors and responses and might be used as evidence of specific affect receptors. In fact, recent research measuring facial responses rather than neurophysiological or somatic responses has produced such evidence (Izard, 1977). Thus, when facial and possibly some bodily and vocal responses are considered evidence of differential responding, there seems to be some support for the hypothesis of specific emotional receptors or at least of specific elicitor–response connections that may be mediated by specific receptors. This conclusion should be qualified, however, since facial expressions are subject to socialization influences. Thus, evidence of patterned facial responses associated with specific elicitors does not in itself support the argument for specific emotional receptors.

Because of the confusion about whether specific receptors exist, any discussion of their developmental course is inconclusive. If one chose to regard the face as a receptor rather than as the reflection of a specific receptor (Tomkins, 1980), then one could discuss the development of facial expressions under the topic of emotional receptors. We do not do this, since the evidence of facial neuromusculature as a receptor site is still lacking. The development of facial expressions is therefore discussed in the section on emotional expressions.

Definition of General Receptors

In the discussion of specific receptor sites, the notion that an elicitor triggers a specific receptor, either through biological connections or through past associations, was suggested. In this model, a one-to-one correspondence is hypothesized between the activation of the specific site and an emotional state. In the general receptor model, however, the elicitor is believed to act on a set of sites, which produces a general emotional response (often called *arousal*) rather than a specific emotion. All emotional elicitors activate the same neurophysiological structures (systems), and all produce the same arousal condition. Rather than postulating a specific center, associated with a specific state, the discussion of a general receptor system focuses on receptors that are involved in the modulation of arousal. This modulation of arousal, in turn, leads to a specific emotional state. Because of the vastness of the literature, only a brief summary is provided here regarding some of the major structures and brain mechanisms as they pertain to arousal. For a more complete review, see Gellhorn (1968) and Pribram (1980).

The neural structures most directly involved in emotional behavior appear to be the hypothalamus and the limbic system. The hypothalamus, in interaction with other structures of the limbic system, acts as the neural control center to influence regions in the lower brain stem that control the functioning of the ANS. The ANS acts directly on the muscles and the internal organs to cause some of the bodily changes characteristic of emotion and indirectly through the stimulation of the adrenal hormones to produce others. Other hormones are secreted by the pituitary gland on direct signal from the hypothalamus. Most of the physiological changes that occur during an emotion result from the activation of the sympathetic division of the ANS as it prepares the body for emergency action. Such changes may include blood pressure and heart rate increases, respiration, dilation of pupils, perspiration increases, decreases in secretion of saliva and mucus, blood-sugar-level increases, decreases in digestion, and penile erection. These same responses may also occur during the excitement associated with states such as joy or sexual arousal. For other emotions, like sorrow or grief, some of these bodily processes may be depressed or slowed down.

Although these bodily sensations are not related to specific emotions, they may determine the intensity of the emotional experience.

The ability of an elicitor to activate the general receptor system might be the consequence of either biological predisposition or learning. Thus, for example, a loud noise, rather than activating a specific receptor site, may produce general arousal through a predetermined neurophysiological connection. On the other hand, an elicitor might act on the general receptor system through a learned association. For example, the receipt of a telegram may activate the general receptor system to produce an arousal state.

Development of General Receptors

The developmental features of the general receptor system (i.e., arousal) have received some attention in the research literature. Bridges (1932), Emde et al. (1976), and Sroufe (1979b) have posited a sequence of emotional development based on the gradual differentiation of emotional states from a basically undifferentiated state of arousal. Through both maturation and the modulation of general arousal, the young organism acquires an increasingly differentiated emotional system.

If only general arousal receptors are innate at birth and are affected by all emotional elicitors, then the development of state specificity involves either the development of specific affect receptors or the development of associations. In the first case, the development of specific affect receptors may occur through (1) the maturation of certain nervous system structures from general to specific; (2) socialization experiences; or (3) the interaction of these two factors. In the second case, the acquisition of associations does not imply an increased differentiation of emotional receptors as a consequence of development. Rather, additional cognitive processes are acquired. This view suggests that developmental specificity may not occur at the receptor level at all but at a cognitive-interpretive level. General arousal, an undifferentiated affect, may gain specificity through development as a consequence of accumulating associations and new cognitive structures.

Emotional States

Definition of Emotional States

An emotional state is a particular constellation of changes in somatic and/or neurophysiological activity that accompanies the activation of emotional receptors. Emotional states can occur without the organism's perception of these changes. Thus, an individual can be angry as a consequence of a particular elicitor and yet not perceive the angry state. A specific emotional state may involve changes in neurophysiological and hormonal responses as well as changes in facial, bodily, and vocal behavior. However, since facial, bodily, and vocal behaviors quickly come under social control, they are treated as emotional expressions in a separate section.

Two views exist concerning emotional states. According to one, these states are associated with specific receptors; indeed, they are the activation of these receptors (Izard, 1977; Tomkins, 1962, 1963). In the second, emotional states are not associated with specific receptors and do not exist as specific changes. Instead, a general receptor system (arousal) is thought to underlie all emotional states (Mandler, 1975, 1980; Schachter & Singer, 1962). Other processes, such as cognitive evaluation, may produce the specific emotion.

Cognitive processes may play several roles in emotional states. Certain elicitors may evoke cognitive processes, which in turn elicit specific emotional states. In such cases, cognition is necessary for the elicitation of a specific state. Guilt is a good example. One must have certain cognitions for guilt to occur, since it is the perceived transgression of particular rules that produces the guilt state. Transgression implies an elaborate cognitive process in which an individual compares an action with some standard and finds the two discrepant. The cognition (i.e., the perceived transgression) acts as the elicitor of or the mediator between specific behaviors and the specific state. The behaviors themselves do not lead directly to the specific state; they must be interpreted for the specific state to occur.

Cognitions are also related to the way an emotional state is experienced. This relationship occurs as the evaluation of a general arousal state (Schachter & Singer, 1962). Here, cognitions lead not to specific states but to specific experiences. A modification of this view might be suggested in which a general arousal state becomes a specific state through cognitive processes. In this case, specific *states* as well as specific *experiences* are produced by cognitive processes. For this to occur, cognitions would have to act on the general state, modifying it in such a way as to make it specific in nature. For example, some elicitor may trigger a general arousal state. The individual may then interpret the arousal state in such a way as to alter the general arousal to a state that is specific. Although there is no empirical support for such a process, such a mechanism might exist. In this view, cognition plays a role, both as an elicitor or mediator of specific emotional states and as a mediator of general arousal.

When receptors are activated, an emotional state, either specific or general, is produced. Critical to this definition is a focus on changes from previous levels of activation rather than on the absolute level. Change can occur as either an increase or a decrease in activity level. For example, heart rate increases have been associated with anxiety and fear (Campos, Emde, Gaensbauer, & Henderson, 1975; Waters, Matas, & Sroufe, 1975), while heart rate decreases have been associated with attention or interest (Graham & Clifton, 1966; Lacey *et al.*, 1963; Lewis, Kagan, Kalafat, & Campbell, 1966).

If emotional states are the consequence of physiological or somatic changes, they exist as long as receptors continue to fire. Receptors can be assumed to continue their activity after the immediate elicitor is terminated. However, if receptor firing either returns to its resting base or remains at a constantly high level for an unspecified period of time, the state associated with the original change may be said to be present no longer. However, it may be the case that a consistently high level of receptor activity maintains the emotional state. The existing emotional state of an organism may eventually provide a new background against which subsequent changes can be viewed.

Emotional states, then, are for the most part transient, patterned alterations in ongoing levels of neurophysiological and/or somatic activity. Is it possible that organisms are always in an emotional state? While it is difficult to imagine, if one considers the variety of different states possible (e.g., interest, anxiety, happiness, passion, boredom), the notion of perpetual emotional states becomes more viable. Even if receptor change involves only variations in the level of a general arousal state, the notion remains valid. Thus, it becomes difficult to imagine being awake and not being in some emotional state or at some level of arousal. It is important to remember that an emotional state is not the same as an emotional experience. Thus, an individual need not be aware of the state for it to occur.

It is not likely that all neurophysiological and/or somatic changes constitute emotional states. Which changes are critical, however, is unknown. If specific affect receptors exist, then any change in these would be sufficient to produce an emotional state. If there are no specific receptors and only a general receptor system, it is less clear whether every change in the general system constitutes an emotional state.

Development of Emotional States

In discussing the developmental issues pertaining to emotional states, two issues need to be addressed. The first concerns the nature of different states and how they are derived. The second pertains to the developmental course of states once they emerge. Many of the issues raised in the discussion of receptor development appear again in discussions of emotional states. For example, if emotional states are viewed as specific, the question of how specific states are derived must be addressed. Two general models are possible. According to one, specific emotional states are derived from developmental processes that turn general states into discrete states. Such processes may be purely maturational, or they may be interactive, involving the organism with its environment. The second model does not depict a role for development in the emergence of specific states. Rather, discrete emotional states are assumed to be innate.

In the first model, the infant has two basic states (or one bipolar state) at birth, a negative (distress) state and a positive (satiated) state. Subsequent states emerge through the differentiation of this basic bipolar state. Differentiation theories focus on both the modulation of the bipolar state and the general arousal system. Hedonic tone and arousal may be the dimensions necessary to generate specific emotional states. (This idea is elaborated in Chapter 5.) Figure 7 illustrates Bridges's (1932) differentiation hypothesis. This theory has been adopted by others, including Spitz (1965), Sroufe (1979b) and Emde et al. (1976), who have added a contextual dimension to the scheme.

The way in which the interface of arousal and hedonic tone de-

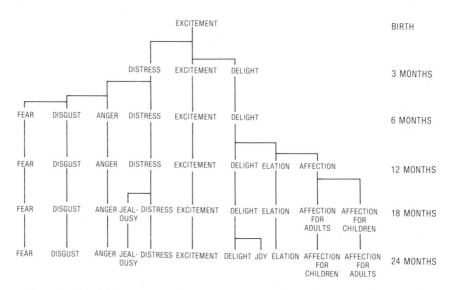

Figure 7. The differentiation of emotions over age. (Adapted from Bridges, 1932.)

velops into specific emotional states remains speculative. It has been argued that both mother–child interaction and maturation underlie the process of differentiation (Als, 1975; Brazelton, Koslowski, & Main, 1974; Sander, 1977). The regulation of the child's state (i.e., arousal and hedonic tone) may be the mechanism leading to differentiation. Although some theorists stress that emotional differentiation is determined more by biological than by interactive factors (Emde et al., 1976), the combination of the two forces seems most likely. While the regulation of hedonic tone and arousal through caregiver–child interactions certainly modifies or alters the intensity and quality of each dimension, the derivation of specific emotional states remains without empirical support (see Chapter 5).

A much simpler developmental model concerning differentiation could be considered from a purely biological perspective. For instance, a simple biological model can be imagined in which undifferentiated emotion becomes differentiated as a function of maturation. According to such a view, the rate of differentiation and the unfolding of differentiated emotional states is programmed according to some physiological timetable. There are no examples of such a process, although one might examine the "pleasure" areas within the brain to see whether they have a developmental course. The differentiation from general to specific structures is common in morphology; there is no reason not to consider such a possibility in emotional development. The most likely explanation of emotional development is that the differentiation of emotional states occurs as a function of maturation, socialization, and cognitive development (Chapter 5). Whatever processes underlie this differentiation, the model is developmental in nature.

An alternative model is that emotional states are discrete states that are preprogrammed in some sense and need no further differentiation (Izard, 1978; Izard & Buechler, 1979). They exist at birth, even though they may not emerge until a later point in development. This view is unlike the differentiation model in that discrete emotional states do not develop from an original undifferentiated state but are innate at birth in an already differentiated form. In the "discrete systems model" (Izard, 1978), specific emotional states emerge either in some predetermined order or as needed in the life of the infant. They may co-occur with the emergence of other structures, although they are independent of them. The emotion system essentially operates according to biological directives.

Some investigators claim that infants exhibit highly differentiated emotional expressions at birth or shortly thereafter and that these differentiated expressions reflect differentiated states. Oster (1978), for example, believes that eyebrow knitting is an expression of puzzlement related to problem solving. The connection between this facial expression and such a complex emotion exemplifies the discrete-emotions theory. Parents certainly think that their children are capable of highly differentiated emotions quite early. Pannabecker *et al.* (1980) reported that parents believed that infants as young as 12 weeks have 10 of the 11 emotions asked about in their questionnaire. Clearly, parents expect to see a variety of emotions in infants earlier than Bridges's (1932) differentiation hypothesis would predict.

Izard has examined in much detail the facial musculature patterns of young infants through an elaborate measurement system (Izard, 1979b; Izard & Dougherty, 1982). Using this coding system, he has demonstrated the existence of several discrete emotional expressions in infants as young as 1 month. There is little evidence, however, that these discrete emotional expressions correspond to internal emotional states this early in life. In the next chapter, a model of the developmental relationship between expressions and states is presented.

A modification of this strong biological-determinism model is one in which distinct emotional states exist early in life but unfold in interaction with other processes. Emotional states are not produced in a developmental sense, but they cannot emerge until other structures have matured. For example, guilt and shame occur as a consequence of some violation of a standard. When the prerequisite cognitive capacities have developed, they may activate an already existing guilt or shame state. It is as if there exists a button called "shame/guilt" and the pushing of this button awaits the development of a set of cognitions. In contrast, one might posit that the developing cognitive capacities themselves produce the emotion. That is, the shame or guilt button does not exist as a prewired structure but emerges as a consequence of cognitive development. These models of cognitive growth that activate emotional states already programmed can be contrasted with developmental models in which discrete emotional states are the product of biological determinism.

These different models address the conceptual difference between experience and structure found in the arguments of Hume and Kant. In one case, experience produces a structure (Hume, 1739/1881). In the other case, experience is assimilated into innate structures (Kant, 1781/1958). In the study of emotional development, the question that one must address is whether emotional states are preformed and depend only on the development of cognitions or whether cognitions themselves produce the emotional states (structures). Such a distinction is rather fine but may have important theoretical implications.

The theoretical importance of the distinction can be illustrated in the study of fear. Is each fear state the same as other fear states, regardless of the circumstances, or do fear states differ as a function of the elicitor? For example, is the fear state produced by a loud noise the same as the fear state produced by the association of a white laboratory coat with the pain of a needle? Are emotional states independent of or dependent on particular elicitors? If emotional states are independent, they need not be created by the elicitor.

This distinction appears repeatedly in discussions of development as the fundamental issue concerning the role of experience in the production or change of a structure. Piaget, for one, has addressed this issue. Beilin (1971) suggested that Piaget's theory is a preformational one: although experience is necessary for the production of a structure, the structure exists independent of the experience. In the same way, cognition may be necessary for the emergence of emotional states, but emotional states may not be produced by the cognitions.

The first major issue related to the topic of emotional states concerned the origin of discrete emotional states. The second major issue focuses on the developmental changes in emotional states once they have emerged. For example, 8-month-old children may show behaviors reflecting fear at the appearance and approach of a stranger, and 2-year-old children may exhibit fear behaviors when they have broken their parents' favorite lamp. Do similar fear states underlie the fear expressions in both cases? Although the elicitors of states and the children's cognitive capacities are different in these two cases, the emotional states may be similar.

Major developmental changes may occur in (1) the events that produce emotional states; (2) the behavioral responses used to reference states; and (3) the cognitive structures of children. Whether the emotional state itself changes as a function of development is difficult to determine. However, there may well be important physiological and neural changes that differentiate young and old organisms. Age changes in heart rate variability (Lewis, Wilson, Ban, & Baumel, 1970) and changes in hormonal levels are two physiological processes associated with emotional states that change over time. These and other changes may be such that once an emotional state emerges, it does not remain constant over time. Rather, the constancy of an emotion may be a function of experience more than state. That is, the phenomenological experience of the emotion seems to be independent of the physiological changes in state that may occur as a function of age. Thus, one of the important distinctions between state and experience may be that emotional experience remains constant each time it is produced even though emotional state may vary as a consequence of elicitors, responses, and cognitive representations that change with age. The emotional experience may serve to organize the variations in the corresponding emotional states that are produced by different elicitors, responses, and cognitive capacities into a coherent whole. In short, subjective experience of a particular emotion may be always the same, with the possible exception of intensity differences, although the state may differ.

The issues related to the development of emotional state are complicated by the fact that emotional states are internal processes for which there are no good measures. Moreover, emotional states are often confused with emotional expressions. While it is possible to measure emotional expressions, the correspondence between the two is not necessarily perfect (see Chapter 5). Thus, the development of emotional state is an issue that is not well explained and that has little empirical support.

Emotional Expressions

Definition of Emotional Expressions

Emotional expressions are those potentially observable surface changes in face, voice, body, and activity level that accompany emotional states. Emotional states are considered constellations of changes in somatic and/or physiological activity that accompany the activation of receptors. Emotional expressions are the manifestation of these state changes. Elaborate coding systems have been designed to measure the facial muscular changes associated with children's emotions (Izard & Dougherty, 1982). For adults, Ekman and Friesen (1978) have identified more than 1,000 possible combinations of muscle movements in the face. Their measurement system, the Facial Action Coding System (FACS), lists more than 1,000 major prototypes and variations of each basic emotion. The evolutionary history of facial musculature suggests that facial expressions, as manifestations of internal states, are a development unique in humans (Als, 1975). The most-attended-to areas of the face and the areas that seem to reflect the most differentiated emotional states appear around the eyes and the mouth.

Other manifestations of emotional states have been less well described (see Chapter 7). Bodily postures seem to reflect emotional states (Argyle, 1975). For example, sitting upright and forward when someone is speaking is associated with interest and attention, whereas slouching and turning away may indicate boredom. Some bodily postures convey sexual interest (Birdwhistell, 1970). For example, when courting, adults often throw the pelvis out to display more of the lower parts of their body. More work on bodily manifestations of internal states (particularly fear, aggression, and sexuality) has been conducted with animals than with humans. This may be the case since the facial expressions of animals are less differentiated than those of humans. As a consequence, the emotional states of animals may be better reflected in bodily expressions than in facial movements. However, it is likely that for humans, too, there are elaborate bodily displays of emotion in need of greater clarification.

Vocalizations are one of the least understood aspects of emotional expression, although they seem to be important conveyors of emotional states. Indeed, vocal expressions are extremely powerful and may have as a property the ability to elicit similar emotional states in others. They may be much more contagious than facial or bodily expressions of emotion. For example, movies are much funnier when seen with others who laugh out loud than when seen in a silent theater. Because of their contagious nature, vocal expression may be the target of early socialization efforts to eliminate them from children's behavioral repertoire. Although not well understood, it seems to be the case that vocal displays of emotion are considered inappropriate in many cultures, certainly in the middle-class American culture. People are not supposed to laugh too loudly when happy, to cry too intensely when sad or frustrated, to growl when angry or revengeful, or to groan in pain. Adults report that the vocal manifestations of emotions are particularly embarrassing.

Scherer (1979, 1982) has recently developed techniques for analyzing the frequency patterns in infants' vocal expressions and has related these patterns to different emotional states. For example, average pitch frequencies can be used to determine the anxiety or tension level of the vocal expression.

Locomotion and spatial location may be other modes of expressing emotions. For example, running away from and running toward an object are locomotive responses associated with negative and positive emotions (Ricciuti & Poresky, 1972). Indeed, it is infants' movement away from an unfamiliar toy or person, independent of facial expression, that is often used to reference fear (Schaffer, Greenwood, & Parry, 1972). Following and clinging to the primary caregiver may also reflect fear in young children.

Although there are some data on emotional expressions in each of these four different modalities (facial, postural, vocal, and locomotor), the relationships among them have received almost no attention. It seems reasonable to assume that sobering, crying, and running away form a cohesive pattern of responses that reflect the emotional state of fear. The particular modality used to express an emotion might be a function of specific rules of socialization or a response hierarchy in which one modality has precedence over another. It may be the case that the least intense emotional states are expressed first in facial, then bodily, then vocal behaviors. Such a hierarchy might be determined either by a set of biological imperatives or by a set of socialization rules. In the absence of empirical data on this problem, the relationship among these different expressive modalities remains speculative. It is reasonable to suppose that the more intense the emotional state, the greater the number of different modalities that would be used to express that state.

The use of one or more channels to express a particular emotion may be determined by a complex set of interactions. One issue of particular interest is the effect on some expressions when one modality is inhibited. Inhibition in a particular modality can be experimentally produced by, for example, preventing children from moving about. Such conditions of inhibition may modify or alter the use of uninhibited modalities. For instance, if children are prevented from running away from an approaching stranger because they are restrained in a high chair, they may express their internal state more intensely through alternative means, such as facial musculature changes. Thus, facial expressions may be affected by whether or not an individual can express emotion through other channels.

Parenthetically, the total inhibition of the expression of emotion may force individuals to manifest their internal states in other ways, such as in the somaticizing of these states and the development of psychosomatic disorders. There is some evidence that people who are not very expressive in external modes (e.g., facial musculature) have more intense manifestations of emotional response in other channels of expression, such as the ANS. Buck, Miller, and Caul (1974) reported that facially unexpressive persons tend to have larger skin conductance and heart rate responses to emotional stimuli than do expressive persons. Again, so little work has been conducted on this issue that one can do little more than speculate about the relationships among modalities.

Emotional expressions have as one of their important functions the communication of internal emotional states. Emotional expression is the public vehicle for private activities. The communicative function of emotional expression is poorly understood. How people respond to particular expressions varies as a function of their values, culture, and age. The communicative function has two parts. One is an elicitor of empathic behavior and the other is an information exchange. The empathic function serves to elicit in another the particular emotion that one is feeling (contagion). The information function serves to tell others what the person is feeling and allows them to adjust, to facilitate, or to inhibit the emotion. Emotional expressions can be intentionally produced in the absence of emotional states in order to influence those to whom the expressions are directed. Feigning disappointment or anger, for example, can be used to manipulate other people. Such deceptions serve a wide set of social needs. For example, when a friend falls down while walking, although one may feel like laughing, it is socially desirable to act concerned.

The intentional production of emotional expressions can also be used in a mock fashion. The exaggerated expression of a particular emotion has a complex social function, often taking the form "I am surprised but don't want to tell you I am, so I act oversurprised." Thus, the person informs the receiver that she or he really does possess a surprised state but wishes to deny the state while at the same time expressing it. The elaborate socialization rules that govern emotional expressions are explored in Chapters 6 and 7.

The communicative value of expressions could be discussed in detail (Buck, 1981, 1982). It involves what people know about other people's knowledge of expression and the meaning of that expression. It also involves the ability to control and manipulate one's own behavior intentionally. Thus, any discussion of the communicative function must consider the cultural rules involving deception. Such a discussion underscores the fact that emotional expressions are separate from emotional states and experiences. Furthermore, it suggests that one of the primary socialization tasks is learning the rules of emotional expression in particular situations (see Chapter 6).

Development of Emotional Expressions

Theories of the development of emotional expressions depend on whether emotional expressions are believed to be directly connected to emotional states. Even more central to the issue of the development of emotional expression is the particular system used to measure expressions. Because the measurement systems for coding expressions other than facial ones are scarce, little is known about the development of other expressions. Historically, more attention has been paid to facial expression; most of the information about emotional development derives from studies of facial expression. Even here, however, the data are limited. Rather than specifying particular types of "faces," most studies have focused on the development of particular features. The most widely studied feature of facial musculature has been smiling. The development of smiling is not discussed here, since it is reviewed in Chapter 7. Suffice it to say that there seems to be some evidence of maturational unfolding (Emde & Koenig, 1969).

Another developmental problem concerns the issue of context. Emotional expressions are connected to states and to elicitors, and the likelihood of observing an emotional expression depends on the nature of the connections. That is, an investigator must know what is likely to make a child afraid in order to produce and measure fear expressions. Since emotional elicitors have a developmental course (discussed above), and emotional expressions are produced by elicitors, the study of the development of expressions is more complicated than it would seem initially. The failure to observe an expression in response to a particular elicitor does not constitute grounds for concluding that the expression is not present at that age, since it might appear under other circumstances.

A final difficulty in studying the development of emotional expressions concerns the meaning assigned to expressions. One would hope that the measurement system used to measure emotional expressions would be independent of any cultural or social meaning system, and that an X face means X. However, since particular situations must be selected if one is to observe particular expressions, a bias is introduced into the measurement system: investigators regard particular faces to reflect what they expect them to mean. For example, the stranger approach situation, thought to elicit fear, is used to produce expressions that are interpreted as fear. In fact, it is uncertain whether infants in this situation are fearful, wary, or attentive. Since wary and attentive faces, as measured by current systems, have much in common, the context and its meaning must be used to interpret the face. The highly detailed measurement systems of Ekman and Friesen (1978) and Izard (1979b) may not be subject to such difficulties because they measure expression independent of context.

The developmental course of emotional expressions, then, is uncharted as yet. Nevertheless, parents have no difficulty in responding to questions designed to examine their beliefs about when children first express emotions (Pannabecker et al., 1980). Generally, parents tend to agree about when they think their children first show a particular emotion. It remains to be determined whether their responses are a function of when emotions actually emerge or whether their answers reflect the belief system of their society. It is likely that if such questions were asked of parents in different cultures or at a different historical time, different results would be obtained. Cultures that place a strong emphasis on particular emotions may perceive their emergence earlier than other cultures. Thus, while 84% of American parents see anger in their babies within the first three months (Pannabecker et al., 1980), it may be the case that in cultures characterized by less aggression, parents would see the emergence of anger somewhat later.

The development of emotional expressions can be considered both in terms of the ability to produce various expressions and in terms of the ability to recognize or discriminate among expressions. Although there is a considerable literature on children's ability to discriminate facial expressions as well as their differential preference for certain facial expressions, little systematic work has been done on the nature of the discriminable aspects of those features. An important theoretical issue is raised. For the most part, investigators have concluded on the basis of such discrimination and preference data that infants are capable of facial differentiation. In fact, the data may reflect not the ability to discriminate emotions but a preference for a highly specific aspect of the face that has a different salience. In contrast to sad faces, smiling and fear faces are both characterized by an open mouth with teeth exposed. Is the discrimination of sad versus happy based on differences in the hedonic qualities of the faces or on teeth exposure? In order to conclude that infants can distinguish facial expressions, such dimensions would have to be controlled. However, by controlling them, the facial expression itself is altered.

There is little conclusive evidence about when infants are able to discriminate gross facial configurations (Charlesworth & Kreutzer, 1973; Ekman & Oster, 1979; Oster, 1981). Many studies do not find clear evidence of infant discrimination of positive or negative expressions before 5 or 6 months (Charlesworth & Kreutzer, 1973), although La-Barbera, Izard, Vietze, and Parisi (1976) reported that 4-month-olds preferred looking at joy faces to looking at anger or neutral faces. Young-Browne, Rosenfeld, and Horowitz (1977), too, found that infants as young as 3 months could distinguish happy faces from surprised faces, although they could not discriminate happy faces from sad faces.

Recently, Caron, Caron, and Myers (1982) introduced a series of controls in the investigation of facial discrimination in order to separate what they considered the irrelevant aspects of facial expressions from the more critical features. Their work strongly suggests that not until

7 or 8 months of age can infants discriminate facial expressions independently of such irrelevant details as "toothy smiles." The careful
demonstration of the role of superfluous stimuli in facial discrimination
studies underscores the problems in studying facial discrimination.
Infants do not discriminate expressions much before the beginning of
the second half of the first year of life.

The development of facial expression is one of the areas of research
receiving the most attention in the infancy literature. With the more
elaborate measurement systems currently being developed, along with
the exploration of contextual variables that influence expressions, a
more complete description of emotional expressions should be forth-
coming. The major developmental issue related to emotional expressions appears to concern the time of their first emergence. Once produced, their developmental course may be primarily a function of the
elicitor–expression relationship and socialization factors, which will
be discussed in the next chapter.

Emotional Experiences

Definition of Emotional Experiences

Emotional experience is the interpretation and evaluation by individuals of their perceived emotional state and expression. Emotional
experience requires that individuals attend to those sets of stimuli previously discussed as emotional states and expressions. The attending
to these stimuli is neither automatic nor necessarily conscious. In the
former case, emotional experience may not occur because of competing
stimuli to which the organism's attention is drawn. An example of this
follows. The car a woman is driving suddenly has a blowout in the
front tire. The car skids across the road, but the woman succeeds in
bringing it under control and stopping the car on the shoulder of the
road. Measurement of her physiological state as well as of her facial
expression might show that while bringing the car under control her
predominant emotional state was fear. Because her attention was directed toward controlling the car, however, she was not aware of her
internal state or expression. She only experienced fear *after* she got out
of the car to examine the tire. Emotional experiences thus require organisms to attend to a select set of stimuli. Without attention, emotional
experiences may not occur even though an emotional state may exist.
Thus, patients may not experience pain at the dentist if they are dis-
tracted through the use of earphones and loud music. This is not to say

that at some level a painful state does not occur. Rather, it is simply not experienced as pain.

The emotional experience may not necessarily be conscious, either. If one is willing to distinguish between conscious and unconscious experiences, it may be the case that emotional experiences occur at different levels of consciousness. Such an analysis forms the basis of much psychoanalytic thought. For example, an individual may be in an emotional state of anger. That is, with the proper measurement techniques, one would find a pattern of internal physiological responses indicative of anger. Moreover, this person may act toward those objects or persons who have made her angry in a way that suggests she is intentionally behaving in response to an internal state of anger. Nonetheless, the person may deny that she feels angry or is acting in an angry fashion. Within the therapeutic situation, such people might be shown that (1) they are angry and (2) they are responding intentionally as a consequence of that anger. The therapeutic process may further reveal that unconscious processes are operating in a fashion parallel to conscious ones. Defense mechanisms function to separate levels of awareness. However, the power of repression is such that although awareness is not at a conscious level, unconscious awareness still exerts powerful effects. Slips of the tongue, accidents, and classes of unintentional conscious behavior may all be manifesting intentional unconscious awareness (Freud, 1960). Thus, people may experience their internal states and expressions and be aware of this experience, or they may experience them in an unconscious mode in which the conscious perception of the experience is unavailable. The problem of unconscious experience remains a significant problem in Western thought (Jaynes, 1977).

Emotional experience occurs through the interpretation and evaluation of states and expressions. Thus, emotional experience is dependent on cognitive processes. It is impossible to talk about interpretation and evaluation without discussing both the ability to interpret and evaluate (i.e., the cognitive processes involved) and the rules governing the interpretation and evaluation that are the product of socialization. Cognitive processes involving interpretation and evaluation are enormously complex and involve various perceptual, memory, and elaboration processes. Events need to be perceived and compared with previous experience. Thus, for example, changes in autonomic activity must be perceived and evaluated against prior state conditions. Interpretation involves comparisons with other events and complex labeling.

Evaluation and interpretation not only involve cognitive processes that enable organisms to act on information (i.e., changes in emotional states) but are very much dependent on socialization to provide the content of the emotional experience. The particular socialization rules are little studied and not well understood. This particular topic is covered in Chapters 6 and 7.

For some, the emotional experience is part of the emotional state. James (1890) defined emotions as "the bodily changes [that] follow directly the *perception* of the exciting fact and our feeling of the same changes as they occur" (p. 449). In order to experience an emotion, a precipitating event ("exciting fact") must occur and cause a bodily change. The conscious feeling of that change is the emotional feeling. Thus, emotion is not the precipitating event, nor the bodily change associated with that event, but the conscious feeling of that bodily change. Although the nature of the bodily change has been questioned (see Chapter 3), proponents of James's theory have maintained that the conscious feeling of bodily changes is as central to the concept of emotion as are the bodily changes themselves.

The conscious feeling of James has become, at least for some (e.g., Schachter & Singer, 1962), a cognitive-evaluative process that determines what to call the physiological change. Schachter and Singer follow a long tradition of investigators who have maintained that the somatic change is not specific to any particular emotional experience but is a general arousal state. This conclusion is, in part, based on the fact that sets of physiological responses that covary with any given emotional experience have not been found. The nature of any specific emotion is thought to be determined by the organism's evaluation of its aroused condition. This evaluation may involve contextual cues, past experience, and individual differences.

The theories of James and of Schachter and Singer are similar in that the elicitor produces a bodily change, which is experienced by the organism. The experience of the organism, defined as a conscious feeling by James or a cognitive-evaluative feeling by Schachter and Singer, is the feeling or emotion. For Schachter and Singer, the evaluation and interpretation are dependent on the context in which the change takes place. Thus, for experiences of either joy or fear, there may be a general, undifferentiated state change. What differentiates these experiences is the context in which the state change takes place. The sight of a mother who has been away may be interpreted as joy, whereas the sight of a stranger constitutes fear.

Not all theories of emotional experience need be as tied to the context, nor do all suggest that the underlying emotional state is the same. However, all emotional experience does involve an evaluation and interpretation of an internal state, the context, and the immediate eliciting stimulus. The context might constitute the social environment, a particular location, the type and number of others available, and the internal states and eliciting stimuli, as previously discussed. Emotional experience is therefore not an automatic response connected in a one-to-one relationship to emotional state. Rather, emotional experience, more than any other component of emotional activity, is the most cognitive and learned aspect of the emotional process. Cultural and individual differences are apt to be most apparent in this aspect of emotion.

Development of Emotional Experiences

The development of emotional experiences is one of the least understood aspects of emotion. An earlier discussion raised the possibility that emotional experience occurs at both a conscious and an unconscious level. While the development of experience at the conscious level has received some attention, study of the development of unconscious experience has been quite limited. Since it has been argued that emotional experience does not necessarily have a one-to-one relationship with emotional state, the development of experiences may occur long after the emergence of emotional states. Therefore, while newborns may show an emotional state of pain when pricked with a pin, it would not necessarily follow that they have an emotional experience of pain.

Emotional experiences require that the organism possess some fundamental cognitive abilities, including the ability to perceive and discriminate, recall, associate, and compare. Emotional experiences also require a particular cognitive ability, which is associated with the development of the concept of self. Emotional experiences take the linguistic form, "I am frightened" or "I am happy." In all cases, the subject and the object are the same—oneself. Until an organism is capable of self–other distinctions, such subjective experiences may not be possible (Lewis & Brooks-Gunn, 1979; Mahler, Pine, & Gerbman, 1975). Finally, emotional experiences are learned through the behavior of others toward oneself. They are a consequence of how others interpret one's emotional states and expressions.

Emotional Experiences and General Cognitive Capacities

Emotional experiences require those cognitive processes necessary for the organism to perceive and discriminate elicitors of particular behaviors as well as the particular behaviors themselves (internal phys-

iological changes as well as overt emotional expressions). As was suggested in the review of facial recognition and discrimination in infants,
children are generally unable to demonstrate this ability before 6 months
of age. The cognitive processes and conceptual abilities necessary to
carry out the perception of emotion in others as well as in oneself are
probably lacking before then. Schaffer's (1974) demonstration that children cannot make simultaneous comparisons prior to 7 or 8 months of
age would also suggest that infants are not capable of experiencing
emotions prior to this point. Campos and Stenberg (1981) also failed
to find support for the existence of cognitive capacities that would
facilitate this ability prior to the last part of the first year. Such findings
support the belief that the critical dimension of development of emotional experience is the ability to experience one's own emotional state.

Some emotional experiences may require a higher level of cognitive
processing than others. Thus, some emotional experiences may develop
earlier than others. For example, fear probably emerges earlier than
shame, since the former requires less cognitive and evaluative processing than the latter. These early experiences may then serve to facilitate the development of later experiences, since they may facilitate
both the development of self and the production of the cognitive-evaluative structures needed for subsequent emotional experiences. The
earlier experiences may be those that others have labeled the *primary
emotions*, while the latter may be those labeled *secondary* or *derived
emotions* (Plutchik, 1980a; Tomkins, 1962). The notion of derived versus primary emotions need not imply that one set is any more biologically rooted than the other, merely that one set requires less evaluative
ability. A model stressing cognitive evaluation rather than biological
determination should be open to experimental verification, since cognitive evaluation and consciousness, as well as emotional experience,
can be measured in young children.

Emotional Experiences and the Concept of Self

If emotional experience is the consequence of an evaluation (whether
conscious or not) of one's bodily changes, then two processes are necessary for most emotional experiences: (1) the knowledge that the bodily
changes are uniquely different from other changes (i.e., they are internal
rather than external) and (2) an evaluation of these changes. Each needs
to be considered.

Internal and external stimuli differ to the degree to which they can
be verified by others: external events are verifiable by others; internal
experiences are not. The distinction between internal and external events

can be considered in many modalities. For example, in perception, one can verify that a tree is in the corner of the yard. However, each person's experience of that tree is an internal event and is neither similar to others' experiences nor verifiable.

The internal–external distinction for emotional development is important because it addresses the difference between experience and expression. If one believes that facial expression, as well as other expressive behavior, is equivalent to an emotional state or experience, then others can view an internal event through an examination of its external manifestation. If, however, one does not subscribe to the view of a one-to-one correspondence between expression and experience, then all one can say is that there is an external manifestation of some unperceived internal event. Nevertheless, emotional experiences are internal events by nature.

The internal–external distinction is also relevant to the concept of self. Internal stimuli have a location inside oneself, external stimuli outside oneself. The development of the infant's ability to make an internal–external distinction is worth exploring, since one might reasonably assume that the ability to distinguish between stimuli "out there," which are verifiable by others, and stimuli occurring within and having limited verifiability is related to self-awareness. Verification of internal stimuli is possible through the use of empathy. By having experienced internal stimuli, one is able to understand and appreciate the description of another's internal state or experience. Empathy connects people's internal experiences.

The evaluation of internal stimuli or bodily changes has been conceptualized as a perceptual-cognitive process similar to the information processing of other stimuli, the only difference being that the information to be processed is located within the body. The distinction between processing information emanating from inside versus outside the body may not be minor. Certainly information emanating from inside the body is more immediate and impinges directly on the person. Whether such differences result in different processes associated with processing internal and external information is difficult to determine.

Such evaluation may involve the process of self-awareness. Self-awareness is an information-processing and decision-making event related to internal stimuli. It logically requires an organism possessing the notion of agency. The term *agency* refers to the aspect of action that makes reference to the cause of the action, that is, not only who or what is causing the stimulus change but who is evaluating it. The stimulus change itself may have the effect of both alerting the organism and forcing it to make some type of evaluation.

The evaluative process should be similar to other cognitive processes, such as the learning of efficacy. The ability of the organism to cause events to occur would seem to require some as yet undefined notion of self. If infants can cause an outcome to occur repeatedly through their behavior (e.g., in secondary circular reactions), then they have learned some of the causes and consequences of that behavior. For certain associations between events, infants have learned the notion of their own agency (e.g., "I" causes something to happen). Although it is difficult to define the "I," it is an "I" that is different from others. "I" has a location even though "I" moves in space, two processes underlying a sense of permanence. This "I," different from others, having an internal and external location and permanence, is the first stage in the development of the concept of self. Thus, in the same way that infants learn to affect their world, infants may also learn to evaluate their actions in the world.

In summary, emotional experiences require a set of stimulus changes that are located in the body and that are evaluated by the person. Both location and evaluation assume that a notion of self exists. Somatic changes are internal stimulus changes located only within one's own body, a location synonymous with "me." Evaluation of these changes assumes consciousness, or self-awareness, as well as cognitive ability. In addition, the evaluation process itself requires an agent of evaluation. It is most difficult to construct a sentence about the evaluation of internal stimuli that does not use a self-referent. The phrase "I am experiencing some internal changes, X," means "I am feeling X." The source of the stimuli and the agent evaluating the stimuli are the same; this interface is the self. To understand the development of emotional experiences, it is necessary to understand the development of self. (See Chapter 5 for a discussion of the development of self.)

Emotional Experiences and the Social Environment

Emotional experience is also derived through the social world; emotional experiences are the social consequence of how other people interpret one's states and expressions. A detailed discussion of how the interpretation of others' verbal and nonverbal behaviors may affect one's emotional experiences is presented in the next three chapters. Here, the topic is discussed only in order to illustrate how the social environment can affect the development of emotional experience.

The development of emotional experience may depend on how the social world responds to children's emotional states and expressions and to the context in which they occur. For example, a caregiver seeing an infant cry in response to a pinprick may interpret the emotional state of the infant as pain. The caregiver's interpretation may be both verbal and behavioral. Different responses will be elicited by different sets of expressions in different contexts. These expressions and the contexts in which they occur are what adults use to interpret their own internal states and those of others. In this way, infants become, in part, what others think them to be (Lewis & Brooks, 1975; Mead, 1934). Thus, the very act of interpretation and evaluation by the social environment provides the rules by which children learn to evaluate and interpret (i.e., to experience) their own behaviors and states.

This model can be used to understand the development of emotional experience. Contextual cues are determined by infants' interactions with and knowledge about their social world. The caregiver provides the bulk of both the early knowledge and the interactions. Infants' evaluations are determined initially by (1) the elicitor, which produces (2) bodily changes, and (3) the responses (both verbal and nonverbal) of the caregiver in response to these bodily changes. The correlation between infants' overt expressions, the emotional feelings, and the caregiver's verbal labeling (e.g., "Don't be afraid") and behavioral responses (e.g., holding and comforting) may provide the information necessary for children to form an emotional experience, one that is consistent with what others expect.

The evaluative aspects of emotion (e.g., Schachter & Singer, 1962), the conscious feeling (James, 1890), and self-awareness (Lewis & Brooks, 1978) need further study in terms of the development of particular emotional experiences. Emotional experiences can occur only after certain cognitive and social underpinnings are present. Over the first two years of life, children acquire these faculties and, with them, the ability to experience emotions. While emotional elicitors may produce specific emotional states and expressions, it is not until self-awareness exists that one can speak of infants as having certain emotional experiences.

✄✄✄✄✄✄✄✄✄✄✄✄

In this chapter definitional and developmental issues related to the components of *emotion* were discussed. In the discussion of emotion and its development, five components were considered: elicitors, receptors, states, expressions, and experiences. For each of these, biological, socialization, and cognition influences were discussed. The contributions of these factors to developmental phenomena were also considered. Emotions are often poorly defined in the research literature, and readers may not know whether the investigator is referring to expressions, states, experiences, or some combination. At times, these terms are used synonymously. However, important distinctions need to be made. From both a theoretical and an empirical point of view, a careful analysis of emotion must be conducted. Without such a clarification, emotional expressions may be misrepresented as emotional states or experiences when this is not necessarily the case. Whether the structural analysis we have presented is sufficient remains to be seen. Nevertheless, it provides a framework for the further exploration of emotional development. In the next chapter, the task of integrating these different features into a comprehensive theory of development is undertaken.

5

The Development of Emotion

In the preceding chapter, five components of emotion were defined. The developmental issues related to the individual components were discussed, as well as possible models of development. For the sake of simplicity, each component was dealt with separately. Not considered were the various interconnections among these components or how development might affect the interconnections. It is now necessary to consider developmental models in terms of the *connections* among these features.

This approach is unique. Normally when investigators discuss emotional development, they focus on the development of a particular component. Consequently, theories, or partial theories, exist about the development of emotional states and about the development of emotional expressions. What such accounts lack is any consideration of the development of the relationship between these components. There are few explanations of the relationship between emotional states and expressions or between emotional states and experiences. In this chapter, our attention will turn to developmental issues pertaining to the interconnections among the components.

The complexity of this task should be obvious from the previous chapters. Given the differences among investigators about the meaning of terms, the lack of agreement about appropriate measurement systems, and the relative scarcity of empirical data, the conceptualization, not to mention the testing, of a comprehensive theory of development is far from possible. However, certain portions of developmental theory are open to greater clarification, explication, and empirical testing. It is these broader issues that will be addressed. Although socialization issues will be mentioned in this chapter, the topic is so involved that it will receive a detailed treatment in Chapters 6 and 7.

In discussing the various approaches to developmental theory, a broad conceptual framework is offered in which to place the prototypic models of emotional development as well as our own approach to development. While our approach is based on an analysis of emotion into its components, it is recognized that many theories make little distinction among these features. Nevertheless, we believe that our approach has heuristic value in its structural analysis of emotional development. The theory posits a role for both biological and socialization forces in the emotional process, placing particular emphasis on the effects of socialization and culture in emotional development. Finally, a primary role for the notion of self in the development of emotional experience is incorporated in the theory.

In this chapter, the general model of emotion will first be described. The model contains the five components of emotion discussed individually in Chapter 4. The model is of particular value in its focus on the relationships among the components as they relate to (1) the unfolding of particular emotions at specific points in time; (2) the cycling of emotions throughout the life span; and (3) the development of emotions. In the discussion of this topic, the general forms of the biological, socialization, and interactive models of development are outlined. Finally, several rather specific developmental issues are raised: (1) the differentiation of emotional expressions or states; (2) individual differences in state differentiation; (3) the development of the connection between states and expressions; and (4) the development of the self and its relationship to emotional development. For the most part, these specific topics address issues related to the connections among the components rather than the components *per se*.

A Model of Emotion

Five components of emotion are critical to the model: elicitors, receptors, states, expressions, and experiences. Now that we have described the major features of these components and some of the developmental issues associated with each, they will be brought together into a model of emotion that can be used to analyze development in the young child. The model allows one to view emotion in several ways. First, the emergence and the unfolding of a particular emotion can be described at a fixed point in time in the life of an individual. The model is applicable to describing the occurrence of an emotion in adults as well as in children. Second, the model can be used to describe the cycling of emotions throughout the life of an individual, either in

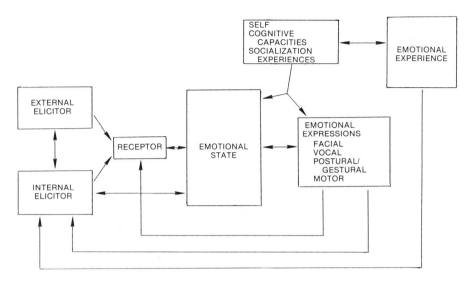

Figure 8. A structural model of emotion.

terms of the movement from one emotion to another or in terms of
recurring episodes of a particular emotion. Third, the model provides
a conceptual frame of reference for viewing the general development
of emotion. The model is presented in Figure 8.

The Unfolding of a Particular Emotion

The model in Figure 8 describes the emergence and the unfolding
of a particular emotion in both children and adults. One must recognize
that throughout the life span, developmental changes may occur, especially in response to socialization pressures. Nevertheless, at some
point, developmental changes become less rapid and may stabilize.

The emotional process depicted in Figure 8 is set in motion by
internal and external elicitors. These elicitors activate receptors, which
produce emotional states. Emotional states, in turn, generate emotional
expressions. Emotional states and expressions become emotional experiences through the mediation of the self and other cognitive processes and through socialization experiences. This description suggests
a unidirectional quality in the emotional process that is not intended.
Although most models of emotion tend to be unidirectional, there are
probably strong cycling effects in the process. The multidirectionality

among the components of the model is indicated through the use of double arrows.

Multidirectionality can be found in the specific relationships between pairs of these components. External and internal elicitors may affect each other so that an internal elicitor alters the quality of an external elicitor and vice versa. For example, if an external event were to cause a drop in an individual's blood sugar level, this physiological event might act as an internal elicitor to affect the individual's response to the original external elicitor. Thus, the same external elicitor can produce different internal elicitors, which, in turn, produce different external elicitors.

Because little is known about emotional receptors, examples of the multidirectionality between elicitors and receptors or between receptors and emotional states cannot be offered. However, the multidirectionality between an elicitor and an emotional state can be documented. For example, a mother's approach (an elicitor) may produce an aroused state in the child. Her continued approach (the same elicitor in some sense) is different as a consequence of the child's aroused state. Thus, the same eliciting condition may be altered by a change in state, attesting to the multidirectionality of this portion of the model. Generally, investigators do not attempt to measure changes in the emotional state of a subject during the presentation of an eliciting stimulus because of the obvious difficulties in assessing (and monitoring) ongoing state changes. Thus, they have come to adopt the rather static view that elicitors remain constant and produce single emotional states.

There are some data to suggest that repeated presentations of an elicitor may produce changes in the emotional state. Sroufe, Waters, and Matas (1974), for instance, found that in response to repeated presentations of a stranger's approach, children first smiled, then began to fret and cry. In other words, elicitor X, by altering the state of the organism, may affect the consequence of subsequent elicitors X. Although different trials were employed in this study, the results seemed to apply equally well to a situation in which the stranger, rather than approaching the child, stood close to the child. The child's first response might be to smile; if the stranger maintained his behavior (i.e., continued to stand near the child and did not move), the child's positive state might change to one of wariness.

A word of caution is in order here: the issue of what constitutes an elicitor is extremely difficult and may depend on somewhat arbitrary definitions of when one elicitor ends and a new one begins. Moreover, the interaction between state and elicitor may be more powerful for some children than for others. For instance, children who are temperamentally irritable or those who are unable to modulate their own states probably experience more variability in elicitor–state outcomes.

Other examples of the multidirectionality in the unfolding of an emotion involve emotional expressions and experiences. Emotional expressions themselves can be elicitors. For example, hearing oneself laugh can make an already positive experience more positive. In fact, according to James's (1884; 1890) theory of emotion, it is the individual's behavior, that, when perceived, produces the emotion. Thus, running away from a fearful event acts as an emotional elicitor in addition to the original elicitor that triggered the running away. Emotional experience itself can influence the other components, including expressions, states, and elicitors. This issue is considered later. Thus, even within the static model represented in Figure 8 some of the dynamic interactions between the experience and the other components are evident.

Up to this point, the focus of the discussion has been a dynamic emotional process that occurs within a limited period of time. In a sense, a particular elicitor activates a system in which oscillation among the various components occurs. This oscillation ultimately manifests itself in a phenomenological sense as an emotional experience. When analyzed, the phenomenological experience may be a single emotion or a mixture of emotions, the mixture being a function of the degree of oscillation in the process or an interaction between this oscillation and socialization experiences. Thus, the model addresses the issue of mixed emotions and raises the possibility that mixed emotions might be the culmination of a set of temporally sequenced events that occur in an oscillating system.

As previously stated, it is extremely difficult to analyze an ongoing emotional process. Thus, emotions are generally divided into finite temporal bouts, each beginning with an elicitor and separated from previous emotional states. Such a procedure is questionable, inasmuch as any division of sequential events is arbitrary. In order to be understood, interpersonal experiences must be viewed in sequence (Fogel, 1977, 1982a,b; Kaye & Fogel, 1980; Lewis & Lee-Painter, 1974; Sackett, 1979). The same considerations that apply to the analysis of interpersonal experiences must also apply to the analysis of ongoing emotional sequences (see Chapter 4).

The Cycling of Emotional Life

The model depicted in Figure 8 has heuristic value in explaining the emergence and the unfolding of a particular emotion from the moment that an emotional elicitor acts on the organism to the time when

the emotion is subjectively experienced. The same process that underlies the emergence of a particular emotion may also underlie the cycling
of emotions through the life span. In fact, the emotional life of an
individual may be best envisioned as a series of emotional bouts. There
may be nothing discrete about emotions other than the need of individuals to impose temporal constraints on subjective experiences. In
the discussion above, it was shown how the continuation of a particular
emotion is maintained by the multidirectionality of the process. Likewise, the movement from one emotion to another is made possible
through an emotional elicitor's continual action on the organism,
which can, through state changes, produce different sequences of emotions. Some of these subsequent emotions are likely to be quite dissimilar.

The model as presented does not explain how emotions are terminated or how new emotions arise, since it does not take into account
either the role of the social world in the production of children's emotions or children's cognitive characteristics. In other words, the model
may be better suited to describing the process activated by an internal
or external elicitor, which culminates in an emotional experience. If
the individual has no other information, the emotional experience may
become the new elicitor. Thus, there will be a continuous recycling of
the same emotion over time.

The need to account for the termination of the process leads to the
consideration of how other information, the introduction of new elicitors or the termination of old ones, enters the system. For example,
the appearance of a new event or the termination of the old event may
alter the cycle. Thus, a stranger approaching from behind on a dark
night may produce fear in an individual. As the stranger walks past
the individual, however, the fear is terminated. Or the achievement of
a goal may terminate a particular emotion.

It is also possible that the new elicitor will appear in the form of
the response of another person. Because the emotional process is
embedded in the social life of the organism, this social environment
must play a critical role in the regulation of particular emotions. For
example, being scolded for laughing at someone else's silly behavior
may terminate the state of humor and elicit shame. Most models fail
to provide a clear articulation of how the emotional process fits into
the social life or into the plans and goals of the individual. While the
issue of how social and cognitive factors may affect each of the five
components of emotion has been considered previously (see Chapter
4), their effect on the system as a whole needs further clarification.

In short, the model, when embedded in the ongoing life of the organism, has some heuristic value in explaining the cycling of emotions in the organism. The cycling of emotions, as we envision it, has a long-term temporal dimension, unlike the unfolding of a discrete emotion, which is generally of a much shorter duration. Although both analyses are more or less restricted to a given developmental level, the model also has implications for the overall emotional development of an organism.

The Development of Emotion

The discussion so far has considered the flow of emotional life within any particular developmental period. The model can also be used to explain emotional processes across developmental levels. The developmental process may create the particular components necessary for the occurrence of an emotion. Developmental processes may also connect components, as well as produce the multidirectionality of those connections. For example, emotional elicitors may activate emotional states that, in turn, feed back and affect elicitors. However, emotional states may not influence emotional experience or be influenced by experience during the first half year of life, since young infants do not yet have the cognitive prerequisites for experiencing an emotion (Lewis & Brooks-Gunn, 1979). The inability to experience an emotion, then, affects both the unfolding of the particular emotion and the feedback system. In this example, the necessary cognitive structure, and thus the experiential component of emotion, is missing because it has not yet emerged in the development of the individual.

Likewise, particular socialization practices, associated with different developmental levels, may alter the cycling process. For instance, when faced with a fear-eliciting situation, the male child may have a fear state and display fear expressions. The imposition of external socialization pressures, however, may modify this emotional bout in such a way that fear expressions will be missing at a later point in time. With special equipment, it might be possible to document the emotional process and discover where and how the process is changed as a result of socialization so that an elicitor no longer produces the original state–expression sequence. From a developmental point of view, our focus should be on (1) the creation of these components; (2) their interconnections; and (3) the rules governing them. In the adult stage of development, these features exist in their mature forms, and all components participate in the normal flow of emotional life.

The model in Figure 8 is also useful for contrasting two general theories of emotional development. Specifically, the following discussion makes use of the model to delineate the differences between biological and socialization interpretations of development. Although our discussion gives the strong version of each view, restricting accounts of emotional development to either position exclusive of the other does an injustice to each. Nevertheless, the strong form of an argument often provides the means for generating testable hypotheses.

A Biological Interpretation of Emotion

In the discussion of the development of particular components in the previous chapter, both the biological and the socialization models were used as explanatory devices. As indicated, the biological model of emotional development is derived from Darwin's (1872) theory that emotional expressions have adaptive significance in the life of the organism, and consequently, they are programmed within the biological structure of the organism. From this point of view, it could be argued that there is a strong evolutionary trend toward an increasingly differentiated facial musculature, the primary function of which appears to be the production of facial expressions. Two caveats are in order. First, evolutionary theory does not allow for the distinction between behaviors or structures that are adapted for and those that are not (Gould, 1977). Second, there is little reason to believe that facial musculature is necessarily connected to internal states. Although facial musculature and facial expressions may be biologically determined, the assertion that they are related to internal states of the organism does not logically follow.

According to biological models, emotions occur as the consequence of strong biological forces that rely on maturational changes rather than cultural factors to explain development. Emotional development is regarded as a complex process in which elicitors, receptors, states, and expressions are biologically linked and influence one another in an unlearned fashion. The biological interpretation of emotion is currently represented in the work of Izard (1971, 1977). According to Izard and Dougherty (1982),

> emotion expressions are innate and emerge ontogenetically as they become adaptive in the life of the infant and particularly in the infant-caregiver communication. (p. 98)

Furthermore,

> the data from these investigations [studies showing that certain emotions have similar facial expressions across widely different cultures] provide a sound basis for inferring that the fundamental emotions are subserved by

innate neural programs that are part of the substrate of qualitatively distinct
states of consciousness. (p. 98)

Biological interpretations posit (1) specific elicitor–receptor connections, as in IRMs; (2) specificity of CNS receptors; (3) unlearned
connections between receptors and states; and (4) unlearned connections between states and expressions, states and experiences, and
expressions and experiences. The strong connection between particular
emotional expressions and states as well as between expressions and
experiences was also postulated by Izard and Dougherty (1982):

> It is reasonable to infer that the link between facial expression, neurochem-
> ical processes and emotions, and certain actions or action tendencies *is the
> inner emotion experience and its motivational properties.* (p. 101; emphasis
> added)

The role of biological factors in the development of the specific
components of emotion has already been discussed (Chapter 4), and it
is unnecessary to articulate these issues again. It has also been shown
that biological differences in individuals in the form of temperamental
characteristics play a role in the modulation of environment–state connections (Chapter 2). For example, a temperamentally difficult child
may find a particular elicitor aversive, whereas a temperamentally easy
child will find the same elicitor pleasurable. Such biological processes
affect the one-to-one correspondence between elicitors and states. However powerful the effects of the culture may be, it is difficult to ignore
the pervasive role of maturational processes and biological differences
in emotional development.

The development of elicitor–receptor connections, the specificity
of receptors, and the connections between receptors and states and
among states, expressions, and experiences all are based on the same
data. States are defined by expressions; thus, a one-to-one correspondence between them is assumed. This assumption, in turn, suggests
the specificity of emotional states based on a demonstration of differences in emotional expressions. Specific states required the assumption
of receptor specificity insofar as specific elicitors produce specific
expressions. Evidence of the universality of emotional expressions is
used to argue that these expressions are not culturally controlled but
are determined by biological mechanisms. The data for such claims are
limited to the demonstration that discrete emotions have unique expressions (Ekman *et al.*, 1972; Izard, 1977). The conclusions from these data
are untested, and the argument is circular.

The importance of data on facial expressions should not be under-
estimated, however. Such data certainly support the view that partic-

ular configurations of facial muscles are the result of biological and maturational processes. The slowly accumulating evidence of the emergence of differentiated facial expressions as a function of age, if verified, confirms the view of a systematic developmental unfolding in one aspect of emotion.

The crux of the argument is the degree to which this is primarily a maturational process or an interactive process, which is connected to other developmental processes. For example, certain facial expressions may be subject to a slow, sequential unfolding. It is important to examine the relationship between this maturational process on the one hand and the development of states on the other. In one case, fear faces may be elicited by fear stimuli only after the maturation of particular facial muscles. This process may take approximately six to eight months to occur and may occur independently of any other process. Could one say, in the absence of a fear face, that a child younger than 6 months of age had a fear state? If a one-to-one correspondence is postulated between expressions and internal states, one would be forced to conclude that a fear state cannot exist in the absence of a fear face. Under this same assumption, one would be forced to acknowledge the existence of certain emotional states that probably do not occur until well after their facial expressions appear. For example, contempt faces in infants younger than 1 year (Izard, 1979b) are difficult to attribute to an underlying state of contempt this early in life. Thus, emotional expressions may appear according to a biological timetable, dependent on certain elicitors, yet independent of any internal state.

The maturation of the neuromusculature of the face and facial expressions of emotions can be viewed as co-occurring with, although independent of, the growth of other processes and structures which are primarily cognitive. In some sense, then, the biological models of emotion, at least as they involve facial expressions, may require two separate processes: the development of the facial neuromusculature and the simultaneous development of some other process(es). At this point, it is difficult to separate biological forces from cognitive influences.

As will be discussed at length both in this chapter and in the next two chapters, the connection between expressions and states may be subject to strong socialization forces. Thus, the natural correspondence between emotional expressions and states, if it exists, can exist for only a short period prior to socialization. Even so, studies of mother–infant interaction indicate that strong pressures exist from the beginning of life to alter the correspondence between expressions and states (Brooks-Gunn & Lewis, 1982). By 2 years of age, children can be observed to produce facial expressions on request, and they have a rudimentary knowledge of how people are supposed to feel in particular situations (see Chapter 6).

These pieces of evidence suggest that the link between expressions and states, even early in life, may be tenuous at best. Nevertheless, studies examining the development of specific emotional expressions in response to a constant elicitor provide valuable and interesting information. Studies such as these are important not so much for what they reveal about the maturation of certain states but for what they reveal about the nature of faces and the development of expressions.

The connections between emotional experience on the one hand and emotional states and expressions on the other are the connections in the model that are the least clarified by biological explanations. The extent to which experiences are mediated by the development of the concept of the self and the extent to which the development of the self has strong maturational roots are the extents to which strong biological models posit a link between experiences and states. Although such a connection may exist, emotional experiences are psychic events and, as such, lack a direct correspondence to emotional states and expressions.

A Socialization Interpretation of Emotion

Both socialization and biological models are built on the same five components illustrated in Figure 8. The strong form of socialization or learning models of emotional development contrasts with biological models in that it does not posit (1) CNS specificity or (2) any necessary connection between components such as elicitors and states, states and expressions, states and experiences, and expressions and experiences. Even though it may be possible to find specific elicitors that result in predictable outcomes (e.g., fear in response to sudden, loud, or unexpected events), in general, elicitors probably have little innate correspondence to receptors or states.

This belief is based on the view that an elicitor is a percept constructed by the organism. The correspondence between "what is" and "what is perceived" is not necessarily direct (Neisser, 1967). The process of socialization that establishes the connections among the components can be viewed as the communication of a culturally defined meaning conveyed through selective responsivity. The degree to which the social environment shares similar meanings for coherences of behaviors and situations across individuals or cultures is the degree to which the socialization process creates common emotional states, expressions, and experiences in these same individuals. Universality, therefore, may be built into the similarity of cultures and the responses of individuals within these cultures rather than inherent in the genetic code of the individual.

The relationship between states and expressions, as discussed in the previous section, may be biologically determined, although the evidence is not entirely clear. Certainly, one of the primary roles of socialization centers on the relationship between internal emotional states and their external expressions. Consequently, there is little reason to assume that socialization does not determine the link between them. Further investigation of this process from a developmental perspective is presented later.

Whether or not one chooses to view elicitors and responses (states or expressions) as having a strong biological connection, there is likely to be little relationship between emotional states and experiences. Consider the following example: Two people are riding on a roller coaster. Each is subjected to the same elicitor (rapid drops) and each has similar physiological responses (e.g., increased heart rates). Nevertheless, their emotional experiences may be entirely different. For one, the ride may be experienced as excitement and exhilarated joy, whereas for the other, the ride may produce fear. In the strong version of socialization models, the connections among elicitors, states, and experiences are considered learned.

In the next chapter, the socialization of emotion is considered at great length. Although the chapter is not structured around the five components of emotion, numerous examples are presented in the chapter that show how the connections between elicitors and states may be learned, how expressions and states may be masked, and how experiences may be altered as a function of conscious and unconscious processes.

Any developmental theory based entirely on the strong forms of either the biological or the socialization interpretations of our structural model is bound to miss the complexity of emotional development. For several reasons, neither version of the model is sufficient to explain emotional development fully. One reason may be that different emotional states have different developmental courses. For instance, fear may have a different history from shame or guilt. The primary emotions may be those that fit a more biological description, whereas learned emotions may be better described by a socialization model. Even within a particular emotional experience different models may be required. For example, fear may be caused by different processes, some of which may be biological (e.g., startle) and some of which may be learned (e.g., phobias).

More than one model may also be necessary to explain emotions at different developmental levels in children's lives. It is likely that biological models are better suited to explaining development in very young organisms, whereas socialization models are more appropriate at later states of development. In Chapter 4, in this chapter, and in the next two chapters, it is argued that maturation, biological processes, and socialization forces all play key roles in the developmental sequence that starts with a relatively undifferentiated organism and results in a highly differentiated, cognitively aware individual capable of engaging in a rich affective life. Part of this affective life includes the ability to deceive both others and oneself. Throughout the volume, the emphasis is on the interdependence and interplay among these processes.

Specific Developmental Issues

Although developmental processes affect the entire emotional process, at this point we will focus on developmental issues related to the specific connections between components. Four topics are of particular interest: (1) facial or state differentiation, (2) individual differences in state differentiation, (3) the development of the state–expression relationship, and (4) the development of the self.

Facial or State Differentiation

Since the publication of Bridges' (1932) classic article on emotional development, there has been some interest in, but not a great deal of research on, emotional states and expressions as seen from a developmental perspective. Two major developmental hypotheses have been suggested. In one, emotional states and emotional expressions are at first relatively undifferentiated and consist of a positive and a negative hedonic tone (Bridges, 1932; Emde et al., 1976; Spitz, 1965; Sroufe, 1979b). Development involves the slow differentiation of this bipolar hedonic state into a set of finely differentiated states and expressions possessed by adults in all cultures. Differentiation is thought to occur through the interplay between the young organism and the social environment and through the development of certain cognitive structures. No theory has yet articulated precisely how differentiation occurs, although it is assumed to be associated with biological maturation, increased cognitive capacities, and social experience.

A second developmental hypothesis has been outlined more recently by Izard (1978; Izard & Buechler, 1979). According to this theoretical framework, infants are endowed at birth with already differentiated, discrete emotional states and expressions. Although particular states and expressions may not appear during the early stages of development, they are hypothetized to exist in a "preexpressed" form, almost like a tooth prior to its eruption from the gums. The only developmental feature involves the timing of their appearance, which is related to the social experiences and presumably the cognitive level of the child.

A version of this hypothesis assumes that very young infants have differentiated emotional states (Oster, 1978). Insofar as these states are not produced by or supported by cognitive structures, there is little reason to challenge the position. All that is required for the occurrence of the emotional state–expression is a particular elicitor.

Both major hypotheses are based on the assumption that the external manifestation of emotion corresponds to an internal emotional state. Thus, little distinction is made between emotional states and expressions. Both models incorporate a role for social and cognitive factors in the developmental process. How these factors influence the development of different emotions is a question left unanswered for the most part. In the case of the first hypothesis, little is known about how social and cognitive factors provide an impetus for the differentiation of specific emotions from the original bipolar hedonic state. In the case of the second hypothesis, the roles of social experience and cognition are even less clear, since the hypothesis is predicated on the notion of predetermined differentiation. Consequently, these factors are necessary only for the expression but not for the creation of emotional states. In fact, Izard (1978) argued that emotion and cognition are two separate systems with separate maturational courses. At times, these systems co-occur to form combinational, affective-cognitive structures.

Whichever developmental model one prefers, the challenges for developmental theory remain (1) to specify the nature of early emotional life; (2) to trace the increasing complexity of emotional life over time; and (3) to determine the processes responsible for this increased complexity. These tasks are basic to any developmental theory. The difficulty of constructing a satisfactory developmental theory is increased by the problem of determining the relationship between external manifestations of emotion and internal emotional states. Ultimately, it may be necessary to settle for a developmental theory of emotional expression and its relationship to particular elicitors, since the measurement of internal states remains problematic and historically has been a difficult problem to solve.

One approach to the issue of the differentiation of emotional states is to construct a developmental model based on two factors: emotional elicitors and the child's past experience (see Figure 9). In this model, elicitors initially produce certain states: positive elicitors produce positive states, and negative elicitors produce negative states. Although these states may be transient at first, prolonged exposure to a particular class of elicitors may result in more enduring emotional states. These enduring states, in turn, may serve to modulate subsequent interactions between elicitors and states. Thus, for example, a child who has been repeatedly exposed to positive elicitors will have a positive enduring state. Subsequently, a new elicitor either positive or negative, may interact with the enduring positive state to produce a new transient state.

Past states or experiences in interaction with a concurrent state produced by an elicitor are factors that can be used to show how a simple bipolar positive–negative differentiation can become a continuum of states varying in intensity from highly positive to highly negative. Figure 9 characterizes this process in two stages. At developmental level A, the earliest developmental period, a positive elicitor leads to a positive state and a negative elicitor leads to a negative state.

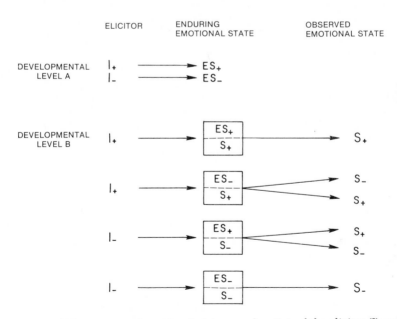

Figure 9. The differentiation of emotional states as a function of the elicitor (I) and an enduring state (ES): An ontogenetic analysis.

After the child has been exposed to a series of positive and negative states, these states become enduring negative (ES_) or positive (ES_+) emotional states. These positive and negative states then serve to modulate the elicitor–state experience of developmental level B. In the case where a positive elicitor producing a positive state (S_+) interacts with a previous positive state, the result is a large positive state. In the case of a positive elicitor's interacting with a negative state, the result is either a smaller positive or a small negative state. The same result could be obtained in the case of a negative elicitor producing a negative state (S_) that interacts with a previous positive state. However, when a negative elicitor interacts with a previous negative state, the consequence is likely to be an intense negative state.

Developmental period B, in Figure 9, illustrates four different degrees in the intensity of emotional states as a consequence of a particular elicitor. This analysis, which accounts for an increased differentiation of hedonic tone from initial bipolar states, addresses differentiation only in the degree of positive and negative tone. It makes no claim regarding qualitative differences of emotional states or about the development of such differences. It may be that qualitative differences in emotional states can be explained simply by intensity and hedonic tone differences. Tomkins's (1981) discussion of affect differences as a function of differences in the density of neural firing addresses this issue.

This model of differentiation requires a mediating variable, such as an enduring emotional structure that is a consequence of accumulated past experiences. The degree of differentiation and the nature of individual differences reside in the nature of the distribution of elicitors. These, in turn, are a function of the socialization experiences of the child. Socialization effects may occur either directly, in terms of the caregiver's interactions with the child, or indirectly, in terms of the way in which the caregiver protects the child from encountering certain stimuli.

The focus of this analysis is primarily on how past experiences might influence present emotional reactions. Past experiences are related to the nature of socialization experiences. Absent from the discussion is any consideration of individual subject characteristics that might account for differentiation and for individual differences in emotional outcomes.

Individual Differences in State Differentiation

The developmental issue just discussed concerned the differentiation of emotional states. A second developmental issue pertains to the development of individual differences in enduring emotional states that we have labeled *moods* or *personality*. In Chapter 2, considerable attention was devoted to defining moods, personality, and their relationships to emotional states. We speculated on the processes that might lead to individual differences in enduring emotional states. Although little research has been devoted to examining these processes, a discussion of them is necessary for a theory of emotional development and individual differences. The following account of individual differences is offered not as a complete theory but as a starting point for further discussion of the issue.

Our model of the differentiation of emotions and individual differences in emotional states requires that three variables be considered: elicitors, temperament, and states (transient and enduring). A child who has experienced many positive states in the past should be relatively less vulnerable to the effects of a particular negative elicitor. In contrast, a child who has been repeatedly subjected to negative elicitors is likely to develop a negative enduring state. The introduction of a negative elicitor will have a very different effect on this child from its effect on the child with the positive enduring state. The differentiation of negative and positive states may be viewed as the consequence of the interaction of particular negative or positive elicitors and the enduring state created by past experiences.

Figure 10 illustrates this model of individual differences. In this figure, two subjects are represented as they might respond to two different classes of elicitors, one positive (I_+), the other negative (I_-). S_1 is a child with a history filled with many positive elicitors, and S_2 is a child with a history of negative elicitors. In social terms one child has been better cared for than the other. Referring to Figure 10, S_1 in Case A and S_2 in Case C both experience a positive elicitor. However, for S_1 as opposed to S_2, the positive state produced by the positive elicitor is mediated by a series of previous positive states (ES_+), as a result of which S_1 experiences an intense positive state. For S_2, the positive state interacts with a negative enduring state (ES_-), the consequence of which is either a less intense positive state or a slightly negative state. Likewise, a negative elicitor is likely to result in an intensely negative state for S_2, but a less intense negative or even a slightly positive state for S_1.

Temperamental differences must be considered in any discussion of individual differences. Rather than postulating enduring states solely as a consequence of past experiences (see Figures 9 and 10), we should also consider enduring states as a function of subject variables. In this new analysis, enduring states can be acquired either as a consequence

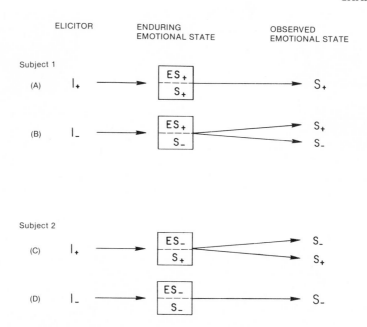

Figure 10. The differentiation of emotional states as a function of the elicitor (I) and an enduring state (ES): A between-subjects analysis.

of temperament or as a consequence of the combination of temperament and enduring states that emerge from past experiences. In Figure 11, temperament is added to the enduring state variable of Figure 9. Temperament, in addition to past states, becomes the mediating variable, and emotional state outcomes, as produced by an elicitor, are a consequence of the mediation of temperament. Thus, a positive elicitor (I_+) impinging on an easy-temperament child (T_+) may produce an intensely positive state (S_+). The same positive elicitor (I_+) acting on a difficult-temperament child (T_-) may produce a less intense positive state (s_+) or even a negative state (s_-). In a similar fashion, a negative elicitor (I_-) impinging on a difficult temperament child (T_-) may produce an intense negative state (S_-). The same elicitor acting on an easy temperament child (T_+) is likely to produce a less intense negative state (s_-) or even a positive state (s_+).

This model allows one to consider both developmental changes and individual differences in emotional development. Moreover, it recognizes the importance of previous social experiences and the personal characteristics of the individual, whether they are related to tempera-

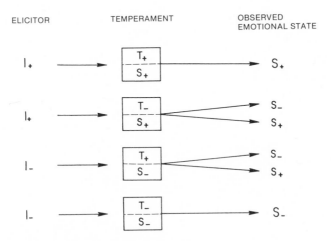

Figure 11. The differentiation of emotional states as a function of the elicitor (I) and the child's temperament (T) and state (S).

ment or past experience, to the relationship between elicitors and emotional states.

The Development of the State–Expression Relationship

The assumption that states and expressions (especially facial expressions) share a one-to-one correspondence underlies much of the work in the study of emotional development. In addressing the issue of their correspondence, two questions can be asked: (1) When is there a relationship between state and expression? And (2) what is the nature of the socialization process that affects this relationship?

In the developmental model outlined below, the maturation of the facial musculature is related to emotional state in a curvilinear fashion. Figure 12 illustrates this relationship for two different emotions. In each case, in the first period, facial expressions are unrelated to states; in the second period, there is a correspondence or synchrony between expressions and states; and in the third period, expressions once again are only loosely related to states.

In the first period of development internal emotional states are generally undifferentiated and independent of differentiated facial configurations. Examples of the early asynchrony between states and expressions are found in research on early infant smiling (e.g., Emde & Koenig, 1969; Wolff, 1963). The infant's earliest smiles are considered

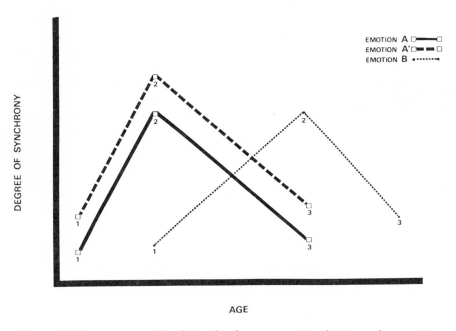

Figure 12. The developmental relationship between emotional states and expressions.

"endogenous" because they do not occur in response to external elicitors and do not seem to be related to positive states. Endogenous smiles often are observed when infants are asleep, and they appear to be correlated with spontaneous CNS activity and REM sleep. One is reluctant to think of these facial expressions as related to anything more than a general excitation of the nervous system.

A similar explanation may apply to observations of specific "faces" observed in very young infants (Izard et al., 1980; Oster & Ekman, 1978; Pannabecker et al., 1980). In this period, the changes in the infant's neuromusculature and the patterning of facial expressions that have been observed are probably related to a "start-up" or "rehearsal" mechanism in which facial expressions share little synchrony with underlying emotional states. This speculation gains support from the likelihood that many of the emotional faces observed early in life do not match the undifferentiated internal states assumed to exist in young infants. In other words, infants may show differentiated facial expressions even though their internal states may be undifferentiated. Alternatively, asynchrony may exist if the facial neuromusculature of very young infants is insufficiently developed and does not correspond with the set of discrete emotional states that some theorists assume exist early in infancy. Whether the early emotional states of infants emerge from an undifferentiated state (Bridges, 1932) or emerge as discrete from the start (Izard, 1978) is an unsettled issue. In either case, asynchrony could exist if the facial musculature of the infant is either more differentiated than the internal states (in the first case) or less differentiated than the internal states (in the second case).

The second period of development is marked by a greater synchrony between facial expressions and internal states. In this phase, different patterns of facial expressions correspond (to a large degree) with differentiated emotional states. This relationship may exist because (1) biological factors have joined states with expressions, and socialization has not yet separated the two; and (2) children's cognitive structures have not matured sufficiently to enable the children to control their emotional expressions apart from underlying states. That is, even if social reinforcement and socialization rules were operative, the cognitive structures necessary for emotional deceit may not yet exist, and the situational knowledge about appropriate social behavior may not have yet been acquired. During the second period, then, one is likely to find the greatest synchrony between facial expressions and internal states.

Implied in this view is the assumption that there is a biological force that automatically creates a synchronous relationship between emotional expressions and states. Equally likely is the possibility that the socialization experiences of the child may create the synchrony between expressions and states. There is evidence that parents reinforce emotional expressions which correspond to what they regard as appropriate behavior (Brooks-Gunn & Lewis, 1982). In this way, synchrony may be established between the internal emotional states of the child and the child's overt expressions, a synchrony that is the result of an interaction between environmental and biological factors rather than the result of biological factors alone. This idea is discussed in more detail in Chapters 6 and 7.

In the third period of development, facial expressions and internal emotional states are once again independent. Unlike in Period 1, however, when the lack of correspondence was due either to undifferentiated internal states or to an inability to express discrete states through a finely articulated facial musculature, the asynchrony of Period 3 is probably due to the acquisition and maturation of cognitive structures and to the cumulating effects of socialization pressures. Although children may have a particular emotional state and the corresponding facial expression, they may have learned to mask the state by disassociating the "appropriate" facial expression from it.

The three periods described above are schematized in Figure 12 in terms of the child's age and the degree of synchrony between facial expressions and internal emotional states. The courses of two different emotions (A and B) are depicted in this figure, from which several points can be made. First, asynchrony may exist at different times for two different reasons: (1) because of the biological immaturity of the organism (in Period 1) or (2) because of the impact of socialization and cognitive forces (in Period 3).

Although all emotions follow the three-stage process, different emotions may develop according to different time schedules. Because each emotion has its own timetable, determined in part by both biological and socialization factors, it is not possible to state the specific ages for the emergence and the developmental sequence of emotions. Synchrony may exist for one emotion at the same time that another emotion is in a period of asynchrony. Emotions that emerge early from an undifferentiated state will probably reach a period of synchrony earlier than emotions that appear later. Thus, a fear face that reflects a fear state should appear earlier than a guilt face that reflects guilt. In fact, for any particular child, the fear face that corresponds to an internal state of fear (Period 2) might occur at the same time as the guilt face that does not correspond to an internal state (Period 1). If this is the case, *the assumption cannot be made that by demonstrating a correspondence between a facial expression and an internal state for one emotion, we have learned anything about the correspondence for any other emotion.* Each emotion has a unique temporal sequence in terms of the time that the facial expression first appears and the time that it corresponds with a differentiated internal state. There is no reason to believe that all emotions follow the same timetable, even though they follow the same developmental course.

So far, implicit in the discussion is the notion that the time frame between any two developmental periods is equal and is independent of the specific emotion. This may not be the case, however. The third point illustrated in Figure 12 is that emotions may differ not only in their time of emergence but also in the rate at which they pass through the three periods. Thus, for Emotion A, the amount of time between Periods 1 and 2 is shown to be shorter than for Emotion B, whereas the time between Periods 2 and 3 is longer for Emotion A as compared with Emotion B.

Fourth, the asynchrony of the third period may vary, with some emotions (e.g., Emotion A in Figure 12) retaining more synchrony than others (e.g., Emotion B). The degree of asynchrony in the third period may be a function of (1) the nature of the particular emotion; (2) the degree to which the expression has been the target of socialization; (3)

the particular situation that elicits the emotion; and (4) the degree to which the expression is under the child's cognitive control. Socially disruptive emotions, such as anger, are probably more quickly and more intensely socialized than other emotions, such as happiness. Furthermore, even though an emotion may have been subject to intense socialization pressures, there may be special circumstances in which it may be more or less appropriate to express that emotion. For example, it may be acceptable to express fear when a large dog lunges but not when going to the doctor ("Big boys don't cry"). If a child has not yet fully acquired the cognitive capacity necessary for controlling the expression apart from the underlying state, then the state–expression relationship in Period 3 may be less asynchronous.

Finally, two levels of Emotion A (A and A') are portrayed in Figure 12. The course of Emotion A' suggests that greater synchrony is possible as a function of the intensity of the eliciting stimulus and thus the intensity of the underlying state. It may be more difficult to disassociate facial expressions from very intense emotional states. Thus, intense stimuli are more apt to produce a greater synchrony between facial expressions and internal emotional states than are less intense stimuli (Lewis, Brooks, & Haviland, 1978). In fact, one way to judge the power of an emotional elicitor may be to establish the degree of synchrony between the subsequent emotional expression and state.

In studying facial configurations and their relationship to internal emotional states, it is crucial to keep this developmental sequence in mind. With this analysis, investigators can study emotional development while recognizing that faces and states may not be related to one another for very different reasons.

The relationship between states and experiences strongly parallels the relationship between expressions and states shown in Figure 12. In the first stage or period of development, states and experiences may be unrelated because the child has not yet acquired a concept of self. Thus, the child may have an emotional state in the absence of experience. The second period is one of synchrony between states and experiences. This stage does not necessarily imply a one-to-one biological connection between the two, although such a connection may exist. Synchrony here must be viewed as the acquisition of a socially acceptable and defined code of emotional experience (i.e., the social meaning assigned to the coherences between certain internal events). This connection between experience and state is acquired through socialization. Consequently, this second stage, unlike the second stage in the development of the connection between state and expression, may be determined less by biological factors and more by the meaning system of the culture.

In the third period, states and experiences again do not necessarily correspond. It may be possible in this stage for the child to experience an emotion without necessarily having a corresponding state. This possibility is assumed on the basis of clinical data showing that adults with spinal cord injuries may experience particular emotions at a cognitive level although the physiological underpinnings of this inexperience (i.e., the emotional state) are missing (Buck, 1980).

The Development of the Self

Emotional experience has been defined as individuals' interpretation and evaluation of their perceived emotional state and expression. To have an emotional experience requires that the person be able to attend to and differentiate a set of internal events, processes that require elaborate cognitive capacities. It also requires that the person be able to distinguish self from other, that is, to make reference to the fact that it is "I" to whom these events are happening. Finally, people must interpret these events in the context of the meaning systems that they have acquired through interactions with others. The first capacity involves general cognitive processes that have been discussed elsewhere. The second involves the development of a concept of self, which we consider in this section. The third addresses general issues of socialization, which are the focus of the next chapter.

The development of the self during the period from infancy has been discussed in two recent volumes (Kagan, 1981; Lewis & Brooks-Gunn, 1979). Lewis and Brooks-Gunn have tried not only to trace the developmental course of the self-concept but also to relate its development to emotional experiences and to cognitive development in general. Because of the central role of the self in the socialization model of emotion, it is worthwhile to summarize its developmental course at this point.

Studies of the development of the self have as their focus self-awareness, particularly the ability to recognize oneself. Such views of the self are restricted, however. As theories of the self have pointed out, featural descriptions of the self require only rudimentary forms of social knowledge. Nevertheless, the use of self-recognition indexes in infancy provides an opportunity to explore empirically what otherwise is a metaphysical issue.

The self is conceived of as having both subjective and objective aspects. The subjective self is the "me" and the objective self is the "I." The subjective self is referred to as the *existential self* in an attempt to stress that this aspect of self is simply that which is different from others. The existential self is viewed as the first and most universal aspect of the self. The objective self is labeled the *categorical self* to indicate that the self, as different from others, has particular characteristics such as gender, height, strength, competence, and age. These characteristics may be universal, but they may also be particular to a culture and to a historical time. The categorical self has a developmental sequence: some characteristics emerge early and remain invariant (e.g., gender); some emerge early and are variant (e.g., age); and some emerge later and are variant (e.g., strength).

The existential self is difficult to study since it has no concrete features. It is not unlike object permanence in this regard, since the permanence of objects is a property of the object independent of its aspects. Thus, the self–other distinction that defines the existential self is similar to the distinction underlying the permanence of objects. In fact, object permanence, person permanence, and self permanence may represent one and the same process (Lewis & Brooks-Gunn, 1979). It is difficult to conceptualize an infant's ability to maintain the existence of an object independent of its experiencing the object without a notion of self permanence and self–other knowledge. That is, how can I know that an object exists independent of me without a "me"? Thus, the emergence of object permanence during the third quarter of the first year of life very likely co-occurs with the emergence of self permanence. As shall be shown, self permanence requires the ability of the organism to maintain its identity across a series of transformations in the same way that the identity of an object is maintained across transformations.

In a series of studies involving mirrors, still photographs, and video feedback, Lewis and Brooks-Gunn (1979) demonstrated that infants recognize themselves within the first quarter of the second year of life. Self-recognition is dependent on two features of reflective surfaces: (1) the contingent feedback of the surface, namely "The image does what I do," and (2) the use of distinct features, that is, "It looks like me." Infants first require the experience of contingency in order to recognize themselves; not until 18 months or so is featural representation sufficient for self-recognition.

From these data as well as from the data of others (e.g., Amsterdam, 1972; Bertenthal & Fischer, 1978; Gallup, 1979; Papoušek & Papoušek, 1974), the following age points are viewed as significant in the development of the self. The first period occurs between birth and 3 months of age. In this period, the self is relatively undifferentiated from others, and the action of the self is relatively undifferentiated from the action and reaction of others. Interactions with the social world result in simple action–outcome events. During this period, there is a general learning of co-occurrence in which actions and response connections are being formed.

The second period occurs from 4 to approximately 8 or 9 months of age, during which the capacity to differentiate the self from others emerges. Although self–other differentiation exists, children's sense of self is limited by the particular interactions that occur. Actions on objects and people start to have intentionality as secondary circular reactions emerge. Not only do children recognize that actions and re-actions are related, but they come to recognize their own agency. Thus, they can, in a rudimentary way, intend certain simple actions. The consistency and regularity of the social environment and the logical necessity imposed on children's interactions with objects provide the environmental support for the emergence of the self–other distinction through secondary circular reactions.

The emergence of self permanence between 9 and 12 months of age characterizes the third period. Children now not only can differ-entiate self from other through their actions on the other but also can maintain the self–other distinction independent of action and context. The existential self can be said to exist, since self permanence has now been achieved. Even though a form of self–other differentiation existed prior to this third period, its dependence on specific actions means that the infant's notion of self is transient. The emergence of self perma-nence allows the construction of the categorical self. Thus, the third period is characterized by the beginning of self permanence as well as the beginning of the self as having specific characteristics. The emer-gence of an ability to compare as well as the ability to differentiate the self from the other provides the mechanisms for the acquisition of the categorical self. This same period is characterized by attempts to pro-duce new actions on old objects as well as old actions on new objects, that is, the emergence of means–ends behavior.

The fourth period, from 12 to 18 months of age, marks the continued consolidation and development of the third period. The consolidation of self permanence and the use of others in the social environment contribute to a further articulation of the categorical self. Intentional behavior and the use of symbolic processes allow children to recognize themselves in mirrors, independent of their actions, and also in still pictures and in movies.

Finally, in the fifth period, beginning around 18 months of age, children are capable, through advanced symbolic behavior, of articu-lating an elaborate categorical self. The increased use of others, the effects of elaborate socialization rules, and the actions of others in articulating children's sense of "I" as having specific properties enable children to generate categories that undergo further developmental changes. This period terminates in the stage of the "terrible twos," in which many of the interpersonal difficulties appear to be a function of children's use of self in social interactions.

This developmental sequence in the concept of self plays an important role in emotional development, at least at the level of emotional states and experiences. Emotional experience requires a sense of self. If the developmental sequence follows that which has been outlined, not before 9 months of age, when a self–other differentiation occurs, does it make sense to talk about emotional experience. This age may represent the earliest time that emotional experience could occur. Since emotional experience also requires other capacities, it may actually be some time after this before emotional experience can be said to emerge. In particular, the emergence of self permanence and of self categories, as well as the cognitive capacity of simultaneous comparison, should enable children to experience the more primary emotions, especially those requiring fewer cognitive underpinnings.

In addition, the increased articulation of the self–other distinction and the formation of the categorical self in the fourth and fifth periods should contribute to the development of the more complex emotional experiences that accompany social emotions, such as empathy, guilt, embarrassment, and shame. These experiences as well as the corresponding states require not only self–other differentiation and self categories but also the ability to use socialization rules and the ability to have, maintain, and compare standards of behavior in specific situations. Thus, the connection between the development of the self and emotional experience suggests that emotional experience may have a developmental course that parallels that of self development.

From such an analysis, one is forced to the logical conclusion that emotional experiences cannot exist until approximately 9 months of age. The separation of states from experiences in our structural model suggests that the 9-month-old infant whose hand is burned on a hot stove may respond with a state of pain yet not experience that pain. This assertion challenges our subjective belief that the child actually experiences the pain state. The absence of experience may be less difficult to accept when one imagines the pain of a child 6 months old or even 6 weeks old. Such a conclusion follows from logical necessity in the structural model of emotion.

Why does this conclusion seem untenable? One possibility is that the development of self occurs earlier and is available for use. Another is that states and experiences are themselves inseparable (Izard & Dougherty, 1982), and thus experience accompanies state. Still another possibility is that adults tend to attribute to creatures considered "like me" the same experiences or feelings as they have (Pannabecker et al.,

1980). In some sense, empathy impinges on the belief system in spite of the logical necessity to conclude otherwise. Indeed, this should be the case: the survival of the species may depend on the socializer's belief that the young organism is "like me." In fact, as we suggest in Chapters 6 and 7, the fact that adults attribute certain experiences to infants before they could possibly have such experiences may be the necessary first step in a developmental process, the outcome of which is that children learn to experience certain emotions that other members of the culture also experience.

The development of the self should also affect emotions indirectly to the extent that the development of the self provides the means for establishing social relationships (Lewis, 1982b). Children's relationships with the critical people in their lives, often referred to as *attachment relationships,* have been assumed to influence emotional development by (1) modulating emotional experiences when they occur and (2) contributing to the production of certain emotions. The first influence is reflected in the ability of the attachment figure to modulate the child's degree of fear through the quality of their relationship. The second influence depends on the assumption that securely attached children are better able to explore their environment, are more curious, and thus emerge as more competent individuals (Ainsworth *et al.,* 1978).

The cognitive structure that is called *self* emerges through a combination of processes. Some of these processes are maturational in nature, others have a learning component, in particular the child's early interactions with objects and people. The mediating variable between interactions and relationships may be the emergence of the self (Lewis, 1982b). The development of the self—including the ability of the child to differentiate self from other, to conserve a concept of self over transformations, and to generate categories about the self—provides the opportunity for experiencing emotions or any process in which self-awareness is necessary, such as empathy or trust. The indirect effects of the development of the self through the establishment of social relationships contribute to the emergence of a rich emotional life that can result only when children can view themselves as well as viewing themselves in relationship to others.

✖✖✖✖✖✖✖✖✖✖✖✖

The specific issues related to the developmental theories of emotion that are discussed in this chapter represent only a partial list of possible issues. A comprehensive theory, including an explanation of the development of specific components as well as the connections among these components, may never be available, much as a complete theory of cognitive development is not a likely possibility. Nonetheless, an analysis of emotion into components and an examination of the development issues pertaining to these components and their connections provides the structural framework for continuing the search.

6

How and When to Express Emotions

> Not only ideas, but emotions too, are
> cultural artifacts.
>
> Geertz, 1973, p. 81

In the study of emotion, a large amount of effort has been expended in measuring emotional behavior and tracing its developmental course. In general, the guiding principle of this task has been the assumption of biological models that posit a fixed and universal connection between facial expressions and emotions. Following Darwin (1872), many investigators have focused on the measurement of infants' facial expressions and occasionally on the connection between stimuli (situations) and emotions as expressed in the face (e.g., Ekman et al., 1972; Emde et al., 1976; Izard, 1977; Tomkins, 1962, 1963). Less often, the affective qualities of vocal behavior and bodily responses are examined (e.g., Argyle, 1982; Buck, 1982; Scherer, 1979, 1982; see also Chapter 8).

While the neuromusculature of facial expressions and the relationship of emotional expressions to particular situations are important topics for study, the ways in which emotions might be socialized have been neglected for the most part. This issue, the socialization of emotion, particularly through the interaction of the child with the social environment, is the focus of this chapter and the next. In order to understand the particular role of the parent–child interaction in the socialization of emotion, it is necessary to consider first some of the general issues pertaining to this topic.

157

Issues in the Socialization of Emotion

The two prototypical models of emotion that were used in the last chapter to contrast various theories of emotional development provide a good starting point for analyzing the socialization of emotion (Hochschild, 1979). The biological model is concerned primarily with the relationship of emotions to biologically given instincts or impulses. Biological factors provide answers to most of the critical questions now posed in the study of emotion. Thus, for example, the measurement of emotion focuses mainly on the constant and universal aspects of expression rather than on individual differences in expressions that may require socialization interpretations. Moreover, when they are recognized, socialization factors are usually considered only when questions about how emotions are stimulated and expressed are raised. To quote Hochschild (1979):

> The image that comes to mind [in considering the biological view] is that of a sudden automatic reflex syndrome—Darwin's instant snarl expression; Freud's tension discharge at a given breaking point of tension overload; James and Lange's notion of an instantaneous unmediated visceral reaction to a perceived stimulus, the perception of which is also unmediated by social influences. (pp. 553–554)

In other words, emotions are viewed as analogous to knee jerks or sneezes, unlearned, biologically controlled, and subject to relatively little socialization influence.

In the interactive or socialization view, attention is focused on the ways in which social influences affect "feeling rules." Feeling rules imply something more active than a reflex and must be considered since "we do feel, we try to feel, and we want to try to feel" (Hochschild, 1979, p. 563). Thus, in socialization models, emotions are not regarded as fixed or universal phenomena, nor is emotional development viewed as the unfolding of various and combinatorial maturation systems. Instead, the fundamental questions posed by socialization models concern how emotions might be socialized. This approach does not deny the importance of organismic functions; rather, it stresses the equally important role of socialization and learning in emotional development.

In order to explore the role of biological and social factors in emotional development, it is useful to keep in mind the structural features of emotion (see Chapters 4 and 5). These are elicitors, receptors, states, expressions, and experiences. According to biological models, the connections among these components are innate and fixed. Thus, elicitors activate receptors that, in turn, produce certain states. States are inferred from the expressions that accompany them. Emotional experiences, the subjective interpretation of states, are often not considered in biological discussions of emotion.

The socialization view regards these components of emotion as less biologically determined and more subject to socialization influences. Indeed, the connections among these features may be produced by the socialization process itself. For example, emotional states and experiences may be related through the socialization experiences of the child. It may be that an emotional experience is not connected in any direct way to expressions or states and that the socialization task is to connect them. That is, the caregiver must match what the society expects an individual to experience given a particular emotional expression (presumed to reflect an emotional state) with a set of elicitors.

Consider this example. One-year-old children might cry if a tower of blocks falls over or if they strike their leg against a pointed object. In both cases, the expressions and presumed state are of distress. The socialization model posits that socializing agents define the children's emotional experience both through the labeling of the children's expression and through their behavior toward the children. In the first instance, when the tower of blocks falls down, a child's mother is likely to tell the child, "You are frustrated," and then help the child build the tower again. Both verbal and nonverbal actions may serve to socialize feelings of frustration in the child. In the second case, the mother as the socializing agent may say to the child, "You are in pain" (instead of frustrated), and accompany the labeling with a different set of behaviors, such as holding and comforting. Thus, the emotional state as referenced by external behaviors such as crying may be linked to two totally different emotional experiences through differential socialization practices. From a psychopathological point of view, "incorrect" labeling and behavioral responses in the face of particular elicitors and particular expressions, and presumably states, may produce "inappropriate" emotional experiences. The experience is "inappropriate" or psychopathological only to the degree that it is unique and is incompatible with what others might feel in similar situations.

This example should alert the reader to the possibility that socialization plays a dynamic and critical role in all aspects of emotional development. Although a universality and fixity may exist among the components at certain points in development (see Chapter 5), the role of socialization in altering or modifying these connections is central and is in need of examination.

In this chapter and the next one, some of the more critical areas in the socialization of emotion are outlined in terms of five feeling rules. The first two feeling rules—how to express emotions and when to express emotions—are the focus of the present chapter. The other feeling rules—how emotions are managed, how emotions are labeled, and how emotions are interpreted—are discussed in the next chapter. These chapters present data from several studies on the socialization of infants' emotional expressions, children's knowledge about situations and emotions and about complex emotional experiences, and the labeling of children's emotional states. The development of psychopathology as a consequence of the socialization of emotion is also considered in Chapter 7.

Although Chapters 6 and 7 are organized around five feeling rules that are learned as the consequence of socialization processes, each of these rules could be related to the structural analysis of emotion in the following ways. The first rule, "how to express emotions," involves the components of expression, state, and elicitor. The issues related to this feeling rule concern whether facial musculature changes are innate, whether facial expressions reflect internal feeling states, and the role of elicitors in producing expressions. The second rule, "when to express emotions," primarily focuses on the elicitor–expression relationship. The rule also applies to the connection between states and expressions. The experience component is involved to the extent that people know what they are supposed to experience under certain circumstances.

The third rule, "how emotions are managed," is perhaps the least relevant to the structural analysis. The point of this rule is that emotion is part of social behavior and that the rules governing social behavior also govern emotional behavior. In some sense, other people may serve as elicitors of emotional information. The fourth rule, "how emotions are labeled," fits into the structural analysis primarily at the level of experience. This rule targets the labels given to emotional expressions and the expression–experience relationship. Finally, the fifth rule, "how emotions are interpreted," governs the relationship between states and experiences and between elicitors and expressions.

How to Express Emotions: The Use of Display Rules

In response to the question of how to express emotions, some might automatically answer that the question is meaningless, since strong biological imperatives connect emotional expression to emotional state. Emotional expression involves a complex patterning of behaviors, including facial, bodily, and vocal responses. This complex patterning is innately programmed, and the emergence of these patterns at early ages is evidence of their unlearned nature (Emde et al., 1976; Izard, 1977).

Theorists who take a strong biological perspective would therefore assert that the question of how to express emotions must be answered in terms of a predetermined and biologically controlled expression system. However, as was pointed out in Chapter 5, and as some theorists with a strong biological view recognize (e.g., Ekman, 1977), a simple biological account is insufficient for explaining emotional behavior. The answer to the question of how to express emotions is incomplete without a description of the socialization rules that govern emotional expression.

Consider the following example.

Lucy is 20 months old. While her mother works on a law brief at home, Lucy plays quietly in the backyard. Through the window, the mother witnesses the following scene: Lucy runs to get a toy at the far end of the yard. She falls on her knees and starts to cry. Immediately, she looks up but sees that no one is paying any attention. She stops crying and walks to the back door of the house. As she approaches the door, she starts to cry again.

This is an example of facial expression and vocal behavior that are not totally determined by the precipitating event. Whereas Lucy's first cry is probably related to her pain, her subsequent cry has more to do with her attempt to communicate a specific message to her mother. This conclusion is supported by the fact that Lucy first looked around to see if anybody was watching. Lucy's ability to produce her facial expression and vocal behavior at will suggests that these behaviors are at least partially under her control and are not necessarily directly related to an underlying state of pain.

How to express emotions is an important feeling rule that all members of a culture learn. Its choice as the first feeling rule does not imply that this particular rule is learned before all others. There is no good evidence to indicate when children start to learn particular rules governing emotional expression, although observations of mother–child interaction patterns suggests that some of the socialization of these rules occurs in early mother–infant interactions (Brooks-Gunn & Lewis, 1982). Before addressing the socialization rules that govern emotional expression, individual differences that are not socialized but are biologically determined must be considered.

In any discussion of emotional expression, it must be kept in mind that even theories associated with biological positions allow for individual differences in expression. Ekman (1977), for example, recognized that certain facial expressions may vary both within and across individuals. A particular facial expression, such as fear, may have a different constellation of features from individual to individual, although the general features remain the same. Therefore, individual differences in the expression of emotion are acknowledged even though these expressions are thought to be biologically determined. These differences are not surprising when one considers the complex set of neuromusculature changes involved in any emotional expression. Such variations need not be socialized. For example, individual differences in expressions of surprise may take the form of eyebrows raised higher in one person than in another or one eyebrow raised higher than the other in one individual on one occasion but not on another. Such individual differences may not be the result of socialization factors. On the other hand, they may reflect learned differences.

A second source of variation in the expression of emotion that may not be a function of socialization is attributed to race. Although the issue of racial differences is highly controversial, racial differences in temperament have been reported in newborns and very young infants (Brazelton, Robey, & Collier, 1969; Freedman, 1979a,b; Wolff, 1977). The most consistent finding is that Oriental and American Indian infants show a more placid temperament than Caucasian babies. Such findings suggest the existence of group differences in emotional expressions that may not be due to socialization factors. Thus, socialization factors do not play the only role in individual and group differences in emotional expressions. Their role is nevertheless influential in the acquisition of the feeling rule of how to express emotions.

In Chapter 5, a developmental model based on the relationship between facial expression and internal state was articulated. In this model, the developmental sequence was divided into three periods. In the earliest period of development, it was suggested, facial expressions are disassociated from internal states because of the relatively undifferentiated nature of the state system. Implied is the view that facial expressions have little meaning vis-à-vis internal states, certainly to the organism itself. The second period is characterized by an association between expressions and states. Although the connection between expressions and states in this period may be in part a function of socialization influences, some correspondence between expressions and internal states can be assumed. It is not until the third period that the strong force of socialization affects emotional expressions, especially expressions related to the facial musculature. In the following section some of these socialization pressures are explored.

The suppression and modification of emotional expression are seen every day, yet few studies exist on this topic. Emotional expressions are modified according to a variety of social rules. Jokes are laughed at even though they are not funny because people are concerned about the feelings of others and how these people might react. Thus, people often produce emotional expressions that do not correspond to internal emotional states. People are as capable of suppressing emotional expressions as of masking internal states. For example, men often suppress fear expressions to show how brave they are.

Most, if not all, of the research on masking emotions has focused on masking facial expressions rather than the other bodily or vocal expressions. Although much of the discussion in this section concerns facial behavior (in part, reflecting the emphasis of the research literature), it should not be forgotten that the masking of emotional expression can also occur at a postural or vocal level. Thus, for example, when people feel angry in a situation when anger should not be expressed, they do not make a fist or strike out in anger. Likewise, the modification of tonal quality is likely to result from socialization forces: people do not usually growl when angry.

The use of language is an alternative way that internal emotional states might be masked. For example, an emotion may be enhanced, denied, or made ambiguous through a discrepancy between what people say about what they feel and how they act. Thus, a person may look sad; his facial, postural, and tonal features all indicate to the observer that the individual is sad. Yet, the individual may say that he is not sad, denying the fact. Or rather than denying that he is sad, the individual might say that he is tired.

The facial and bodily expressions of the individual may be more correctly identified when the observer has information about the particular situation eliciting the expressions. In this example, it is impossible for the observer to know from the person's facial and postural behavior whether he is sad or tired without the person's verbal explanation (e.g., "I am not sad, but I was up all night studying"). On the other hand, the person might say he is tired but not provide an explanation for the discrepancy between the nonverbal and the verbal expressions. In this case, language is used to conceal the emotion both from the person himself and from the observer.

In another instance, a person may not show any expressive behavior associated with a particular emotion because of certain socialization rules. In this case, language may be used as a substitute for the missing expressions, thereby providing a powerful means for masking internal emotional states. For example, a person might say that she is angry when she does not look angry because a socialization rule says "It is appropriate to say you are angry but not to look angry." People in therapy may find it easier to express anger first at the verbal level and only later at the behavioral level. This example suggests that language may facilitate the expression of a particular emotional state either immediately or at a future time.

Language, then, can be used to deny, to clarify, to substitute, or to enhance emotional expression. In studies of emotional behavior, experimenters filter out the content of the message, since it has been demonstrated that language is a powerful and deceptive stimulus (Rosenthal, 1967; Scherer, 1982). Language may be the most salient and most attended to mode of emotional communication; one of its prime functions is to alter other emotional expressions.

It would be interesting to investigate the socialization rules that are associated with parts of the body other than the face to determine their emergence and course of development. For example, do such rules emerge with the learning of facial masking or are they learned independently? On the one hand, rules governing bodily expressions might be learned after those pertaining to facial expressions, since they are less attended to. However, as appears to be the case for tonal cues, bodily expression rules might be learned earlier than facial rules, since they are more susceptible to shaping. Sounds of distress (i.e., crying) appear to come under social control quite early. As Blatz and Millichamp (1935) have observed, there are between 3,000 and 5,000 episodes of distress in children's first two years of life. Consequently, there appear to be ample opportunities for shaping to occur.

The idea of masking the face has been considered by Ekman and Friesen (1975), advocates of a strong biological position. Their recognition that socialization as well as biology plays an important role in emotional expression should temper the controversy generated by strong forms of socialization and biological theories. These investigators have identified various ways in which facial expressions might be modified (Ekman & Friesen, 1969). These include neutralization, exaggeration, minimization, and dissimulation. Neutralization involves the use of the poker face and thereby the suppression of any expression of emotion. Exaggeration, by making fun of a particular affect, allows the person to express an emotion when the normal display might be inappropriate. Thus, to display an extremely shocked expression serves to minimize the message that one is shocked. It is a social game in which poking fun makes the message being sent less intense. Minimization, on the other hand, involves a marked reduction in the display itself. The form is thereby understated, and the reduced intensity permits a safer transport of the message. Dissimulation of the facial expression involves a discrepancy between the internal state and the expression itself. This discrepancy is manifested through the substitution of one emotional expression for another. In general, substitutions are of positive emotions for negative ones. However, at times, negative emotions may be substituted for positive ones. For example, one might feel happy or relieved when an adversary dies. However, it is more "appropriate" to express sadness instead. In sexual attraction, as well, a positive emotion (interest) may be replaced by a negative one (disgust or lack of interest). Substitution is the strategy preferred by young children when they are asked how they would deceive someone about their true feelings (Saarni, 1979a).

Saarni (1982) also considered the various ways in which expressive behavior may be modified. Four general categories are used to explain modifications: cultural display rules, personal or idiosyncratic display rules, deception, and dramatic or theatrical pretense. The cultural display rules are rules unique to a particular culture that are learned by all members of that culture. Personal or idiosyncratic display rules refer to familial or individual (in some cases, pathological) display rules that occur as a consequence of either (1) a particular individual's history and unique patterns of expressions or (2) biological differences among people. Historical experiences refer to each individual's unique social experiences and the effect of these on expressive behavior; biological differences may be temperamental differences that reflect intensity thresholds and racial differences. The hypertonia and hypotonia found among handicapped individuals certainly affect their emotional expressions.

Deception involves falsifying an internal state through behavior. Intentional falsification in emotional behavior does not necessarily imply awareness. Although the issue of awareness of consciously motivated behavior is beyond the scope of this discussion, it must be noted that deception rules may operate to deceive oneself as well as another. Whistling in the dark is an example of a self-deceptive rule, whereby an expressive behavior is produced in order to deceive oneself about the actual emotional state (fear).

The final category suggested by Saarni, dramatic or theatrical pretense, describes the conscious and intentional "putting on" of a particular emotional expression in order to convey a portrait to another. The theater represents the best and most legitimized attempt at dramatic pretense by presenting characters as if they really feel a particular emotion.

These four categories of modification address the feeling rule "how to express emotion." Unfortunately, the research literature on the socialization of this rule is quite limited. Studies from a developmental perspective are even scarcer. Saarni (1978, 1979a,b), one of the few to investigate this issue developmentally, has studied children between the ages of 6 and 10. She noted an increase over age in children's application of display rules in various described stress situations and in their own personal experience. The complexity of their explanations about why emotional behavior should be managed or displayed in certain ways also increased over age. This research, however, addresses children's knowledge about, not their use of, display rules.

Recently, Saarni (1980, 1982) examined the developmental changes in the spontaneous use of display rules and deception in children between 6 and 11 years old. The children were given a gift in a situation that required them to use the display rule "Look pleased and smile when someone gives you something they expect you to like even if you don't." The results confirmed the fact that children's knowledge and use of complex display rules increases with age. Deception was shown by 50% of the 6-year-olds; 70% of the children older than 6 used deception. Thus, by 6 years of age, many children have already learned the rule "how to express emotions." An interesting gender difference in the learning and use of this rule was found; more girls than boys seemed to have learned and to be applying the rule "Look pleased and smile when someone gives you something they expect you to like even if you don't."

This research represents an important start in understanding the acquisition of the feeling rule, "how to express emotion." Virtually no research has been conducted with children younger than 6 or 7 years old. Thus, the origin and developmental course of this socialization rule is unknown. Observations of mother–child interaction patterns reveal cultural differences that may reflect early socialization processes (Caudill & Weinstein, 1969). Clearly, whether or not a particular culture condones crying in children should markedly affect the display rules learned by children.

A Study of Mother–Infant Interaction

In a recent study of mother–child interactions, interesting developmental patterns in mothers' socialization of infants' expressions were observed (Brooks-Gunn & Lewis, 1982). Such patterns may influence the rules learned by children. Specifically, three categories of behavior were coded: mother or infant vocalizing, mother or infant smiling, and infant crying. The results showed that the mothers were more responsive to infant crying during the infants' first six months of life than during the latter half of the first year or the second year of the infants' life (see Table 4). Yet, maternal responsivity to other infant behaviors, such as vocalizations, increased with age over this same period. Maternal responses to infant smiling increased during the second six months of the infants' life and then showed no developmental change. The mothers were as responsive to their baby's smile when the child was 1 year old as when the child was 2 years old. The data were analyzed in terms of proportions and therefore reflect the base amount of the infants' behaviors. Thus, not only was infant crying decreasing in an absolute sense but the mothers' responses to this level were decreasing as well. These findings suggest that different socialization rules may govern positive and negative expressions even in infancy. To wit, mothers increase their responsiveness to positive expressions of emotion over the first years of their children's life, but they decrease their responsiveness to negative emotional expressions as their children get older.

In Table 4, the data for a group of handicapped children are also presented. These children were observed in the same situation as the normal children (i.e., free play). The data show a reduction in maternal responsivity to infant crying over the first two years, a trend observed in the nonhandicapped sample. Notice, however, that the mothers of the handicapped children were more responsive to infant crying than the mothers of the nonhandicapped children. This finding suggests that even though mothers find it less appropriate to respond to infant crying as the infant gets older, mothers find it somewhat more appropriate if the child is dysfunctional. A developmental pattern in maternal responsivity to handicapped infant smiling is less evident. The mothers of the handicapped children in general showed less responsivity to infant smiling. Maternal responsivity to infant vocalizing also failed to show a developmental pattern; the mothers of the handicapped infants seemed to be less responsive to infant vocalization than the mothers of the nonhandicapped children.

Table 4. Maternal Responses to Infant Behaviors

Maternal response to	Infant age in months		
	2–7	8–16	17–27
Infant vocalization			
Nonhandicapped	.13	.35	.50
Handicapped	.34	.25	.30
Infant smile			
Nonhandicapped	.07	.23	.27
Handicapped	.11	.17	.10
Infant cry			
Nonhandicapped	.21	.08	.06
Handicapped	.31	.13	.09
Total number nonhandicapped	193	167	156
Total number handicapped	16	27	39

The findings from this study make several points. First, they indicate that maternal responsivity to infant crying decreases as children get older. The rule seems to be that "It is inappropriate to express distress through crying; other 'more appropriate' modes should be used." Longitudinal data have shown that infants' distress caused by separation from their mothers by a barrier changes from crying to asking for help between 1 and 2 years of age (Feiring & Lewis, 1979). This trend parallels decreases in maternal responsivity to crying and increases in maternal responsivity to infant vocalization during the same period in children's lives.

Second, the study revealed that mothers are less tolerant of crying in boys than in girls, with a steeper developmental function shown for mothers of boys. This result indicates the operation of a socialization rule pertaining to emotional expression that says, "Boys should not cry when distressed." Maternal reinforcement patterns of emotional expressions in infancy would appear to be responsible for some of the known gender differences apparent at later ages.

The third point pertains to differences in maternal behavior as a function of children's status. In this particular study, the children's status was defined in terms of normal versus handicapping conditions. Even under handicapping conditions crying was less reinforced as an appropriate response to distress. Nevertheless, differences in maternal responsivity to handicapped and nonhandicapped children suggest that general socialization rules, such as those specified above, may be modified according to children's level of functioning.

Implicit in the discussion so far has been the idea that biologically produced emotional expressions can be altered by socialization processes. However, the socialization process itself may actually produce or create certain emotional expressions. The mechanisms underlying this process are not clear. First, the original elicitor would have to be disassociated from the particular response. The mechanisms that are most likely responsible for this dissociation might be imitation, modeling, or contagious behavior (see Chapter 7). Imagine that a particular elicitor produces an emotional expression in an adult caregiver. That response does not necessarily have a one-to-one correspondence with the elicitor. The caregiver's expression then may be imitated by the infant. For example, a noise may cause the mother to smile. The infant sees the mother smile, and the mother's smile causes the infant to smile. The infant has learned to smile in response to the noise. In this way, emotional expressions may be produced not through the modification of an original expression but through the creation of an entirely new one. Infants are capable of imitating the facial expressions of others (Field, Woodson, Greenberg, & Cohen, 1982; Kaye, 1982; Meltzoff &

Moore, 1977) and their emotional expressions can be created or modified through interactions with the caregiver (Feinman & Lewis, in press; Feiring, Lewis, & Starr, 1982). Thus, the mechanisms by which the socialization process might actually create emotional expressions appear to be in place at very early ages.

The discussion of the modification of emotional expression through socialization and the various rules governing such processes presupposes that very young infants are capable of producing emotional expressions that can be shaped or modified by the environment. Reviews of the research literature indicate that facial expressions associated with a wide variety of adult emotional states can be observed in infants (Charlesworth & Kreutzer, 1973; Ekman & Oster, 1979; Izard, 1979b; Oster & Ekman, 1978). There is some controversy about the time of appearance of these facial expressions. Although mothers think that infants are capable of expressing many of the primary emotions in the first months of life (Pannabecker et al., 1980), sophisticated analyses of infants' facial musculature show that some of these expressions do not appear until later in the first year (Izard et al., 1980).

In short, the feeling rule "how to express emotions" has received some attention in the research literature. The data from the study of mother–infant interaction indicate that socializing agents may differentially reinforce certain emotional expressions and thereby alter the connection between innate expressions and internal states. Research on the use of deception by adults and children alike, and on facial masking in particular, indicates that faces and states are not directly related. The fact that external expressions do not necessarily reflect internal emotional states opens the door to an investigation of the socialization rules governing emotional expression. The developmental issues associated with masking and deception still need to be explored. It is clear that the socialization of expressions begins in early infancy and that its effects can be seen throughout the life span in the everyday behavior of people. Thus, regardless of the strength of the biological position one prefers, it is necessary to recognize the existence of socialization rules governing the expression of emotion.

When to Express Emotions: Knowledge of Emotions by Situation

Clearly, certain emotions are produced by specific elicitors in an automatic fashion. A sudden, intense stimulus event with a fast rise time is likely to cause organisms to startle independent of their intention or control. Nevertheless, people seem to know what emotions are usually produced or are expected in certain situations. This knowledge is an important aspect of emotional experience, since knowledge of the situational rules can be used either to mask an experienced emotion or to facilitate the production of the emotion.

This knowledge is considered under the feeling rule "when to express emotions." This second feeling rule suggests that children may acquire knowledge about what emotions are expected in particular situations apart from their actual experiences. The demonstration of such knowledge challenges the notion that an internal emotional state is directly elicited by a stimulus event, the central point of the first feeling rule.

When to express a particular emotion that is not automatically produced by an elicitor requires some understanding of the cultural norms concerning emotional states and expressions. Knowledge of the situation is one source for determining what ought to be expressed. Knowledge of the situation may have a direct impact on emotional states by providing the motivation to feel a certain way. This idea requires that one accept the proposition that people can make themselves feel certain ways because of particular events. Indeed, everyday experience suggests that this assumption is not very farfetched. Moreover, since modeling and contagion are facilitating processes, that others feel X can and does facilitate my feeling X.

It is the case that adults of a culture possess similar information about the feeling states of others in particular situations. Such information about situationally appropriate emotions may be obtained from (1) direct observations; (2) indirect sources such as the reported experiences of others or from books; and (3) empathic processes. The knowledge that adults have about socially appropriate emotions in the context of particular situations can be illustrated in everyday examples such as laughing at the boss's joke. A more direct test of the extent of this knowledge is to ask people directly about what emotions or emotional expressions should occur in particular situations. Schwartz and Weinberger (1980), for example, asked adults to imagine how they would feel in certain situations or how others would feel in the same situation. Their college-aged subjects were able to identify feelings associated with normative situations. They knew not only that situations produce differential emotional responses, but also that the patterning of responses differs by situation (see Chapter 2).

A Study of Adults' Social Knowledge of Emotions

In order to examine further what people know about how others feel in certain situations, we gave the following task to 11 adults. Each subject was shown a list of emotions that included happiness, sadness, anger, fear, embarrassment, competence, love, anxiety, sympathy, guilt, shame, elation, excitement, frustration, jealousy, passion, pity, remorse, surprise, joy, and relief. The subjects were asked to answer seven questions about what people feel in certain situations by selecting emotions from the list or by providing other emotions not listed. They were not given any information about how many emotions to select. The prominence of each emotion selected in response to the questions was indicated by placing a number above each emotion, with "1" being the emotion most likely to be experienced. The seven questions asked were

1. What do you think people feel at the wedding of a friend?
2. What do you think people feel at their own wedding?
3. What do you think parents feel at the wedding of their child?
4. What do you think people feel at their graduation ceremony?
5. What do you think parents feel at their child's graduation ceremony?
6. What do you think people feel at a friend's funeral?
7. What do you think people feel at a parent's funeral?

Several important issues are raised by the results of this study. First, none of the subjects had any difficulty in reporting what they thought people would feel in these situations. That is, it is not unreasonable to ask adults in our culture (1) what they think others might feel and (2) what they think others might feel in particular situations. Second, it is clear that the perceived feelings of others vary according to the situation. This variation by situation appears to have face validity: graduations and weddings are characterized by happiness and excitement (the most prominent emotions) and death is characterized by sadness. There is more excitement about both the graduation and the wedding of the self than about the graduation or wedding of a friend, but there is also more anxiety.

The specific results of the study are presented in Tables 5–11. It can be seen that there was almost universal agreement among the subjects that the graduation of a friend produces happiness: 10 of 11 subjects selected happiness as the most prominent emotion (see Table 5). (It should be noted that the responses of Subject 11 were somewhat unusual and reflect the idiosyncratic nature of emotional experience.) The second most prominent emotions were excitement and pride. Jealousy and envy, when they were selected, were the least prominent emotions.

The responses to the next situation, graduation of the self, showed a slightly different picture (see Table 6). Happiness, still the most pre-

Table 5. Emotions Associated with Graduation of a Friend

Subject 1	Happy	Excited				
Subject 2	Happy	Proud	Elated	Excited	Love	
Subject 3	Happy	Excited	Proud	Surprised		
Subject 4	Happy	Love	Proud			
Subject 5	Happy	Excited	Jealous			
Subject 6	Happy	Jealous				
Subject 7	Happy	Excited				
Subject 8	Happy	Excited				
Subject 9	Happy	Proud	Admiration	Envy		
Subject 10	Happy	Proud	Elated			
Subject 11	Glad	Bored	Pleasant	Cynical	Proud	Relieved

dominant emotion, was now combined with pride and excitement. The second most prominent emotion also reflected a happy, excited, elated dimension. Notice that in the graduation of self, negative emotions appeared more often than in the graduation of a friend. Fear, sadness, and anxiety were selected by 8 of the 11 subjects, with fear usually seen as more prominent than anxiety or sadness.

In the next situation, the wedding of a friend, happiness again was chosen as the predominant emotion, and excitement and joy were the next emotions selected (see Table 7). Two instances of jealousy as well as two instances of sadness are observed in the subjects' responses. In general, weddings of friends seem to be associated with happiness and excitement along with some jealousy and sadness.

Compared with the wedding of a friend, one's own wedding was felt to be accompanied by more intense emotions as well as more negative emotions (see Table 8). Whereas happiness was selected as the first or second emotion by 8 of the 11 subjects for the wedding of a friend, happiness was chosen only twice as the most prominent emotion for the wedding of the self. Love, joy, and excitement were selected more frequently, indicating that more intense emotions were thought to occur at one's own wedding. Negative emotions were also seen as likely responses to one's own wedding. Anxiety, nervousness, and fear appeared among the first two predominant emotions in the responses

Table 6. Emotions Associated with Graduation of the Self

Subject 1	Happy	Excited	Fear	Competent	Sad			
Subject 2	Happy	Relieved	Sad	Competent	Anxious			
Subject 3	Proud	Elated	Relieved	Fear	Competent	Happy	Sad	Joy
Subject 4	Excited	Happy	Relieved	Anxious Fear				
Subject 5	Happy Competent	Proud	Fear	Relieved	Anxious			
Subject 6	Excited	Happy	Elated	Joy	Relieved			
Subject 7	Proud	Competent	Elated	Excited	Joy	Happy		
Subject 8	Excited	Anxious	Proud	Happy				
Subject 9	Happy	Sad	Relieved	Excited	Proud	Anxious		
Subject 10	Happy	Elated	Proud Competent	Relieved				
Subject 11	Pleasant	Relieved	Bored	Cynical	Nervous	Glad	Competent	Proud

Table 7. Emotions Associated with Wedding of a Friend

Subject 1	Happy	Excited					
Subject 2	Joy	Excited	Elated	Happy			
Subject 3	Love	Joy	Excited	Happy			
Subject 4	Happy	Excited					
Subject 5	Happy Elated	Love	Excited	Nervous			
Subject 6	Happy	Joy	Elated				
Subject 7	Excited	Joy	Happy	Proud			
Subject 8	Happy	Affection	Nostalgic	Sad			
Subject 9	Happy	Sad	Nostalgic				
Subject 10	Happy	Excited	Jealous				
Subject 11	Gay/ Bubbly	Happy	Amused	Elated	Envy	Skeptical	Jealous

of 4 subjects. Perhaps the most different response to the wedding of the self compared with the wedding of a friend was fear. For the wedding of the self, 5 subjects selected fear as a typical response, and 10 selected nervousness or anxiety. Thus, the wedding of the self, unlike the wedding of a friend, clearly was thought to produce a mixture of intense feelings, both positive and negative.

For the wedding of one's child, 6 of the 11 subjects identified happiness as the predominant emotion (see Table 9). Unlike for the wedding of self and friend, sadness was thought to occur at the wedding of one's child. Of the 11 subjects, 10 selected sadness as one of the emotions in this situation. Excitement was also chosen as a predominant emotion, along with pride. Although pride was selected by several subjects for the wedding of the self, it was selected much more frequently for the wedding of one's child. These results confirm the view that the weddings of children elicit mixtures of happiness and sadness, with some pride.

Not surprisingly, in the most negative situations, death of friends and parents, the most predominant feeling was one of sadness. For the death of a friend, 8 subjects identified sadness as the predominant emotion, and 2 selected sympathy (see Table 10). Anger was selected

Table 8. Emotions Associated with Wedding of Self

Subject 1	Excited	Love	Happy	Fear	Anxious			
Subject 2	Anxious	Fear	Excited	Happy				
Subject 3	Love	Anxious	Excited	Joy	Happy			
Subject 4	Love	Excited Nervous	Happy Elated Joy	Proud	Fear	Passion		
Subject 5	Love	Happy Elated	Anxious	Fear	Excited	Passion	Sad	
Subject 6	Excited	Love	Anxious	Elated	Joy	Happy		
Subject 7	Love Excited	Elated	Joy	Passion	Proud	Happy	Fear	
Subject 8	Joy	Love	Proud	Excited	Hopeful	Anxious		
Subject 9	Excited	Love Joy	Happy	Anxious	Relieved			
Subject 10	Happy	Excited	Anxious	Sad				
Subject 11	Happy	Joy Nervous Elated	Relieved	Belonging/ groundedness	Security	Ambivalence	Sad	Doubt

Table 9. Emotions Associated with Wedding of One's Child

Subject 1	Love	Excited	Happy	Proud	Sad			
Subject 2	Happy	Sad	Love	Joy	Relieved			
Subject 3	Happy	Excited	Anxious	Elated	Sad			
Subject 4	Happy Joy Sad	Love	Anxious Fear	Proud				
Subject 5	Proud	Happy	Love	Sad	Anxious	Fear		
Subject 6	Happy	Excited	Love	Elated	Joy	Anxious	Proud	Sad
Subject 7	Elated	Joy	Excited	Love	Proud	Happy	Sad	Relieved
Subject 8	Joy	Proud	Hopeful					
Subject 9	Excited	Joy	Sad	Proud	Love Happy	Fatigue		
Subject 10	Happy	Sad	Love	Elated				
Subject 11	Happy	Competent	Relieved	Sad				

Table 10. Emotions Associated with Death of a Friend

Subject 1	Sad	Remorse	Surprised							
Subject 2	Sad	Remorse	Frustrated							
Subject 3	Sympathy	Pity	Sad	Frustrated	Remorse	Angry				
Subject 4	Sad Sorrow	Angry Frustrated	Love	Fear Guilty Pity	Sympathy					
Subject 5	Sad	Remorse	Frustrated	Angry	Guilty					
Subject 6	Sad	Anxious	Remorse	Pity	Fear	Sympathy				
Subject 7	Sad	Remorse	Fear	Frustrated	Angry	Guilty				
Subject 8	Sympathy	Grief	Frustrated							
Subject 9	Sad	Empty	Surprised	Love	Pity	Fear	Frustrated			
Subject 10	Sad	Remorse	Angry	Excited	Pity					
Subject 11	Wrung-out	Sad/loss Deserted Nurturant Responsible Love	Vulnerable Small	Angry	Cheated	Anguish	Numb	Fear	Depressed	Miserable

by 6 subjects as a typical emotion, although in all but one instance, anger was not one of the two prominent emotions. Remorse was more likely to be selected after sadness as the most predominant feeling. Guilt was selected by 3 subjects. Frustration, on the other hand, was chosen by 7 subjects.

The death of a parent revealed interesting and significant differences in perceived emotions compared with the death of a friend (see Table 11). Sadness was still thought to be the predominant feeling by 8 of the 11 subjects. Anger was also identified by 4 subjects. However, unlike the death of a friend, the death of a parent was thought to elicit fear by 5 subjects. Although only 3 subjects selected guilt as a likely response to the death of a friend, 5 selected guilt for the death of a parent.

These results have important implications for the study of emotion and emotional development. It is clear that people have knowledge of emotions by situations. The adults in this study understood the requirements of the task. It is also clear that such knowledge is generally

Table 11. Emotions Associated with Death of a Parent

Subject 1	Sad	Remorse	Surprised				
Subject 2	Sad	Remorse	Fear				
Subject 3	Angry	Frustrated	Fear	Guilty	Remorse	Sad	
Subject 4	Sad Sorrow Love	Angry Frustrated Pity Remorse	Sympathy				
Subject 5	Sad	Guilty	Angry	Frustrated	Remorse		
Subject 6	Sad	Frustrated	Fear	Anxious	Pity	Remorse	
Subject 7	Sad	Sympathy	Fear	Anxious	Remorse	Angry	Guilty
Subject 8	Grief						
Subject 9	Sad	Empty	Love	Guilty	Remorse		
Subject 10	Sad	Remorse Guilty	Relieved				
Subject 11	Wrung-out	Deserted Lost Love	Vulnerable	Numb	Fear		

available in our society. The results of the study point to a strong consistency across subjects in their choice of the emotions most likely to be elicited by the situations. Adults seem to know *prior to the elicitation of an emotion* what emotion(s) the situation will elicit.

Where does this knowledge come from, how does it occur, and what is its developmental course? The 11 subjects differed in their firsthand experience with the particular situations. Not all of the subjects were married or had children who had graduated from school. Yet, the answers of those with firsthand experience and those without did not differ. This finding suggests that learning what emotions are appropriate in what situations does not require direct experience. How, then, might these rules be learned? It is not unreasonable to expect that the rules governing emotions can be known in the same way that other cultural rules that pertain to eating, dressing, or social behavior are known. The socialization of these cultural rules needs to be examined, especially as it applies to learning when to express and feel particular emotions.

The sources for experiencing these rules are many. They may be learned by observing the behavior of other people in similar situations. For instance, children may observe their parents' response to the death of a parent (the children's grandparent) and use this cue as the source of knowledge about the appropriate emotion. Knowledge may also be acquired in a more indirect fashion, such as through films, radio, television, or novels.

The extent to which these sources reflect the cultural rules is the extent to which children acquire knowledge about culturally appropriate emotions. Psychopathology may result if children observe or learn "incorrect" emotional reactions. For example, children in a particular family might witness boredom or lack of interest rather than sadness and guilt or fear when a parent or grandparent dies. In this case, the children may learn a deviant social rule: "You should be bored when someone dies." Because of the prevalance of the cultural experience, however, such idiosyncratic experiences might affect the rules acquired by children only in the absence of other "more appropriate" experiences.

How do people come not only to know about feelings but to feel? The answer is quite complex and probably involves the processes of empathy and generalization. In the particular task in our study, adults were asked what others might feel in certain situations. Although they were not asked directly, it was assumed that the subjects would feel these emotions themselves. Observations of the subjects as they responded to the task reflected both facial and emotional behaviors corresponding to the emotions they selected. This finding raises the issue of private acts. It suggests that people know about the private acts (e.g., emotions) of others through their own experience of similar private acts. People use information about themselves in order to understand and share the feelings of others. Thus, for example, I may know about your pain through the experience of my own, regardless of whether it is the same experience of pain. Such processes would seem to facilitate the understanding of the emotions of others as well as the situations that produce them (see Chapter 2).

Children's knowledge of how other people feel in certain situations is an area of research that has received considerable attention because it overlaps with two other areas of study: the development of social knowledge and the development of empathy. Data show that children 3 to 6 years of age understand the "appropriate" people to interact with in different situations (Edwards & Lewis, 1979). For example, 3-year-olds know to play with peers, to go to adults when hurt, and to go to older children when seeking information. Although not directly related to knowledge of situationally appropriate emotions, these data indicate that young children are capable of situational analyses and have very clear social preferences as a function of particular situations.

There is also some research that suggests that children as young as 2 years are capable of empathic behavior and show some under-standing of the emotions of others. For example, a father showing sad-ness may be comforted, held, and patted by his 2-year-old child (Borke, 1971). There is no way of knowing in this situation whether the child has any understanding of the situation that elicits the emotion or whether the child is responding solely to the father's expression of sadness. Whether knowledge of the feelings of other people is derived through empathy or other learning processes is quite complex and no research exists to suggest an answer.

Of specific interest to the present discussion are studies showing that at relatively young ages, children know about how others feel and how they feel in certain situations. The source of this knowledge may be an understanding of expressions produced by the other person rather than an understanding of the emotions associated with the situation per se. Thus, for example, children's knowledge about situations may be derived primarily through their observation of another person's be-havior in a particular context. This observation may, in turn, provide information about the situation. On the other hand, children may un-derstand the situational requirements apart from the behavioral expres-sion of emotion. The studies most relevant to children's knowledge about situationally appropriate emotions are studies that do not provide the emotional behaviors as cues to the feeling.

In many of these studies, children are told a brief story and are shown a picture depicting the situation (e.g., Borke, 1973; Feshbach & Roe, 1968). For example, the story might be about a birthday party or a broken toy. The children are asked, "How does the child in the story feel?" or "How would you feel?" The extent to which the picture does not contain aspects of emotional behavior is the extent to which the children's answers reflect their knowledge of situations through cues other than behavioral expressions. The results from such studies suggest that by age 4, and sometimes as young as age 3, children can give what would be considered by adults the appropriate response to the situation (Borke, 1971, 1973; Mood, Johnson, & Shantz, 1974). Shantz (1975), in a review of this literature, suggested that simple situations eliciting happy responses are reliably understood by children as young as age 4. Between 4 and 7, children show an increasing ability to understand situations eliciting fear, sadness, and anger.

Similar results are reported by L. Camras and J. Brusa (personal communication, 1981), who interviewed kindergarten children about their knowledge of appropriate emotions in specific situations as well as about the intensities of these emotions. The children were told a number of different stories, including the following: "My friend came home from school one day and his mother told him that the family dog had just had puppies. My friend didn't even know his dog was going to have puppies." The children were asked about the presence or absence of several emotions—in this example, happiness, surprise, and disgust. They were also asked about the intensity of the emotion ("a lot" or "a little"). A preliminary analysis indicated that the kindergartners were able to judge both the presence and the intensity of the emotions that other children might have in various situations. They also recognized that more than one emotion may be elicited by a situation. In the example about the dog, the children reported that the feelings associated with this situation included equal amounts of happiness (mean = 1.50) and surprise (mean = 1.56) and some disgust (mean = 0.67), on a 3-point scale of intensity.

The process of identifying feelings appropriate to particular situations appears to be facilitated by a similarity between the subject and the child in the story. When the person in the situation is more like the subject (i.e., similar in age or of the same gender), the subject's ability to report the emotion accurately is facilitated (Shantz, 1975). Such findings suggest that empathy and therefore the self may play an important role in the process.

It is interesting to note that when both situational and facial cues are provided in the story, younger children tend to rely more on the information provided by the situational cues. Studies containing ambiguity because of a discrepancy between the situational and facial cues have shown that children differentially use situational and facial cues in judging the emotion of the person in the story. In one study, preschool children (3–5 years of age) were found to base their judgments more on situational cues, whereas elementary-school children (5–7 years) used expressions more often (Burns & Cavey, 1957). Too few data exist on this topic to confirm the developmental trend, especially since there is evidence that adults, like the younger children, frequently use situational cues (Tagiuri, 1969). Situational cues also seem to have a more powerful effect on adults' emotional responses than do their own facial expressions (Laird, 1974). Regardless of the source of the knowledge, it appears that children as young as 4 years old have already acquired some situational knowledge about when emotions occur.

A Study of Children's Social Knowledge of Emotions

In most studies of children's knowledge of emotions, investigators ask children to use verbal labels rather than facial expressions to identify the appropriate emotion. Rarely are children asked to show how a face would look in a particular situation. The type of experiment we have in mind is similar to the game that Casey and his grandfather play in the following example:

Casey has gone to his grandfather's house for the weekend. At 2 years Casey is a verbally precocious child who is highly sociable and enjoys being with other people. His grandfather is an actor who encourages Casey's dramatic flair. One game they like to play together is "make a face." In this game, the grandfather asks Casey to make different kinds of faces. First, he may ask Casey to make a sad face, for example. Casey indeed makes something resembling a sad face, narrowing his eyes and frowning. Next, the grandfather may ask Casey to make a happy face. For an instant, Casey's face resumes its neutral position and the frown disappears. His eyes then open wide and a grin fills his face. Casey's grandfather follows these faces with requests for others, including, possibly, a sleepy face and an angry face. Before he becomes bored with the game, in each instance Casey produces a face that approximates that of the adult version of the appropriate face.

This example highlights the fact that around age 2 some children are capable of producing some facial expressions when requested to do so. It also indicates that the verbal labels of particular emotions are already associated with particular facial configurations. Had we continued to observe the game, we would have seen the grandfather ask Casey what kind of face a little boy would make if he got a big chocolate ice-cream cone. We would have seen that Casey was capable of producing a happy face, whether as a consequence of his learned association between past ice-cream cones and his feelings when receiving them or as a consequence of general knowledge about what people feel in certain situations. As a function of past associations, as a function of the knowledge of emotions associated with particular situations, or as a function of empathy, Casey showed an ability to produce facial expressions appropriate to imagined situations. Specific events and facial expressions are mediated through cognitive processes that may be as simple as associations or as complex as empathy.

Recently, we conducted a pilot study with eight children, aged 2, 3, and 4. We first asked the children to make different faces, after which they could ask the experimenter to make faces. The faces the children were asked to make included: happy, angry, sad, surprised, sleepy, scared, afraid, silly, and "like when you eat something that doesn't taste good" (i.e., disgust). We did this experiment to determine whether children this young could associate verbal labels with particular facial configurations. With the children's permission, photographs were taken of each face they made. The children were then told several stories in which the chief character (a little girl named Felicia) experienced specific events that were likely to elicit specific emotions. For example, in one story, Felicia dropped an ice cream cone. The subjects were asked to describe the way Felicia might feel ("What kind of face would Felicia make?"), to make a face like the one Felicia might make, and to select from a set of four pictures of Felicia making different faces the face that she would make in the story.

Our preliminary findings suggested that children as young as 2 are capable, when asked, of making faces that approximate adult faces, although the faces made by the 2-year-olds were less differentiated than those made by the 4-year-olds. The 2-year-olds produced happy, sad, angry, and surprised faces. By age 4, the children had little trouble making happy, sad, angry, funny, surprised, and scary faces. This result may be due to several factors. First, the facial musculature of 2-year-olds may be less differentiated than that of 4-year-olds, and they may have less voluntary control over it. Second, 2-year-olds may know fewer verbal labels applying to the faces; thus, they may produce fewer faces not because they are less capable but because they do not know the association between the verbal label and the face. Finally, 2-year-olds may become bored with the game faster than older children and therefore they make fewer faces.

The preliminary findings also indicated that the 2-year-old children could make faces and point to faces that were likely to occur in par-

Table 12. Children's Knowledge of Emotions by Situation

Situation	Emotions							
Graduation—friend								
10-year-old	Happy	Elated	Love	Jealous				Remorse
13-year-old	Happy	Excited	Proud	Jealous	Bored			
Graduation—self								
10-year-old	Elated	Excited	Happy	Joyful	Competent	Proud		
13-year-old	Proud	Relieved	Happy	Anxious	Sad			
Wedding—friend								
10-year-old	Happy	Love	Joyful					
13-year-old	Happy	Excited	Proud	Jealous	Surprised			
Wedding—self								
10-year-old	Elated	Excited	Happy	Passion	Joyful	Love	Vain	
13-year-old	Joyful	Love	Anxious	Fear	Proud			
Wedding—child								
10-year-old	Love	Happy	Sad	Proud	Excited			
13-year-old	Happy	Proud	Anxious	Sad	Excited			
Death—friend								
10-year-old	Sad	Angry	Remorse	Frustrated	Cried	Remorse		
13-year-old	Sad	Pity	Sympathy	Angry	Frustrated			
Death—parents								
10-year-old	Sad	Angry	Frustrated	Cried	Guilty	Passion		
13-year-old	Sad	Angry	Guilty	Relieved	Fear		Remorse	

ticular situations. Specifically, they identified happy, sad, angry, and disgust faces appropriate to the stories.

These data lend support to the proposition that children acquire knowledge about the contexts for socially appropriate emotions quite early. Whether children in different cultures with different feeling rules would also possess this knowledge is not known. A test of the proposition would require two different cultural rules for emotional expressions in the same context. For example, in the United States, when someone accomplishes a goal, the rule is to feel pride over this achievement. This emotion may be expressed through smiling and general excitement as well as verbally. In another culture, such as that of the Zuñi Indians, however, embarrassment (or shame) may be the rule that is taught in response to personal achievement (Benedict, 1934). Children who succeed may be taught to lower their eyes, hang their heads, and maintain neutral faces. We suspect that American and Zuñi children would respond differently to our test items.

Further confirmation of the proposition that children know about when to express emotions is provided by the finding that children respond similarly to the task we gave to 11 adults. Two children, a 10-year-old girl and a 13-year-old boy, were asked to identify which emotions people would feel in each of seven situations. Their responses are quite similar to those of the adults (see Table 12). For example, they also thought that people feel more anxiety and fear at their own graduations and weddings than at the graduations and weddings of friends. Even the wedding of a child produced mixtures of happiness and sadness, the most prominent emotions chosen by adults, even though these two subjects are children themselves.

Thus, there is some evidence that children, perhaps as early as age 2, but certainly by age 6, have knowledge about when to express emotions. We might expect differences in this ability to vary as a function of children's general intellectual capacity as well as the nature of the socialization process, although no data have addressed this issue. Thus, cognitive differences as well as gender differences and even social class differences (insofar as social class represents a subculture in a given society) should be examined. All that can be said at this point is that much of this knowledge about when to express emotions is acquired early. Only additional investigations can further clarify this issue.

Single versus Mixed Emotions

One rather interesting aspect of the issue concerning what people know about when to express emotions is reflected in subjects' selection of multiple emotions rather than a single emotion in response to particular situations. In our study of situational knowledge, subjects were not instructed to rate each emotion nor to choose only one emotion as a response to a situation, yet only one subject selected a single emotion in response to a test situation, and that was grief toward the death of a parent. In all other cases, every subject chose more than one emotion as a consequence of each situation. All subjects seemed to think that more than one emotion would be experienced in the different situations.

The implications of this particular finding are broad. A careful analysis of the subjects' responses indicates that the first emotion identified as the likely response seemed to be the one that best reflects society's expectations of situationally appropriate emotions. Thus, death was experienced as sad and graduations involved a mixture of happiness and excitement. However, the identification of many emotions in response to particular situations indicated that other emotions might also be expected. Some of these other emotions might also fit the general expectations of society. For example, weddings of children were typically experienced as both happy and sad. Other emotions, usually appearing at the end of a subject's list, seemed to have a more personal or idiosyncratic value. It seems that the first emotions selected may reflect the perceived cultural expectations, whereas the emotions selected later may have had personal meaning to the subject. Such individual choices probably pertain to personal experiences and emotional reactions, and consequently, they may have a clinical value. Certainly, the subject who selects surprise as the emotional response to the death of a parent would be clinically different from the subject who regards relief as the predominant emotion.

These findings, as well as the results of studies of college students (G. Schwartz, personal communication, 1979) and of children (L. Camras & J. Brusa, personal communication, 1981), demonstrate that people recognize that situations, although eliciting a primary emotion, may, in fact, produce mixtures of emotions. Emotions are not simple events; consequently, situations are likely to evoke not single emotions but multiple emotions. The belief that elicitors activate one emotion rather than multiple emotions is probably incorrect, although it is useful as a shorthand method for characterizing emotional experiences.

The findings of these studies also underscore the fact that there are few labels in the English language for mixed emotions. The absence of unique labels for mixed emotions, despite the existence of mixtures of experience, is rather peculiar. An analogous case might be if one could use only primary colors to describe all colors. Fortunately, the English lexicon includes terms for mixtures of colors. Aqua, for example, is a mixture of blue and green, and purple is the mixture of red and blue. The terms aqua and purple have meaning in themselves apart from the colors that comprise them. Whether the language can be adapted to include terms that convey mixed emotions is not known. Certainly some terms do exist. For example, melancholia is a mixture of sadness, anger, and grief, and depression is considered a mixture of anger and sadness. It does not seem unreasonable to create a term that might capture the feeling of happiness and sadness felt on the graduation of one's child. Those who have experienced the feeling might readily understand and be receptive to a new label. The absence of such terms may reflect the low regard that people (at least, English speakers) have for the careful demarcation of specific emotions. Or it might reflect the rather "primitive" level of language associated with emotional experiences. Despite the scarcity of adequate labels for complex emotional experiences, it is the case that situations produce mixtures of emotions rather than single emotions and that children as well as adults know that this is the case.

The third issue raised by our findings follows directly from this fact. If situations produce mixed rather than single emotions, then investigators must realize that when they construct an experimental situation to elicit a particular emotional behavior, they may have unknowingly created a situation that produces more than one emotion. Moreover, as the research indicates, this mixture may not be homogeneous, at least in the case of low-intensity emotions. In fact, the responses of individual subjects tended to be rather heterogeneous (see Tables 5–11). In this event, the relationship between specific elicitors and emotional responses that investigators seek to establish may be difficult if not impossible to obtain. If an elicitor produces mixed emotions, then the responses observed are likely to be associated with various emotional states and experiences.

G. Schwartz (personal communication, 1979) reported that individual differences were found for 20 adult subjects on their ratings of the amounts of happiness, sadness, anger, fear, anxiety, and depression associated with particular situations. Situations such as "Your girl or boy friend leaves you for another," "You are accepted at Yale," or "Your dog dies," each resulted in a different psychophysiological pattern of mixed emotions. An examination of the data for each individual revealed a heterogeneous distribution of responses to these situations. When the subjects were grouped, however, no psychophysiological patterns were observed. The pooling of subjects around situations cannot result in clear psychophysiological responses because although each subject experiences the same situation, she or he may have very different emotional responses. Moreover, these emotional responses are themselves mixtures of emotions. Consequently, the assumptions that (1) all subjects experience the same emotion and (2) only one emotion is experienced do not have empirical support.

Thus, in order to study emotional responses, it is necessary that investigators confirm with each subject that the elicitor experienced by the subject is the elicitor presented by the experimenter. The belief that experimenters know which elicitors produce which emotions is presumptuous, and it may be necessary to replace or at least supplement experimenter phenomenology with subject phenomenology. Through such a procedure, and with the recognition that situations and elicitors usually produce complex patterns of feelings, the study of emotion may be advanced.

Whether particular emotional expressions are prewired to certain elicitors is an issue that needs to be explored further. However, it is the case that children learn early in life that many situations are associated with particular emotional states, expressions, and experiences. The specific socialization rules that govern the acquisition of this knowledge have not been determined. Certainly, the social experiences of children with significant others play an important role. For example, data were described in this chapter that demonstrate how mother–child interaction patterns differ for three particular emotional behaviors. The direct effect of mother–child interactions may influence the development of both expressions of and knowledge about the appropriateness of certain behaviors and feeling states in particular situations.

Indirect effects may also play a role in the acquisition of situational knowledge about emotions (Lewis & Feiring, 1981). For instance, children may observe the interactions between their parents or among relatives in particular situations. A child might witness the joy and relief of her mother and father when the mother completes graduate school. Thus, the child learns indirectly, through observation, that particular emotional experiences are associated with specific events. The degree to which the others play a significant role in the child's life is the degree to which such observations may influence the child's understanding of emotions.

What is important to consider from these examples is the proposition that if subjects already know what emotional state or expression is appropriate in a particular situation in the absence of the elicitor itself, then it is difficult to argue logically that an elicitor causes an emotional state in an experimental situation. In other words, the experimental method that attempts to control and manipulate variables to demonstrate causality is potentially flawed when a subject, prior to the manipulation of the independent variable, can tell the experimenter the likely outcomes of the dependent variable. For example, imagine an experimental situation in which one group of subjects is deprived of food for a period of time and another group is not. If the subjects in the deprived group produce more food-oriented responses when shown ambiguous pictures, an experimenter might argue that food deprivation results in increased food orientation. If, however, the subjects who are not deprived but are informed of the experimental procedures also know and report that there would be an increase in food-oriented responses, then the experimenter cannot logically conclude that food deprivation *causes* an increase in food-oriented responses. In an analogous fashion, the knowledge acquired through socialization about which emotional states and expressions are appropriate in particular situations precludes the empirical demonstration of a causal relationship between experimental situations (elicitors) and certain emotional states and expressions.

The socialization of this knowledge about the relationship between emotional states and situations is critical to children's adaptation to their social environment. That children possess this knowledge quite early indicates that the process of its transmission takes place soon after birth and constitutes one of the important lessons of early childhood. The role of empathy may be particularly important in this process. Although children can learn either directly or indirectly about what other people are likely to feel or what emotions they are likely to express in particular situations, the demonstration that children have this knowledge at very young ages suggests that the standard methods of learning may not underlie the information acquired. It appears that too many trials over too many situations would be required when learning is conceived of in the traditional, trial-by-trial, slow-acquisition, or didactic sense. Empathic processes may be a means through which children come to know how other people experience emotions in certain situations.

The literature on role taking and empathy is controversial (Ford, 1979). Some investigators (Borke, 1971) believe that children are capable of some forms of empathic behavior at very early ages. Others, taking a more Piagetian view, have argued that empathic capacities emerge later in childhood (Flavell, 1974; Flavell, Botkin, Fry, Wright, & Jarvis, 1968; Laurendeau & Pinard, 1970; Piaget & Inhelder, 1956). It would seem that empathic ability requires the development of certain cognitive structures, such as a concept of self. In order for role taking or perspective taking to occur, it is necessary that children be able to perceive themselves in the place of the other, and in the case of empathy, to experience what the other person is feeling. One cannot conclude with any confidence from the available data that young children possess empathic capacities. Nor is there any empirical evidence to suggest that empathic processes enable children to come to know about the feelings of others in particular situations. Nevertheless, it is possible that such processes play an important role in children's acquisition of this information. Until nonverbal measures of empathic processes are devised and more developmental data are available on children's knowledge about situationally appropriate feelings, this question cannot be answered empirically. If it is the case that empathic abilities are acquired early in life, then it is quite possible that empathic process may underlie children's knowledge about when to express emotions.

Situations have expectations about emotional reactions associated with them. These expectations constitute the socialization rules that appear to be learned. This being the case, it is necessary to ask where the situational knowledge comes from, how it is acquired, and what its developmental course might be. It seems reasonable to assume that emotional experiences can be learned as other cultural rules are learned. Both the learning process and individual variations in the acquisition of this knowledge must be understood if we are to understand more fully the socialization of emotion.

❧❧❧❧❧❧❧❧❧❧❧

Two feeling rules were discussed in this chapter: how to express emotions and when to express emotions. These rules have not been explored in much detail from a developmental point of view. The research described in this chapter suggests that both rules are affected by socialization factors. The examples of Lucy's use of expression and Casey's knowledge of situationally appropriate emotions underscore the fact that these rules are acquired early in life and develop rapidly. These rules are important in children's adjustment to their social niche both in terms of their immediate impact on children's behavior and their influence on children's subsequent development.

This discussion should serve as a point of departure for a complete research program investigating developmental changes in these feeling rules across the first six years of life. This suggestion does not imply that there is sufficient information with respect to later points of development but only that there is a serious lack of knowledge about the early age periods. In the following chapter, three additional feeling rules are considered.

THE SOCIALIZATION OF EMOTION

How Emotions Are Managed, Labeled, and Interpreted

In Chapter 6 the discussion of the socialization of emotion began with a consideration of Geertz's (1973) proposition that emotions, like ideas, are cultural artifacts. The socialization of two feeling rules—how to express emotions and when to express emotions—was considered. The first feeling rule applies to the relationship between emotional expressions and internal states. Issues related to the elaborate display rules that govern the expression of emotions in any culture were considered as well. The second feeling rule—when to express emotions—is related to the social knowledge that accompanies the elicitation and display of emotions. Research examining what people, both adults and children, know about which emotions are associated with which situations was described.

In this chapter, three additional feeling rules are described. These rules include how to manage emotions, how to label emotions, and how to interpret emotions. Following the discussion of how to interpret emotions, issues related to developmental psychopathology as one possible outcome of the socialization of emotions are addressed.

How Emotions Are Managed: The Use of Others

Under the topic *managing emotions*, many issues might be considered. For example, one could discuss ego control, impulse regulation, and self-monitoring of behavior. Mischel (1974), for example, has tried to delineate the dimensions and the developmental course of self-regulation. One particularly noteworthy aspect of children's self-regulatory behavior, which has been explored mainly by Russian psychologists, is the use of language as a self-regulatory mechanism (Zivin, 1979). This research shows how children use language to manage their behavior. In the classic experiment, children are required to inhibit a motor response under one of two conditions: (1) children are instructed to repeat to themselves certain messages, such as, "Don't press the button when the light goes on"; or (2) children are not allowed to repeat any messages. The results indicate that response inhibition is more successful when children are allowed to use language to manage their behavior.

The issue of managing behavior is clearly relevant to the study of emotion inasmuch as people learn to inhibit emotional expressions that society deems inappropriate and even to inhibit their awareness of certain emotional states. In a sense, this activity constitutes managing emotions through inhibition. Many examples of managing emotions through inhibition come to mind. In a recorded reading of his poetry (Caedmon Records, 1960), Dylan Thomas mentioned that he was once in a restaurant with Matthew Arnold and was quite upset when Matthew "laughed much too much." According to the social norm expressed in this example, the vocal expression of the emotional state is inappropriate, at least when displayed in public. In fact, one rule in managing emotions may involve disassociating the vocal component of emotional expression from the rest of the response. For example, the vocal display of anger is usually regarded as inappropriate. Adults and even children in our society learn not to growl in anger. However, it is interesting to note that when the armed forces train soldiers to act aggressively toward the enemy, they instruct them to vocalize anger. Thus, bayonet practice and hand-to-hand combat may involve lessons on screaming when stabbing an imaginary enemy. The vocal expressions of fear (e.g., screaming in terror) are often considered inappropriate. Young children, especially boys, learn to inhibit vocal expressions of fear, and while women are allowed to scream in fright when a mouse scurries across the floor, it certainly would not be appropriate for men to do so. Even the expression of sadness at deaths and funerals may need to be inhibited. Crying, a major component of sadness, is suppressed early. One of the most common behaviors in the comforting repertoire of adults involves saying, "There, there, that's okay, *don't cry*." In short, both positive and negative emotions need to be managed.

One wonders why there is such strong social pressure to manage the vocal component of emotional expression through inhibition. One strong possibility is that vocalizations of emotion are particularly powerful elicitors of emotions in other people. Thus, the management of

the vocal component of emotional expression may be necessary to coun-
teract the strong contagious effect. A similar explanation might apply
to the need to manage facial and bodily expressions of emotion as well.
The social requirements may be to control and manage the most contagious element(s) of the emotional expression.

Large differences can be found in individuals and in situations in
which the management of emotions takes place. Cultural and gender
differences may affect some of these management rules as well. For
example, in the American culture, women are usually perceived to be
more emotional than men. The social rule seems to allow women to
display many behaviors that reflect emotional states and experiences.
Men, on the other hand, are taught early to manage or to inhibit manifestations of emotion.

There is some evidence that females may manage their emotional
states less well than males. For example, females may be less able than
males to deceive an observer by expressing an emotion not necessarily
felt (De Paulo & Rosenthal, 1979a,b). Females may perform less well
on deception tasks because they experience less social pressure to manage their emotions and consequently have less practice in doing so.
The fact that more women than men seek therapeutic help might reflect
gender differences in their willingness to recognize emotional difficulties and to effect change rather than gender differences in psychopathology.

Gender differences may particularly be evident in the expressions
of particular emotions. For instance, girls may be allowed to express
more sadness and fear, whereas boys are allowed to express more anger.
In addition to anecdotal accounts of gender differences in emotional
expressions, there are some data indicating that young boys (5 years
old) report more anger compared with girls when asked about how they
would feel in certain situations (L. Camras, personal communication,
1981). The results of the research presented in this volume also suggest
that gender differences exist in the emotional expressions of children
younger than age 2 (see Chapter 11). In support of these differences,
Saarni (1981) reported gender differences in children's knowledge of
what emotions cartoon figures are experiencing.

Gender differences may be influenced by differential socialization
experiences, in particular, differences in parents' responses to children's behavior, or they might be the result of different biological dispositions. One particular gender difference reported in the literature is
that females show longer durations of orienting and interest (Haviland
& Lewis, 1975; Malatesta, 1981). There is also some evidence to suggest
that females, when showing interest, may have greater "eye-openness"

(Haviland & Lewis, 1975). That is, holding brow raising constant, the degree to which the eyelids open is greater for female than for male infants. This phenomenon is apparent from the time the infant is a few weeks old through the first years of life.

This biological difference does not necessitate concomitant state differences, however. Biological differences in facial expressions may or may not be related to biological differences in state. Indeed, such differences are likely to be differences without meaning. It is the culture that imparts particular meanings to biological differences in accord with the particular constructs or biases of the culture. Through the responses of the culture which are associated with its constructs, the meaning of the behavior is realized. For example, eye-openness implies naiveté and receptivity. Whether eye-openness is fact has any correspondence to those internal states, the fact that the culture assigns that meaning to the behavior and the fact that the behavior is differentially distributed between genders suggest that the socialization process itself may produce the meaning. Although it is not possible to determine the extent to which gender differences in emotional expressions are determined by socialization or biological factors, it is important to consider both as possible sources.

Cultural and social class differences may also be factors in the management of emotions, although no strong data exist on this topic (Ekman, 1972, 1977; Goffman, 1959). There is some evidence of social class as well as gender differences in the management of aggressive behavior in American society to the effect that the lower class may exhibit more aggressive behavior than the middle class, and boys show more aggression than girls (see Feshbach, 1970; Zigler & Child, 1969). Such differences, however, depend on how aggression is measured. If aggression is measured in terms of physical violence, then the lower class is found to engage in more physical violence than the middle class, and males are found to be more physically violent than females. If other forms of aggressive behavior are included in the measurement, such as vocal aggression, physical competition, and guilt induction, then many of the social class and gender differences in aggression disappear. What this analysis reveals is that the management of aggressive behavior may be quite different as a function of social rules. Thus, the middle class may show more aggression in the form of guilt induction compared with the lower class, whereas the lower class may show more aggression in the form of physical violence. The socialization task is to teach the children of a particular class the management rules of aggression (or any emotional expression) that conform to the values of the particular social class.

The management rules of emotional behavior appear to be quite different in the middle-class Anglo-American society from those in the black or Hispanic cultures. Simple greeting patterns that mark enjoyment or pleasure in seeing a person, such as shaking hands and embracing, may vary both within and across cultures. Strong differences in expressive behavior can be observed as a function of geographical area: Northern Europeans (e.g., the English) are more physically reserved in public than Southern Europeans (e.g., the Italians). Even the distance maintained between people when they speak varies according to the culture. For example, Spanish speakers tend to stand closer to each other than English speakers.

The developmental factors in the management rules of emotional behavior that produce individual and group differences have barely been explored. The few data that do exist suggest that some of these management rules are probably learned through reinforcement patterns, an issue discussed in the previous chapter. Thus, the different socialization practices detected in studies of mother–child interactions (Brooks-Gunn & Lewis, 1982; Malatesta, 1981) may not only inform children about the social rules governing particular behaviors but also teach children through direct interactions how to manage particular responses, and perhaps states, through inhibition.

Although a case can be made that biological differences exist in the levels of certain emotions experienced by males and females, it seems more likely that gender differences in emotional expression are produced by socialization differences. One might ask whether the socialization rules that govern the management of emotional expressions need to be learned for each particular situation or whether children learn "metaprinciples" that apply to particular emotional expressions. For example, is an individual who learns to manage a particular emotion through inhibition likely to inhibit other emotions as well? Do male children who are taught to hide feelings of fear also express less happiness and sadness?

This issue is particularly seminal insofar as it interfaces with the debate over the nature of emotional development. If specific emotional states and expressions develop from a general, undifferentiated emotional system, then socialization processes may impact on discrete emotions by affecting the general system. If, however, socialization rules are acquired after emotional differentiation occurs, then they must be learned around specific emotional states and expressions. In other words, if each discrete emotion has its own developmental track, then rule learning may take place around specific emotional states regardless of when the rules are learned. On the other hand, if metaprinciples are involved, then it is conceivable that the particular developmental model that one chooses is irrelevant; children may learn from particular situations a metarule that generalizes to subsequent situations and emotional states and expressions. Such rule learning would require a more mature cognitive capability than is required if management rules are learned through particular early interaction experiences.

The discussion so far has focused on the management of emotions primarily through the inhibition of emotional expressions. Although this management technique is quite important, other management rules, including the use of others in managing emotions, can be considered. Some of this rule learning is similar to that described in the section of the last chapter on how to express emotions. The examples used to illustrate management through inhibition are also relevant to a discussion of the role of others in managing emotional states and experiences. For example, people tend to laugh more when others are laughing than when no one else is around, and they tend to cry more when others are crying.

The contagious element of emotion may also affect oneself. In adults and children alike, crying may facilitate more crying. Applying James's (1884) theory of emotion, one might argue that one's own crying signals that one is having a sad experience. Attending to oneself can trigger either a continuation of a state or an even more intense manifestation of that state. Contagion is probably associated with other emotional states and expressions as well. For example, sexual experience is likely to be enhanced by the experience of one's partner. Sex therapists treating low levels of sexual arousal may concentrate on enhancing the experience of the couple at the interpsychic level, so that the pleasure of one partner increases the pleasure of the other (Leiblum & Pervin, 1980). The contagious aspect of emotional expression underscores a potential need to manage expressions through inhibition in order that emotional experience can be regulated. Thus, one aspect in managing emotions, for both elicitation and inhibition, involves a strong social component.

Social Referencing and Indirect Effects

Social influences can affect people's emotional states and expressions either directly or indirectly. Direct effects are defined as the product of interactions that reflect the influences of one person on the behaviors of another when both are engaged in mutual interaction. Two classes of indirect effects can be identified (Lewis & Feiring, 1981; Lewis

& Weinraub, 1976). Of importance to this discussion is the class of indirect effects resulting from the interactions among members of a system that occur in the presence of a person but that do not directly involve that person. For example, an indirect effect that can be observed in the context of the family derives from the interactions between the parents that are observed by children. In these interactions, children may learn things about the mother, the father, and their interactions even though the interactions do not directly involve the children. In another example, an indirect effect may be produced by mothers' emotional behaviors toward other people on children's responses to those people, especially when the children do not already know those people.

This class of indirect effects is also referred to as *social referencing* (Campos & Stenberg, 1981; Feinman & Lewis, in press; Lewis & Weinraub, 1976). In a general sense, social referencing is the use of another's behavior to form an understanding. For example, social psychologists report that adults' judgments can be modified by the judgments of other adults (Asch, 1956; Sherif, 1958). The use of others in forming beliefs and attitudes, feeling states and expressions, and appropriate behaviors toward either particular situations or particular people is an important concept of many social psychological theories (Bandura, 1977; Festinger, 1954; Mead, 1934; Schachter, 1959; Sherif, 1958). The process of social referencing involves two aspects of change in behavior. Underlying one change is compliance, whereby individuals alter their behaviors and feelings in accord with the behaviors of those around them. Social referencing in this case is rather limited; the term *compliance* rather then *referencing* applies better. On the other hand, social referencing may refer to the changes in or the creation of specific schemata or mental activities that arise when individuals truly believe the behavior of others.

The use of social referencing is crucial with respect to emotions, both in terms of simple compliance and in terms of the creation or alteration of particular schemata. Although the research literature contains many examples of social referencing by adults, relatively little has been written on this topic within a developmental perspective. Yet social referencing may constitute an important process through which children use other people to manage their own emotional expressions and states.

Social referencing seems to bear some resemblance to imitation. The processes underlying imitation and social referencing may be different, however. Indeed, imitation may involve a more holistic, biologically determined process. Although some investigators claim to have observed imitation in infants in the first days of life (Field *et al.*,

1982; Meltzoff & Moore, 1977), these results are controversial. Clear demonstrations of nonreflexive imitation cannot be made in infants before 6 months of age (Hayes & Watson, 1981; Kaye, 1982; Lewis & Sullivan, 1982).

The skills needed for social referencing are also being learned at this time (Campos & Stenberg, 1981; Feiring et al., 1982). For example, during this period, infants become wary of unfamiliar objects and people, and when confronted by these new events, infants are likely to turn toward the caregiver (Feinman, 1980; Feinman & Lewis, in press; Haviland & Lewis, 1975; Rheingold & Eckerman, 1973). The newly acquired capacity of infants to attend to two events at the same time (Schaffer, 1974) enables them to attend to the new event as well as to the caregiver's response to that event. Infants also begin to distinguish among and react to the emotional expressions of other people after 6 months of age (Caron et al., 1982; Charlesworth & Kreutzer, 1973).

Thus, the abilities of infants to imitate, to make simultaneous comparisons, and to perceive the emotional expressions of others all seem to emerge in the same period as the skills needed for social referencing are learned. Therefore, it is not unreasonable to assume that children's ability to manage their own emotions is mediated by their attention to and their use of the social environment.

This form of indirect learning has many advantages insofar as it allows learning to occur within the context of the children's social environment. Not only does the social environment teach children directly, but through social referencing, children can learn the rules of the reference group indirectly. This form of learning is particularly efficient, since it allows children to acquire knowledge from many people in a nondidactic manner.

Empirical evidence of the indirect influences on children's emotional and social behaviors toward strangers is provided by a study conducted by Feinman and Lewis (in press). In this study, the responses of 10-month-old infants to a stranger were observed under two conditions. Both conditions employed a standard stranger approach in which a smiling and nonvocalizing female stranger moved slowly toward the infant, who was seated next to the mother. In one condition, the mothers spoke warmly to their infants about the stranger as she approached. In the second condition, the mothers used a neutral tone to speak to the infants about the stranger. After approaching, the stranger sat down beside the infant and for a full minute busied herself. During this time, the mother did not talk. Observations of infants' toy offering, smiling, and gesturing behaviors to the stranger revealed that the infants whose mothers spoke to them about the stranger in a positive tone showed significantly more positive behavior toward the stranger than the infants whose mothers used a neutral tone to talk about the stranger.

These results suggest that by the time infants are 10 months of age, their social and emotional behaviors toward an unfamiliar person can be influenced by their mothers' behavior toward that person. Whether the infants would have responded with more fear had their mothers' message been negative was not explored because of the investigators' concern about producing strong fear in the children. Klinnert, Campos, Sorce, Emde, and Svejda (1982) have recently conducted similar referencing studies and have confirmed the fact that young children are capable of using others (i.e., mothers) in managing their social and emotional behaviors. Exactly what cues of the mothers' message the infants used is unclear, since both facial and vocal messages were available. It is possible that the infants used the tonal quality of the maternal voice for social referencing, especially in light of Scherer's (1982) demonstration that the quality of voice cues can be discriminated by infants and are related to specific emotional states.

Individual differences in social referencing (i.e., in managing emotions through the use of others) are probably related to many factors, not the least of which are children's perceptual ability, their ability to comprehend the message, and their ability to control their own emotional states. One factor that might affect individual control of emotional states is the child's temperament. Indeed, children with difficult temperaments have trouble modulating and controlling their social and emotional behaviors (Thomas & Chess, 1977). Temperament has been found to play a significant role in children's use and interpretation of the mother's message as a means of managing their emotional response to a stranger. Specifically, children with easy temperaments may be better able to manage the mother's positive message regarding the stranger than children with difficult temperaments (Feinman & Lewis, in press). Thus, individual differences in managing emotions may be a function of temperament differences among children. Such a finding underscores the interaction between biological and social factors in the emotional process.

Social Transitivity as a Particular Case of Social Referencing

The results of studies of social referencing indicate that other people influence children's social and emotional behaviors. However, these studies do not address the question of whether some individuals are more critical than others to the social referencing process. The differential effects of social relationships on the use of social referencing are the focus of the topic labeled *social transitivity* (Lewis, Feiring, & Weinraub, 1981; Lewis & Weinraub, 1976).

If one is to understand children's use of others in social referencing, children's relationships to the other people must be considered. The following formulation has heuristic value in understanding children's relationships with other people (Lewis & Feiring, 1981):

$$C \ r \ Person_A = f \ (C \leftrightarrow Person_A) + [(C \ r \ Person_B) \times (Person_B \ r \ Person_A)]$$

This formula states that the child's (C) relationship (or response) to $Person_A$ is a function of a direct effect (namely, the child's interaction with $Person_A$) plus an indirect effect (in this case, the child's relationship to $Person_B$ and $Person_B$'s relationship to $Person_A$).

If $Person_A$ in this example is a stranger, then there is no direct relationship between the child and $Person_A$ and the formula becomes

$$C \ r \ Person_A = f \ [(C \ r \ Person_B) \times (Person_B \ r \ Person_A)]$$

In this case, the child's relationship to $Person_A$ (the stranger) is a function of the child's relationship to $Person_B$ and $Person_B$'s relationship to $Person_A$. Thus, two pieces of information are important in determining the child's response to a stranger.

Since in most studies of social referencing (e.g., Feinman & Lewis, in press; Klinnert *et al.*, 1982) only the mother is present to serve as a referencing agent, the importance in the child's emotional response of the child's relationship to the referencing agent cannot be tested. An additional condition is needed to observe the effects on the child's response of someone other than the mother interacting with the stranger. By observing the effects of the child–other relationship as well as the other–stranger relationship on the child's interaction with the stranger, the notion of social transitivity can be tested.

The term *social transitivity* is used to indicate a parallelism between the general notion of transitivity and transitivity as applied to social relations. Recall that in tests of transitivity, A's relationship to B and B's relationship to C logically dictate A's relationship to C. For example, in the case of sticks, if A is longer than B and B is longer than C, then logically A must be longer than C. A similar conceptualization can be applied to the notion of social transitivity: the relationships of A to B and of B to C influence the relationship of A to C. However, in the case of social transitivity, the relationships among the elements are not bound by logical constraints as they are in formal transitivity problems.

To examine whether children's relationships to other people affect their relationships to a stranger through the responses of other people to that stranger, Feiring et al. (1982) conducted the following study. Of particular interest were (1) whether a stranger's response to others would influence infants' behaviors toward that stranger and (2) whether the mother was a more potent conveyor of emotional information for the child than another person.

In this study, three groups of 15-month-old children were exposed to one of three conditions. In Condition I, the children observed their mothers interacting in a positive way with Stranger$_1$ for three minutes. During Condition I, another stranger (Stranger$_2$) was in the room but did not interact with the mother, Stranger$_1$, or the child. In Condition II, the children observed Stranger$_1$ interacting in a positive way with Stranger$_2$ for three minutes. During the positive Stranger$_1$–Stranger$_2$ interaction, the mother was present in the room but did not interact with either stranger. In Condition III, there was no interaction among Stranger$_1$, the mother, or Stranger$_2$. Rather, all three sat and read magazines for three minutes.

Following the Stranger$_1$ manipulation in each condition, the stranger greeted the child and then attempted to engage the child in play. Stranger$_1$ called the child by name and then offered the child a toy that she carried in her purse. Coaxing the child to play, Stranger$_1$ sat on the floor and attempted to involve the child in playing with the toys in the room. After three minutes, the stranger said good-bye and left the room.

The child's relationship to the person interacting with Stranger$_1$ was expected to be important in defining the other indirect component and hence in affecting the child's subsequent play with Stranger$_1$. As a result, it was hypothesized that there would be more positive behavior from the children toward Stranger$_1$ when the children observed the mother acting in a positive manner toward Stranger$_1$, as compared with when the children observed a positive interaction between Stranger$_1$ and Stranger$_2$. Moreover, it was hypothesized that the mother–Stranger$_1$ condition would facilitate a more positive child–Stranger$_1$ interaction than the Stranger$_1$ no-interaction condition (Condition III). Whether Stranger$_2$'s interacting with Stranger$_1$ (Condition II) would be different from no interaction (Condition III) was difficult to predict. Given the formula for social transitivity, one might hypothesize no difference since the (S$_2$ r C) term was essentially zero. However, since Stranger$_2$ had certain things in common with both the mother (she was also an adult female) and the child (she was in the same room as the child), the (S$_2$ r C) term may have been greater than zero. If the (S$_2$ r C) term was slightly positive rather than zero, Condition II should have been more positive than Condition III.

In this experiment, the primary dependent measure was the amount of play behavior that the children were willing to engage in with $Stranger_1$ during the three minutes of play. The results showed that toy play with the stranger varied as a function of the condition. For the "offer or accept toy" category of behavior, 7.8 occurrences were found for Condition I, 6.1 for Condition II, and 4.9 for Condition III. Also of interest was how fast the children were able to make friends with $Stranger_1$. Whereas the level of accepting or offering toys did not change during Condition II or Condition III, a marked increase in accepting or offering toys was observed over the three-minute period for Condition I. By the third minute, these differences were significant. Although little negative behavior was directed by the children toward $Stranger_1$ in any of the three conditions, the children in Condition III showed the most wariness toward the stranger during the stranger's initial approach.

The data suggest, then, that for children as young as 15 months of age, indirect effects are already important in mediating social interactions. Moreover, the finding of some difference, although not significant ones, between Conditions II and III suggests that at this age, children may be learning some things about strangers through their interactions with another person. However, it appears that children need to have a significant relationship with the other if strong indirect effects are to occur, a finding that supports the notion of social transitivity. As indicated above, indirect effects may be best facilitated when an individual at any age has some relationship with another person who, in turn, is interacting with a third person. This relationship may be based on several dimensions, some of which have been considered in the literature on imitation and modeling (Bandura, 1977; Lewis, 1979). Among the possible dimensions are the degree of similarity between oneself and the other, the relationship between oneself and the other, and the recognition of the power of the other.

The studies in which mothers' emotional responses to a stranger influence their children's behaviors toward the stranger demonstrate the general proposition that the management of emotions by even young infants is mediated in part by the social environment. These results and the findings of individual differences in the management of emotions as a function of temperament suggest that the social environment through both direct interaction and indirect mediation may affect children's social and emotional behaviors.

The management of emotions is, of course, an enormously complex issue. As was mentioned previously, the topic of impulse control and ego development has received much attention in the research literature. The omission of this topic in the discussion does not reflect its lack of importance but reflects our focus on the socialization of feeling rules. The role of the early social environment in producing coping or adaptive abilities in young infants cannot be ignored, as these abilities obviously impact on children's later ability to manage emotions. The attachment literature represents an extension of this topic, stressing the secure relationship of children to the mother and examining how this secure attachment affects children's later social competence (Ainsworth et al., 1978). Direct evidence is still lacking to connect the quality of the attachment relationship in early life to the later ability to control or manage one's emotions, although there is evidence that mother–infant interactions help regulate emotional behavior (Erikson, 1950; Hartmann, 1939/1958). A complete discussion of the management of emotions would need to include these topics. However, since the focus of this chapter is on feeling rules in general, this brief discussion must suffice.

How Emotions Are Labeled: The Acquisition of an Affect Lexicon

One aspect of the socialization process that is seldom investigated is the acquisition of a lexicon of emotion terms. While many investigators have noted the existence of complex mixtures of emotions (e.g., Ekman & Friesen, 1975; Izard, 1977; Plutchik, 1980a,b; Schwartz & Weinberger, 1980), labels for such mixtures are usually not part of the English language. Indeed, very little is known about the labeling and use of affect terms for even discrete or primary emotions. If one takes the position of social anthropologists that cognitive concepts and language are intimately related (for example, consider the well-known example of the ability of Eskimos to differentiate types of snow, which is reflected in the number of words for snow in their language), then the study of children's acquisition and use of affect terms becomes even more important. Even the experience of smell depends on the labels available to describe odor (Cain, 1979).

There is evidence that children have some understanding of their emotional experiences and the emotions of others prior to the acquisition of specific linguistic labels for those emotions. For instance, 18-month-old children who exhibit empathic behavior by patting a bereaved parent indicate through appropriate behavior that they have at least a rudimentary understanding of the parent's particular experience, although they cannot yet put a label on that experience (Borke, 1971). Although this behavior may represent children's ability to understand the parents' experience, such behavior might also be considered a conditioned response to a particular elicitor or a reflex-like behavior, neither of which would necessarily imply any understanding on the part of the children.

Even when children's linguistic abilities emerge, they may be unable to use appropriate lexical terms although they may have other emotional expressions. For example, consider the example of Benjamin, whose family moved from one house to another when he was 2 years and 9 months old (Lewis & Brooks, 1978). Benjamin had spent all of his life in the first house. One week after moving to the new house, he was asked whether he liked it. "This house doesn't taste good," he said, as he stuck out his tongue. Such examples underscore the fact that children may well have emotions that can be articulated through their behaviors in the absence of appropriate linguistic labels.

The acquisition of affect terms by children may reflect the overlap among language acquisition, cognitive capacity, and emotion in a manner similar to the way that the affect terms of a culture may reflect important underlying properties of the social experience of that culture (Geertz, 1959; Shott, 1979). Lutz (1981) has described ways in which cultures differ in the availability of affect terms and their referents. However, the relationship between the use of such terms by particular cultures and cultural differences in experiences has not yet been studied. In Chapter 1, evidence was presented that within our own culture, at least within the academic part of that culture affect terms and the study of emotion in general focus on the negative end of the emotional spectrum. For example, textbook discussions of children's emotions contain more about sorrow, gloom, and sadness than about laughter and humor, and more about jealousy than about sympathy. Without question, the most lengthy discussions have focused on fear and anger. In every textbook surveyed, one or both of these feelings were allotted the largest number of pages of discussion.

How this bias toward certain aspects of emotional experience rather than others relates to the particular goals and values of a society is not clear. The Puritan background and the northern European influence on the dominant group in the American culture, with its emphasis on impulse control, work, and guilt, imply that it may be no accident that our intellectual searchlights are focused on negative feelings rather than on whimsy, play, and delight. Even the study of positive emotions,

such as humor, is often devoted to their psychopathological implications (e.g., Freud, 1960; Levine, 1979). Unfortunately, too little information on cultural differences in the psycholinguistics of emotion is
available to allow more than a hypothesis on the interconnection between the use of affect terms in general and cultural phenomena.

In the same way that knowledge of cultural rules about the use of
affect terms may be valuable for understanding the structure of particular cultures, knowledge of how children acquire and use affect terms
may be of some importance in understanding the structure of children's
emotional experience. Although studies on children's acquisition of
language are numerous, there are few data on children's acquisition of
emotion labels. Researchers have studied the acquisition of nouns, verbs,
pronouns, and more recently personal pronouns, but the acquisition of
words to label emotions is not usually examined. Although some studies have focused on the language of emotion—that is, how children and
adults talk about their feelings (e.g., Davitz, 1969; Lewis, Wolman, &
King, 1972a,b; Wolman, Lewis & King, 1971, 1972a,b)—very little is
known about how labels are acquired for these feelings. Amen (1941)
found that by 4 years of age, children have already acquired a limited
number of affect terms, including happy, sad, mad, angry, and scared.
Izard (1971) reported that children can discriminate emotions earlier
than they can label them, and that although the recognition and discrimination of emotions increase with age, emotion labeling is not strongly
related to age. The recognition and labeling of the basic emotions of
joy, sadness, anger, and fear develop earlier than those of emotions
such as contempt and shame. Izard concluded that the ability to recognize emotions exceeds the ability to produce appropriate labels for
them. More recently, Zahn-Waxler, Radke-Yarrow, and King (1979) have
found that as early as 2 years of age, children begin to understand and
even produce verbal labels for emotional behaviors such as crying and
laughter.

Where affect terms come from and how they relate to children's
experiences of emotion are not clear. Some data have been collected
about how parents provide information about emotions to their preschool children (Greif, Alvarez, & Ulman, 1981). During a task in which
parents read a picture book to their children, the parents' references to
emotions were coded as statements, questions, explanations of emotions related to causal or situational factors, or information about the
ways in which emotions can be inferred from bodily or facial cues. The
results showed that 71% of the parents mentioned emotions to their
children, usually in the form of statements or questions. The most
frequently labeled emotions were anger, joy, and distress. Whereas the

mothers showed no difference in their use of affect labels to sons and daughters, the fathers were twice as likely to mention emotions to their daughters than to their sons. Although not significant, there was a tendency for the mothers to mention anger to their sons more often than to their daughters. Finally, when instances of the children's spontaneous use of affect terms were coded, it was found that of the 20 instances that occurred, 17 of the labels were produced by girls.

Language development, in particular the acquisition of phonetic and lexical abilities, appears to be related to the use of language by people around the child, including parents, siblings, and peers (Lewis & Rosenblum, 1977). A good way to begin the study of the acquisition of affect labels, therefore, is by studying the language of children's principal caregivers. By determining the context of the affect labels used around children, investigators may be better able to relate that context both to the children's use of affect terms and to their expressions and experiences of those emotions.

There are many methods for recording the language that mothers use in talking to their children. Usually, mothers are asked to behave naturally and talk to their children either in a nonstructured situation or in a teaching situation. The corpus of mothers' language is gathered from these situations, and particular features of their language are studied. Such methods are favored because they capitalize on the spontaneous use of language by mothers and children and because a large corpus of naturally occurring language is usually obtained. The disadvantage of these techniques, however, is that they do not tap aspects of language that are related to situations unlikely to occur or likely to occur only with low probability when the language corpus is being recorded. In particular, mothers' affect language is less apt to be observed in some situations than in others. Therefore, in order to study the use of such language, investigators must restrict or focus the situations in which the language corpus is gathered. As a consequence, the language data are likely to be highly restricted to the particular situation in which they are collected.

To counter this problem, it is important to look at situations that have general importance in children's lives. Good situations are not easily produced, since information about situational constraints is limited, especially from a developmental perspective (Lewis, 1978). However, one situation in which affect terms are likely to occur is the "attachment situation" (Ainsworth & Wittig, 1969). The attachment situation seems to meet the requirements outlined above, since by its nature it is (1) a restricted situation eliciting a spontaneous sample of mothers' language; (2) more likely to elicit affect terms because of its stress on children and parents; (3) a prototypical measure of an important affect (attachment); and (4) generalizable and predictive to other situations (Ainsworth *et al.*, 1978).

The attachment situation, therefore, is a good situation for studying mothers' language and use of affect terms. Even in this situation, however, the range of affect expressions is likely to be limited. The enormous literature on attachment suggests that the feelings that the situation elicits are those of fear, anger, and unhappiness rather than joy, delight, or interest. Thus, the affect labels produced in this situation cannot be generalized to other, less stressful situations.

Maternal Affect Labeling: A Study of Infant Distress

In order to investigate at least some aspects of maternal affect labeling, the following data were collected on 111 one-year-old infants and their mothers during a 5-minute reunion period in an attachment situation (Lewis & Michalson, 1982c). This reunion period occurred after a 15-minute free-play episode in which the mother and the infant engaged in unrestricted play and after the mother's departure from the playroom for not more than 2 minutes. This situation constitutes a modified "strange situation" in which attachment behaviors can be observed. A similar version, using one separation and one reunion episode, was used by Waters *et al.*, (1979).

Use of Affect Terms

Of the 111 mothers, only 26% used any affect labels during the five-minute reunion, and 74% used no affect labels. Four categories of affect labels were used by 29 mothers. Seven mothers said that their child was "tired/sad"; seven used "angry/mad"; seven used "scared/upset"; and eight used "miss me." Thus, even though most mothers used no affect labels, those who did used only four different ones that were appropriate to the situation. This finding confirms the belief that particular situations limit the number of different affects observed. In this situation, the emotions elicited were not positive.

Labelers versus Nonlabelers

Because all the mothers faced an upset child when they returned to the room, the next question asked was what maternal variables distinguished the mothers who labeled ("labelers") from the mothers who did not ("nonlabelers"). The maternal variables available for study included socioeconomic status (SES), Wechsler Adult Intelligence Scale (WAIS) verbal subscale score, and maternal internality–externality measured by the Rotter Internality-Externality Scale (Rotter, 1966). No significant differences were found on any of these variables between mothers who labeled and those who did not, although higher SES mothers were somewhat more likely to use affect labels than lower SES mothers. Other investigators have reported the use of affect concepts to be more prevalent in the language of the middle class than in that of the lower class (Bernstein, 1961; Hess & Shipman, 1965). There was also a tendency for labelers to have higher WAIS verbal scores.

Labeling and nonlabeling mothers were also compared on specific maternal behaviors toward their infants during reunion. These behaviors included vocalizing, looking, smiling, teaching, holding, approaching, and establishing proximity (moving within arms' reach of the child). Also compared were maternal initiations and maternal responses, which measured whether the mothers initiated contact with the child or responded to the child's initiation. No differences between labelers and nonlabelers were found for any behavior except maternal response; the nonlabelers were more likely to respond to their infants than the labelers.

Differences within Labelers

Because few differences between labeling and nonlabeling mothers were found, the next question asked was whether there were any differences within the group of mothers who labeled their children in terms of the labels they used. The results showed that the mothers with higher verbal WAIS scores more frequently labeled their children "scared/upset" or "miss me," compared with mothers with lower verbal WAIS scores, who used the terms "angry/mad" and "tired/sad." The lower SES mothers used "angry/mad" relatively more often than did the higher SES mothers. The SES difference in the use of "angry/mad" is intriguing in light of findings from other studies showing social class differences in the expression and acting out of anger and aggression: lower SES mothers and children tend to show more physical aggression than higher SES mothers and children (Feshbach, 1970; Zigler & Child, 1969). Additional evidence of group differences in the differential use of anger labels is provided by the finding that mothers tend to label anger more in talking to sons than in talking to daughters (Greif et al., 1981). Also, American children are more likely than French children to recognize and label anger (Izard, 1971). Whether the differential use of affect labels on the part of the mothers facilitates group or individual differences is a highly speculative issue. Still, the labeling of specific emotions as a function of social class is a provocative finding.

Finally, mothers of boys used "miss me" more than mothers of girls. The use of the term "miss me" more for boys than for girls may have important behavioral implications, especially from a psychoanalytical point of view, which suggests that mothers may be more seductive toward their male than toward their female children (Sroufe & Ward, 1980). "Miss me" is an intriguing label. The use of this particular label may have more to do with the feelings of the mother than with the feelings of the child, since the child did not show signs of missing her.

What about other maternal behaviors, besides labeling, that might have covaried with the children's emotional behaviors and with maternal labeling behavior? Did the mothers' reunion behaviors differ as a function of how they labeled their children's distress? The mothers who labeled their children "scared/upset" held their children more than the mothers of the other three groups. The mothers who showed less proximal behaviors labeled their children "miss me" more than the other mothers. The mothers who were more responsive to their children's behavior used "scared/upset" and "tired/sad" more than "miss me" and "angry/mad." The fact that "miss me" and "angry/mad" children both elicited low levels of maternal responsivity may have had different causes. "Angry/mad" children were characterized by throwing themselves about and pushing and throwing toys; such behaviors are not conducive to maternal responsivity. The use of "miss me," on the other hand, did not appear to be related to the children's distress.

Labeling as a Function of Infant Differences

After examining maternal differences in labeling behavior, the characteristics of the children that might have caused the mothers to produce the particular affect terms they did were examined. Specifically, IQ (Bayley Mental Development Index) and gender were found not to be related to the mothers' use of affect terms. Maternal labelers did not have children who were more upset than the children of nonlabelers, since all the infants were upset when the mothers left the room.

Although the infants' behaviors did not influence whether mothers used affect labels, they did influence the specific label used. The mothers labeling their children "angry/mad" had children who tended to throw themselves on the ground or to throw and push toys around. The use of the label "tired/sad" was applied to children who showed depression, which was expressed in behavioral terms by a marked reduction in activity as well as a "tired appearance." The use of "scared/upset" was applied to children who cried and often assumed a bodily posture of wishing to be picked up, accompanied by a pleading look at the mother. In these cases, maternal labeling behavior appeared to be related to the behavioral characteristics of the infants. Although the infants labeled "miss me" showed no consistent behavioral pattern, their main response could be characterized as looking away from the mother or looking at a toy and not paying attention to the mother as she entered the room.

The mothers labeled their infants' experiences according to the eliciting situation and according to the infants' behavior in that situation. Moreover, their labeling behaviors covaried with their other behavioral responses to distress. Not all cases of maternal labeling followed these patterns, however. These exceptions are the focus of a later section on developmental psychopathology.

One reason that some mothers labeled their children's emotional behaviors and others did not is that these children may have expressed certain behaviors other than distress, which facilitated maternal affect labeling. To examine this question, 30 nonlabeling mother–infant dyads were selected at random from the 82 dyads in the nonlabeling group for a comparison with the 29 labeling mother–infant dyads. In the 30 nonlabeling dyads, 26 children exhibited behaviors similar to the 29 children who were labeled. These 26 infants showed behaviors that fitted into three affect categories: "scared/upset" (16 children), "miss me" (6 children), and "angry/mad" (4 children). None of the children appeared tired or sad, and 4 showed no clear affect patterns. There appeared to be no differences in maternal nonverbal behaviors between these 30 nonlabelers and the 29 labelers. The results suggest, then, that the mothers' use of affect labels was not attributable to the infants' behaviors, although the particular label used was influenced by the infants' behavior.

Individual Differences in the Use of Affect Labels

Although limited in the number and kinds of different affect labels studied, this investigation demonstrates that mothers use affect labels prior to their children's acquisition of language. Of interest is the fact that the mothers' use of affect labels in this particular situation was rather infrequent. Only 26% of the mothers used affect labels of any sort in this stressful situation. This is not to say that the mothers did not express any emotion toward the children: indeed, they did. In most cases, they picked up and comforted their children either through direct physical contact or through distractions. The mothers neither scolded nor hit their children when they showed distress. Thus, the mother–child interactions appeared synchronous vis-à-vis the children's emotional expressions and the mothers' nonverbal responses. For the most part, however, the mothers did not use verbal affect labels. Whether the low level of maternal affect labeling was due to the relatively infrequent use of affect labels by mothers in general or was due to the fact that the children were only 1 year old and without language is not known. The finding that by the time children reach preschool age, over 70% of parents are using affect terms (Greif et al., 1981) suggests that the children's age may be a significant factor. Even so, the observation of any affect labeling with 1-year-old children is an important finding in need of further exploration. This is especially true in light of data suggesting that mothers *attribute* three of the affects observed in the study ("sad/tired," "angry/mad," "scared/upset") to children of this age (Pannabecker et al., 1980), even though the mothers may not actually *apply* these labels to their children's behavior.

Most of the mothers who used affect labels in the attachment situation used them in a way that appeared to be related to the behaviors produced by the children. Thus, some mothers may have provided affect terms for their children as a function of the children's behavior. Even though no maternal characteristics were found to distinguish labelers from nonlabelers, the mothers who produced these labels may have been providing their children with a linguistic experience that would facilitate the children's later acquisition of affect terms. Although no data are available on this topic, there is evidence that mothers who use more elaborated language have children who are able to differentiate their environment better than children whose mothers use more restricted language (Bernstein, 1961; Hess & Shipman, 1965). The same may be true in the realm of affect: mothers who use a greater number of and more differentiated affect terms may have children whose emotional experiences are more differentiated.

The inability to differentiate labeling from nonlabeling mothers may have been due to the fact that the critical dimensions of the people who used affect terms were not obtained. In addition to verbal fluency, certain types of interpersonal sensitivity and concern with emotional experience may characterize these people. It is tempting to consider labeling mothers and nonlabeling mothers somehow different; yet, it must be kept in mind that labeling and nonlabeling pertain to particular situations and emotions. Other situations likely to elicit different emotions might have produced a different subset of "labelers" and "nonlabelers." This is another dimension of socialization to be explored. If people are differentially sensitive to emotional moods (e.g., if depressives are more sensitive than nondepressives to other peoples' depression), then the mother's mood state may be the critical factor differentiating those who label from those who do not label particular emotional states. In the present study, the labeling mothers may have been more sensitive to negative emotions than to positive emotions. Thus, a general sensitivity to emotional states may be less important for labeling particular emotions than a selective sensitivity. Although there is little empirical evidence to support this hypothesis, moderate correlations have been found between mothers' and infants' emotional expressions, particularly between their displays of anger (Malatesta, 1981; Malatesta & Haviland, 1981).

It is important to note once again that the mothers' labeling behavior was a function of both the specific behaviors expressed by the infant and the particular context. The mothers did not label the children's behavior solely on the basis of these behaviors in the context of separation. The use of behaviors and situations in labeling the infants' emotions facilitates the association of behaviors and situations in the constellations of emotional experience that are known as "sad/tired," "angry/mad," or "scared/upset."

The same mothers and children were observed in the same situation when the children were 2 years old. A preliminary analysis of the data shows a significant increase in the number of mothers who labeled their children's emotional behaviors. However, the labeling did not appear to be consistent. That is, the mothers who used affect labels when their children were 1 year old were not necessarily the mothers who labeled their 2-year-old children's behaviors.

Studies such as this provide important information on the affect lexicon used by children's caregivers. When accompanied by data on children's use of affect terms, such studies should contribute significantly to a theory on the socialization of emotion. The types of labels used in children's social environment provide children with information that may influence their own emotional experiences. The social environment provides children with labels for their internal emotional states and external expressions. The social environment also conveys culturally appropriate meanings to feelings in the context of certain situations. Finally, the social environment provides children with a language of emotion that may facilitate the differentiation of more subtle emotions. The potential for idiosyncratic labeling also comes from the social environment. By providing incorrect labels, the social environment may set the stage for later psychopathology. This potential developmental outcome, as a function of affect mislabeling by the social environment, is discussed in the final section of this chapter.

The particular study of maternal affect labeling illustrates the type of research needed on the issue of language acquisition and emotional expression. While a great deal of information is available on language acquisition, studies of the acquisition of emotion labels are scarce. Neither the developmental sequence of the labels acquired nor the relationships between emotional labels and other aspects of emotional development have been examined. The study of emotional language is confounded by the fact that the acquisition of language appears to be associated with general intellectual development. Therefore, word acquisition may interact with other cognitive skills and mask the relationship between affect labels and emotional behaviors.

Despite this problem, several fundamental questions still need to be asked concerning not only the developmental acquisition of the affect lexicon and the relationship between affect terms and other behaviors but also individual differences. Is the observation that males are more aggressive than females and females more affiliative than males related to differential maternal use of the lexicon. Do social class differences in social and emotional behaviors also appear in the language?

Lewis and Cherry (1977) have argued for a model of language development in which language acquisition, including semantic, lexical, pragmatic, and syntactical development, is both an end product of the socialization of children (i.e., a set of skills that adults seek to establish in children) and a means for socializing other aspects of behavior. In the first case, adults wish to teach children the language. Thus, the general rule is "Talk to them, read to them, point out word–object relationships, and encourage conversation." On the other hand, language is used to socialize children, to teach children particular rules that are regarded by the society as important. For example, 2-year-old girls are asked more questions than boys, whereas more imperatives are directed toward boys (Lewis & Cherry, 1977). Moreover, girls are more likely than boys to be responded to when they ask a question (Cherry, 1975).

These findings may fit within a general socialization pattern that promotes specific gender differences in behavior. There are some data that suggest that one socialization task of mothers is to move male children physically further away from them than female children (Goldberg & Lewis, 1969; Lewis, 1972). In order to realize this socialization goal, mothers may ask their sons fewer questions then their daughters, because question asking requires a social exchange that is incompatible with physical distance. Question asking requires (1) engaging the other; (2) looking at the other; (3) remaining close to the other; and (4) taking turns. Questions, then, do not effect distance and separation from the mother. On the other hand, commands such as "Get that toy" are less likely to keep the child close and to produce interaction. One way to keep children close may be to ask questions. Consequently, the socialization of gender differences in proximity behaviors may be facilitated by the language that parents use.

The language of a culture is the particular code in which the various social roles and tasks are embedded. The symbol system of this code must match the symbol system or meaning of the behaviors of the individuals in the system. In this regard, the acquisition of an affect lexicon and the particular uses of affect terms may share important associations with emotional development in general. When we turn to the consequences of emotional labeling, the importance of the acquisition of the language code becomes even clearer.

How Emotions Are Interpreted

In the structural analysis of emotion (see Chapters 4 and 5), emotional state was regarded as separate and distinct from emotional experience. This distinction may have a heuristic value, because it allows for the development of states apart from experiences and because it allows both biological and social factors to play roles in the emotional process. States are associated with biological, especially physiological, processes, and experiences are related to psychological and phenomenological events. In discussing "how emotions are interpreted" as a feeling rule that is socialized, it is necessary to consider expression, state, and experience as distinct components of emotion. Young organisms indicate that they have emotional states through their emotional expressions. Thus, for example, when pricked with a pin, even very young infants cry, and their facial expressions and crying may be different from their expressions when they are wet or hungry. How do children develop experiences from emotional states? Much of the developmental process may be viewed as the acquisition of experience from state. In this analysis, the child is seen as the agent, and the focus of inquiry is on the manner in which children create an emotional experience from an emotional state. A similar question can be raised from the viewpoint of adults: How do adults infer that children have a particular emotional state? The insights gained in the discussion of the child as agent may help in articulating the processes that adults use. In fact, adults' interpretation of children's states may provide material for children to construct emotional experiences.

In Chapter 5, it was suggested that in order for children to have an emotional experience, it is essential that there be some mediation between the state and the experience. The minimal structure necessary for that mediation was considered the cognitive underpinning of a sense of self. Not until infants can distinguish between self and other are they capable of deriving emotional experiences from their states. Thus, the experience of fear is different from the state of fear, inasmuch as there is a self, or an "I," to which that state can be attached (e.g., "I am afraid"). The development of the self, then, provides the minimal structure facilitating emotional experience, and not until a self–other concept emerges is it reasonable to think about emotional experiences. However, such a structure, essentially cognitive in nature, is probably insufficient from a developmental perspective to explain this transition or to explain the emotional experiences of adults. The meaning rules, or the interpretation rules that are applied to children's behavior, must also be taken into account in explaining the acquisition and development of emotional experience.

One set of meaning rules that may be critical is the interpretation of infants' emotional states by their caregivers. The interpretation of one's state by another constitutes the basis of meaning for specific behaviors. For example, children may cry in pain when they hit their leg and in frustration when a tower of blocks falls over. In both cases, crying may reflect a distressed state, undifferentiated in terms of experience until it is differentially responded to by the caregiver. In the first case, the mother's behavior and corresponding label, "It hurts," may provide a social experience that conveys the meaning of pain. This meaning may be embedded in a social context consisting of the labels that people give to behaviors and the events that produce pain. Thus, the interpretation of others may represent an important means through which children learn to interpret their own emotional states.

Relatively little information exists about how adults interpret the emotional states and expressions of infants. The labeling study reported in the previous section of this chapter indicates that mothers interpret infants' emotional states in terms of specific behaviors in a particular context. The restrictions of the situation and the small number of subjects did not allow for a full understanding of what mothers think about all of the emotional states of their infants. Mothers may also need to be asked directly about their perceptions of their children's emotions. Since mothers see their children in a variety of situations over an extended period of time, their reports might reflect their knowledge about the emotions of their children.

In a recent study, approximately 590 mothers were asked about the emotions of their children younger than 18 months old (Pannabecker et al., 1980). Of interest were (1) when the mothers thought particular emotions first emerged in their infants and (2) what emotions they saw in their infants at the time the questionnaire was administered. The emotions asked about were joy, surprise, anger, distress, interest, fear, shyness, sadness, disgust, contempt, and guilt.

The mothers' data on their infants' emotions were grouped by three-month intervals, according to the infants' ages, to produce six age groups on which analyses were performed. Interest, joy, surprise, anger, disgust, and fear were perceived by 66% of the mothers to appear in the first three months of life. In contrast, shyness, sadness, disgust, contempt, and guilt were thought to be present by fewer than 33% of the mothers of the youngest age group.

Four basic patterns of emotional development could be depicted from the mothers' reports. First, interest, joy, surprise, and anger were observed in almost all infants in the early periods and showed relatively little increase after 6 months of age. Second, the time when sadness, disgust, contempt, and guilt first appeared showed a steady increase as a function of the children's age. However, none of these emotions were seen in all infants, at least by the time the infants were 18 months old. Third, distress and fear were seen by mothers in nearly 60% of the children in the first three months and in 80–90% of the children in the oldest age group. Shyness presented a fourth pattern of development. Very little shyness was seen in the first three months of life, but the appearance of shyness increased monotonically to 90% of the children by 18 months. No differences were found in maternal perceptions of emotions as a function of the children's gender or the mothers' educational level or child-rearing experience.

The investigators also studied a small group of mothers of newborn infants. Of the 26 mothers contacted, interest and joy were seen by 95%, anger by 87%, distress by 65%, surprise by 68%, sadness and disgust by 40%, and fear by 35%. Although none of the mothers reported signs of guilt, 8% reported seeing shyness. These results confirm the data of the first study and indicate that even mothers of newborns perceive many emotions in their children.

Several explanations of these findings are possible. In the first place, the maternal reports might not have been reliable, and the data reported may not be replicable. However, the collection of data from a second sample of newborns and their mothers casts doubt on this interpretation. If these findings are reliable, how can they best be explained? Surely, any theory of emotional development must be taxed by such findings. How does one explain that 87% of the mothers of newborns saw anger in their children and more than 40% saw sadness and disgust? That even 8% saw shyness is still difficult to accept.

In trying to explain these findings, one must first question the basis of the mothers' reports. The mothers may have seen specific facial expressions reflecting these emotions. Alternatively, they may have interpreted their infants' general behaviors as what they themselves would have felt in similar situations. In the Pannabecker et al. (1980) study, it is not clear whether the mothers were referring to expressions, states, or experiences. The infants' expressions may, in fact, have been present. Izard et al. (1980) have argued that almost all of the facial expressions of these emotions appear within the first year of life. Consequently, it is possible that the mothers' reports were based on their actual observations of their infants' facial expressions.

Is one to believe that these emotional expressions reflect discrete emotional states in such young infants? According to the model of development described in Chapter 5, it is unlikely that expressions are connected in a one-to-one fashion with internal states in very young infants. Thus, even if the mothers were correctly observing their infants' expressions, this observation may have had little to do with the infants' emotional states or experiences. In other words, the mothers may have observed the behaviors of their infants in particular situations and interpreted these behaviors as if their children possessed these states. If, however, emotional states and expressions do exist in a differentiated form at birth or shortly thereafter, the mothers' reports might have reflected their sensitivity to their infants' emotional states.

Although there are few data to support the notion that parents interpret or label specific behaviors in context or use information about individual differences in this process, there is some reason to believe that this is the case. For example, individual differences in mothers' labeling behavior were found in the study of maternal affect labeling described previously.

Unfortunately, no data on the mothers' emotional states were reported by Pannabecker et al. (1980). Perhaps mothers who are more distressed, fearful, joyous, or interested, for example, are more likely to see these same emotional states in their children. The qualities of the social environment over and above the developmental sequences observed may play a role in the perception and labeling of children's emotional states. The data reported by Pannabecker et al. (1980) suggest that for at least some emotional states, mothers seem to be attuned to their likely developmental sequence. Shyness is one example. But even here, the fact that over 40% of the mothers saw shyness in 4- to 6-month-old infants suggests that the developmental sequence they were observing may have been colored by other factors. It is not likely that shyness occurs in 4-month-old infants. Furthermore, over 30% of the mothers reported seeing guilt in children 10–12 months old. Yet, guilt would not be expected to occur until children can adopt a standard and recognize a violation of that standard.

In short, these data suggest that caregivers may overestimate the emotional development of their children. By interpreting their children's behavior in specific contexts, caregivers may attribute to the children certain emotional states that, in fact, may not yet exist in an undifferentiated form. This interpretation does not necessarily reflect an inappropriate socialization process or individual psychopathology (although this could be the case, as will be discussed later) but may play a productive role in the actual creation of these emotional states and experiences.

Parents tend to overestimate and possibly to interpret incorrectly many aspects of children's behavior. An example is the tendency of mothers to overestimate infants' imitative abilities (Lewis, 1979; Lewis & Sullivan, 1982; Waite & Lewis, 1979). When a group of mothers were asked whether their babies could imitate the behavior of others, 15% of the mothers said that their infants could imitate at the newborn state, 52% said at 3 months, and 35% said at 6 months (Waite & Lewis, 1979). Yet, when one looks at infants' imitative behavior and records the number of times infant behavior follows the behavior of the mother (e.g., tongue protrusions), one finds that the co-occurrence of infant–maternal behaviors is quite frequent. In experimental situations, they co-occur on an average of 30–40% of the time (Lewis & Sullivan, 1982). Consequently, if mothers observe whether an infant repeats what they do, they would, in fact, find evidence of imitation, even in infants younger than 14 days. Mothers are likely to interpret this sequence of events as an example of their infants' ability to imitate.

What has been overlooked by some investigators and left out of the mothers' interpretation is the phenomenon of base rate (Tversky & Kahneman, 1974). It is important to establish not only the co-occurrence of a select behavior but also the base occurrence of that behavior. In the case of imitative tongue protrusions, the investigator must record not only the co-occurrence of infant–mother tongue protrusions but also the occurrence of infants' tongue protrusions when the mothers perform another action, such as shaking their heads. When this base rate is taken into account, the data on infant imitation become controversial. Imitation prior to the development of means–end ability can only be reflexive; therefore, nonreflexive imitation cannot be said to exist before infants are 6 months old (Kaye, 1982; Piaget, 1951).

These data indicate that mothers interpret their infants' behavior as if the infants are imitating. Although this interpretation may not be correct with respect to what the children are in fact doing, it may play a significant role in promoting mother–child interactions and in fostering nonreflexive imitation. The ways in which interpretation may facilitate the acquisition of imitation are not clear. However, several possibilities might be suggested. Mothers' belief that children are actually imitating them may make mothers more interested in interacting with their children. This interest, in turn, may increase not only the frequency of their interactions but also the contingency of the interaction. The contingency itself may direct the children's attention to the co-occurrence of behaviors and thereby promote increased circular reaction skills and imitation. In this event, the interpretations by mothers, although incorrect, may facilitate the acquisition of the very capacity that they already attribute to their children.

The general socialization rule may be that in order to teach children a particular capacity or set of skills (or, in the case of emotions, meanings and interpretations), the socializing agent must "preview" such capacities in order to promote the children's acquisition of them. Previewing may involve attributing skills and capacities to infants before they actually exist. In fact, as was suggested, the process of interpretation may serve to facilitate the skills. Everyday experience indicates that this view of the socialization process may have merit. Family therapists often use such rules in helping families to alter interpersonal behaviors. For example, a parent's belief that a child is a liar and a thief may in itself foster lying and stealing in that child. Rather than focusing on the fact that children do not tell the truth, therapists may suggest that parents focus on the truthfulness of the child and thereby foster in the child a belief that she or he is not a liar.

This type of attributive or interpretative process may also play a role in emotional development. It has already been demonstrated that such attribution may affect "appropriate" sex-role behavior by assigning different meanings to behaviors (e.g., eye-openness) as a function of the infants' gender. Attribution by adults may foster a wide range of capacities in infants, including those considered emotional. Parents attribute emotions to children before children may have such states and certainly before children experience these emotions (Pannabecker et al., 1980). The function of this attribution may be to help children learn to interpret their own states. Children's ability to interpret their own states may be realized both through the specific labels that parents apply to their children's behaviors and through the types of behaviors that the parents exhibit. Parental attribution and interpretation may be translated into specific behaviors, including labeling, which, in turn, affect children's experience. In such an analysis, emotional states become emotional experiences through the interaction of children with their social environment.

The implications of this view are vast. For example, consider the implications for cultural differences. If Culture A interprets State 1 as X and Culture B interprets State 1 and Y, then the emotional experiences of children in Culture A will be different from the experiences of children in Culture B, even though the underlying emotional state may be the same. Such a view of the socialization of emotion is in sharp contrast to more biological views, in which states are biologically connected to experiences as well as to elicitors. A fuller discussion results from considering the possible psychopathological outcomes of emotional development from both the socialization and the biological viewpoints.

Implications for Psychopathology

Both the socialization history of the individual and a biologically programmed neuromusculature underlie emotional expression. In combination, these give rise to the expression of emotion. As has been pointed out by others, emotional expression is a communicative process, the function of which is to inform others as well as oneself about personal feelings (Buck, 1981, 1982; Ekman & Friesen, 1975; Izard, 1977; Tomkins, 1962, 1963). The social environment interprets the emotions of children through observing their behavior in particular contexts. Thus, it can be said that the social environment acts on children (1) by prescribing the nature of their emotional expressions and (2) by interpreting their emotional states through an observation of their expressions in context. For example, girls are more likely to be reinforced for smiling (Malatesta & Haviland, 1981). Furthermore, it is commonly assumed that females are more sociable and affiliative than males because they show more smiling behavior. Such a dual process reflects the particular meaning system of a particular society or culture.

Personality differences and psychopathology related to emotional states, expressions, and experiences involve a complex set of factors, including differences in temperament and cognitive abilities. Deviations in the normative socialization practices of a culture may also influence subsequent personality development and psychopathology. Idiosyncratic child-rearing practices may occur at the level of the socialization of particular emotional expressions. Some children may not be allowed to express fear or distress if such behaviors are negatively reinforced. As was seen in the study of maternal socialization practices, negative reinforcement or the absence of reinforcement can result in the elimination of certain components of emotional expression (Brooks-Gunn & Lewis, 1982).

What might be the consequences of the elimination or alteration of these components? Two consequences in particular may contribute to psychopathology. First, the absence of certain types of emotional expressions may have a direct effect on emotional states and expressions. For example, individuals' emotional experiences are determined by perceiving and interpreting (1) their personal state and expression, (2) situations, and (3) the behaviors of others. The degree to which an expressive component is missing is the degree to which the ability to experience an appropriate state may be impaired. Second, the idiosyncratic socialization of emotional expressions may affect how others react to the individual. Given that emotional expressions communicate the individual's internal state to other people, the inappropriate socialization of these expressions, inappropriate vis-à-vis the cultural norm, might cause the individual to be misinterpreted by others.

Another way in which the socialization of emotional expressions may be related to subsequent personality deviations pertains to the interpretation given those expressions by significant others. For example, it may be the case that a child's emotional expressions are appropriate vis-à-vis the cultural norm. However, the caregiver's interpretation of those expressions may not be appropriate. For example, in the study of maternal affect labeling described earlier, the labels used by mothers to interpret their 1-year-old children's distress behaviors were examined. In general, the mothers, when they labeled their children's behavior, correctly identified the emotion from the children's behaviors. For example, the mothers labeled their children's behavior as "angry" if their children threw toys around or did not want to be picked up. They used the label "miss me" when the child ignored them and did not run to them when they returned (indicating that the child, in fact, did not miss the mother). "Scared" was applied to children who cried and assumed a bodily posture indicating a wish to be picked up, accompanied by a pleading look at the mother. Finally, the label "tired/sad" was applied to children who showed a marked reduction in activity. These labels reflected the mothers' interpretations of their children's internal states.

By monitoring their children's emotional expressions in this fashion, the mothers generally adopted what is considered the normative interpretation of emotional behavior. There were several occasions, however, in which a mother's labeling behavior contradicted the independent judgments of an observer about her child's general emotional expression. For example, one mother labeled a child who acted scared "angry," and another mother labeled a frightened infant "sad." Such mislabeling of children's emotional states based on a misinterpretation of expression by the socializing agent may have important implications for the development of psychopathology. Since psychopathology may be the consequence of both the characteristics of the child and the interpretation of people around the child, evidence of a discrepancy or "mismatch" between these two factors could potentially be used to identify children at risk for later psychopathology. In addition, such discrepancies reveal, and thus promote the study of, the interaction of biological factors and socialization in emotional development.

This misinterpretation in mothers' labeling and behavioral response has the potential to affect the children's development in two ways. First, it is in disagreement with the normative values of the society and therefore puts the children at risk with respect to their behavior toward others. Second, it teaches children inappropriate labels with respect to their internal state. While such an analysis is offered at the level of speculation, it provides a model of psychopathology that is based on deviations in the normal socialization of emotions. The socialization model of psychopathology is applicable only if one assumes that states, expressions, and experiences are not isomorphic and that the socialization of expression results either in the acquisition of socially appropriate emotions or in deviant behavior.

The implications of a socialization model as it affects psychopathology stand in some contrast to the implications inherent in other models of psychopathology. It is worthwhile to outline the major features of these models if we are to understand the contributions of each. In conventional biological models, a certain elicitor, M, is assumed to produce an emotional state, N, with accompanying expressions and motoric behaviors. For example, M might be a common fear elicitor, such as the uncontrollable approach of a stranger. Presumably N, a fear state, is directly translated into a fear experience.

In conventional models, it is assumed that state N (fear) is produced by the elicitor whether or not fear is experienced. A fear state may not be experienced if the individual employs a set of defense mechanisms such as suppression, inhibition, repression, or denial. This might be the case for a 14-year-old boy who does not wish to let others or even himself know that he is afraid of an approaching stranger. These defense mechanisms imply that an underlying state, N, exists even though the individual may be unable to experience N. The defense mechanisms rob the individual of psychic energy and prevent him from freely experiencing the underlying state. Implied in these models of psychopathology is a one-to-one relationship between an elicitor and a state and between a state and an experience. Psychopathology is largely a consequence of the individual's inability to connect the experience to the existing state. Consequently, the role of therapy is to break down the defense system and to allow the subject to experience the underlying emotional state.

This model has, in fact, a strong socialization component inasmuch as it assumes the child's particular emotional experience is inhibited or suppressed as a result of socialization. Nevertheless, the model implies that a particular emotional experience is directly connected to a specific emotional state. However, if one believes that socialization processes *always* intervene between the state and experience, through the attribution or interpretation of others, then an alternative model is necessary.

Socialization models, in contrast to biological models, suggest that *experience and state may not be connected in a one-to-one fashion and that the socialization task is to connect them.* That is, socialization involves matching what the culture expects children to experience with an emotional state that is reflected by a set of expressions in a specific situation and in the presence of certain elicitors. In other words, rather than experiencing fear as the automatic consequence of a fearful state, children may experience fear only to the degree to which they have been socialized through the interpretation, labeling, and interactive behavior of others to do so.

For instance, if in the early socialization period a child's emotional state, expressed by wary looking and inhibition of activity in response to the approach of a stranger (an elicitor) is interpreted by the social environment as angry rather than fearful, the child might experience anger and not fear. Here, the child's failure to experience fear would reflect not the presence of defense mechanisms such as repression, denial, or suppression but the fact that the child never learned to experience fear under these circumstances.

Such a model of the socialization of emotions requires therapeutic practices that are different from those prescribed by more conventional models. Whereas in biological models the therapist's task is to put the patient in touch with repressed experiences and to release the psychic energy bound up with defense mechanisms, the therapist's task in socialization models is one of reeducation. The psychopathology here is not so much a consequence of repression and the dissipation of psychic energy as of the fact that the child, through the mismanagement of a socialization process, has come to experience an inappropriate emotion, A, vis-à-vis the situation. The inappropriateness of emotion A is reflected in the fact that other members of the social group experience a different emotion under the same conditions and think it inappropriate for the child to experience emotion A. Such children are at risk because of their deviance vis-à-vis others in their social network rather than because of their inability to recover a suppressed or repressed experience.

This model recognizes within-group differences in socialization processes by which the same stimulus through different meaning systems and socialization practices may result in culturally different emotional experiences. Examples of cultural differences in emotional experiences are widespread. One particular example is a cultural difference in feelings related to personal achievement. In the Western tradition, there are elaborate models of competence that emphasize a strong positive emotional experience as the natural consequence of personal achievement. Yet, other cultures may find it inappropriate to recognize personal achievement because it tends to separate one from the group. Among the Zuñi Indians, for example (according to Benedict, 1934), the individual with undisguised initiative and greater drive than his or her fellows is apt to be branded a witch and hung up by the thumbs. Consequently, the socialization task for American and Zuñi parents may be quite different and may involve promoting the emotional experience of competence in response to achievement in one case and the emotional experience of shame or guilt in response to achievement in the other.

Socialization models do not necessarily exclude the role of defense mechanisms in affecting the emotional experience of people. Certainly, such mechanisms are at work. The present discussion is meant to suggest that socialization factors probably play a more complex role in the emotional life of children and adults than has previously been acknowledged and that they may be responsible for some aspects of psychopathology not normally considered. Thus, such considerations should broaden the perspective on the processes involved in emotional development as well as in psychopathology and at the same time suggest the use of less conventional psychotherapeutic strategies.

The results of the study of maternal labeling presented earlier showed that in general, mothers interpret their children's states and experiences through the combined use of the situation and their children's behavior. Their attributions tend to match what the social group would accept as the "true emotional experience." Nevertheless, mislabeling did occur occasionally. What are the possible outcomes if mothers consistently mislabel their children's behavior across many situations? How will these children interpret their own behavior if the behavior of significant others is inappropriate to the behaviors and situations that exist? Several possibilities can be imagined. First, one might adopt a more biological point of view and answer that children's emotional experiences have a high correspondence to their internal states, independent of the behavior of others. Thus, in those cases in which mothers labeled "tired/sad" children "angry/mad," according to this view the children would feel "tired/sad" despite the mother's mislabeling behavior.

A second possibility derives from a "mixed-feeling model," in which children's experiences are influenced both by their own states and by the labeling of others. This mixed feeling might be a combination of "angry/mad" (the mother's label) and "tired/sad" (the children's state). An analogy to the development of bird songs comes to mind. In Marler's (1977) study, Bird A was raised by Bird B with the consequence that the call of Bird A was a mixture of the calls of Species A and Species B. Social experience may act on and alter an underlying biological process but cannot eliminate it. The result is a behavior that is due neither to socialization nor to biological tendencies. Similarly, children may experience a combined feeling of "tired/sad" and "angry/mad" as a consequence of the mother's mislabeling of the emotional state.

The third possibility comes from an inhibitory view. Children may really experience sadness, even though their mothers label them "angry/mad," but because of the labeling, sadness is inhibited through some mechanism like repression or denial; the primary emotional experience that emerges into consciousness is anger. According to this model, the children really are sad. That is, the children's behaviors express their true emotional experience, but they have inhibited this sadness through the mothers' socialization and instead feel angry. The task in psychotherapy is to remove the inhibitory effect and allow the children to feel their sadness.

A fourth model involves the substitution of experience rather than an inhibition. Through particular socialization processes, children may learn to interpret certain emotional states and experiences as anger rather than sadness. There is no inhibition of sadness. The sadness originally associated with the elicitor has not been altered through socialization but has been replaced by another experience. The psychotherapeutic technique would involve reeducating these children and teaching them that others experience different emotions in the same situation.

One or all of these models may be valid. The existing data do not allow the rejection of one in favor of another. The majority of the mothers in the maternal affect labeling study did not label their 1-year-old children's emotional behavior. Thus, other models are needed to address the question of how children's emotional states become related to emotional experiences in the absence of maternal labeling. The first model described earlier (the biological model) can be applied to this question as well as to the problem of mislabeling. Recall that in this model, the emotional experience is automatically connected to the emotional state and consequently is little affected by either incorrect labeling or the absence of labeling by the socializing agent. The absence of labeling, then, would not produce psychopathology, according to the biological model.

Another possibility is that if the social environment fails to provide children with appropriate labels for their emotional states, the children will be unable to label, or less able to recognize and thus to experience, their own internal states. In this case, psychotherapy might involve supplying the children with affect labels appropriate to their internal states and the circumstances eliciting those states, thereby "creating" a new emotional experience. The role of the therapist would not be to *reeducate* but to *educate* the child.

A final model states that even though mothers do not label their children's emotional behaviors, they nevertheless provide an interpretation and evaluation of children's emotional states through their nonverbal responses to children's emotional behaviors. In other words, children learn to interpret and evaluate, and thus to experience, their emotional states not only through the verbal labels provided by the social environment but also through the nonverbal behaviors of significant others. Indeed, it is possible that children rely on nonverbal behaviors as much as, if not more than, verbal affect labels to connect their emotional states with emotional experiences. According to this model, the failure of mothers to label their children's emotional behaviors may not result in psychopathology as long as their nonverbal responses to their children's emotional behavior are appropriate to the underlying emotional state of the children and the eliciting situation.

In summary, in the socialization model, society or culture, in the form of caregivers or significant others, may intervene in both emotional development and emotional behavior. First, society gives meaning to emotional expressions and, potentially, to emotional states. In biological models, expressions and states assume a one-to-one correspondence. Thus, the interpretation of emotional expressions may break that correspondence. In socialization models, the connection between expressions and states is not biologically established. Thus, the interpretation of emotional expression serves to create the connection. The relationship between states and experiences in the socialization model allows for the development of, as well as the alteration of, experience as a function of interpretation by others. The interpretation of others may affect emotional elicitors as well. Although little consideration has been given to this notion, the fact that some people may interpret an emotional elicitor as not fearful but as friendly immediately underscores the critical role of interpretation in all aspects of the emotional process.

To view emotion as a biological process independent of the social milieu and to view emotion as having meaning independent of social experience is to overlook the evolutionary history and adaptive significance of emotional behavior. The meaning of emotional behavior would seem to necessitate the view that the social context, through the interpretation of others, is a vital force in the ongoing emotional life of the organism. From a developmental perspective, the social context helps to define the consequence of the emotional process.

✕✕✕✕✕✕✕✕✕✕✕✕✕

The five socialization rules that have been addressed in the last two chapters reflect some important factors that must be considered in the study of emotional development. These feeling rules appear to play a significant role in the emotional life of children. One cannot argue that children's emotional states and experiences are unaffected by socialization processes and that therefore one need only study their biological origins. Nor can one consider socialization processes solely in terms of how socialization acts on a fixed and universal unfolding of emotional life. It may indeed be the case that socialization only affects (in part) biologically given aspects of emotion. Yet, socialization models are required to explain the creation and development of emotions from even the earliest time of life. By analyzing emotions into various components, both the universal and fixed biological rules governing emotional life and their interface with socialization processes may be considered.

It should not be surprising to discover, as has been the case in other areas of early development, that models depicting socialization and biology as separate factors accounting for different amounts of the variance in the emotional process actually explain very little of what happens in everyday life. Such models are probably fictitious. Rather, the inseparability of the biological and the socialization components should be stressed.

The view of emotional development described in Chapters 4, 5, 6, and 7 does not readily incorporate separate and independent roles for biological and socialization influences, even during the first stages of a child's life. The fact that parents of newborns already interpret their children's behavior in emotional terms and respond according to that interpretation must be considered in any account of emotional development. At the same time, however, the consistency in the appearance and development of emotions such as fear suggests that this process cannot be regarded as independent of maturation. The development of emotion is a complex process in which biological and socialization factors must interact. Finally, any model of emotional development and developmental psychopathology must be sensitive to children's individual differences. Such individual differences may be a function of temperament, the children's ontogenetic stage, and other individual abilities (e.g., cognition), as well as the cultural and family rules that govern emotional life.

8

The Measurement of Emotion

The relationships among theory, measurement, and results are often confused. Clearly, the measurement techniques not only of psychology but of science in general may affect dramatically the results obtained as well as the theories generated. The implications of this view are broad and suggest that the ideal of an absolute and independent truth, one separate from measurement and observer bias, is not only unattainable but should not even be expected (Lewis, 1982a).

To some degree, human observation and measurement may actually create the phenomena being studied. For instance, in quantum mechanics, the study of subatomic particles undermined the belief in a reality unaffected by human action. As Max Born wrote about the changes brought about by quantum mechanics, we have been

> taught that there exists an objective physical world, which unfolds itself according to immutable laws independent of us; we are watching this process like the audience watches a play in a theatre. . . . Quantum mechanics, however, interprets the experience gained in atomic physics in a different way. We may compare the observer of a physical phenomenon not with the audience of a theatrical performance, but with that of a football game where the act of watching, accompanied by applauding or hissing, has a marked influence on the speed and concentration of the players, and thus on what is watched. In fact, a better simile is life itself, where audience and actors are the same persons. It is the action of the experimentalist who designs the apparatus which determines essential features of the observations. Hence there is no objectively existing situation as was supposed to exist in classical physics. (Clark, 1972, p. 413)

Such a view should not discourage one but should lead to a greater appreciation of the connections among theory, measurement, and results.

In studying emotion, these connections are perhaps more complex than in other areas of psychology because the investigator is confronted with the measurement of the various aspects of emotion that were articulated previously. These aspects may require different measurement strategies. For instance, the measurement of emotional elicitors requires the observation of specific stimuli and contexts. It may also require the measurement of a subject's personal interpretation of these stimuli. On the other hand, the measurement of emotional receptors requires recording internal physiological processes in particular locations of the central or peripheral nervous systems. The measurement of emotional states focuses on changes in at least three systems of the body: the somatic nervous system, the central nervous system, and the autonomic nervous system. Finally, studying emotional experience requires the measurement of the organism's subjective state. Thus, the measurement of emotion is complicated by the number of different components that comprise the emotional system. The failure to specify which aspect is being measured can lead to much confusion.

Thus, to assume that the measurement of a physiological change in response to a specific elicitor represents the entire emotional activity is to neglect the other components of the emotion. It is likely to be the case that an emotional elicitor—that is, a particular stimulus selected by the experimenter—may not be the same emotional elicitor perceived or experienced by the subject. For example, a fearful stimulus, such as a mask, may be perceived as fearful only by some subjects. A concern only about the measurement of particular facial musculature changes without concern about the measurement of the emotional elicitor (in this case, the measurement of the subject's perception of the fearfulness of the stimulus) limits our understanding of emotional activity. Likewise, to assume that the measurement of CNS change is the measurement of emotional experience is to misrepresent the nature of the phenomenon being studied. The assumptions made about emotion and its various components may act as a restricting influence on what is measured and how it is measured.

Emotions as Private Acts

A distinction can be made at the level of emotional experience between public and private acts. The same distinction may be made for emotional states. It seems reasonable to assume that emotional states or experiences are public to the degree that a strong correspondence exists between observable behavior and the internal state or experience. Observable behavior refers to both overt behavior, such as facial, bodily, and vocal responses, and covert behavior that can be measured only through the use of instruments that monitor internal physiological changes. However, in some cases, emotional states and experiences may share little correspondence with observable behavior. In discussions of the socialization of emotion (see Chapters 6 and 7), and in discussions of public emotional behavior (Ekman, 1977; Goffman, 1959), there is evidence against a one-to-one correspondence between emotional states and experiences, and observable behavior. Indeed, the socialization practices of particular cultures may be predicated on altering or even modifying such correspondences.

How, then, do people come to recognize and respond to the emotions of others? Despite the private nature of these activities, there seem to be three ways in which the emotions of others might be known or studied: (1) introspection, (2) empathy, and (3) attribution.

Introspection

Introspection means individuals' personal reports about their internal processes and feelings. Although introspection has been renounced as a scientific method, it is interesting to note that at the turn of the century, when Wundt (1897) was advocating a public view of psychology as a "brass instrument science," he was privately working on the problem of introspection. Introspection suffers from all of the difficulties of subjective reports, not the least of which is the fact that naive subjects in general are not accurate reporters of external situations (Loftus, 1979). The use of sophisticated trained observers may eliminate some of the problem, however.

Whether or not subjective errors and biases can be eliminated from introspective methods, it is clearly the case that introspection has become the method of the experimenter (Lewis *et al.*, 1978). The experimenter constructs situations that are intended to elicit particular emotional responses. In order to design such experimental situations, it is necessary that the scientist introspect as to which situations are likely to produce which emotions. Landis's (1924) unpleasant laboratory experiments, such as chopping off the head of a live rat to elicit strong emotional response, or Ekman, Malmstron, and Friesen's (1971) showing of facial surgery for the purpose of eliciting surprise and disgust are representative of this particular use of introspection. One might think that there would be some inquiry into the relationship among the experimenter's introspection, the experimental situation, and the emotions elicited; however, in the very intense laboratory situations that have been used, it is assumed that the experimenter's introspection is accurate, and rarely is the validity of the experimenter's assumption tested.

Although children seem to learn early about the accepted relationships between particular situations and specific emotional responses (see Chapter 6), the assumption that a particular elicitor will result in a particular emotional state is predicated on the experimenter's personal introspection and may or may not correspond to subjects' experiences. The failure to investigate the subjects' perceptions and interpretations of the elicitor may cause investigators inadvertently to group together subjectively different elicitors and thus distort the meaning of the group response. Although many people have difficulty talking about emotions because of inexperience with and inhibitions about articulating private feelings, and because language itself is inadequate for conveying emotional nuances, introspection as a methodology is necessary for understanding emotional activity (Schwartz, 1982).

Empathy

A second way to know about people's emotional states or experiences is through empathy. *Empathy* can be defined as an emotional response to another's condition. It requires the ability to imagine oneself in another person's place and in that way to know what the person is thinking, feeling, or perceiving based on personal experiences in similar situations. True empathic ability enables one to *experience* the feelings of another person through thinking how one would feel oneself under similar circumstances. For example, an empathic response might be verbalized as "If I were in that situation, I would feel afraid."

The use of empathy would not appear to be a reliable method for the laboratory, although it is widely used in everyday experiences and is a field of study in its own right. The development of empathic behavior is of considerable interest (Ford, 1979). Some data indicate that children as young as 2 years can imagine themselves in the place of another and act in an empathic fashion (Borke, 1971; Masangkay et al., 1974). Most developmental psychologists, however, follow Piaget and Inhelder (1956) and envision empathic ability as proceeding along a more delayed developmental path (Flavell, 1974; Flavell et al., 1968; Laurendeau & Pinard, 1970).

Empathic behavior might make its appearance in laboratory settings in two indirect ways: (1) in designing situations to elicit specific emotions and (2) in interpreting behaviors. The first way, discussed previously, involves the process by which the experimenter selects situations to elicit specific emotions on the basis of personal criteria.

These criteria can take the form of knowing what people generally feel in certain situations, or imagining what one would feel if one were in a similar situation. Empathic responses may also be used in the interpretation of specific behaviors in specific contexts. An experimenter, for example, may observe a young child watching intently and cease moving or playing with toys as a stranger enters the room. Imagining how she might feel in this situation, the experimenter concludes that the child is afraid and therefore labels the child's emotional state as one of fear. In this situation, the child's behavior could be interpreted either as fear or as interest, but because the experimenter uses an incorrect empathic response, the child's state gets labeled fear.

Attribution

A third method used to assess the feelings of others is attribution. Through attribution, emotions are inferred by assigning a meaning to a complex set of events. Attribution assumes that there exists a set of behaviors in a particular context that one can use to infer what other people are experiencing. For example, there is a general consensus, at least in Western society, that young children who scream at the approach of a stranger are experiencing fear. Such an assumption can be derived from empathy or general knowledge. Both behavior and context are essential in attributing emotions to others. Since it is impossible to know whether a person is actually experiencing the emotion, however, it is necessary to settle for the statement, "acting as if. . . . "

Knowledge of both behavior and context is required before attributing a specific emotion to another person because, as we will discuss later, neither the behavior independent of the context nor the context independent of the behavior permits the identification of a particular emotional state or experience. This is the case for two reasons. First, a behavior such as crying may be elicited under extremely different circumstances and may reflect different emotional states. For example, crying at a funeral and crying at the unexpected appearance of a loved one do not reflect similar internal states. Second, different behaviors may be elicited under very similar circumstances, i.e., the same situation may elicit different emotional behaviors and states. For example, when a mother returns home after a brief absence, her child may run to greet her on one occasion; yet, at another time, the same child may cry and run away on her return. Presumably, the same situation has elicited different emotions, joy and anger.

Emotions are public insofar as emotional expressions are observable and insofar as the socialization process fosters correct attributions (i.e., attributions that match the internal feelings of other persons) or accurate empathic responses. The implication of these conclusions for a measurement system is important: any measurement task that requires an observer entails the same processes that observers use in everyday experience to infer emotions. At this point in the study of emotion, investigators must be satisfied with a measurement system that cannot inform them about internal states in a direct way. In the everyday observation of emotions, two classes of events guide both attributive and empathic processes. In order for one to infer emotional states and experiences, both select behaviors and the particular contexts in which these behaviors occur must be considered simultaneously. In a similar fashion, both behaviors and contexts are necessary to measure specific emotions. The study of emotion must take both of these factors into account.

The Meaning of Behavior

A review of the literature on emotion indicates that for children of all ages, there is no single behavior that can serve as a necessary and sufficient reference for any emotion. Even crying, perhaps the most likely candidate, fails to meet this requirement, since crying may signal feelings of anger, sadness, or even joy. The inhibition of activity can also indicate different states, such as thoughtfulness, attention, or fear. A given stimulus that initially evokes smiling and laughter may, with repeated presentations, evokes crying. Indeed, on different occasions, some stimuli may produce a number of different responses in a particular child (Sroufe et al., 1974).

The patterning of facial expressions has been regarded as a behavioral system that has a one-to-one correspondence with specific emotional states (Ekman et al., 1972; Ekman & Friesen, 1975; Izard, 1971, 1977; Tomkins, 1962). Yet, it must be recognized that individual differences, socialization processes, and cultural display rules act in such a fashion as to mask the face, thus undermining the unique relationship between certain facial expressions and internal states. Perhaps the most likely time for the existence of a one-to-one correspondence between facial expressions and states is in the early period of life before socialization processes have had a chance to alter the meaning of expression. However, cultural and individual differences are already apparent, even at the beginning of life, making a one-to-one correspondence difficult to demonstrate (Caudill & Weinstein, 1969; Freedman, 1974).

As was noted in Chapter 5, the relationship between emotional expression and state is complex. The relationship may involve a developmental history in which expressions and states are unrelated at first because of the immaturity of the child, become related as a consequence of biological and social forces, and then become unrelated as a function of the socialization of expression.

Finally, when other response modes are blocked, facial expressions may take on an attenuated or exaggerated meaning. Thus, for example, children unable to run away from a stranger may show more fear in their faces than children who are able to move away. Thus, even if the face is used to measure emotions early in childhood, a simple correspondence between expression and state is difficult to infer. It may be safer to assume that there is little correspondence between a single response and a particular emotion.

If such an analysis is correct, then perhaps patterns of interrelated responses instead of specific responses should be studied. Such a complex set of responses might include measures of facial, vocal, bodily, and physiological activities. Unfortunately, few studies have looked at more than a single response system. Typically, studies of emotional behavior focus either on physiological responses or on facial responses. Although there are exceptions, which will be discussed later, researchers, for the most part, have used discrete responses to assess children's emotions.

Since behaviors may not necessarily correspond to specific emotional states, some investigators have focused on emotion systems (e.g., Bischof, 1975; Bretherton & Ainsworth, 1974). Emotion systems are regarded as uniquely organized sets of responses integrated within the nervous system of the organism. Each system is thought to be functionally independent of other systems in terms of the stimuli that elicit it and the neural structures that subsume it.

Unfortunately, the systems approach has its own pitfalls. Most of the data on this topic suggest that no single system independent of other systems is elicited by a class of events. For example, it has been postulated that attachment behaviors constitute an attachment system (Ainsworth et al., 1978). However, stimuli that activate the attachment system also are likely to activate exploration, affiliation, and even fear systems as well (Bretherton & Ainsworth, 1974; Bronson, 1972; Sroufe et al., 1974). Other examples of the interdependence of emotion systems abound. For example, studies of stranger fear during infancy illustrate well the evocation of multiple systems. The approach of strangers is likely to evoke smiling and prolonged gaze behaviors, which suggest the activation of interest and affiliation systems, as well as gaze aversion, lip quivering, and crying behaviors, which implicate the activation of a fear or aversion system (Feinman & Lewis, in press; Haviland & Lewis, 1975).

Thus, an emotion system may be no better at imparting specific meanings than are single response measures independent of either the subject's personal report or the experimenter's knowledge of the stimulus event. Nevertheless, given the obvious failure of single responses to serve as meaningful markers for emotional states, patterns of responses and the use of multiple response measures may offer the best solution to determining the relationship between behaviors and internal states or experiences.

Before examining in detail the different response modalities that have been used to measure emotions, two important measurement issues should be addressed. These concern (1) differences in patterns of behavior observed as a function of individuals, groups, and developmental processes and (2) the distinction between the occurrence of an emotional response and its intensity.

Individual, Group, and Developmental Differences

The measurement problem is made increasingly complex by the fact that patterns of emotional behavior may differ among groups of individuals, among members of the same group, and even within the same individual at different times. Genetic and developmental factors, cognitive and motor abilities, and cultural experiences, as well as immediate antecedent events, may all act to alter the structure of response patterns in an individual.

Differences in socialization practices as a function of children's gender may result in strikingly different patterns of emotional response for boys and girls. For example, if motor activity is discouraged in girls but encouraged in boys, one would expect girls and boys to differ in response patterns that use the large muscles of the body. When faced with a fear stimulus, boys may run away, or at least use gross muscles as part of their fear response, whereas girls may rely on other behaviors to express fear, such as facial and vocal responses. It is not that girls are incapable of large muscle activity, but it may not be part of their fear repertoire if the socialization process has lessened the likelihood of its occurrence.

Genetic differences also may contribute to the responses comprising a particular system. For example, potential group differences among individuals in temperament variables have been identified (Freedman, 1974; Thomas & Chess, 1977; Wolff, 1977), especially in reactivity to external stimuli. It is possible that individuals differ genetically in the amount of stress they experience as a consequence of an intense stimulus (Buss & Plomin, 1975).

Developmental differences are particularly salient to a discussion of the meaning of behavior, since the capacities critical to the expression of emotion themselves may vary with age (Lewis & Starr, 1979). How can physical withdrawal serve as a measure of fear in children too young to crawl? Is gaze aversion an index of fear in infants too young to walk but an index of distraction or lack of interest in toddlers? Does a given behavior or a set of behaviors maintain a consistent relationship with the underlying state or experience over age, or is a more fluid combination of behaviors, open to transformation over time, required in order to infer a particular emotion (Lewis, 1967). Currently, there is insufficient information to answer these questions. Developmental inquiry in general, however, must recognize that various alternatives are possible.

Thus, although the underlying emotional state or experience may remain constant across the life span, behavior(s) in its service may change as a result of developmental processes. In this way, no single behavior over time serves as a sufficient marker for the emotional state. Nevertheless, it may serve as a referent at a particular time. Such an analysis suggests that patterns of responses or even psychometric factors are critical in tracing the course of development. It is possible that the underlying state may be reflected by the changes in a class of behaviors undergoing transformation as they constitute a particular factor (Emmerich, 1966; Lewis & Starr, 1979). Alternatively, some continuity in emotional behaviors may exist over time, although the underlying structure that they serve may not remain constant. Crying is a good example: we cry throughout our lives, but we cry in early childhood and in later life for different emotional reasons. Such problems in measurement are perhaps minimized by studying adults of a single culture or of one gender, as is sometimes done. However, any discussion of the development and measurement of emotion and of individual differences in expression necessitates a careful consideration of such issues.

Response Intensity

In an earlier discussion, a distinction was made between transient and enduring emotional states. The former were considered "emotions" and the latter "moods" (see Chapter 2). In both cases, the issue of intensity is of critical concern. It may be said that the more intense an emotion is, the more likely it is to be related to (or to become) an emotional mood. Thus, a person who responds with intense fear to a fear elicitor may feel fear more readily another time and may be afraid for longer periods of time and over more fear situations. The single fear response evolves into a fearful mood.

The failure to measure intensity may preclude a study of the relationship between particular emotional responses and moods. Since the measurement of moods requires, by definition, multiple and prolonged observations of emotional behaviors (see Chapter 2), information about the relationship between response intensity and frequency of occurrence is critical to this measurement.

The measurement issues regarding the intensity of emotional behavior have been only partially explored. Traditional measurement techniques often do not provide a way to measure intensity directly; rather, they assess intensity in terms of the frequency or the duration of a particular response. Intensity has also been assessed through physiological measures. More reactive heart-rate increases, for example, may be associated with greater emotional intensity. Although the issue of emotional intensity is occasionally addressed in theoretical discussions of emotion, either in terms of arousal or as one dimension of emotion (see Chapter 3), the limited response repertoires sampled in empirical studies and the failure to observe patterns of responses have impeded the study of response intensity.

An exception exists, however, in the case of children's responses to fear-eliciting stimuli. In an attempt to articulate differences in the intensity of an emotional state or experience, a distinction has been made in the research literature between wariness and fear (Bronson, 1972; Rheingold & Eckerman, 1973; Sroufe, 1977). For example, screaming and crying in response to the approach a stranger seem to be more intense manifestations of fear in young children than the cessation of playing and movement accompanied by "sobering" facial expressions. It is important in measuring fear to distinguish between these two classes of behavior. If both sets of behavior are judged to represent fear and no distinctions are made between levels of fear, any individual variations in fear expressions and states will be missed.

The intensity of an emotional response may, of course, have less to do with the specific characteristics of a situation and/or a socialization process than with the arousal thresholds of individual children. Such variations in response thresholds are one dimension of temperament (Thomas et al., 1963). As has already been stated, the intensity of a response, temperament, personality, and mood are probably highly related. Thus, response intensity, as a reflection of either mood or a predisposition toward the development of a particular mood, becomes a critical measurement problem.

Components of Emotional Behavior

The measurement of emotional behavior requires the consideration of a variety of possible response modalities. Although most studies have focused on facial expressions, this exclusive concern with facial expressions as a measure of emotion is rather perplexing. While studies of facial expressions are a part of the Darwinian tradition, Darwin (1872) himself described not only specific facial expressions related to different emotions but postures and vocal behaviors as well. Thus, the exclusive use of facial expressions may represent a historical error. Clearly, a measurement system that considers behaviors in addition to facial expressions is necessary.

Ricciuti and Poresky (1972) have proposed a dimensional analysis of emotion similar to those conceived by others who are less restrictive in their views of what responses constitute appropriate measures of emotion (e.g., Schlosberg, 1952, 1954). Specifically, Ricciuti and Poresky argued that three interrelated components or dimensions are necessary in measuring emotions. These dimensions are hedonic tone, directionality, and arousal.

The first dimension, hedonic tone, measures the pleasant–unpleasant aspect of emotion and is manifested in its clearest form in facial and vocal behaviors. For example, pleasurable aspects of emotion may be reflected in behaviors such as smiling, whereas unpleasant feelings may be conveyed by frowning or crying.

Directionality, or approach–withdrawal, is a second dimension of emotion. This dimension is distinguished as stimulus-seeking, -maintaining, or -enhancing, on the one hand, versus stimulus-terminating or -avoiding, on the other. Directionality may be best reflected in postures or movements that are directed either toward or away from the elicitor. This class of behaviors has received little attention in the study of children's emotion, which is surprising, since bodily movements communicate considerable amounts of information (Argyle, 1975; Buck, 1982; Weitz, 1974, 1979). When children run away from a stranger and hide behind their mother neither facial nor physiological responses can be used to attribute fear, but the locomotive cue is quite sufficient. In conditions where mobility is restricted because children are either too young to crawl, are restrained in some way, or are physically handicapped, postural cues may be used to assess directionality. For example, a novel toy placed in front of a child in a high chair may cause the child to pull away his or her hands or push away from the object if the child is afraid (Schaffer et al., 1972).

Finally, an emotional reaction may include arousal characteristics, reflected by internal physiological changes and by changes in activity and motility levels, response intensities, and the number of response systems activated. In laboratory studies of emotion, arousal may be measured directly by monitoring changes in physiological responses, such as heart rate acceleration and deceleration. Although many advances have been made in the measurement of physiological parameters of emotion and motivation (Black, 1970; Grossman, 1979; Levi, 1975; Pribram, 1980), little success has been achieved in identifying responses that are unique to specific emotions. However, such measures may reveal changes in the general level of arousal associated with the activation of any emotion. In naturalistic settings, where it is not feasible to monitor physiological responses, changes in infants' overt activity levels as well as changes in the intensities of their responses may be used to assess the arousal dimension of emotion.

In any measurement system of emotion, then, it is desirable to obtain facial, vocal, bodily, and physiological indexes of behavior. The research literature on each of these response modalities is reviewed in the following sections.

Facial Expressions

The study of emotion as expression was pioneered by Darwin (1872). His work on facial expressions and bodily posturing as signals of emotion in both humans and animals has been substantiated for the most part (Ekman, 1973b). Much of Darwin's work has been carried forward by animal ethologists, although there is a growing interest in the facial expressions of human beings and their measurement (e.g., Ekman et al., 1972; Izard, 1971, 1977; Tomkins, 1962, 1963). There is evidence that many facial expressions have the same meanings in most human societies (Eibl-Eibesfeldt, 1970; Ekman, 1972, 1973a) and may be found in blind children and children who are both blind and unable to speak (Eibl-Eibesfeldt, 1973; Thompson, 1941). These studies suggest that there are certain invariances in nonverbal expressions that occur across the human species.

Studies of the facial expressions of infants and young children have a long history and include baby biographies with accounts of emotional behavior (Dennis, 1936), descriptions of gross behavior (Watson, 1924), and adults' impressions of infant expressions (Bridges, 1930, 1932).

Recently, attempts have been made to construct a systematic mapping of infants' and young children's faces (Demos, 1982; Izard, 1979b; Oster, 1978; Oster & Ekman, 1978; Young & Décarie, 1977), similar to the ethograms developed for nonhuman primates (Chevalier-Skolnikoff, 1973), older children (Blurton-Jones, 1971), and adults (Ekman & Friesen, 1978; Grant, 1969).

The measurement of facial expressions is difficult, however. Facial expressions are easily altered by suggestion, and even young children learn early in life the display rules for expressing emotions (Saarni, 1979a,b, 1980; see also Chapter 6). Another problem arises when a single response is used to infer an emotional state. Thus, smiling alone, without a careful consideration of other aspects of the face, or even other bodily responses, cannot reliably be used as the indicator of a particular emotion.

Very global behaviors, without careful coding systems, are sometimes used in studies of fear. Such behaviors may be distorted by the investigator's expectation of what ought to be seen. This may be labeled as a case of *selecting the signal.* Indeed, one of the issues in the measurement of emotion focuses on the use of a holistic versus a constructive approach (Lewis *et al.*, 1978). In the holistic approach, the experimenter rates the subject using broad categorizations. In the constructive approach, the experimenter rates each section of the face separately with facial patterns constructed from the individual parts. In both cases, facial patterns are obtained, the latter method having the advantage of avoiding contamination by both general impressions as well as a reliance on one aspect of the face (e.g., the mouth) in the determination of the nature of the emotion.

Some facial expressions seem to be more easily identified than others, the more easily identified ones being enjoyment and surprise and the less easily identifiable ones being pity, fear, and rage. Even children can usually identify expressions fairly accurately, meeting adult standards somewhere around the age of 14 (Oster & Ekman, 1978). However, without knowing the context of the particular facial expression, observers may have difficulty interpreting what they see. Bridges (1930) and Sherman (1927a,b) have demonstrated that without situational information, the perception of infants' emotions is not reliable, although it is above chance for most emotions.

Bodily and Vocal Expressions

Much more is known about facial responses than is known about other expressions of emotion, especially in infants and young children.

Nonverbal expressions involving parts of the body other than the face have been studied primarily in animals and in human adults. The use of bodily postures in adults to communicate internal states has received some attention in the nonverbal communication literature (Argyle, 1975; Mehrabian, 1968, 1969, 1972; Scheflen, 1964, 1972). Approximately 1,000 different postures are anatomically possible, although each culture selects and uses only a limited repertoire (Hewes, 1955). At a distance, bodily postures may have more signal value than changes in facial musculature, inasmuch as they are larger, more visible, and subject to less control (Ekman & Friesen, 1974; Ekman, Friesen, & Scherer, 1976). Postural responses can be observed in animals with basically undifferentiated facial musculature. In dogs, tail wagging and tail-between-the-legs are certainly responded to as if they reflect different emotions. Across species, differences in the meaning of a response must be considered as well. For example, the movement of a dog's tail is regarded as an indication of pleasure, but in a cat, it may signal displeasure. These everyday examples call attention to two issues: first, bodily responses are good indicators of emotions; and second, no single response can be considered sufficient to infer a particular state.

Infants' bodily responses have received little attention in the nonverbal communication literature. Yet, it is not difficult to distinguish bodily responses of tension (e.g., shaking arms and legs or clenching fists) from responses of relaxation (e.g., resting or playing quietly). Postural movements toward and away from an object may signal an emotional state, as may gestural movements such as raising one's arms or hitting and throwing. In a recent study, we found that mothers of 1-year-olds frequently used children's bodily responses to infer and label emotional states. For example, throwing objects or kicking were used by mothers to infer anger (see Chapter 7).

In the absence of facial behavior, bodily cues may become particularly important in determining the underlying emotional state. Consider children who run away from a stranger and hide behind their mother. Neither facial nor physiological responses can be observed. However, the postural and locomotive cues are sufficient to label the state as one of fear or shyness. In conditions where mobility is restricted because children are either motorically immature or unable to escape, as from a high chair, postural cues may carry much of the emotional message. The response of children when a familiar toy is placed on the surface of the high chair or a friend approaches often takes the form of reaching or leaning toward the object or person. Proxemics, a topic of investigation in the nonverbal communication literature (e.g., Goffman, 1963; Hall, 1968; Scheflen, 1975), has also received little attention in the infancy literature. Yet, in everyday encounters, behaviors such as following and clinging tightly to a caregiver are used as indexes of emotional states.

Another category of behavior that can be used in determining an emotional state is vocal expression without the cues provided by formal language (Davitz & Davitz, 1959; Scherer, Koivumaki, & Rosenthal, 1972). Tomkins (1962, 1963) has argued that an important aspect of facial expression is the concomitant use of vocal behavior: laughing when happy, crying when sad, growling when angry, and groaning when impassioned. Vocal expressions of emotion in infancy and early childhood have been little studied, although several researchers looked at crying (Frodi, Lamb, Leavitt, & Donovan, 1978; Lester, 1978; Wolff, 1969; Zeskind & Lester, 1978). Recently, Scherer (1979, 1982) has developed techniques for investigating the audio frequencies of vocalization as a measure of emotional state. Such studies are uncommon, however.

Physiological Indexes

The James (1884, 1890) hypothesis that somatic and visceral activity produces the conscious feeling of emotion gradually gave way to Cannon's (1927, 1931) hypothesis that activation through discharge from a subcortical structure to the cerebral cortex determines emotion (see Chapter 3). Both theories recognize two aspects of emotion: (1) a physiological event (visceral, muscular, or neural) and (2) the conscious feelings of this change. The focus of research generated by these theories changed from an interest in the felt change to a study of the physiological manifestations of the change (Black, 1970; Fehr & Stern, 1970; Levi, 1975).

The focus on the ANS and sympathetic activity led to the use of the galvanic skin response (GSR) as a physiological measure of emotion or activation (Sternbach, 1966). Numerous studies were performed to determine whether subjects would be "activated" by different sorts of tasks, including electrical shock (Seward & Seward, 1934), free association (Jones & Wechsler, 1928), pleasant and unpleasant odors (Shock & Coombs, 1937), and various laboratory conditions, including loud noises, burning oneself with a lighted match, eating candy, and quizzes (Bayley, 1928; Patterson, 1930). In general, the "stronger" the stimulus, the shorter the latency and the more extreme the GSR (Strongman, 1978).

Other peripheral measures of ANS activity used to study emotion and activation include blood pressure, heart rate (HR), and respiration. The history of the use of blood pressure and HR is as long as that of

GSR. For the most part, the earlier findings indicated a consistency in the pattern of ANS activity; namely, during arousal all ANS systems change. In the early 1950s, Lacey, Batemen, and Van Lehn (1953) reported that the autonomic nervous system does indeed respond to experimentally imposed stress "as a whole" in the sense that all autonomically innervated structures exhibit equal increments or decrements of function.

Further investigation, however, revealed differences in response specificity as a function of the organism's transaction with its environment. Thus, while GSR was shown to be relatively undifferentiated in terms of tasks requiring the organism to "take in" or exclude information, HR deceleration seemed to be more differentiated. Lacey *et al.* (1963) demonstrated that HR deceleration was a concomitant of the taking in of information (e.g., attending), whereas HR acceleration was related to external stimulus rejections, such as the solution of mental arithmetic problems (Steele & Lewis, 1968). This differential HR response appeared to hold across a wide age range. Continuing research on HR changes has raised an important issue concerning the relationship between the CNS and the ANS. Lacey and his associates argued for a more immediate relationship, while others believe that HR changes are more related to general bodily quiescence than to a CNS–ANS relationship (Obrist, Webb, Stutter, & Howard, 1970).

The physiological research literature indicates a shift away from a focus on emotional responses *per se* to a more general focus on ANS reactivity to stimulation in general. Overall, the studies tend to be restricted to situations that the experimenter judges to elicit stress or attention.

While it was originally thought that different emotional states might be associated with different patterns of physiological response, the data provide little support for such a contention (Lacey & Lacey, 1970). There has been little success in differentiating the various emotions through the use of physiological responses or response patterning, although the intensity of emotion may be related to the intensity of the physiological response. Whether the failure to detect any physiological response patterning in emotion resides in the methods used or in the theory itself must be determined by future research and technological advances. Theories based on the notion of a general arousal state in combination with the subject's cognitive evaluation of that state raise the possibility that there may be no set of specific physiological responses corresponding to discrete emotions (Schachter & Singer, 1962).

With few exceptions (e.g., Campos & Johnson, 1966), most of the research using physiological indexes of emotional expression in infants and young children has centered on a single response, HR change. Following Lacey's work on HR change as a function of organisms' intended transaction with their environment, Kagan and Lewis (1965) and Lewis *et al.* (1966) demonstrated that HR deceleration is an important concomitant of attending in infants. Subsequent research on the HR response suggests that across a large age range, HR deceleration is related to taking in and attending to external stimulation when the organism is in an alert state (Graham & Jackson, 1970; Lewis, 1975). Moreover, the level of HR deceleration seems to be directly related to the degree of attention, which affects performance on a subsequent task (Lewis, 1974). If attention is related to emotional states such as curiosity and exploration, the demonstration of a change in HR response associated with attention provides some evidence of an indirect relationship between emotion and physiological responses.

In addition to attention, investigators have measured HR changes in infants in the visual cliff situation. The finding that 9-month-old infants show HR acceleration when placed over the high side of the cliff has been interpreted to indicate fear, although no behavioral manifestations of that fear may be evident (Schwartz, Campos, & Baisel, 1973). In an earlier study using 55-day-old infants, HR deceleration was obtained when infants were placed over the deep side of the cliff (Campos, Langer, & Krowitz, 1970). The deceleration in this case might reflect infants' attention—rather than fear—at being off the ground. In general, physiological measures of emotion have not received the attention they might. No doubt the requirements of elaborate equipment and complex data reduction have contributed to a lack of interest in their use.

Measurement Methods and Their Relationships

Basically, three methodological approaches have been used to study emotion. Two of the methodologies derive from James's (1884) hypothesis: (1) introspection, or the direct questioning of subjects about their feelings, and (2) physiological measures of emotion. The third methodology emerges from the work of Darwin (1872), who emphasized the surface aspects of emotion (facial and bodily) rather than a feeling or physiological response. Although a long tradition of research exists for each of these measurement methods, some of which are reviewed above, very little work has been done using more than one measurement method (Lewis *et al.*, 1978). While studies of emotion are generally restricted to the use of a single method, at times two or more measures may be taken within the same method (e.g., HR change and GSR). In

the following sections, the use of more than one methodology to examine emotional responses is discussed.

Introspection and Facial-Bodily Expressions

It is difficult to find any studies in which facial or bodily expressions of emotion and subjective accounts are examined concurrently
(Schwartz & Weinberger, 1980). Introspection is used, for example, in
studies in which subjects are asked to pose for photographs by imagining a situation in which they feel the emotion that they are supposedly
expressing. The investigator, however, seldom questions whether the
subject actually acts on the suggestion or whether this approach actually
improves the pose. Introspection is an instruction, not a condition of
the study.

Another experimental condition that uses some form of introspection was discussed previously. It involves the process through which
the experimenter creates a condition and measures the subjects' facial
or bodily responses. Although the condition is assumed to be emotional
based on the introspection of the experimenter, it is necessary to find
out how the subjects view the manipulation and to relate their subjective reports to the other measures obtained.

In infancy, introspection is not a relevant methodology, since infants are not capable of self-report. Yet, introspection on the part of the
experimenter is widely used. Placing the infant on a visual cliff is
believed to induce fear in infants mature enough to "understand" that
this is a fearful situation. The physiological and facial responses that
occur in this situation are assumed to be concomitants of fear. Relying
on the introspection of the investigator in designing studies of emotion
is not an unreasonable procedure. However, caution must be taken,
since the assumption that children will react with the same emotion
as the experimenter may be faulty, especially in the case of young
organisms who certainly cannot categorize their experiences as adults
do.

The possibility exists that even if infants exhibit emotional responses similar to those of adults, there may be little relationship between the expression and the feeling. This relationship may develop
as a part of children's socialization experiences. The caregiver's responses may be the causal event relating expressions to feelings (see
Chapters 5, 6, and 7). Thus, the integration of measurement methods,
particularly those using facial expression and physiological response,
takes on a special significance in the study of emotional development.
The lack of any introspection or self-report on the part of infants sug-

gests that careful attention must be given to the relationships among the other response systems available for study.

Introspection and Physiological Indexes

Although in recent years many advances have been made in the measurement of the physiological and biochemical parameters of emotion (Black, 1970; Fehr & Stern, 1970; Grings & Dawson, 1978; Levi, 1975), there has been little progress in identifying responses that are specific to particular emotions. Most research continues to focus on the physiological parameters of stress and arousal without attempting to be more specific about emotions. An interesting study has been reported by Siminov (1969). In this study, actors were asked to imagine being shocked with electrical stimulation, and their physiological responses were measured. The results revealed that a high degree of similarity existed between the physiological responses that accompanied the imagined shock and the physiological responses produced by a real shock. If the introspection of the experimenter is considered, there is a wide variety of studies looking at the physiological indexes of emotion-producing situations (Hamburg, Hamburg, & Barchas, 1975). As previously noted, the relationship between the experimenter's perception of the situation and the subjects' feelings about the situation is relatively unexamined.

Facial-Bodily Expressions and Physiological Indexes

The relationship between facial and bodily expressions of emotion and physiological indexes has also been little attended to, with a few interesting exceptions. The results of one study show some relationship between HR acceleration and expressions of disgust, as well as HR deceleration and expressions of surprise, during a film of facial surgery (Ekman et al., 1971). Although there are unresolved difficulties with this study and the results are not conclusive, it represents the integrated approach needed in the study of emotion. Such studies are scarce.

Recent studies by Buck and his associates suggest that there may be an inverse relationship between naturally occurring facial expressions and physiological indexes such as HR or GSR (Buck, Savin, Miller, & Caul, 1972). Either one or the other was used by subjects to express emotion in relatively mild laboratory situations. These studies support an earlier suggestion by Jones (1950, 1960) that different individuals tend to be "internal" or "external" expressors of emotion.

Although facial and bodily behavior were not analyzed, Siminov

(1969) measured both voice intonation by spectral analysis and changes in HR and found that changes in voice intonation and HR were related to stress. The subjects in this study were Russian astronauts circling the earth and the moon.

Several studies in infancy have included concurrent measures of HR responses and facial expressions. Waters *et al.* (1975) found that wary infants (determined by facial expression) were more likely to exhibit HR acceleration than less wary infants. Campos *et al.* (1975) undertook a more extensive study of infants' cardiac and behavioral reactions to an approaching stranger when the mother was present and when she was absent. Unlike in the Waters *et al.* (1975) study, the investigators time-locked filmed records of the infants' facial responses to a polygraph writeout. Mean facial expressions and mean HR responses both showed covarying changes during distress. However, this result is not proof of a relationship between HR acceleration and distressed facial expressions; mean data are insufficient for this purpose. Although Campos *et al.* may have overstated the relationship between HR acceleration and fear, their time-locking and measurement procedures have contributed much to the study of faces and HR response.

A more recent study by Lewis *et al.* (1978) also explored the relationship between HR responses and facial expression on the approach of a stranger. The results of this study did not show a clear relationship between HR changes and facial responses when the data were examined on an individual subject basis. Upset, fearful faces were not associated with HR acceleration any more than were smiling, happy faces. In fact, the only relationship between facial expression and HR was between attentive faces and HR deceleration. This relationship confirms the findings from other studies dating back to the mid-1960s showing HR deceleration to be associated with attending to external events (Graham & Clifton, 1966; Kagan & Lewis, 1965; Lewis *et al.*, 1966). Thus, although a relationship between physiological indexes and facial expressions may yet be found, the existing data offer little support for such a contention.

Other Response Relationships

Not all combinations of response relationships have been considered. Nevertheless, one combination is of particular interest: the relationship between facial and bodily activities. Although the relationship between facial and bodily activity has not been documented, it is possible that facial and bodily responses are related to one another in an additive or substitutive fashion. For example, under intense fear, children may show both facial and bodily cues that indicate fear. On the other hand, children may "prefer" one set over the other. Indeed, as was suggested previously, it may be the case that the inability to use one modality may activate the use of the other. Facial expressions of fear may be intensified when children are prevented from escaping (Lewis, 1980). Thus, studies in which children cannot move away from an approaching stranger may find more facial expressions of fear than studies in which children can flee. This hypothesis seems reasonable if one of the functions of flight is to inform the stranger about the internal state of the organism. In the absence of this response, the approaching figure must be informed by other means, and facial expressions become a good alternative. In other words, the inability to express emotion through bodily movement may accentuate facial expressions. From a general systems point of view, the blockage of one set of behaviors from a larger set may serve to intensify the remaining set of behaviors.

The Concept of Synchrony

The search for the relationships among physiological measures of emotion has been a long one. For the better part of a century, many investigators have assumed that no true experience of emotion occurs without concomitant bodily changes. The latter are considered a reflection of the former. Except for studies of facial musculature based on the assumption that changes in facial musculature represent such bodily changes, there are few data confirming the consistency among the behaviors used to indicate emotion. Differential patterns of responses thought to indicate emotion have not been found.

In discussing synchrony, we focus on the relationship between ANS responses and emotional behavior, since more work has been conducted in this area. To date, little relationship has been found between ANS functioning and emotional behavior. The lack of a relationship is not surprising in light of the findings that within the ANS itself, there is relatively little response specificity and covariation (Lacey & Lacey, 1970). Given that the responses within the ANS do not covary in a predictable way, it would be unusual to find a high correspondence between emotional behavior and ANS activity. The relationship between cardiac deceleration and attention in infants and young children seems to be one instance in which a relationship exists (Lewis & Goldberg, 1969a).

If there is little empirical support for a notion of general synchrony among response systems, is the notion of synchrony useful? The lack of synchrony found in many studies may be explained in several ways. First, synchrony may not exist, in which case it would not be possible to obtain synchrony in experimental studies.

Second, measurement problems may confound the search for synchrony. It may be that once the measurement of facial expressions and physiological responses is refined, a stronger relationship between the two will emerge. The measurement of facial expressions in infants and young children is still in its early stages of development. In the last two decades, the study of the cardiac response has received much attention. Sampling procedures, base-level effects, and state changes have been explored. This information should be valuable to a study of synchrony. Even if adequate procedures existed for measuring facial expressions and physiological changes, important issues must be faced concerning the measurement of their covariation. Group averaging may mask the phenomenon, and issues of adequate time-locking need further consideration (Lewis et al., 1978). It is still too early to conclude that there is no relationship between an ANS response and a behavioral manifestation of emotion.

Third, asynchrony may be a structural property of the nervous system. Both synchrony and asynchrony may be essential for efficient functioning; organisms need both to initiate and to terminate behavior. It is this principle and its accommodation that may influence synchrony (Lewis et al., 1978). While synchrony might be efficient in any action (i.e., all response systems acting together provide the most powerful response set), it would not be efficient for stopping that response or action. If all response systems are equally activated and covary when activated, there are no response systems left to stop the ongoing behavior.

It is hypothesized that a critical feature of the nervous system is its ability both to activate and to terminate ongoing behavior. Hull (1943) discussed the notion of retroactive inhibition, and more recently, Solomon and Corbitt (1974) have proposed a competitive or opponent-process theory of appetitive behavior. Both these theories are designed to explain how organisms stop behaving as well as how they behave. It is possible that the asynchrony within the ANS itself and between the ANS and other behavioral systems serves to stop the organism's ongoing behavior. The lack of covariation, therefore, is the structural process that creates "drag" on the responses of the organism, thereby allowing for the termination of ongoing behavior. The amount of drag or, conversely, the efficiency of a response may be a function of the number of covarying responses: the more drag or efficiency needed, the more the covarying or noncovarying responses. Thus, in any response-producing situation, there is a competitive system: response synchrony or covariation for more efficient behavior and response asynchrony for the termination of ongoing behavior.

Fourth, asynchrony may be observed when the level of stimulation is low. In situations where the need to act predominates, in cases of extreme stress, or in cases where efficient processing is required, more responses may covary. These cases may be exemplified by situations of emergency where survival is in danger and states of high arousal are necessary. Under these conditions, covariation may be more likely. That is, in high-arousal conditions, response sets may be activated faster and may take longer to terminate. Termination may be effected by the general inhibitory activity of responses, a kind of neuronal fatigue. In everyday situations, characterized by low levels of or little arousal, response sets are more likely not to covary (see Chapters 5 and 6).

Attentive behavior, which could be placed at a moderate level on an arousal continuum, would be expected to reflect some relationship between two response systems. Synchrony and covariation of response systems are a function of the competitive need for action and for cessation of action and depend on the nervous system's resolution of this conflict, with high states of arousal leading to more covariation. The results of studies measuring infants' HR responses and facial expressions (Campos et al., 1975; Lewis et al., 1978) make sense from this perspective. Very frightened infants, left alone without their mothers and being approached by a stranger in a strange manner, are in a high state of arousal; facial expression, motoric activity, and HR are more likely to show a high correspondence. When the infant's mother is physically close, an approaching stranger is less arousing and therefore causes less covariation among the response systems. This theory of synchrony suggests that empirical studies may find different degrees of synchrony depending on the situations used.

Although there are few data on the topic, it does not seem unlikely that a fifth source of asynchrony involves individual differences in nervous system synchrony. Some organisms, as a function of some combination of temperament, nervous system efficiency, and socialization, may show more covariation of systems than others. Prideaux (1920) found that adults who showed large and/or frequent GSR also showed less overt emotional behavior than less GSR-responsive individuals. Similar findings have been reported by Buck et al. (1972, 1974). This lack of synchrony has been used to categorize individuals into "internalizers," those who express emotions internally, as in GSR, and "externalizers," those who express emotions externally, as in facial changes (Jones, 1950, 1960). Individual differences in arousal level may also affect synchrony, since arousal level may act as a mediating factor, organizing both the behavioral manifestations, such as facial expression, and ANS responding: the higher the arousal level, the more synchrony among systems. Thus, individual differences in arousal level and the ease of evocation may be related to synchrony.

Age differences may constitute a special case. According to the developmental theory described in Chapter 5, one would expect to find more synchrony prior to socialization (and the advent of deception). That is, socialization pressures may disengage facial expressions from somatic responses. There may be age differences in synchrony that are not a function of socialization but a function of arousal level. As we stated earlier, there may be a relationship between synchrony and arousal level: greater synchrony corresponds to higher arousal levels. It may be that at particular points in development, infants show higher arousal levels in response to certain situations. These higher arousal levels may facilitate the synchrony and result in greater covariation of behavioral responses with ANS functioning. Thus, in a situation designed to evoke fear (e.g., the stranger-approach situation), infants may be more aroused, although not necessarily more fearful. This heightened arousal should result in a higher covariation between facial expression and HR responses.

A final possible reason for the lack of synchrony found in many studies of emotion is related to a concept of mixed emotions. It is possible, and even highly likely, that situations do not elicit "pure" emotions (see Chapter 6). Rather, mixtures of several emotions may occur, the consequence of which might be the activation of competing sets of emotional responses. These competing sets of responses underlying mixed emotions may appear as asynchrony in the system.

At this point, many issues concerning the measurement of emotional behavior remain unanswered. Investigators do not know whether one set of responses reflects an emotional state better than another. Nor do they understand the relationships among sets of responses or how they change as a function of development and culture. Clearly, as children develop, new responses appear. In addition, as children continue to develop, mature forms of expressions change. As new responses are added, old ones may become inappropriate. For example, in Western cultures, crying is acceptable in the the opening years of life; however, it is discouraged in preschool children. Thus, the meaning of crying as an index of emotion will change over time (Lewis, 1967). Finally, there are probably vast individual differences in the responses that children use to express emotions. It appears that different children use different responses or combinations of responses. While the source of these differences has not been determined, many probably originate in temperament differences or in different familial patterns of interaction.

Stimulus or Contextual Meaning

The argument has been made that the attribution of emotion requires a knowledge of both the behaviors elicited and their context. The matrix made up of both behaviors and contexts provides the means for referencing particular internal states. Judgments concerning emotions cannot be made from a knowledge of responses in and of themselves. For example, although laughing reflects a joyous state most of the time, the context in which this behavior is expressed is critical for making a correct inference about the internal state or experience. Being told whether the context is the hearing of a good joke or of the news that one's friend just died constitutes an essential component of the meaning of any facial or vocal expression. Adults know and children soon learn (see Chapter 6) that it is sometimes important to hide "real" feelings and to substitute false cues. Thus, laughter at a boss's joke may mask the true feeling of boredom or even disgust.

Dissociation between facial, bodily, and vocal behaviors and internal states may be one of the primary goals of socialization. As a result, cultural differences are observed. For example, Japanese children are taught quite early the difference between public and private acts. This teaching undoubtedly affects their public displays of emotion (Ekman, 1972). Unfortunately, little effort has been devoted to analyzing the situational contexts of emotional behaviors from a developmental perspective. While some progress has been made in increasing the level of complexity of behavioral analyses through the use of interactional techniques (e.g., Cairns, 1979; Lewis & Lee-Painter, 1974; Sackett, 1979), less effort has been directed toward situational analyses (Clarke-Stewart, 1974; Lewis & Freedle, 1973, 1977; Parke, 1979a).

This lack of interest in and information about contexts was acceptable as long as only a few situations were used to study behavior. These situations were laboratory-based, for the most part, and the behaviors observed were assumed to be impervious to situational variations. Thus, for example, experimenters generally believed that seeking help, approval, or affection (behaviors associated with dependency) could be measured in any situation; individual differences in the amount of behavior shown were assumed to reflect individual traits or characteristics. Likewise, little attention was paid to the dimensions of the context used to measure the attachment relationship between mother and infant, since attachment was assumed to reflect an underlying relationship between the dyad, a relationship that remains invariant across situations (something akin to a trait). In the past decade, however, concerns have been expressed about whether the laboratory or the field is more appropriate for studying behavior (Bronfenbrenner, 1979; Hartup, 1973; Parke, 1976).

The failure of developmental theory to take situational variables into account is in part due to the focus of genetic epistemology on the emergence of similar structures under different circumstances. In fact, the major determinant of behavior was thought to be the genetic unfolding of invariant sequences and behavior. This lack of concern about situations or contexts as affecting both structures and processes, such as equilibrium–disequilibrium, has been a major theoretical obstacle to the study of context (Riegel & Meacham, 1976).

Studies of the differential effects of the laboratory versus the field (i.e., the home) on children's behavior represent an attempt to examine the behavioral context (e.g., Bretherton & Ainsworth, 1974; Skarin, 1977). The research is predicated on a belief in "natural situations" and "natural behaviors." However, the argument that having identified the natural situations, one can then study the natural behaviors of subjects negates the basic assumption that behavior is influenced by context and that there is no single context that is best for observing behavior. The issue of whether to study behavior in the laboratory or in the field pertains to the broader issue of the nature of the situation. In the following sections, issues related to the situation will be the topic of concern, not because the situation necessarily plays a central role in behavior (Mischel, 1977), but because in order to understand development, one must understand the interaction between behaviors and situations.

The Nature of the Stimulus

American psychology has, for the most part, not been receptive to the study of the nature of the stimulus, being more concerned with observing, categorizing, and assigning meaning to responses. By either ignoring the situation or holding it constant, it has been thought that through the careful study of behavior, one could come to understand and predict individuals' perceptions, motivations, cognitions, and actions within their environment.

The basic experimental paradigm can be characterized as the control of the stimulus and the observation of dependent responses. In the traditional experimental design, experimental and control subjects receive different stimuli (stimulation), and differences in their responses are measured. The careful manipulation of both the stimulus (stimulation) and the response is essential, because a cause-and-effect relationship is being tested. Sophisticated techniques for the observation, measurement, and classification of responses have been developed. However, a strong asymmetry is inherent in such procedures inasmuch as responses emanate from the subject, whereas the stimuli are controlled by the experimenter. For example, it is the experimenter who varies the size or shape of a stimulus, while it is the subject who responds. This asymmetry raises problems, since the determination of a causal relationship between stimulus and response requires as much knowledge of the stimulus as of the response.

The interaction between the stimulus and the subject is well illustrated in studies of perceptual development in infancy. In particular, the scanning ability of infants has been shown to vary as a function of age (Haith, 1976; Salapatek, 1969), a finding reported for older children as well (Zaporozhets, 1965). Salapatek (1969) found a developmental trend in whole–part perception, with younger infants engaging in less perception of the whole. For example, young infants are more likely to fixate on an angle of a triangle than to scan the whole figure. A similar finding was obtained when faces were used as the stimulus (Haith, 1976). Initially, the contour of a face was scanned; only after 5 weeks of age did infants look at the internal features of the face. These developmental changes in what infants look at when a stimulus is presented have important implications for understanding the meaning of infants' responses.

J. J. Gibson (1960) reflected on this problem and the general lack of concern about the stimulus: "It seems to me that there is a weak link in the chain of reasoning by which we explain experience and behavior, namely *our concept of the stimulus*" (p. 694; emphasis added). While Gibson had several interesting ideas about the stimulus and how it might be studied, his article caused little change in the traditional research approach. The historical and philosophical roots of the issue were strong (Hamlyn, 1961), and it was thought best to leave tradition alone.

Later, the traditional view that the stimulus is controlled by the experimenter was once again challenged, this time by Orne (1973). Orne pointed out that the mind of the subject as well as the subject's past experience affect the nature of the stimulus and its effect on the subject's

behavior. That is, the subject's response depends on the subject's perception of the stimulus and its meaning.

Taxonomy of Situations

Once one has recognized the important role of the stimulus in the
meaning of behavior, issues related to the stimulus must be addressed.
In this discussion, attention is focused primarily on the situation, although issues pertaining to situations apply to stimuli and environments as well (Fredericksen, 1972; Lowenthal, 1972; Pervin, 1975).

The study of the situation is filled with complications (Mischel,
1977; Murray, 1938; Pervin, 1968). First, in trying to develop a taxonomy of situations, everything must be included. Pavlov correctly
noted that a "stimulus [or situation] could be anything in the terrestrial
world" (Gibson, 1960). Given the inclusive nature of this problem, the
second problem in the study of the situation offers little relief: Who
shall define the situation? According to one view, situations can be
defined in objective and measurable characteristics (Barker, 1965; Rotter, 1955; Sells, 1963). For example, experimenters may define the situation in terms of a room size, a measurable characteristic. An alternative view holds that the situation should be defined in terms of the
subject's perception of it (Endler & Magnusson, 1974). In this approach,
one would study how individuals characterize their environment. Any
situation must be specified in terms of the particular individual experiencing it (Bowers, 1973). A third position is based on arguments
for a taxonomy in terms of an interaction between the objective situation
and the individual's perception of it. If the environment exists independent of the individual's perception of it, there is little reason to ask
the subject to define the stimulus. In this case, the experimenter defines
the situation. If, on the other hand, the environment exists only as the
subject experiences it, the definition or characterization of the situation
will require the subject's participation. Situations must be specified by
the individuals experiencing them.

Independent of these considerations is the issue of how to define
the situation, regardless of whether it is defined from the experimenter's
or the subject's perspective. For example, situations can be defined in
terms of physical properties that vary along several dimensions (e.g.,
temperature and area). Situations can be defined in terms of location,
such as rooms or buildings. Daily activities such as washing or going
to bed, and adaptive functions are other means of categorizing situations. The requirements of situations, the skills involved, or the emotions elicited are additional dimensions. Finally, social characteristics,

including the people involved, might be used to define the situation. Classifications across specific dimensions or combinations of dimensions might be feasible. Certain dimensions might be more interrelated than others. Obviously, the taxonomy of situations presents an enormous problem to investigators (Pervin, 1975).

Some of the dimensions suggested above may be less critical to certain research studies than to others. Thus, one solution to the problem may be to characterize situations in terms of the problem to be studied. The taxonomy or methods derived from this solution will not generalize to all cases, however. Nevertheless, until more empirical effort is made to understand the crucial dimensions of situations, the problem must remain abstract.

In the study of emotion, situations and stimuli are viewed as emotional elicitors. Situations are defined in terms of the emotions they elicit. Various dimensions of situations can be varied so that one can determine which are critical to the elicitation of the emotion. The problem of this approach is that it is difficult to avoid defining situations without circularity. There is little solution to this problem, but it offers a starting point for investigation. Ethologists have adopted this approach to study behavior in context. For instance, they look at fighting behavior to study aggression and copulation to measure sexual states.

Two aspects of the context of emotional behavior have been examined in the infancy literature: (1) the physical properties of the central stimulus and (2) the contextual cues provided by prior events and current conditions (Lewis, 1980). The physical characteristics of specific stimuli, particularly social stimuli, that influence children's responses have been studied for a limited number of emotions, primarily fear and happiness. Among the social characteristics that may elicit fear are the person's age, gender, size, degree of familiarity, and manner of behaving. For example, children have been found to respond more positively to strange children than to strange adults (Brooks & Lewis, 1976; Lewis & Brooks, 1974). Gender differences in the social stimulus have also been reported, indicating that male strangers elicit more fear than female strangers (Benjamin, 1961; Greenberg, Hillman, & Grice, 1973; Morgan & Ricciuti, 1969; Shaffran & Décarie, 1973; Skarin, 1977). Height may also be the important social characteristic (Feinman, 1980; Weinraub & Putney, 1978).

In addition, children's prior experience with the class to which the stimulus belongs may have an important impact on their response. Thus, for example, a stranger or even a familiar person wearing a white laboratory coat may evoke an emotional state of fear independent of the person and dependent on the children's past experience with white coats. More generally, with repeated exposure to a particular stimulus, involving cognitive processes ranging from simple stimulus habituation to complex assimilations, children may show response changes to the same stimulus. Two equally novel toys may evoke very different responses depending on the state of the child, the state itself being dependent on the history of past events. The first novel toy presented to the child may evoke arousal, interest, exploration, and pleasure. The second presentation to a child already aroused may provoke upset as the arousal threshold is raised beyond the pleasurable level and the child cannot control the arousal.

From a more cognitive point of view, a consideration of this temporal sequence of stimuli in terms of both immediate and more remote antecedent events invokes some hypothetical memory capacity that allows children to recognize previously experienced events and to alter their responses accordingly. The development of such cognitive structures, especially in early childhood, is essential if past experiences are to have an effect on the child's current emotional state.

The broader context in which emotional behavior is observed may be more important than the characteristics of the primary stimulus. Yet, little attention has been given to the context in the study of children's emotions. One reason for the failure to consider the situation may be the assumption that experimenters already know the critical dimensions of the contexts and how they interact with the emotional response. This may not be the case, however. For example, the approach of a stranger, once thought to elicit fear may produce both fear and greeting behaviors (Bretherton & Ainsworth, 1974; Haviland & Lewis, 1975). If experimenters are prepared to find only fear behaviors in fear contexts, they run the risk of misinterpreting the subject's response. This narrowness of focus may be the cause of many discrepancies in the fear literature. The wide eye gaze and cessation of activity observed in infants when the stranger approaches can also be observed when infants look at a visual array of geometric forms. That is, wide eye gaze and decrease in activity accompany attending and are not specific to fear.

The experimental manipulation of context is usually carried out in laboratory studies, although the contextual dimensions of naturalistic environments must also be investigated. This investigation is particularly important to understanding the socialization of emotion. Adults and children alike know that certain contexts are more likely than others to elicit particular emotional states, independent of the behaviors elicited by the context (see Chapter 6). Funerals are likely to elicit sadness, while circuses are likely to elicit delight. Weddings may elicit a mixture of emotions. Knowledge of the emotions likely to be elicited

by the context occurs as a consequence of an elaborate process of socialization that includes past experiences, empathy, and the responses
of others to children's own behaviors. Situational knowledge about
emotions may exert a powerful impact on their expression as well as
on the perception of emotions in others. Knowledge about contexts may
be learned as a type of script, similar to that described by Abelson
(1976). This script prescribes the conditions under which one is more
likely to see certain types of emotions. In addition, attribution and
empathy may be used to decide in which situations one is likely to see
certain emotions. Whatever the processes underlying this knowledge,
at some point early in development contextual information is used in
understanding and interpreting emotional behavior.

ᕱᕱᕱᕱᕱᕱᕱᕱᕱᕱᕱᕱᕱ

In this discussion on the measurement of emotion, the point was
made that no single measure, whether facial, vocal, bodily, or physiological, or any combination of measures is likely to be isomorphic to
discrete emotional states. While it would be desirable to find such a
measure or set of measures, research to date is not encouraging.

Likewise, it was stressed that there is no one-to-one correspondence
between situations (or emotional elicitors) and emotional states. How,
then, can investigators study emotional states, whether transient or
enduring? First, it is unreasonable to expect that one can construct a
measurement system in which behaviors and/or situations have a one-
to-one correspondence with emotional states. Moreover, measurement
systems that do not consider the subjects' reports of their emotional
experience are bound to be subject to error. However, introspective
techniques themselves raise additional difficulties.

These conclusions fly in the face of everyday experience. Generally,
people have little difficulty in recognizing and responding to both the
transient emotions and the moods of other people. The discussion of
behaviors and situations suggests that it is the relationship between (1)
the situations or stimuli that elicit behavior and (2) the specific behaviors elicited that provides the best means for inferring the emotional
state that another person is experiencing. Behaviors acquire meaning
in the context of other behaviors and the situations that produce them.
Likewise, situations derive meaning from the behaviors that they evoke,
both as a natural consequence (e.g., unlearned responses) and a function
of a particular culture (e.g., learned responses). Both elements form a
matrix in which meaning can be established.

The measurement instrument that is described in the following chapters was constructed with the use of these propositions. The instrument employs both sets of behaviors and sets of situations to assess children's enduring emotional states. Inferences concerning both transient and enduring emotions are based on the information generated from the behavior–situation matrix.

9

Construction of the Scales of Socioemotional Development

Up to this point, our discussion has been primarily theoretical. We now focus our attention on the concrete problems of scale construction. Our ultimate desire was to construct a measurement instrument that could (1) measure several different emotions in infants and young children between the ages of 3 months and 30 months; (2) measure emotions in settings that engage infants in everyday, naturally occurring situations; (3) measure emotions through a variety of behaviors, including facial, vocal, postural, and locomotive; and (4) measure differences among infants in terms of single emotions as well as patterns or configurations of emotions. In constructing the measurement scales, a series of questions were raised about which emotions should be studied, where these emotions should be studied, which behaviors should be used to reference the emotions, and which situations would be most likely to activate these emotions. These questions are the focus of the discussion in this chapter. The empirical aspects of the scale construction are described in the following chapter.

Which Emotions Should Be Studied?

The first task in constructing the scales was to decide which emotions to measure. Whereas the emotional experiences of adults appear to be quite varied and many different emotions can be studied (Davitz, 1969), it is not clear that the emotions of infants and young children are as numerous or as differentiated. Indeed, one of the research goals was to determine the extent to which emotions are differentiated during infancy. Nevertheless, in order to examine the relationships among emotions it was necessary to select various emotions that might be observed in young children.

Five emotions were targeted for study: fear, anger, happiness, social affiliation, and competence. These particular emotions were chosen for several reasons. First, they represent both positive and negative emotions. Moreover, expressions of these emotions can be seen in the natural behaviors of children. Whether the expression is tied to an underlying emotional state is an issue of theoretical debate (see Chapter 5). However, parents and casual observers generally have no difficulty in spotting these emotions in children's behaviors. Finally, other researchers have been interested in these emotions during infancy. More research has been conducted on fear and affiliation, in the form of attachment and peer relationships, than on the other emotions, although each has received some attention. For example, happiness is likely to be studied in terms of smiling. No claim is made that these emotions constitute the complete emotional repertoire of infants. Although additional emotions might have been selected, the constraints of time and effort restricted our choice to these five.

Whether social affiliation and competence are emotions may be questioned by some, since they are not usually included in taxonomies of infants' emotions (Izard, 1977). We chose social affiliation as an emotion to be measured, since we believe it comes as close to the feeling of love as can be measured. One operational definition of love is movement toward or proximity to another person. Although affiliation is sometimes studied as the personality dimension of introversion–extroversion (Eaves & Eysenck, 1975), we included it in our scales as a measure of social attraction or, in some cases, of love. Competence was included as an emotion in the scales in order to measure the positive feelings that children have about themselves, feelings translated into actions on their environment. Adler (1927), in his notion of mastery, regarded this feeling state as a powerful motivator of human behavior. Even though our classification of social affiliation and competence as emotions is somewhat unconventional, their importance as feeling states must be acknowledged. In our scale construction, these five categories of feelings are referred to as *socioemotional* rather than *emotional*.

The research pertaining to each of these emotions is reviewed briefly in the following pages, with particular attention paid to the situations that other investigators have used to elicit these emotions and the behaviors used to measure them. Many of these situations and behaviors were included in constructing our scales.

Fear

At least five different kinds of fear have been studied (Lewis & Rosenblum, 1974b). One type is unlearned and occurs when the organism experiences an intense, sudden, and unexpected change in the level of energy reaching the sensory systems. Such stimuli probably account for a relatively small percentage of fear responses, particularly as they become increasingly associated with other events over time. Learned fears, in contrast, probably account for a much larger portion of children's fear behaviors (Watson & Rayner, 1920). Yet learned fear and its pattern of generalization across stimuli have not been studied extensively.

A third kind of fear is seen in infants' negative response to strangers (e.g., Brooks & Lewis, 1976; Décarie, 1974; Lewis & Brooks, 1974; Morgan & Ricciuti, 1969; Schaffer, 1966; Skarin, 1977; Sroufe, 1977). The development of stranger fear has generated much research and is discussed in detail later. Violation of expectancy is a fourth type of event that produces fear when infants are unable to assimilate, or make sense of, a change in a familiar stimulus (Kagan, 1974). Fear is particularly likely to occur if the new event cannot be ignored but impinges on the child and causes a loss of control (Gunnar, 1980; Gunnar-Vongnechten, 1978; Lewis, 1980).

A fifth kind of fear involves loss of the mother. Not only may the mother's departure evoke expressions of fear in infants (Tennes & Lampl, 1964; Weinraub & Lewis, 1977), but her inaccessibility and/or unresponsiveness may also elicit distress behaviors (Goldberg & Lewis, 1969; Young & Lewis, 1979).

These types of fear are quite different, yet all are characterized by an emotional response that is distinguishable by a negative hedonic quality and some form of avoidance behavior. Fear is also referred to as *anxiety* or *wariness* in the research literature.

Fear Situations

The most frequently and thoroughly analyzed fear during infancy has been fear of the stranger (Lewis & Rosenblum, 1974b; Sroufe, 1977). In the standard stranger situation, a stranger enters the room where the infant is situated, pauses, walks slowly toward the infant, pauses, extends her arms in a pick-up gesture, touches or actually lifts the infant, then withdraws from the room. The infant's behaviors are observed in response to the stranger at various phases in the approach sequence.

In addition to strangers, other situations that have been described in the research literature as potential elicitors of fear in infants include masks (Morgan & Ricciuti, 1969; Scarr & Salapatek, 1970; Sroufe et al., 1974; Sroufe & Wunsch, 1972); the visual cliff (Gibson & Walk, 1960; Scarr & Salapatek, 1970; Schwartz et al., 1973); an unfamiliar environment (Sroufe & Waters, 1977); separation from the mother (Tennes & Lampl, 1964; Weinraub & Lewis, 1977); and novel, unusual, or startling toys, such as the jack-in-the-box, mechanical animals, or "nonsense toys" (Ricciuti & Poresky, 1972; Scarr & Salapatek, 1970; Schaffer et al., 1972).

Empirical studies have revealed that many different dimensions of these stimulus situations can influence the infant's fear responses. For example, several studies using the stranger situation have demonstrated sex-of-stranger differences that indicate that male strangers elicit more fear in infants than do female strangers (Benjamin, 1961; Greenberg et al., 1973; Morgan & Ricciuti, 1969; Shaffran & Décarie, 1973; Skarin, 1977). However, the height of the stranger relative to the infant may be a more potent factor in evoking fear than the stranger's gender (Weinraub & Putney, 1978). Consequently, when height differences between male and female strangers are controlled, sex-of-stranger differences tend to disappear (Brooks & Lewis, 1976; Lewis & Brooks, 1974). Age-of-stranger differences have also been reported in studies of stranger fear. In general, adult strangers are much more likely to evoke fear in infants than are child strangers, who usually are not regarded as fearful at all (Brooks & Lewis, 1976; Greenberg et al., 1973; Lewis & Brooks, 1974).

In addition to the physical characteristics of the stranger, the stranger's behavior also may influence the nature of infants' emotional responses. For example, the sight of a stranger across a room is not likely to provoke fear in many infants, but as the stranger approaches, touches, and attempts to pick up the infant, increasingly negative reactions are more likely to be observed (Bronson, 1972; Brooks & Lewis, 1976; Campos et al., 1975; Cohen & Campos, 1974; Greenberg et al., 1973; Lewis & Brooks, 1974; Morgan & Ricciuti, 1969; Schaffer, 1966; Skarin, 1977; Tennes & Lampl, 1964; Waters et al., 1975). The effects of proximity interact with other aspects of the stranger's behavior, however. For instance, a smiling, talking stranger does not frighten many infants (Bretherton & Ainsworth, 1974; Rheingold & Eckerman, 1973), nor does a stranger playing peek-a-boo in the infant's immediate proximity (Morgan, 1973; Morgan & Ricciuti, 1969). Overall, fear expressions are much more likely to be observed in studies where the stranger acts in an intrusive manner (Sroufe, 1977).

In addition to the physical characteristics of the stimulus, certain dimensions of the broader context in which the stimulus appears are likely to affect the nature of infants' emotional responses. For example, familiarity appears to be a critical aspect of the situation in determining the likelihood of observing fear. Infants typically exhibit more fear in an unfamiliar environment than in their own homes (Bretherton & Ainsworth, 1974; Castell, 1970; Skarin, 1977; Sroufe et al., 1974). Furthermore, increasing the amount of time that infants have to become familiar with the strange environment and the stranger may decrease the amount of fear observed (Bretherton, 1978; Ross, 1975; Sroufe et al., 1974; Trause, 1977). The presence of a familiar person also tends to alleviate fear in most infants. Thus, infants show more stranger fear in the absence of their mothers than in their presence (Campos, Emde, Gaensbauer, & Sorce, 1973; Emde et al., 1976; Ricciuti, 1974; Skarin, 1977) or even when they are separated from their mothers by a few feet (Bronson, 1972; Morgan & Ricciuti, 1969).

In addition, the mother's own response to the stranger's presence is likely to influence the infants' reaction (Feinman & Lewis, in press; Haviland & Lewis, 1975). In particular, infants have been observed to be less afraid of and to make friends with a stranger in a shorter amount of time when the mother demonstrates a positive rather than a neutral attitude toward the stranger (Feiring, Lewis, & Starr, 1982). The effect of the mother's behavior on an infant's responses is also apparent in findings of separation anxiety showing that the amount of distress that infants display on being left alone is mediated by the manner in which their mothers choose to leave them: mothers who inform their infants about their departure and who instruct them about what to do once they have gone have infants who show less distress than do mothers who simply leave (Weinraub & Lewis, 1977).

Two additional aspects of the stimulus situation that may affect infants' emotional expressions have been demonstrated in studies of infants' responses to masks. The importance of the stimulus agent is demonstrated in results that show that more infants are afraid of masks when they are worn by a stranger than when they are worn by the mother (Sroufe et al., 1974; Sroufe & Wunsch, 1972) or presented on sticks (Morgan & Ricciuti, 1969). In fact, in the latter two instances, masks may evoke smiling and laughter in infants. However, laughter and smiling are substantially reduced and instances of fear behavior are increased when mother-wearing-mask is preceded by stranger-wearing-mask. Thus, the antecedent events as well as the nature of the stimulus agent may moderate or enhance expressions of fear.

Fear Responses

Facial, physiological, bodily (postural, gestural, and locomotive), and vocal responses have all appeared in the research literature as indexes of fear. Infants' facial expressions of fear were first described by Darwin (1872). Most empirical studies have used at least one of the following facial expressions to reference fear: sobering, frowning, pouting, wrinkling or screwing up the face, lip trembling, and "cry face."

Several studies have suggested that the physiological response of heart rate acceleration indicates fear and accompanies infants' fearful responses to strangers (Campos et al., 1973, 1975; Skarin, 1977; Waters et al., 1975) and to a visual cliff (Schwartz et al., 1973) and also appears when the infant enters an unfamiliar environment (Sroufe & Waters, 1977). Results from a more recent study show that heart rate responses do not covary with facial expressions of emotion when the data on individual subjects are examined. In particular, neither fearful nor happy faces were found to be related to heart rate responses (Lewis et al., 1978).

Bodily and vocal indexes of fear have been used less often, although fear expressions associated with bodily tension (e.g., "freezing") and flight (e.g., "crawling or running away") are used in everyday situations to infer fear. In conditions where mobility is restricted because the infant either is physically immature or is restrained, postural cues such as pulling back or turning the head can be used to measure fear (Lewis & Brooks, 1974; Morgan & Ricciuti, 1969; Ricciuti, 1974; Schaffer, 1966; Skarin, 1977; Waters et al., 1975). A few studies have included negative, distress vocalizations such as whimpering or crying in their measures of infants' fear. Indeed, some investigators have concluded that of all the responses, crying is the only valid measure of fear and that its absence indicates that the infant is not afraid (Rheingold & Eckerman, 1973).

The lack of consensus among investigators regarding which measures are appropriate indexes of fear is undoubtedly a major source of the inconsistencies in findings reporting the number of infants who exhibit fear under different circumstances. For example, more fear is observed in studies that accept sobering as an index of fear (Scarr & Salapatek, 1970) than in studies that rely on crying or fussing (Rheingold & Eckerman, 1973).

The reliability or consistency of measures of emotional expression has been researched in more detail for fear than for any other emotion. In general, the results show variable reliability in fear-of-strangers measures for infants age 4 months and older. When assessments are separated by very short periods of time, reliabilities are greater, with correlations ranging between .65 and .91. When periods of several months separate the measurements, reliabilities may drop to as low as .32 (Bronson, 1972; Morgan, 1973; Robson, Pedersen, & Moss, 1969). When different strangers are used to assess fear at two points in time, only moderate consistencies in fear responses may be obtained (Morgan, 1973; Shaffran & Décarie, 1973).

Response consistency over a two-month period has been tested for fear of the visual cliff, jack-in-the-box, and masks, as well as for fear of strangers, with variable success reflected in correlations ranging between .32 and .74 (Scarr & Salapatek, 1970). Fear reactions to a mechanical dog and a loud noise show virtually no short-term stability (Ricciuti & Poresky, 1972; Scarr & Salapatek, 1970).

Reliability can also be assessed by examining the consistency of responses across different situations designed to elicit fear. Scarr and Salapatek (1970), investigating infants' fear reactions to six different stimulus events, reported relatively little situational consistency. Not surprisingly, reactions to the "startle" toys (jack-in-the-box, mechanical dog, and cap pistol) were the most related to each other ($r = .51$) but were not related to fear responses to the stranger or to the visual cliff. On the other hand, fear of masks was significantly related to all of the other fears. Ricciuti and Poresky (1972), in contrast, failed to find any consistency in infants' fear reactions to two startle stimuli (jack-in-the-box and a buzzer).

Anger

Compared with the research on fear, very little empirical work has been done on the development of anger and frustration. Yet, anger is frequently cited as a primary emotion, and observers have described "angry" cries and faces in very young babies (Izard et al., 1980; Sroufe, 1979b; Watson, 1924; Wolff, 1969). Whereas distress and avoidance behaviors characterize fear, anger is more likely to be reflected in expressions of protest and movement toward a stimulus, often in response to an interruption in an ongoing activity or a failure of events to conform to specific expectations. For example, children may display anger by shoving a child who has grabbed a favorite toy, or children may throw tantrums when their mother turns off the television and announces that it is bedtime. Inanimate objects may also be elicitors of anger, as when a bottle of milk or a pacifier is situated immediately out of an infant's reach or when a mechanical toy fails to work as a child expects it to.

Anger Situations

The range of situations in which anger and frustration have been studied is quite narrow. Watson (1919) elicited anger by physically restraining infants. Interrupting infants' sucking activity by removing the bottle during feeding has been used to examine responses to frustration in 3-month-old infants (Bell, Weller, & Waldrop, 1971; Lewis, 1967), while a barrier placed between the child and the mother has been used as a test of frustration and anger in 1- and 2-year-olds (Bell et al., 1971; Feiring & Lewis, 1979; Goldberg & Lewis, 1969; Jacklin, Maccoby, & Dick, 1973; Pedersen & Bell, 1970; Van Lieshout, 1975). In addition, a few investigators have looked at expressions of anger in infants' natural interactions with their mother, particularly as a reaction of abused and/or insecurely attached infants to separation from and reunion with the mother (Ainsworth, 1979; Ainsworth et al., 1978; George & Main, 1979; Lewis & Schaeffer, 1979; Main, 1977). Research on aggression indicates that frustration and physical attack are potent elicitors of aggressive behaviors in children (Feshbach, 1970). Studies on punishment have consistently found a positive relationship between physical punishment and aggression in children (Feshbach, 1973).

The salient dimensions of these situations in evoking anger have yet to be determined. Some data suggest that the distance of infants from their mothers and/or the desired goal influences their emotional response to a frustrating situation. For example, infants placed farther from the mother in a barrier situation have been observed to show more clinging and less manipulative behaviors (but also less crying) than infants who are initially placed closer to the mother (Jacklin et al., 1973).

The degree of familiarity inherent in the situation does not seem to affect angry reactions in the way that it affects fear responses. In one study examining responses in two different contexts, avoidance of the mother on reunion in a day-care center was found to be correlated with avoidance of the mother on reunion in an experimental laboratory (Blanchard & Main, 1979). No differences have been reported in expressions of anger on reunion as a function of the parent's gender (Main & Weston, 1979).

Anger Responses

Bodily behaviors have been the primary measures in empirical studies of anger and frustration. Responses typically associated with anger include hitting, throwing, stomping, throwing self on floor, throwing toys, kicking, pushing away, withdrawal or rejection of engagement, and breath holding (Gaensbauer, Mrazek, & Emde, 1979; Main, 1981). Mothers report that 1-year-olds are angry when their activity consists of hitting, throwing objects around the room, and throwing themselves on the floor (see Chapter 7).

In response to reunion with the mother after a brief separation, anger toward the mother may take the form of either resistance or avoidance behaviors (Ainsworth et al., 1978; Lewis & Michalson, 1982c; Main, 1977). Some infants protest if they are not picked up when they want to be, or if they are put down when they still want to be held. When picked up, these infants may show ambivalence by resisting contact while at the same time they cling to the mother. In contrast, other infants exhibit even more anger by totally ignoring the mother when she returns, despite her efforts to coax the baby to come to her (George & Main, 1979; Lewis & Schaeffer, 1979). These infants may direct their attention away from the mother, turn away, or move away.

That this avoidant reaction is associated with anger is reinforced by a strong correlation between avoidance of the mother on reunion and angry behavior observed in other, stress-free settings (Ainsworth et al., 1978; Heinicke & Westheimer, 1966; Main, 1981). Moreover, concurrent heart rate records also reveal that these "avoiding infants" are aroused and not merely uninterested in the reunion situation, inasmuch as the postreunion play of these infants is not accompanied by the heart rate deceleration characteristic of involvement with toys (Sroufe & Waters, 1977). Avoidance behavior may thus permit the infant to maintain control over intense anger that threatens behavioral disorganization. At the same time, it may allow the infant to maintain some degree of contact with the mother.

Certain vocal behaviors, too, have been regarded as signs of anger and frustration, particularly when they accompany one of the more active, bodily forms of protest. Among such vocalizations are grunts, fusses, protests, and harsh, shrill crying (Gaensbauer et al., 1979). Without knowledge of the situational context or accompanying behaviors, however, it is difficult to distinguish different types of crying (Müller, Hollien, & Murry, 1974), although spectrographic studies have distinguished angry cries of newborns from other cries (e.g., Wolff, 1969).

Facial expressions of anger and physiological measures have not been extensively used in infancy research, nor has the relationship between different measures of anger been explored. Facial expressions of anger may include frowning or scowling (Gaensbauer et al., 1979; Main, 1981). Repeated failures to link heart rate responses to emotional expressions in any specific way are applicable to expressions of anger as well, although one might expect to find heart rate acceleration in anger-eliciting situations reflecting an activation of the general arousal system.

The reliability of expressions of anger over time or across situations has received some attention in the research literature. Lewis (1967) found that the specific response to a frustrating situation was not related at two age periods. However, the form of the response was. That is, active crying at 3 months of age in response to interruption of feeding was related to actively trying to get around a barrier at 12 months of age, while passive reactions to frustration at 3 months (e.g., closing the eyes) were related to crying at 12 months.

There also appears to be moderate stability ($r = .56$) in the frequency of angry episodes between the third and fourth quarters of the first year of life (Main, 1981). Furthermore, scores for avoidance of the parent in a reunion situation have shown moderate stability over a two-week period ($r = .66$; Ainsworth et al., 1978), over a six-month period ($r = .62$; Waters, 1978), and over an eight-month period ($r = .59$, Main & Weston, 1979). Avoidance at 12 months of age has also been found to be related at 21 months to number of attacks and threats of attacks on the mother, number of episodes of hitting and banging toys, active disobedience in response to maternal commands, and tantrums (Main, 1981). Thus, while a particular expression of anger may change over time and circumstances, and while the situations that provoke anger may differ, the frequency and general form of its expression appear to show some stability over the first two years of life.

Happiness

The research literature is filled with studies of smiling and laughter in infants. Smiling is one of infants' first emotional and social behaviors and thus plays a crucial role in infants' total development. Through differential smiling, infants are able to communicate their wants and desires before they acquire language. Moreover, smiling seems to elicit positive emotions in adults, binding them to the infant. Thus, smiling may have a survival function as well as a social function (Lewis & Rosenblum, 1974a).

While it is generally accepted that smiling and laughter are associated with positive states such as happiness, delight, joy, and pleasure, it is not clear that these behaviors reference these states in any direct way. For example, children are taught early in life to mask negative feelings such as anger and fear by smiling and laughing instead of crying (see Chapter 6). Children also learn that adults are more likely to fulfill their wishes and desires if they smile and display other "appropriate" (i.e., adultlike) behaviors. However, there is more likely to be a one-to-one correspondence between smiling and positive emotions in infancy when the effects of the socialization processes are not fully realized (see Chapter 5). Nevertheless, it is still necessary to know the specific context in which smiling and laughter occur to be able to infer an underlying positive emotion.

For the sake of convenience, the term *happiness* has been selected to refer to positive states that are also labeled *delight, joy,* or *pleasure* in the research literature. The characteristic feature of these states is a positive hedonic tone, usually reflected in a smile or laughter. Most of the early research literature is devoted to tracing the developmental course of smiling and noting the age at which laughter first appears. The more recent literature discusses in more detail the nature of the situational circumstances that evoke smiling and laughter.

Happiness Situations

The kinds of situations found to be most effective in eliciting smiling and laughter in infants differ according to the age of the infant (Sroufe & Waters, 1976; Sroufe & Wunsch, 1972). At first, spontaneous internal changes in the infant's physiological state elicit smiling in neonates during sleep (Emde & Koenig, 1969; Spitz, Emde, & Metcalf, 1970; Wolff, 1963). The earliest waking smiles are elicited by low-level tactile and kinesthetic stimulation, such as blowing on the infant's skin (Emde & Koenig, 1969; Watson, 1924). During the first month, auditory stimuli (particularly a high-pitched voice), a nodding head accompanying vocal stimulation, the mother's voice, and pat-a-cake become increasingly effective in eliciting smiles (Wolff, 1963). At the end of the fifth week, the voice declines in effectiveness as more vigorous and dynamic visual stimulation takes priority over low-level, modulated stimulation in eliciting smiles (Salzen, 1963; Wolff, 1963).

As infants develop, however, dynamic stimulation *per se* does not suffice; rather, smiling occurs as a result of infants' efforts to process, or master, the content of a stimulus event (Kagan, 1971; Shultz & Zigler, 1970; Sroufe & Waters, 1976; Sroufe & Wunsch, 1972; Zelazo, 1972; Zelazo & Komer, 1971). The assimilation of a stimulus into an already established schema, it is hypothesized, constitutes a source of pleasure for the infant when some optimal amount of mismatch between the stimulus and the schema occur. This pleasure is typically accompanied by smiling.

For smiles that occur as a function of mastery and recognition, stationary stimuli are sometimes more effective than dynamic stimuli (Shultz & Zigler, 1970). Social stimuli such as the human face become particularly potent in evoking smiles of recognition (Kagan, 1967; Lewis, 1969). However, as infants' schemata for the human face become more articulated and less effort is required for assimilation, the human face declines in effectiveness (Ambrose, 1961; Gewirtz, 1965; Kagan, 1967; Spitz et al., 1970; Takahashi, 1973). Increasingly complex degrees of incongruity are required to elicit smiling. The infant's own mirror image also can be a highly effective elicitor of smiling, especially during the first year of life (Amsterdam, 1972; Lewis & Brooks-Gunn, 1979).

The stimuli capable of evoking laughter also evolve from intrusive stimulation of a tactile and auditory nature to interest-evoking, social-visual events during the first year of life (Sroufe & Waters, 1976; Sroufe & Wunsch, 1972). At first, physically vigorous stimulation (e.g., tickling) is most potent, followed by less vigorous but more provocative tactile and auditory stimulation (e.g., the mother saying, "Boom-boom-boom"). In the second six months, laughter is directed more toward social and subtle visual situations (e.g., peek-a-boo and the mother crawling on the floor), and 1-year-olds laugh primarily to visual and social items that provide an element of cognitive incongruity.

In short, strong developmental trends have been identified in situations likely to elicit smiling and laughter. These situational trends are from smiling and laughing in response to intrusive stimulation and to stimulation mediated by active attention, toward smiling and laughing in response to the stimulus content. Finally, more active involvement on the part of the infant in engaging the stimulus itself is required for smiling or laughter to occur.

The stimuli potent for eliciting smiling and laughter can at times elicit fear, depending on other dimensions of the context. For example, the sequence of stimulus presentation is a salient dimension influencing the emotional response. Although mother-wearing-mask usually evokes smiling and laughter in infants, the frequency of smiling and laughter declines substantially and more fear responses occur when this situation is preceded by a stranger-wearing-mask (Sroufe et al., 1974). Children's state is another aspect of the total context likely to affect the nature of the response. Events that usually produce laughter may produce crying if children are tired or ill.

Happiness Responses

Studies of positive emotions have relied on facial expressions (smiling or laughter) over other behaviors (e.g., Gaensbauer et al., 1979). Recently, investigators have begun to analyze in detail the facial musculature involved in enjoyment or joy using anatomically based measurement systems (Izard, 1979b; Oster, 1978). Only occasional studies report other behaviors that accompany these facial responses. For instance, in addition to smiling at their mirror image, infants have been observed to vocalize, touch the mirror or themselves, make faces at the mirror, bounce in front of the mirror, or display silly and coy behaviors (Lewis & Brooks-Gunn, 1979).

Investigations of physiological changes accompanying positive emotional states are rare. In one study, heart rate acceleration was found to accompany smiling, although substantially less acceleration occurred during smiling than during frowning and crying (Emde, Campos, Reich, & Gaensbauer, 1978). In contrast, Sroufe et al. (1974) reported heart rate deceleration in response to mother-wearing-mask up to the moment of smiling and laughing, when deceleration was followed by tachycardia associated with vigorous muscle discharge. Whether heart rate acceleration can be attributed to a positive emotional state expressed in smiling (Emde et al., 1978) or whether it is associated with muscular activity (Sroufe et al., 1974) is difficult to determine. Without data analyses on individual cases, it is impossible to eliminate muscular activity as the cause of heart rate acceleration associated with smiling (Lewis et al., 1978).

A close relationship between smiling and laughter is suggested by a substantial literature demonstrating that laughter is a more intense expression of positive affect than is smiling. Laughter requires a steeper gradient and a more rapid fluctuation of tension than smiling (Cicchetti & Sroufe, 1978; Rothbart, 1973; Sroufe, 1979b; Sroufe & Waters, 1976). With incongruous events, especially, laughter may be observed to build from smiling and to fade again to smiling with continued presentations (Sroufe & Wunsch, 1972). However, the frequency of smiling does not appear to be related to the frequency of laughter during the first year of life. Infants who smile a great deal do not necessarily laugh much (Washburn, 1929).

Finally, the stability of expressions of positive affect is still at issue. There is some evidence that the duration of smiling in response to the presence of an adult is consistent over the first six months of life (Tautermannová, 1973). In addition, Shaffran and Décarie (1973) observed infants to be substantially more consistent in their positive responses to a stranger than in their negative responses.

Social Affiliation

In its most intense form, social affiliation reflects the concept of love. In general, social affiliation represents a positive attraction toward conspecifics as well as toward animals and inanimate objects. In the developmental psychology literature, this feeling state has been studied most often in terms of the infant's attachment to primary caregivers. More recently, the child's relationships with persons other than the caregivers have also been investigated (Lewis, 1982b). The work on attachment is extensive and difficult to summarize in a short space; thus, only the more seminal aspects of this topic are reviewed in this section.

From the moment of birth, infants enter into social relationships with numerous people. In addition to the mother and father, infants' siblings, grandparents, aunts, and uncles, as well as other relatives and friends, form a vast "social network" that envelops the infant (Lamb, 1977b; Lewis, 1982b; Lewis, Feiring, & Kotsonis, in press; Weinraub, Brooks, & Lewis, 1977). Only recently has the importance and complexity of infants' interactions with people other than the mother been recognized in the research literature (e.g., Belsky, 1981).

Since Bowlby (1958) introduced the term, attachment has been used to refer to the infant's unique relationship with the primary caregiver (usually the mother), a relationship regarded as necessary for survival. For attachment theorists, the infant–mother relationship is the source of all subsequent social relationships, with the nature of the attachment relationship determining the quality of other relationships (Ainsworth, 1979; Bowlby, 1973). Investigations of the special features of the infant–mother relationship have produced a massive attachment literature showing that the mother may play a central role in infants' subsequent intellectual as well as socioemotional development (Ainsworth & Bell, 1974; Bowlby, 1969; Brazelton et al., 1974; Hunt, 1961; Lewis & Coates, 1980; Lewis & Goldberg, 1969b; Yarrow, 1961; Yarrow, Rubenstein, & Pedersen, 1975).

It is becoming obvious, however, that children's social, emotional, and cognitive development is not solely determined by the infant–mother relationship. Infants are capable of entering into significant relationships with other people as well. Observations of infants' behaviors in everyday situations indicate that infants also have affectionate feelings for fathers, siblings, and grandparents, as well as for other relatives and friends. Moreover, infants' relationships with the father and with peers seem to emerge at about the same time as infants' relationship with the mother (Harlow & Harlow, 1969; Lamb, 1978, 1979; Lewis, Young, Brooks, & Michalson, 1975; Mueller & Vandell, 1979; Parke, 1979b). This evidence suggests that these relationships may be functionally independent rather than direct offshoots of the infant–mother relationship. It is likely that these different relationships serve different functions in the life of the infant, thus satisfying different needs (Lewis, 1982b; Lewis & Feiring, 1979; Weinraub et al., 1977). For example, while the maternal relationship may serve to protect and nurture the infant, peer relationships may promote exploration and play.

Because *attachment* has traditionally referred exclusively to the infant–mother relationship, in the construction of the measurement scales the term *social affiliation* was adopted to refer to the social-emotional relationships of infants with all members of their social network, including the mother. Social affiliation is primarily expressed in behaviors aimed at establishing or maintaining contact with other human beings. The hedonic quality of the response depends on the degree of distress induced by the eliciting situation. The nature of the situations and the forms of behavior used to measure attachment and social affiliation in children are discussed in the next sections.

Social Affiliation Situations

Separation from the mother (Ainsworth & Bell, 1970; Rheingold & Eckerman, 1970; Schaffer & Emerson, 1964), reunion with the mother (Ainsworth & Bell, 1970; Maccoby & Feldman, 1972), and low-stress, "free-play" situations (e.g., Brooks & Lewis, 1974a; Goldberg & Lewis, 1969; Maccoby & Jacklin, 1973) are standard situations used to measure the infant–mother relationship. The quality of an infant's relationship to the mother is generally assessed by means of a highly structured "strange situation" procedure (Ainsworth & Wittig, 1969). This procedure consists of a series of eight episodes in which the infant's behaviors are observed as the mother and a stranger alternately leave and reenter a laboratory playroom in various ·prescribed combinations. Findings from a number of studies indicate that the reunion episode with the mother, particularly the second time it occurs, provides the best measure of the quality of the infant–mother relationship (Ainsworth et al., 1978).

A small but growing literature on infants' relationships with their fathers suggests that when given the opportunity, fathers are as capable as mothers of eliciting affiliative behaviors in infants (e.g., Feldman & Ingham, 1975; Lamb, 1978; Willemsen, Flaherty, Heaton, & Ritchey, 1974). Fathers can be as responsive and competent as mothers in interacting with their infants (Lamb, 1976, 1977a; Parke, 1979; Parke & O'Leary, 1976). Furthermore, there are few differences in infants' behaviors toward their mothers and fathers when measured in structured playroom situations (Lewis & Weinraub, 1976), although at age 1 infants may show a slight preference for the mother (Cohen & Campos, 1974; Lewis, Weinraub, & Ban, 1972). By age 2, however, few sex-of-parent differences are apparent (Lewis et al., 1972). Kotelchuck (1976) reported that infants show very little parental preference during the first year of life. After that, approximately 55% of a group of infants were found to prefer the mother, 25% to prefer the father, and 20% to show no preference. In addition, mothers and fathers seem to elicit approximately equal amounts of separation protest when they leave the room in the strange-situation paradigm (Cohen & Campos, 1974; Kotelchuck, 1976; Spelke, Zelazo, Kagan, & Kotelchuck, 1973).

Even though fathers and mothers have an equal capacity for nurturing their infants, under naturally occurring conditions in the home the two parental relationships may be characterized by different types of interactions. Mothers tend to engage infants more in caretaking activities, and fathers engage infants more in play (Lamb, 1978; Parke & O'Leary, 1976). The quantity of interaction with infants may also differ between fathers and mothers outside the laboratory setting. The data on the number of father–infant interactions suggest that fathers may interact very infrequently with infants (Ban & Lewis, 1974; Pedersen & Robson, 1969; Rebelsky & Hanks, 1971), although there seems to be a contemporary trend for fathers to take a more active role in caretaking activities than they have in the past (Lamb, 1979). In view of the limited number of interactions between fathers and infants, the father's primary effect on the infant may be indirect, being mediated in the absence of the father by the father's relationship with the mother, which, in turn, influences the mother's relationship with the child (Lewis & Feiring, 1981; Lewis & Weinraub, 1976; Lewis et al., 1981).

In general, there is a lack of research on infants' relationships to caregivers other than their parents. One might ask whether infants become attached to regular baby-sitters or to caregivers in day-care centers (Fox, 1977). While there is some evidence that infants can and do develop a discriminating attachment-like relationship with familiar caregivers (Farran & Ramey, 1977; Fleener, 1973; Ricciuti, 1974), when under stress infants seem to prefer their mothers over familiar caregivers or even their fathers (Lamb, 1976, 1978).

As was mentioned earlier, not all social relationships can be identified as attachment. For example, a growing literature exists on infants' relationships with peers (Bronson, 1981; Lewis & Rosenblum, 1975; Mueller & Vandell, 1979). Not only do infants interact with other infants, but they interact in a discriminatory fashion depending on whether the playmate is a friend or a stranger (Bridges, 1933; Doyle, Connolly, & Rivest, 1980; Lewis et al., 1975; Young & Lewis, 1979). The study of sibling relations lags behind even that of peer relations (Lamb & Sutton-Smith, 1982; Sutton-Smith & Rosenberg, 1970). Very little is known about infants' relationships to grandparents, uncles, aunts, and cousins (Feinman, Roberts, & Grumbles, 1982). Such relationships probably have, at the very least, an indirect effect on the infant (Lewis, 1982b; Lewis & Feiring, 1981).

Affiliative relationships are not confined to familiar persons. Infants have been observed to respond positively and even to initiate social interactions with strangers (Bretherton, 1978; Bretherton & Ainsworth, 1974; Haviland & Lewis, 1975; Maccoby & Jacklin, 1973; Morgan & Ricciuti, 1969; Rheingold & Eckerman, 1973; Ross & Goldman, 1977). Unfamiliar children are more likely than unfamiliar adults to evoke positive social responses in infants (Brooks & Lewis, 1976; Greenberg et al., 1973; Lewis & Brooks, 1974).

Social affiliation, then, is manifested in response to a variety of social objects, including mothers, fathers, caregivers, peers, and even strangers. The specific dimensions of these objects that elicit affiliative responses have not been investigated, although it is clear that from the first months of life, infants react differently to various people in the social environment (Lewis et al., 1975; Parke, 1979b). Familiarity seems likely to be a highly salient dimension in determining infants' responses. Findings from several studies show that parents are more likely than strangers to elicit affiliative behaviors (Feldman & Ingham, 1975; Kotelchuck, 1976; Lester, Kotelchuck, Spelke, Sellers, & Klein, 1974; Spelke et al., 1973). Moreover, infants react differently with peers who are familiar compared with unfamiliar peers (Lewis et al., 1975; Young & Lewis, 1979).

The degree of familiarity of the setting and other contextual variables are also likely to affect infants' emotional responses. Laboratory settings usually prove to be stronger elicitors of affiliative behaviors and may elicit different behaviors to different degrees of intensity than are commonly observed in the home (Ainsworth et al., 1978; Brookhart & Hock, 1976). In addition, expressions of attachment have been observed to increase as a function of the amount of time spent with the mother in a laboratory playroom (Brooks & Lewis, 1974b). The number of toys in the setting may also affect the likelihood of observing attachment, with fewer attachment behaviors exhibited in the presence of "more interesting" sets of toys (Willemson et al., 1974).

The degree of stress inherent in the situation is also likely to alter the infants' social behavior (Sroufe et al., 1974). For instance, preference for the mother over the father is more likely to occur under stressful conditions (Lamb, 1976). Finally, the age of the social object may affect infants' social responses, with unfamiliar children eliciting more positive behaviors than unfamiliar adults (Brooks & Lewis, 1976; Greenberg et al., 1973; Lewis & Brooks, 1974).

Social Affiliation Responses

Traditional measures of attachment have been limited to those behaviors aimed at maintaining close proximity to a particular person. Such behaviors include protest (e.g., crying and fussing), approach (e.g., approaching and reaching), proximity-seeking, and seeking to be held. These responses are likely to be manifested in high-stress situations such as separation from and reunion with the mother and in the presence of a stranger (Ainsworth, 1979). In contrast, studies of infant–mother interaction in low-stress, free-play situations have used affiliative measures that generally include touching and staying close to the mother ("proximal" modes of expression), as well as looking, smiling, and vocalizing ("distal" forms of expression; Ainsworth, 1967; Goldberg & Lewis, 1969; Lewis & Wilson, 1972; Messer & Lewis, 1972).

Such behaviors may also express infants' desire to establish and maintain contact with people other than attachment figures. A review of the peer literature shows that affiliative behaviors are not directed exclusively toward "attachment" objects but are directed toward peers as well (Mueller & Vandell, 1979). Thus, signaling behaviors (e.g., crying, calling, and smiling), orienting behaviors (e.g., looking), locomotions (e.g., following and approaching), and active physical contact (e.g., clambering up, embracing, and clinging) can be used to reference social affiliation in response to a variety of social objects.

Attempts in the mid-1970s to establish the consistency of discrete attachment behaviors over periods of time ranging from three minutes to as long as one year and across different eliciting situations were largely unsuccessful (Coates, Anderson, & Hartup, 1972a,b; Maccoby & Feldman, 1972; Masters & Wellman, 1974). As a consequence, the concept of attachment was brought into question (e.g., Rosenthal, 1973). Responses to the challenge were varied. Lewis and his colleagues (Lewis & Ban, 1971; Lewis & Weinraub, 1974; Lewis et al., 1972) provided data indicating that although proximal forms of attachment at 1 year are not related to the same behaviors at 2 years, they are related to distal forms of attachment at 2 years. Others attempted to draw theoretical distinctions between attachment as a bond and attachment as behavior. The necessity of regarding attachment as an organizational construct rather than as discrete behavior was emphasized (Sroufe, 1979a). Recommendations were made for using multiple measures of attachment and considering their interrelationships in an effort to show that only the discrete behaviors used to express attachment, not attachment *per se*, vary over age. Indeed, when patterns of responses are looked at in the strange-situation procedure (e.g., maintaining contact, seeking proximity, and avoiding and resisting the mother on reunion), individual differences in attachment are found to be stable across periods of two weeks and six months (Ainsworth *et al.*, 1978).

Competence

Competence is the most difficult of the five emotions to conceptualize, partly because competence is not generally included in current taxonomies of emotional states (Izard, 1977) and partly because competence is so closely related to the cognitive domain that the distinction between the emotional state of competence and the cognitive notion of competence is not always clear. In its general usage, *competence* usually means individuals' inherent ability to do a particular task as distinct from their actual performance on the task.

As an emotional state, competence refers to the feelings of individuals about their own abilities. *Abilities*, in this instance, refers to a collection of attributes, skills, and even other feelings. Thus conceived, competence is regarded as an important dimension that reflects personal feelings about oneself. In the psychiatric literature, competence reflects mastery and is considered to be a powerful motivational state of the individual (Adler, 1927).

Children's social competence has been of great interest to several investigators, who suggest that this construct should extend beyond measures of cognitive ability to include motivational, affective, and physical measures as well (Anderson & Messick, 1974; Harter, 1978; Scarr, 1981; Zigler, 1979; Zigler & Trickett, 1978). We included competence as a domain in our scales to assess children's feelings about their own sense of mastery and ability. In other words, we wanted to measure how young children feel about themselves. The feelings associated with this construct might be thought of as happiness, when the child's attempt at mastery is successful, or as helplessness, sadness, or anger, when it is not. Whether competence is a feeling state in and of itself remains to be determined. But because it is a special state that affects children's development, we have included it in our scales as a separate domain.

The emotional state of competence is also inferred from a set of observable behaviors, but in the construction of the measurement scales, *competence* was not necessarily meant to refer to a set of basic skills.

Rather, the notion of competence as an emotional state derives from R. White's (1959) theoretical discussion of competence, a concept that has subsequently been developed by other investigators (e.g., Bronson, 1971b, 1974; Harter, 1978; Hunt, 1965; Lewis, 1971; Lewis & Goldberg, 1969b; Wenar, 1964, 1972, 1976, 1978; B. White, 1975, 1978; White & Watts, 1973; Yarrow, 1979; Yarrow & Messer, in press; Yarrow & Pedersen, 1976). Essentially, White (1959) noted that many human behaviors are directed toward having an effect on the environment without satisfying a physiological need. Interactions with the environment that have an effect are likely to be repeated. In other words, White described an intrinsic motivation for competence behaviors.

As infants associate their actions with certain environmental effects, they develop feelings of efficacy, that is, feelings associated with being an effective force in the environment. As a result, infants acquire a perception of themselves as capable of doing things. One aspect of this perception is the feeling of self-confidence that accompanies mastery of the environment. Yarrow (1979; Yarrow & Messer, in press; Yarrow & Pedersen, 1976) has written about competence in terms of a positive self-evaluation associated with the ability to control the environment. Unfortunately, few data have been published on the relationship between mastery and self-evaluation.

At the heart of the competence issue is the notion that in order to feel competent, infants must experience environmental effects as contingent on their own actions. Thus, most of the research in this area is directed at investigating (1) which behaviors are responsive to contingency experiences and (2) the relationship between early contingency experiences and later cognitive and social development. Few descriptions can be found in the research literature of infants' expressions of competence in everyday transactions with the physical and social environments.

Competence Situations

The feelings that one's actions will affect the environment originate from contingency experiences in infancy. The mother is regarded as the most important source of infants' contingency experiences insofar as it is the contingency between the infants' behaviors and her responses that enables the infants to learn that their behavior does have important consequences (Ainsworth, 1973; Ainsworth & Bell, 1974; Lewis, 1971; Lewis & Goldberg, 1969b). Thus, competence may be fostered in everyday situations, such as the mother's answering when the infant cries or smiling when the infant smiles.

Two dimensions of the mother's response may be particularly important in affecting the development of competence (Lewis & Goldberg, 1969b). One is the total amount of stimulation provided to the infant by the mother; the other is the relationship between the infant's behavior and the mother's response. Recently, it has been shown that the mother's frequency of contingency responding may be less important to the development of competence in infants than is the contingency of the relationship between maternal and infant behavior (Lewis & Coates, 1980).

Empirical evidence suggests that infants' early contingency experiences are associated with cognitive and social development. For example, the amount of mothers' contingent responding to infants' crying and vocalizing behaviors is related to learning in a habituation test (Lewis & Goldberg, 1969b). In addition, a positive relationship between mothers' responsiveness to infants' behaviors and infants' competence has been reported (Ainsworth & Bell, 1974; Clarke-Stewart, 1973; Lewis & Coates, 1980). Nonsocial as well as social contingency stimulation has been found to be positively correlated with infant intelligence (Yarrow, Rubenstein, Pedersen, & Jankowski, 1972).

The absence of contingency experience can also affect competence variables in a dramatic fashion. For example, several studies have shown that experience with stimulation over which the infant has no control (i.e., noncontingent stimulation) interferes with later learning (Dweck & Repucci, 1973; Finkelstein & Ramey, 1977; Watson, 1971), creating a condition known as *learned helplessness* (Seligman, 1975; Seligman & Maier, 1967).

Competence Responses

Infants who have been led to believe that their actions have consequences in the environment are likely to seek contingency experiences through exploration of both the physical and the social environments. The response measures used in two longitudinal studies of infant–mother dyads in the home environment are particularly interesting for the purposes of the present study. Wenar (1976) studied "executive competence" in infants from 12 to 20 months of age in terms of the infants' ability to initiate and sustain locomotive, manipulative, and visual regarding activities at a given level of complexity and intensity, with a given degree of self-sufficiency. In another study, Wenar (1978) broadened the definition of competence to include not only infants' spontaneous exploration of the physical environment but also their social initiative in relationship to the mother. Thus, both exploration of the physical environment and initiatives in social interaction were regarded as measures of competence.

B. White (1975, 1978; White & Watts, 1973) has studied competence longitudinally in terms of children's social activities with peers and adults. Among the measures of social competence were gaining adult attention, using adults as resources, expressions of affection and hostility, engaging in role play, expressing pride in achievement, showing competition with peers, and leading–following. White (1975) noted that expressions of competence may be somewhat different in different ages of children. For instance, at 12 months of age, exploration was observed more frequently than mastery activities (e.g., practicing simple skills); mastery gradually became more prominent during the second and third years of life.

Ross (1974) also described age changes in exploratory activities. In the first six months of life, exploration is accomplished primarily by watching and listening activities. Soon, infants explore by reaching for and manipulating objects. Around 9 or 10 months of age, locomotive abilities are added to sensory and manual capacities and provide new means of exploration.

The pleasurable feelings derived from successful mastery of the environment can also be inferred in infants' facial and vocal behaviors. Smiling, grinning, laughing, cooing, and babbling are expressions of positive affect that accompany infants' need to act on and to affect the environment (W. C. Bronson, 1971a,b). Another group of studies has reported that smiling and laughter are likely to accompany infants' successful attempts to assimilate a novel event into an existing schema (e.g., Haith, 1972; McCall, 1972; Shultz & Zigler, 1970; Zelazo, 1972; Zelazo & Komer, 1971). Kagan (1971) found that 2-year-olds tend to smile following the solution of an embedded-figures problem, with a greater probability of smiling's occurring in response to more difficult problems. However, if a stimulus configuration or problem is too novel or too difficult for the infant, or is too familiar or too easy, expressions of fear or lack of interest are more likely to be observed than are expressions of competence.

Finally, a general review of the literature reveals that a variety of early infant behaviors are susceptible to environmental contingencies, including sucking, head turning, vocalizing, and smiling (Thurman, 1978). However, when subjected to contingency experiences, infants seem to learn more than a single response (Brinker & Lewis, 1982). Not only have responses been observed to generalize across situations, but infants have been observed to be generally more competent and efficient learners in new situations (Finkelstein & Ramey, 1977).

Where Should Emotions Be Studied?

Most studies of emotional development are conducted in experimental laboratories. In laboratory-based situations, investigators can both control many of the variables and measure responses that may be difficult to measure in nonlaboratory settings (e.g., physiological responses). Such advantages often are offset by the disadvantages of contrived situations and the limited number of alternatives available. In order to facilitate the exploration of emotional development, it is necessary to use measurement techniques that can be applied not only in the laboratory but in children's natural ecology.

One alternative to studying emotions in the laboratory is to identify other environments that are related to the everyday life of children. Observing children in their own homes comes to mind. Such a technique has considerable merit. However, in order to obtain enough instances of varied elicitors within the home, extremely long periods of observation time would be required. Thus, for example, if one were interested in children's naturally occurring play behavior with peers, an observer would have to wait for a play situation to occur in the home. For pragmatic reasons, the home becomes less viable as an environment for studying children's emotions.

An alternative naturalistic setting is the day-care center. Today, over 40% of preschool children spend at least some time in a day-care environment. Day-care settings contain a larger and more varied array of potential emotion-eliciting situations than either the home or the laboratory. Moreover, one goal of our research was to devise an instrument that might be used to assess children's emotional status in intervention programs as well as to evaluate the effectiveness of intervention programs. Thus, the best environment for constructing the scales seemed to be day care.

The items included in the scales, however, may occur in settings other than day care. Thus, while the scales were constructed in the context of day care, their use should be general. Whether day-care centers constitute the ideal environment for observing differences in children's emotions needs to be determined. Even so, one would expect the relationship between elicitors (situations) and behaviors to be relatively constant across settings, although the particular elicitors producing certain behaviors may be restricted vis-à-vis the general situation. For example, the approach of a stranger might elicit different intensities of fear (or affiliative) behaviors in the laboratory, in the home, and in the pediatrician's office, but it is unlikely that an individual child would be afraid in one setting and not another. In other words, children should maintain their fear ranks with respect to other children even though the intensity of their fear might vary by situation.

Even so, there may be some difficulty in assuming behavioral consistency across environments. If, in fact, the approach of a stranger (or any other stimulus event) is totally dependent on the nature of the event or the situation in which the event occurs, then the complexities involved in measuring emotions may undermine the research efforts. Although pessimistic, such a possibility must be considered. However, the working assumption of the research project was that the scales, or at least some of the scale items, would produce the same behaviors and the same individual differences in environments other than day care. Such environments might include pediatricians' offices and well-baby clinics, as well as homes.

Which Situations Should Be Used?

For the purposes of scale construction, the situations were the items on which the children's responses were to be scored. The situations were selected as items in a complex manner. First, the literature on the five emotions was reviewed. Special attention was paid to the situations that others have used to define and study children's emotions. Of particular interest were situations that might naturally occur in children's everyday environment. Thus, while both the approach of a stranger and the visual cliff have been used as stimuli to evoke fear, only the stranger approach situation was included, since visual cliffs are not likely to be part of the natural environment. In addition to the literature review, observations were made in a day-care setting on 12 infants. These observations consisted of detailed descriptions of emotion-eliciting situations that occurred at the day-care center along with infants' responses to the situations.

From these two sources, lists were made of situations that might evoke each of the five emotions. As one would assume, some situations were likely to evoke more than one emotion. For example, strangers were observed to be effective elicitors of both fear and affiliative behaviors. The solution was to include these situations as potential items for measuring each relevant emotion.

The original assessment instrument consisted of 48 different situations. Because many of these situations appeared as items for different emotions, these 48 situations actually constituted 83 scale items. As a consequence of detailed data analyses (described in the following chapter), the number of situations and items in the scales was reduced.

The revised version of the scales consisted of 37 situations and 48 items. The items included in the scales are listed by emotion in Table 13.Their definitions are provided in Table 14. Social affiliation, as can be seen in Table 13, is measured in both low-stress and high-stress situations. The reader should keep in mind that some item redundancy exists across different emotions; that is, some situations were included as measures of more than one emotion.

Table 13. Items of the Scales of Socioemotional Development

Fear
 When the child arrives at the day-care center ("arrival")[a]
 When the child plays with a surprise toy ("surprise toy")[a]
 When the child breaks a toy ("toy breaks")
 When a peer cries ("peer cries")
 When a peer attacks the child ("peer attacks")
 When the caregiver makes a funny (unusual) sound ("funny sound")[a]
 When the caregiver yells ("caregiver yells")
 When the caregiver forbids the child to do something ("caregiver forbids")[a]
 When the caregiver scolds the child ("caregiver scolds")[a]
 When the child is taken to an unfamiliar place ("unfamiliar room")
 When the child notices a stranger in the room ("stranger")
 When the stranger approaches the child ("stranger approach")
 When the child notices an unfamiliar child in the room ("strange child")

Anger
 When the parent leaves ("mother leaves")[a]
 When the child wants something another child has ("wants something peer has")
 When the child wants something caregiver has ("wants something caregiver has")[a]
 When the child wants something that is out of reach ("wants something
  unreachable")[a]
 When the child plays with a difficult toy ("difficult toy")[a]
 When the child breaks a toy ("toy breaks")
 When a peer receives special attention from a caregiver ("peer gets attention")
 When a peer grabs the child's toy ("peer grabs toy")
 When a peer attacks the child ("peer attacks")
 When the caregiver teases the child ("teased")
 While the child watches, the caregiver hides a toy ("hidden object")
 When the caregiver takes a toy away from the child ("caregiver takes toy")[a]
 When the caregiver takes a bottle or pacifier away from the child ("caregiver takes
  bottle/pacifier")[a]
 When the caregiver physically restrains the child ("physical restraint")[a]
 When the caregiver forbids the child to do something ("caregiver forbids")[a]

---

[a] Item eliminated from revised version of scales. (continued)

Table 13. *(Continued)*

When the caregiver scolds the child ("caregiver scolds")
When there is an obstacle between the child and his/her goal ("obstacle")[a]
When the parent returns ("mother returns")[a]

Happiness
When the child arrives at the day-care center ("arrival")[a]
When the child accomplishes what he/she intended to do ("completes task")[a]
When the child plays with a surprise toy ("surprise toy")
When the child sees self in a mirror ("mirror-self")
When the child sees the reflection of another person in a mirror ("mirror–other")
When a peer acts silly ("peer acts silly")[a]
When the caregiver gives special attention to the child ("interaction–special attention")
When the caregiver praises the child ("praise")
When the caregiver plays peek-a-boo or hide-and-seek ("peek-a-boo")
When the caregiver teases the child ("teased")
When the caregiver makes a funny (unusual) sound ("funny sound")[a]
When the caregiver acts silly ("caregiver acts silly")
When the caregiver offers a snack to the child ("snack")
When music is played or the caregiver sings ("music")

Social affiliation
Low stress
When the caregiver greets the child ("caregiver greets")
When another parent and child arrive at the day-care center ("another mother arrives")
During free play ("free play")[a]
When the child sees some children and caregivers playing together ("group")
When a peer cries ("peer cries")[a]
When the caregiver gives special attention to the child ("interaction–special attention")[a]
When the caregiver returns ("caregiver returns")
When the child notices a stranger in the room ("stranger")
When the child notices an unfamiliar child in the room ("strange child")[a]
When another parent returns to take a child home ("another mother returns")[a]
When the parent returns ("mother returns")

High stress
When the parent puts the child down ("mother puts child down")
When the parent leaves ("mother leaves")
When another parent and child arrive at the day-care center ("another mother arrives")
When a peer receives special attention from a caregiver ("peer gets attention")
When the caregiver leaves ("caregiver leaves")
When the caregiver puts the child down ("caregiver puts child down")
When another parent returns to take a child home ("another mother returns")[a]

Table 13. *(Continued)*

Competence

When the child arrives at the day-care center ("arrival")[a]

When the parent puts the child down ("mother puts child down")

During free play ("free play")

When the child sees some children and caregivers playing together ("group")

When the child wants something another child has ("wants something peer has")[a]

When the child wants something a caregiver has ("wants something caregiver has")

When the child wants something that is out of reach ("wants something
  unreachable")

When the child accomplishes what it intended to do ("completes tasks")[a]

When the child plays with a difficult toy ("difficult toy")[a]

When the child breaks a toy ("toy breaks")

When the child sees self in a mirror ("mirror–self")[a]

When the child sees the reflection of another person in a mirror ("mirror–other")[a]

When the caregiver gives special attention to the child ("interaction–special
  attention")[a]

When the caregiver shows the child how to do something ("demonstration")

When the caregiver tells the child to do something ("command")[a]

When the caregiver praises the child ("praise")[a]

While the child watches, the caregiver hides a toy ("hidden object")[a]

When the caregiver puts the child down ("caregiver puts child down")[a]

When there is an obstacle between the child and his/her goal ("obstacle")

When the child is taken to an unfamiliar place ("unfamiliar room")

Table 14. Situations and Definitions in the Scales of Socioemotional
Development[a]

1. *Arrival*[c]—when the child arrives at the day-care center. The child and parent[b] enter
   the main room of the day-care center. (Watch S from the moment of entry. Note if
   someone other than the parent brings S or if S is asleep).
2. *M puts child down*—when the parent puts the child down. The parent[b] who has
   been holding S, places S on the floor, in a playpen, in a crib, or in a high chair,
   thereby terminating physical contact with S. (If the parent carries S into the day-
   care center, watch for him/her to put S down. If S walks in by him/herself, wait until
   the parent picks S up for whatever reason. If the parent does not pick up S at all
   during "arrival," watch for this situation during "departure." Situation begins when
   parent begins to release S.)
3. *C greets*—when the caregiver greets the child. A caregiver greets S by name, accompanied by "Hi," or "How are you today?" Usually C looks and smiles at S; C may
   also lean toward, touch, or pick up S during the greeting. (Watch for S's response
   from the first word of the vocalization.)
4. *M leaves*—when the parent leaves. S's parent[b] walks out of the room where he/she
   and S were and leaves S behind. The parent may tell S he/she is leaving or may try

[a] *Abbreviations:* S, subject (target child); M, mother, father, or parent substitute (e.g., relative or
  neighbor); C, caregiver or teacher at day-care center; P, peer (another child at day-care center).
[b] Or parent substitute (i.e., relative, neighbor).
[c] Situation eliminated in the revised version of the scales.

(continued)

Table 14. *(Continued)*

---

to sneak out. (Situation begins when the parent puts on coat, picks up purse, moves toward door, or opens door, whichever S notices first.)

5. *Another M arrives*—when another parent and child arrive at the day-care center. After S's own mother or father has departed, another child and parent[b] enter the room where S is. (Situation begins when S looks in their direction.)

6. *Free play*—during free play. No structure is imposed on S's activity. S is unrestrained, toys are available, and S is left to his/her own pursuits. (This situation lacks a beginning and an end and often may be interrupted by peer- or caregiver-initiated behaviors; e.g., peer or C may grab the toy S is playing with. Code S's behavior only during periods of unstructured play.)

7. *Group*—when the child sees some children and caregivers playing together. S looks in the direction of a group of children with or without Cs engaged in a common activity, such as block play, coloring, reading, or games. S may or may not be invited to join the group. The group must consist of *at least* three people, either three children or two children and one caregiver. (Situation begins when S looks in their direction.)

8. *Wants something P has*—when the child wants something another child has. S looks intently at another child who is playing with a toy or holding a "desirable" object. The desirable object may be a bottle or pacifier or a makeshift toy. (Situation begins when S looks in child's direction.)

9. *Wants something C has*—when the child wants something a caregiver has. S looks intently at C who is holding a "desirable" object. The object may be a bottle or pacifier, a toy, or a potential toy (e.g., spoon, cup, or pencil). (Situation begins when S looks in C's direction.)

10. *Wants something unreachable*—when the child wants something that is out of reach. S looks intently at "desired" object, which is not easily obtained (within easy reach for child). For example, S may or may not be able to obtain object by standing on tiptoe and stretching arm or body toward it. Desired object may be a bottle, a toy, or a potential toy. (Situation begins when S looks at object.)

11. *Completes task*[c]—when the child accomplishes what it intended to do. S completes task/activity. Task/activity may or may not have been initiated by S; it may be either productive (e.g., S adds piece to puzzle or block to tower) or destructive (e.g., S pushes over tower). (If S has trouble mastering a play object because it seems too difficult, score #13 "difficult toy.")

12. *Surprise toy*—when the child plays with a surprise toy. S turns the handle of jack-in-the-box causing jack to pop up, or C turns handle and S watches jack pop up. (Situation begins when jack pops up. Note behaviors that follow initial startle response.)

13. *Difficult toy*[c]—when the child plays with a difficult toy. S is confronted with a manipulable, age-appropriate play object that S does not readily or cannot easily master. The nature of the toy will vary according to the developmental level of the child. Toys that require the child to drop a varying shaped block into the appropriate hole or to place a large puzzle piece in the right place are good. However, the source of difficulty could be as diverse as turning the pages of a book, pulling the ring of a music box, or causing the parts of a mobile to shake or bells to ring. This differs from situation #11 ("completes task") in that #11 requires achievement, while #13 requires only an attempt to achieve. (Situation begins when even a "clumsy" attempt is made to manipulate the play object. Remember that if S masters the toy imme-

Table 14. *(Continued)*

diately, the toy should not be considered "difficult," and #11 should be coded.)

14. *Toy breaks*—when the child breaks a toy or sees a broken toy. S is playing with a toy, which breaks while S is handling it (i.e., a piece comes off or a part ceases to work), or S notices that a toy is broken (for example, a doll without a head or a toy car missing a wheel). Toy is broadly defined as any potential play object. (Situation begins when toy breaks or when S looks at broken toy.)

15. *Mirror–self*—when the child sees self in a mirror. S, not further than three feet from a mirror and within the mirror's reflecting radius, looks at the mirror. From S's perspective, no one else is visible in the mirror. (Situation begins when S glances at mirror.)

16. *Mirror–other*—when the child sees the reflection of another person in the mirror. The image of another person, who is behind S, is reflected in the mirror. S, not further than three feet from a mirror, focuses her/his eyes on the image at least momentarily. (Make sure S glances at the image of the other person, however briefly, and not exclusively at her/his own image. Situation begins when S focuses on image.)

17. *P gets attention*—when a peer receives special attention from the caregiver. S notices C interacting exclusively with another child (while S is *not* receiving any attention from an adult). The nature of the interaction is pleasant. For example, C may be holding another child or playing with another child. C must do more than just vocalize to a child. (Situation begins when S glances at them.)

18. *P cries*—when a peer cries. Another child cries or screams. Cry must be of an intensity to be noticed by another person. (Situation begins when cry becomes loud enough to attract attention.)

19. *P grabs toy*—when a peer grabs the child's toy. S is playing with a toy (broadly defined); another child attempts to take it away from S. S may or may not actually be holding the toy at the moment P grabs it. For example, S may be putting blocks in a bucket, when another child walks off with the bucket. Attempt to take may or may not be successful. (Situation begins when peer reaches for toy.)

20. *P attacks*—when a peer attacks the child. Another child hits, kicks, bites, or pushes S, either on purpose or accidentally, or pulls S's hair. (Situation begins when peer touches S.)

21. *P acts silly*[c]—when a peer acts silly. Behavior of another child is designed to elicit smile or laughter from others. For example, peer may don "funny" hat, attempt to stand on his/her head, or make a "funny" face or noise. (Situation begins when peer starts acting silly.)

22. *Interaction–special attention*—when the caregiver gives special attention to the child. C interacts exclusively with S. The nature of the interaction is pleasant. For example, C may hold S or may play with S but must do more than just vocalize to S from a distance. (Situation begins when interaction begins.)

23. *Demonstration*—when the caregiver shows the child how to do something. C demonstrates to S how a toy works (e.g., ring stacks), the functional use of an object (e.g., spoon), or a body movement (e.g., dance, jump, or skip). C may say things such as "Watch," or "Do what I do." (Situation begins when C begins demonstration.)

24. *Command*[c]—when the caregiver tells the child to do something. C tells S to perform a specified act. For example, C may tell S to bring a toy or to put something away. This situation does *not* cover the instance when C tells S not to do something S is

(continued)

Table 14. *(Continued)*

doing or about to do (see #35 "forbid" and #36 "scold"). (Situation begins when C begins the command.)

25. *Praise*—when the caregiver praises the child. C tells S that he/she is a good child or has performed well. For example, C may smile, clap hands, and say something like, "Thank you, that was a good thing you did!" or "That was very good!" (This situation is likely to follow #23 "demonstration" or #24 "command." Situation begins when C begins to speak.)

26. *Peek-a-boo*—when the child plays peek-a-boo or hide-and-seek. C covers either S's eyes or her/his own with a cloth or hands, usually saying something like, "Where's (S's name)?" Then C removes cloth or hands, smiles and/or laughs, and says something like "Peek-a-boo! There you are!" In hide-and-seek, either C or S hides face behind hands, puts a cover over head, or hides behind a piece of furniture. C or S may be partly or totally invisible, and the game is usually accompanied by smiles and laughter. These games may also be played by S with another child. (Situation begins when C or S hides or is hidden.)

27. *Teased*—when the caregiver teases the child. C tantalizes S by holding something desirable (e.g., toy or food) just out of S's reach, or by inhibiting S's movement toward a goal by blocking S's "route" and alternative routes. (If S's path is blocked by an inanimate object, see #42 "obstacle"; if C physically restrains S's progress, see #33 "physical restraint." Situation begins when C holds toy out of reach or blocks path.)

28. *Funny (unusual) sound*[c]—when the caregiver makes a funny sound. C presses a squeaky toy or emits an unusual vocalization. For example, sound may take the form of lip popping, gargling, squeaky voice, or animal noise. Funny sound is not accompanied by other behaviors designed to elicit laughter. (If acccompanied by silly behaviors, see #29 "act silly." Situation begins when C makes sound.)

29. *C acts silly*—when the caregiver acts silly. Behavior of C deviates from normal behavior and is designed to elicit a smile or laughter from audience (evidenced by smile, laugh, or twinkle in C's eye). For example, C may don "funny" hat, make "funny" face, or make a "funny" gesture. The behavior may be accompanied by a funny noise. (If a funny sound occurs in the absence of funny behaviors, see #28 "funny sound." Situation begins when C starts acting silly.)

30. *Hidden object*—while the child watches, the caregiver hides a toy. C places a cover over a toy that S shows an interest in, or C places the toy behind another object. Before toy is hidden, S's interest in "game" must be obtained. Toy is hidden within reach of S. (Situation begins when toy is out of sight.)

31. *C takes toy*[c]—when the caregiver takes a toy away from the child. S is playing with a toy (broadly defined); C interrupts S's play by taking S's toy. S may or may not be actually holding the toy at the time, but the toy is obviously a part of S's play activity (e.g., blocks). (Situation begins when C reaches for toy.)

32. *C takes bottle*[c]—when the caregiver takes a bottle or pacifier away from the child. S is holding onto or sucking on bottle or pacifier, which C removes from S's possession. (Situation begins when C reaches for bottle or pacifier.)

33. *Physical restraint*[c]—when the caregiver physically restrains the child. C inhibits movement of S through physical interference. For example, C might hold S's arms and/or hands to prevent S from doing something, or C might hold S while trying to change diapers. (Situation begins when S is unable to move freely the part of his/her body being held by C.)

Table 14. *(Continued)*

34. *C yells*—when the caregiver yells. C vocalizes very loudly to someone other than S or to no one in particular. (If C yells at S, see #35 "forbid" or #36 "scold.") (Situation begins when C yells.)

35. *C forbids[c]*—when the caregiver forbids the child to do something. C tells S not to do whatever she/he thinks S is about to do. The command not to act is given before S has committed the act (compared with #36 "scold," which is after the fact). "Forbids" emphasizes restraint on activity, while #24 "command" requests action. For example, S has arm raised above another child's head, and C says, "Don't hit!" or S is headed toward the garbage pail, and C says, "Don't mess in the garbage." (Situation begins when C expresses negative.)

36. *C scolds*—when the caregiver scolds the child. C tells S that S shouldn't have acted as S did or that S is a bad girl/boy. The reprimand occurs after S has committed the act (compared with #35 "forbid," which is before the fact). (Situation begins when C expresses negative.)

37. *Snack*—when the caregiver offers a snack to the child. Other than at mealtime, C extends hand, which contains food (e.g., cookie, cracker, fruit) toward S. C may ask if S would like a cookie (or whatever C has) and smile at S. (Situation begins when C extends arm.)

38. *C leaves*—when the caregiver leaves. C walks out of the room where she/he and S were and leaves S behind. C may or may not tell S she/he is leaving. Situation is comparable to #4 "M leaves." (Situation begins when C moves toward door, opens door, or tells S that she/he is leaving, whichever S notices first.)

39. *C returns*—when the caregiver returns. C, who has been out of the room, enters the room. (Situation begins when C is visible to S.)

40. *C puts down*—when the caregiver puts the child down. C, who has been holding S, places S on the floor, in a playpen, in a crib, or in a high chair, thereby terminating physical contact with S. (Situation begins when C begins to release S.)

41. *Music*—when music is played or the caregiver sings. A record player, radio, or music box is turned on and/or C sings, whistles, or hums. (Code whenever there is music.)

42. *Obstacle*—when there is an obstacle between the child and her/his goal. An inanimate object prevents S from traveling where S wants to go. For instance, S may be in an infant walker, which gets hung up on the rug or on a toy, or S may get stuck while exploring some equipment or furniture. (If obstacle is another person, see #27 "teased" or #33 "physical restraint." Situation begins when S encounters obstacle.)

43. *Unfamiliar room*—when the child is taken to an unfamiliar place. C accompanies S (S may be walking by self or be carried by C) to a location where S either has never been before or visits infrequently. The unfamiliar place may be another room in the day-care center or a nearby building, such as the neighborhood bank, a business store, the library, or a museum. C may take S either singly or as part of a group of children. (Situation begins when S enters unfamiliar room)

44. *Stranger*—when the child notices a stranger in the room. An adult (not S's parent or another child's parent) who does not participate in the day-care-center functions enters the room where S is. S may never have seen this person before or at most has seen her/him once or twice. The stranger may be either a male or a female. (Situation begins when stranger enters room.)

45. *Stranger approaches*—when the stranger approaches the child. The stranger who appeared in the previous situation smiles at, talks to, or moves toward S. (Situation begins when stranger begins to smile at, talk to, or move toward S.)

(continued)

Table 14. *(Continued)*

46. *Strange child*—when the child notices an unfamiliar child in the room. A child (infant or toddler), who does not participate with S in the same day-care activities, enters the room. The child may be newly enrolled in the center, may be a "student" from another part of the center, or may be a temporary visitor. The child may be either a boy or a girl. (Situation begins when unfamiliar child enters room.)
47. *Another M returns*[c]—when another parent returns to take a child home. Before S's own mother or father returns to get S, another parent[b] arrives. The situation focuses on the parent's arrival and not on the departure, so if the child's own parent returns before the other parent and child have departed, the situation is still valid. (Situation begins when another parent enters room.)
48. *M returns*—when the parent returns. S's parent or parent substitute comes to get S and to take S home. (Situation begins when parent enters the room. Note if someone other than parent takes S home or if S is asleep.)

Which Behaviors Should Be Used?

In the same way that lists of situations were drawn up from a search of the literature and observations of infants in day-care programs, so also were lists of behaviors made for each emotion from a literature review and observations of the same pilot sample of 12 children. Special attention was given to the children's facial, vocal, postural, and loco-motive behaviors that occurred in response to emotion-eliciting situations. An attempt was made to include behaviors that might be exhibited by infants between 3 months and 30 months of age. Since behaviors may reflect more than one emotion, it was necessary to list some behaviors in more than one emotional domain. For example, "crying" appears in the fear, anger, and social affiliation domains. The behaviors for each emotion and their definitions are listed in Table 15.

Table 15. Behaviors and Definitions in the Scales of Socioemotional Development

Act coy—Appear to be bashful, shy, or "cute," usually by turning face away from person or mirror image yet glancing at person or image out of corner of eye. Activity level is low.
Act silly/Clown—Try to elicit smile or laughter from audience. For example, child may stand on head, put on funny hat, or teasingly withhold toy from another person. May be accompanied by smiles and laughter.
Alternating glance—Look at mirror image then at self or another person (depending on the situation) at least twice in succession.
Attack—Hit, kick, bite, push, run into, or trip over another person, or pull person's hair. Always involves another person.

Table 15. *(Continued)*

Bang/Pound—Hit or kick vigorously an inanimate object (e.g., toy, wall, mirror, but not another person). Can bang or pound either with hand or object.

Bounce—Move body rhythmically sideways or vertically. Feet may be lifted (together or one at a time), but no locomotion takes places. In response to music, the appearance of dancing is given.

Broad smile—Lips are turned outward and upward. Mouth may be opened or closed, and the corners of the mouth are wrinkled. The cheeks bulge outward as the entire face brightens.

Call attention to self—Whimper or fret accompanied by intense look toward another person. Behavior is likely to be observed when the child is trying to accomplish something. (In the same context, a neutral vocalization is regarded as "seek help.")

Call to—Short, discrete vocalization that is directed to another person in an attempt to attract the attention of another person.

Chatter—Continuous, pleasant vocalizations of conversational quality. May or may not be directed toward an object or another person.

Clap hands—Strike hands together at least twice in succession.

Clench fists—Shut hands tightly. Arms may be held close to the side of the body or fists may be extended toward an object or another person.

Create new activity—Use play material in original way, or invent imaginative activity. May be demonstrated either in solitary play or when playing with someone else.

Decrease activity/Hesitate—Slow tempo of activity.

Examine—Manually inspect object. Accompanied by attentive watching.

Eyes glow—Brilliant or sparkling quality to the eyes. May be accompanied by broad smile.

Flail—Wave or shake arms and/or legs (undirected).

Follow—Maintain proximity to another (moving) person.

Follow instructions—Child does, or attempts to do, what someone tells him/her to do.

Freeze—Cease activity. Body is rigid.

Fret/Cry—Unpleasant, distressful vocalization, louder in intensity than whimper and high and discordant in pitch. The facial appearance may be characterized by a general tenseness or trembling.

Frown—The lips are turned down and the face conveys a general unpleasantness.

Grasp/Cling—Hold tightly onto another person or an object (including person's clothing).

Grimace—Tense, mouth, clench teeth.

Hesitate/Decrease activity—Slow down level of activity.

Hit/Kick—Strike part of body (e.g., hand or foot) or object against mirror.

Hold back tears—Pout or pucker.

Hug/Kiss—Put arms around another person, touch another person (or person's clothing) with mouth.

Imitate—Copy behavior of another person.

Increase activity—Speed up tempo of activity.

Initiate own activity—Find own activity without adult supervision. For example, the child may reach for and play with toys or wander around the room examining various objects. (Bringing toys to another person counts as "show/share toy" and not as "initiate own activity.")

Join group—When two or more people are playing, child moves toward them and attempts to enter into their activity. Effect may be cooperative or interruptive.

(continued)

Table 15. *(Continued)*

Kiss/Mouth—Touch mirror image of self or other (depending on the situation) with the lips or mouth.

Laugh/Giggle—Rapid repetition of short positive sounds. Always accompanied by smile.

Lean away—Pull back upper body and head away from another person or object, usually accomplished from a sitting position. Does not involve locomotion.

Lean toward—Incline upper body and head toward another person or object. Behavior is usually accomplished from sitting position and does not involve locomotion.

Look and avoid—Glance at least twice at and away from another person or object. If the child glances and avoids *once*, the behavior is "refuse to look" or "look away."

Look around alertly—Visually examine environment.

Look away—Lower eyes, divert eyes, or turn head away.

Look behind mirror—Visually search behind mirror.

Look behind self—Turn head and direct gaze over shoulder.

Look/Glance at—Focus eyes momentarily on another person or an object.

Look hard at—Piercing gaze directed toward a particular object or person.

Manipulate/Examine—Manually inspect object. Accompanied by attentive watching.

Mouth object—Put object other than part of own body, pacifier, or bottle in mouth.

Move away—Increase distance between self and another person or object.

Move toward—Decrease distance between self and another person.

Not look—See "refuse to look."

Persist/Struggle—Persevere in spite of opposition. When faced with difficulty, child does not easily give up.

Play actively—Lively vigorous activity. Child may pursue one activity at length or move through various activities.

Point to mirror—Finger, hand, or arm is extended in direction of mirror but does not touch mirror.

Point to person—Finger, hand, or arm is extended in direction of person whose image is reflected in the mirror.

Point to self—Finger or hand is directed toward but is not touching own body.

Pout/Pucker—The corners of the mouth are pulled in and may be pulled down slightly. The lips are pushed forward and the mouth remains closed.

Pucker—The corners of the mouth are pulled in and may be pulled down slightly.

Raise arms—Arms are lifted toward person, and desire to be picked up is conveyed.

Reach—Extend arms(s) in direction of another person or object.

Refuse help—Child, who is engaged in activity, pushes away person, who tried to show him/her what to do or how to do something. Push away may be physical or verbal (e.g., fuss, "No," or "Me do").

Refuse to—Ignore; effect of stubbornness (tantrum) is conveyed. For example, the child refuses to respond when spoken to or to obey a directive.

Refuse to look—Avoid looking at object or another person. The child may lower or close eyes, look away, turn head away, or cover eyes with hand or arm. Not look.

Rehearse/Repeat activity—Practice or perform task (activity) again. For example, child may build a tower of blocks, knock it over, and build it again.

Relax—Muscles are free of tension.

Scream—Overwhelmingly loud, piercing vocalization.

Table 15. (Continued)

Search for—Look for person or object that is out of sight. Usually involves movement of hand (removal of cloth covering toy) or body (hunt around room or move toward place where person was last seen). May be limited to visual exploration in very young infants or in cases where movement is restricted (physical restraint).

Seek help—Neutral or pleading vocalization—not a whimper or fret—accompanied by intense look toward another person, or fetching of and returning to original situation with another person.

Select alternative activity—Find another toy or another activity when original activity is interrupted.

Show/Share toy—Child extends object in direction of another person, gives object to another person, or engages in cooperative play with another person.

Shut eyes tightly—Eyelids are firmly pressed together.

Skip/Strut—Locomotion characterized either by alternating hops and steps (skip) or by lifting knees high (strut) in marching style.

Slight smile—Lips are turned outward and upward. Mouth may be closed or slightly open. The smile is "less bright" than broad smile.

Sober—Serious expression. Lips are not turned down (as in frown) or clenched (as in grimace).

Squeal—Positive, high-pitched, excited, intense sound.

Stare—Visual fixation on an object or person.

Stomp—Foot is lifted and brought down forcibly.

Struggle—Wrestle over toy with another person or squirm during restraint.

Suck thumb—Put finger, thumb, pacifier, or bottle in mouth. Any automanipulation.

Tense—Muscles are tight; body is rigid.

Test alternatives—Demonstrate another or several other ways of accomplishing the same goal. For instance, the child may reach as far as possible toward an object that is out of reach, then leave and return with a stool to stand on.

Throw object—Raise or swing arm, releasing and projecting object away from body. Object may or may not be aimed.

Tongue/Mouth—Slight tongue protrusion and/or lip smacking (tongue–lip contact).

Touch—Initiate physical contact with another person or object (including person's clothing).

Touch image—Finger or hand is put on mirror reflection of self or of another person (depending on situation).

Touch self—Finger or hand is put on any part of own body (including clothes).

Tremble—Muscular rigidity accompanied by quivering.

Try to fix—When a toy breaks, the child tries to put it back together again. The endeavor may or may not be successful.

Turn away—The body is moved from facing an object or another person to not facing it.

Vocalize—Pleasant, discrete sound.

Watch intently—Intense, alert visual orientation toward another person or object.

Whimper—Discrete, unpleasant vocalizations separated by pauses and of lower intensity than "fret/cry."

Yell—Very loud vocalization of relatively short duration. Lacks piercing intensity of scream. Vocal protest.

Behavioral Scaling

Throughout the theoretical discussion of enduring emotional states, reference was made to the fact that emotions vary along a dimension of intensity. Children who look up and cease playing when a stranger enters the room or when the mother leaves might be considered somewhat fearful. Certainly, children who scream, hide behind their mother, and clutch her body tightly at the approach of a stranger can also be said to be afraid. It is not unreasonable to assume that the fear exhibited in the second case is more intense than the fear observed in the first case.

Enduring emotional states (i.e., emotional states that last for long periods of time and are easily produced) may also be characterized by their intensity. Although there are no good data supporting the premise, one might assume that children who show fear more readily and are afraid for longer periods of time are likely to show more intense fear as well. This assumption would apply to emotional states in general.

When the behaviors reported in the literature for particular emotions are examined, they seem to vary along a continuum of intensity. To consider only the presence or absence of an emotion in a particular situation is too simplistic an approach to the measurement problems identified in the previous chapters. In order to assess important emotional differences among infants, an assessment must incorporate the level or intensity of an emotion as well as its presence or absence. By scaling emotional behaviors along a dimension of intensity, it becomes possible to differentiate infants according to their emotional expressions, and, by inference, according to their emotional states.

In scale construction, the following procedures were used to scale the behaviors for each of the five emotions. First, the behaviors appropriate to each emotion, obtained through a survey of the literature and observations of children in day care, were written on index cards, one behavior per card. When behaviors were included in more than one emotional domain, they were written on a card for each domain. The cards were shuffled and put into decks. Each deck consisted of behaviors for a different emotion. Since situations in the social affiliation domain elicit different behaviors depending on whether the situation is stressful or not, two decks of cards were made for that domain; one composed of affiliative–high-stress behaviors, the other of affiliative–low-stress behaviors.

The decks of cards were given to 16 developmental and social psychologists, who were asked to rate the behaviors of each deck according to how intense they judged the behavior to be. Specifically, the judges were told:

> This task is part of a project designed to examine the emotions of infants. Each deck of cards contains a group of behaviors that characterize a particular emotion. The task is to rate each behavior on a 5-point scale of intensity (with 1 reflecting low intensity and 5 reflecting high intensity) by sorting each deck of cards into five piles. Thus, each pile will represent a rank on a 5-point scale of emotional intensity. At least one behavior should be in each of the five piles and each deck should be ranked independently of the others.

After each deck had been sorted, the judges were asked to record their behavioral ratings on a special scoring form. Judges took about one hour, on the average, to complete this task.

The reliabilities of the judges' ratings were computed by a repeated-measures analysis of variance according to the formula:

$$r = 1 - \frac{MS_{\text{w. behs.}}}{MS_{\text{bet. behs.}}}$$

The variance due to differences between the judges' frames of reference was assumed to be part of the error of measurement and was assumed not to represent a systematic source of variation (Winer, 1971). The reliabilities of the ratings were quite high for all of the emotions: fear (.96), anger (.96), happiness (.93), affiliation–low stress (.92), affiliation–high stress (.92), and competence (.92).

From the judges' data, mean ratings were computed for each behavior in each emotion. So that the behaviors were distributed evenly across 5 points, the behaviors ordered from low to high mean ratings were assigned ranks by dividing them into five categories. When the number of behaviors within a domain was not divisible by 5, the extra behaviors were placed in the middle ranks. The behaviors and their assigned ranks are shown in Table 16.

Scoring Responses

The behavioral ranks became the basis for scoring the items on the scales. Each item on the scales described a situation and listed behaviors corresponding to the emotion that the situation might evoke. Observers used these items to gather information about behaviors that might occur in particular situations. Each item, then, could be scored by using the rank of the most intense behavior observed in a particular situation. Only behaviors thought to reflect a particular emotion were scored. Thus, if infants showed no fear behavior in a fear situation, a score of 0 for fear was given on that fear item. If infants showed an angry response in a situation designated to measure fear, they were given a 0 for fear. Scores of 0 were also given if infants showed no response at

Table 16. The Ranked Behaviors

Intensity rank	Fear	Anger	Happiness	Social Affiliation		Competence
				Low stress	High stress	
1	Sober face Decrease motor activity Tongue Hesitate	Sober Look away Suck thumb Frown Look hard at	Relax Slight smile	Look/glance at Lean toward Slight smile at	Sober Look/glance at Suck thumb Lean toward	Look at alertly Vocalize Relax Mouth object Chatter Slight smile
2	Stare at Look and avoid Lean away Suck thumb	Pout/pucker Increase activity level Grimace Tense Hold back tears Turn away	Vocalize (pleasant) Eyes glow Chatter	Vocalize (pleasant) Watch Chatter Move toward	Frown Pout/pucker Tense Hold back tears	Eyes glow Reach for Watch intently Broad smile Imitate Bounce
3	Pucker Frown Turn away Tense	Move away Whimper Reach toward Shut eyes tightly Flail Clench fists	Clap hands Play actively Broad smile	Reach toward Touch Broad smile at Imitate	Whimper Watch intently Touch Move toward Reach toward	Flail Skip/strut Manipulate/examine Clap hands Seek help Play actively Persist/struggle

4	Refuse to look Move away Whimper Tremble	Flail Skip/strut Bounce	Show/share toy Laugh/giggle Raise arms Call to	Tremble Raise arms Follow Call to/for	Refuse to... Fret/cry Tremble Move toward Struggle Bang/pound	Squeal with delight Call attention to self Join group activity Show/share toy Select alternate activity
5	Grasp/cling Freeze Fret/cry Scream	Laugh/giggle Act silly Squeal with delight	Follow Search for Hug/kiss	Fret/cry Search for Grasp/cling Yell/scream	Stomp Yell Throw objects Scream Attack	Refuse help Rehearse activity Try to fix Initiate activity Create new activity Test alternatives

all in a particular situation. In this way, items were keyed to measure only those emotions likely to be elicited. It was assumed that 0 scores across many fear situations, for example, would characterize infants who generally were not afraid. It was also assumed that little fear behavior would be elicited by other non-fear-eliciting situations. Thus, emotions were measured only for specific situations, those likely to elicit that particular emotion.

By summing the item scores for each emotion and dividing by the number of items, a mean intensity or "total affect score" for each emotion was calculated for each subject. Although every attempt was made to observe all items, situations that did not occur were not scored, nor were they used to calculate the mean affect scores.

A general question can be raised about whether failing to measure emotions on situations other than those specified biases the results. Although it is true that fearful children, for example, might respond fearfully to situations in which other children would not show fear, it would be hard to argue that fearful children would not also show fear in those situations selected to elicit fear. In other words, although fearful children might react fearfully to situations included in domains other than fear, this does not alter the fact that they are still fearful children and will also show fear in the situations in the fear domain. Consequently, although the measurement system does not include all possible elicitors of particular emotions, it is believed that any missed occurrences will not bias the results or affect the ability of the scales to measure individual differences in children's emotions.

The Scales of Socioemotional Development

After day-care settings were selected as the site for scale development and dictionaries of situations and behaviors were constructed, and after behaviors were scaled according to intensity, the Scales of Socioemotional Development were ready to be tested. The scales, predicated on a matrix of situations and behaviors, took the general format of the sample items presented in Table 17. Table 17 shows four different items. Items 1 and 2 describe the same situation. However, the behaviors to be observed reflect different emotions. Items 3 and 4 measure two other emotions. This format was adopted in constructing the basic instrument used in the investigation of children's enduring emotional states except that the actual instrument used to collect data did not

Table 17. Sample Items from the Scales of Socioemotional Development

---

Item 1: Stranger (fear). When the child notices a stranger in the room, does the child

sober	lean away	move away
decrease motor activity	suck thumb	whimper
tongue	pucker	tremble
hesitate	frown	grasp/cling
stare	turn away	freeze
look and avoid	tense	fret/cry
	refuse to look	scream

Item 2: Stranger (affiliation). When the child notices a stranger in the room, does the child

look/glance at	move toward	laugh/giggle
lean toward	reach toward	raise arms
smile slightly at	touch	call to
vocalize to	smile broadly at	follow
watch	show/share toy	hug/kiss
chatter		

Item 3: Peer grabs toy (anger). When another child (peer) grabs the child's toy, does the child

sober	hold back tears	tremble
look away	turn away	move against
suck thumb	move away	struggle
frown	whimper	bang/pound
look hard at	reach toward	stomp
pout/pucker	shut eyes	yell
increase activity level	tightly	throw objects
grimace	flail	scream
tense	clench fists	attack
	refuse to. . .	
	fret/cry	

Item 4: Peek-a-boo (happiness). When the caregiver plays peek-a-boo or hide-and-seek, does the child

relax	clap hands	bounce
smile slightly	play actively	laugh/giggle
vocalize	smile broadly	act silly
eyes glow	flail	squeal with
chatter		delight

---

reveal the emotion likely to be elicited by each situation (see Appendix A).

✖✖✖✖✖✖✖✖✖✖✖

Based on observations of children in day-care settings and findings from other research on children's emotions, lists of situations and behaviors were composed for each of five emotions. The measurement model guiding the scale construction views emotion in terms of behaviors in their situational contexts. Based on the ratings of a group of psychologists, the emotional behaviors of each emotional domain were assigned ranks from 1 through 5. The ranks were designed to reflect the intensity of the emotion that the behavior reflected. The end result of this process was the Scales of Socioemotional Development, consisting of various situations and behaviors that characterize five emotions. Each item of the scales describes a situation and lists behaviors that correspond to the emotions that the situation might elicit. Items are scored according to the rank assigned to the most intense behavior elicited by the situation.

In the next chapters, the procedures used in the empirical validation of the scale construction are described in detail. The internal consistency of the scales is examined, and the results obtained from data collection using the scales are considered in terms of the theoretical issues raised in previous chapters. Specifically, the issue of whether infants express different and distinct emotions or a general emotional state such as arousal is addressed. Developmental changes in emotional differentiation are investigated. Also considered are issues concerning developmental trends in the expressions of specific emotions and individual differences as a function of children's gender and of the social milieu. The patterning of emotional expressions in individual children and the degree to which these patterns resemble personality types are considered as well. In the final chapter, the clinical application of the scales is described.

10

Internal Properties of the Scales

A survey of the research literature and observations of infants and children in day-care centers allowed us to construct a measurement instrument, discussed in detail in the last chapter. In this chapter, the administration of these scales to two separate samples, the procedures used in this administration, and the results that led to a revised version of the scales are described. The empirical aspects of the scale construction are presented in order to demonstrate that the scales (1) provide a reasonable means for observing individual differences in infants' and young children's emotional behavior in day-care settings; (2) are reliable (that is, different observers can use them and obtain similar results); (3) possess psychometric validity; and (4) generate information about specific emotions rather than general arousal.

Method

Subjects

In the construction of the scales, two samples of infants were observed. One sample consisted of 34 infants enrolled in three day-care centers. The infants had a mean age of 17.0 months and ranged in age from 3 to 30 months. Approximately half were male (n = 18) and half female (n = 16). All were from low-income families. Both white and black children were observed. The length of time that the infants had been enrolled in the day care programs ranged from 1 to 11 months, with an average length of time of 4 months.

Data were collected on a second sample of infants in order to test the replicability of the results obtained from the original sample. Sam-

Table 18. Subject Characteristics: Age and Gender

	Gender		
Age group	Male	Female	Total
Sample 1			
≤12 months (young)	5	4	9
13–18 months (middle)	6	3	9
≥19 months (old)	7	9	16
Total n	18	16	34
Sample 2			
≤12 months (young)	12	1	13
13–18 months (middle)	3	6	9
≥19 months (old)	5	5	10
Total n	20	12	32

ple 2 consisted of 32 infants from one day-care center. The infants had a mean age of 14.4 months and an age range from 4 to 23 months. Of these infants, 20 were male and 12 were female. Like Sample 1, all were from low-income families. The average length of time that these infants had been enrolled in day-care programs was 5 months, with a

Table 19. Subject Characteristics: Age at Entry and Time in Program

	Time in program		
Age at entry	≤3 months (short term)	>3 months (long term)	Total
Sample 1			
≤6 months	4	2	6
7–12 months	2	6	8
13–18 months	4	6	10
≥19 months	7	2	9
Total n	17	16	33[a]
Sample 2			
≤6 months	5	6	11
7–12 months	7	6	13
13–18 months	3	1	4
≥19 months	3	1	4
Total n	18	14	32

[a] The number of subjects totals 33 instead of 34 because the date of entry was not available for one infant.

range between 1 and 19 months. Tables 18 and 19 present the demographic data for each sample.

The infants selected for observation came from a larger population of infants and toddlers enrolled in three day-care programs. Two of the programs were in Trenton, New Jersey; one was in Princeton, New Jersey. Each day-care center conducted an all-day program five days a week for 40–60 infants and young children of low-income families. Two centers had child–teacher ratios of approximately 3 to 1, while one had a slightly higher ratio of 5 to 1. In all of these centers, children of similar ages shared a classroom, with 5–12 children in each room.

Procedures

The construction of a measurement instrument based on the intensity of behavior in response to specific situations produced an observational checklist that could be used to assess the emotional states of children in day-care settings. Five observers were used to collect data on two samples of children. The observers had arrived at the day-care centers by the time the children and their parents (usually the mothers) arrived. Each observer watched a different child each day, staying at the center until the parent returned to take the child home. The observers were instructed to wait for each situation described in the scales to occur. When the situation occurred, the observers checked off on the scales which behaviors the infants exhibited. If it seemed obvious that a situation was not going to occur spontaneously, observers were asked to "arrange" for it to happen. At this point in the procedure, the observers noted only the children's behaviors on the scales. The ranks reflecting the intensity of the behavior were coded on special forms for each item after the data had been gathered (see Chapter 12).

The procedures for collecting the data for both samples of children were similar, although the data for the second sample were gathered with a select subset of items from the original scales. The instructions provided to the observers can be found in Table 20.

Observer Reliability

Two observers collected data on six subjects (three males and three females). Reliabilities were calculated for the behaviors of each domain by dividing the number of agreements by the number of agreements

Table 20. Instructions for Using the Scales

It is important that each observer read this information carefully, since the following points are critical for understanding and correctly using the Scales of Socioemotional Development.

1. Become overfamiliar with the situations in the scales (see Dictionary of Situations). The situations and the child's behaviors in response to the situations happen very quickly. It is recommended that you practice identifying situations and seeing behaviors before collecting any data.
2. Be familiar with the different types of behaviors in the scales (see Dictionary of Behaviors). The behaviors within each situation are arranged in three columns. In the first column are facial behaviors, in the second are vocal behaviors, and in the third are body movements or motor behaviors.
3. Try to be as unobtrusive as possible. The situations should occur naturally.
4. Watch for a situation to occur. In general, the situations are grouped around specific events (e.g., arrival, departure, peer-initiated situations, caregiver-initiated situations, unfamiliar events).
5. When a situation occurs, watch what the child does from the moment the situation begins (as defined in the Dictionary of Situations) until either the situation ends or the sequence of behaviors is interrupted, whichever happens first. (If you don't see the beginning of the situation, don't code the child's behaviors. Wait for the situation to happen again.) Pay particular attention to facial expressions, vocalizations, gross body movements, and the direction of any movement (i.e., toward or away from stimulus).
6. Locate the situation and its corresponding item number on the cover page, then turn to that item in the scales and code the child's behaviors. Check the behaviors immediately after the situation occurs.
7. If the child's behaviors are not specified in that situation, note these behaviors under "Other."
8. If the target child isn't aware of the situation (e.g., never notices the stranger, never glances at the mirror), check "Didn't notice."
9. If the target child notices the situation but doesn't react to it, check "No response."
10. *Caregiver* refers to any adult who stays with the children at the day-care center. The caregiver can never be the child's parent.
11. *Parent* usually refers to the mother or father but includes whoever brings the child to the day-care center or whoever returns to take the child home. This may be a relative of the child, a friend of the family, or a neighbor. Note beside the relevant items who accompanies the child and if this person usually brings or picks up the child. (Ask the caregiver afterward for this information.)
12. Between situations, refresh your memory regarding those situations that haven't yet occurred. You may ask a caregiver to arrange any situations that are under her/his control and that haven't yet occurred. Leave blank any items that weren't observed and that can't be arranged (e.g., peer acts silly).
13. It will take about one day to collect data for each child, because of the number of items and the inclusion of both arrival and departure situations in the scales. Make sure you arrive before the target child does and plan to stay until someone comes to take the child home. It is permissible to collect data during the morning of one day and the afternoon of the next day.
14. Before you leave the day-care center, ask the caregiver whether the child's behavior that day has been at all atypical. If so, record the caregiver's comments along with general comments of your own.

plus disagreements. Observer reliabilities were found to be highest for fear behaviors (91%), followed by anger (90%), competence (90%), social affiliation (89%), and happiness (85%) behaviors.

Test Reliability

Essentially, the issue of measurement reliability centers on the problem of whether a single observation provides a sufficient and reliable measure of how a person behaves. This problem can be addressed in two different ways. The more conventional method is to observe individuals twice within a short period of time. The consistency of their behavior over time can then be calculated through a correlational analysis. On the other hand, it is possible to observe individuals in multiple situations, each of which is known to be a measure of the same trait or ability. In this context, reliability is established by showing that the multiple situations do, in fact, measure the same thing. Both approaches to measurement reliability were used in constructing the scales.

A small sample of infants (two males and two females) was assessed twice on the scales. These infants ranged in age from 11 to 16 months with a mean age of 12.5 months, and all had participated in day care for at least three months. Pearson product–moment correlation coefficients based on the item scores were calculated for each infant between two time periods. The correlations ranged from .93 to .31, with an average correlation of .60. All but the lowest correlation were statistically significant. It was concluded that variable but sufficient reliability existed in the responses of these infants at two points in time.

Since the behaviors of infants are subject to developmental changes, this method of obtaining test reliability is best supplemented by a second method, that of collecting multiple measures of infants' behaviors across a variety of situations. Rather than observing the same behavior in the same situation at two different times, the expression of a particular emotion may be observed over multiple situations in order to measure that emotion. For instance, 13–20 different situations were used to assess each emotional state in the original version of the scales. If the measurement of a particular emotion was random (i.e., not reliable), one would expect to find wide differences in the expression of that emotion as a function of the situation. That is, the situations should not result in consistent individual scores.

In the current research, measurement reliability was tested by calculating coefficient alpha, a measure of the internal consistency or reliability of a group of test items (Nunnally, 1967). High coefficient alphas were obtained for the measures of each emotional state, a finding that will be discussed later. These results were replicated on a second sample of infants, which strongly suggests that the measurements taken in a particular situation were reliable.

In short, three sets of findings indicate that the measurements obtained on each subject represent reliable estimates of emotional expression. First, the observer reliabilities were quite high. Second, although test–retest reliabilities based on observations of a few infants at two points in time were variable, they are comparable to correlations reported by other investigators regarding the consistency of infants' emotional responses over time (e.g., Ainsworth *et al.*, 1978; Bronson, 1972; Scarr & Salapatek, 1970). Finally, measurement reliability based on multiple observations of each emotional domain was found to be quite high for two different samples of infants.

Internal Consistency of the Domain Scales

The internal consistency (i.e., the item reliability) of the domain scales was assessed according to the formula for coefficient alpha:

$$r = \frac{k}{k-1}\left(1 - \frac{\Sigma\,\sigma_i^2}{\sigma_y^2}\right)$$

where k represents the number of items in a domain scales, σ_i^2 represents the item variance, and σ_y^2 represents the total variance (Nunnally, 1967). Coefficient alpha can also be regarded as a measure of the homogeneity of a domain or the extent to which the items of a domain scale are measuring the same emotion. In computing coefficient alphas for the five domain scales, missing data were dropped from the calculations, and the total scores were based only on the items observed for each subject.

Sample 1

Coefficient alphas were computed first on Sample 1 infants for the domain scales based on all of the items of the original scales. The reliabilities were found to be moderately high, with the social affiliation scale having the highest reliability (.75), followed by the scales for happiness (.70), anger (.65), fear (.61), and competence (.59).

Since the primary goal of the research was to construct a measurement instrument of maximum reliability, an attempt was made to improve the reliability of each domain scale by discarding from it items having low or negative correlations with the total score. Thus, coefficient alphas were computed for the domain scales after the items with negative domain correlations were discarded. Then, items with domain correlations less than .05 were discarded, and coefficient alphas were recomputed. This procedure was followed as items with domain correlations less than .00 (negative), .05, .10, .15, and .20 were excluded from the calculations of coefficient alpha.

The results of this procedure showed that the most reliable and homogeneous scales were produced by excluding items with domain correlations less than .20 (see Table 21). Not only was the reliability of each domain scale increased by discarding these items but the reliabilities were improved to the point where all were above .70. In particular, the fear, anger, and competence scales were made substantially more reliable by dropping items with domain correlations less than .20. The reliability of the fear scale increased from .61 to .76, the anger scale from .65 to .85, and the competence scale from .59 to .77. The happiness and social affiliation scales showed somewhat smaller increases in reliability, with the happiness scale increasing from .70 to .74 and the social affiliation scale from .75 to .81.

The items remaining after items with domain correlations less than .20 were eliminated constitute the items of the revised scales. Whereas the number of items in each domain scale ranged from 13 to 20 in the original scales (before any items were excluded), the number of items in the shorter, more reliable version of the scales ranged from 8 to 12. Consequently, the scales not only were more reliable and homogeneous in their revised form but were also more efficient to administer since there were fewer situations to be observed.

Table 22 lists those items dropped for each domain scale. There are a variety of reasons that subjects' scores on these items may have

Table 21. Internal Consistency of the Scales as Items Were Excluded[a]

Domain scale	All items	Excluding items with domain r less than				
		.00 (neg.)	.05	.10	.15	.20
Fear	.61 (13)	.69 (11)	.69 (11)	.71 (10)	.69 (9)	.76 (8)
Anger	.65 (18)	.72 (13)	.72 (13)	.85 (10)	.85 (10)	.85 (8)
Happiness	.70 (14)	.68 (13)	.74 (12)	.74 (12)	.73 (11)	.74 (10)
Affiliation	.75 (18)	.79 (16)	.80 (15)	.80 (13)	.80 (13)	.81 (12)
Competence	.59 (20)	.65 (16)	.65 (16)	.67 (14)	.70 (11)	.77 (8)

[a] The numbers in parentheses indicate the number of items remaining in the domain scale.

Table 22. Items Excluded from the Domain Scales

Fear	Anger	Happiness	Affiliation	Competence
Arrival	Mother leaves	Arrival	Free play	Arrival
Surprise toy	Wants something caregiver has	Completes task	Peer cries	Group
Funny (unusual) sound	Wants something unreachable	Peer acts silly	Interaction/special attention	Wants something peer has
Caregiver forbids	Difficult toy	Funny (unusual) sound	Strange child enters room	Completes task
Caregiver scolds	Caregiver takes toy		Another mother returns[a]	Difficult toy
	Caregiver takes bottle/pacifier			Mirror–self
	Physical restraint			Mirror–other
	Caregiver forbids			Interaction/special attention
	Obstacle			Command
	Mother returns			Praise
				Hidden object
				Caregiver puts child down

[a] Eliminated from both the low-stress and the high-stress sections of the affiliation scale.

been unrelated to other scores. For example, some items may not have occurred frequently enough. "Funny sound," "physical restraint," and "peer acts silly" are items that seldom occurred. Even though some situations may have occurred often enough, few individual differences may have been found on these items. "Arrival," "caretaker takes toy," "caretaker takes bottle/pacifier," "caregiver forbids," and "command" are examples of these items. Finally, some situations may not have elicited any emotional behaviors. An example is "another mother returns." For these reasons as well as others, some items were not useful for observing individual differences.

Eleven situations were eliminated completely in the revised version of the scales. Some situations were eliminated for only a particular emotional state, which resulted in a reduction of 37 items. Thus, the original version of the scales consisted of 83 items, and the revised version of the scales consisted of 46 items, 37 of which were different situations.

Sample 2

The revised version of the scales was used to gather data on the second sample of children to determine whether the high reliabilities of the domain scales obtained with the first sample could be replicated. Coefficient alphas based on data from the second sample were quite similar to those based on the data of the original sample (see Table 23). Increases in reliabilities occurred in the fear and competence scales with coefficient alphas increasing from .76 (original sample) to .95 (replication sample) for the fear scale and from .77 (original sample) to .96 (replication sample) for the competence scale. The reliabilities of the happiness and social affiliation scales were only slightly higher for

Table 23. Internal Consistency of the Revised Scales: Original, Replication, and Combined Samples

	Sample		
Domain scale	Original	Replication	Combined
Fear	.76	.95	.88
Anger	.85	.77	.80
Happiness	.74	.76	.73
Affiliation	.81	.84	.82
Competence	.77	.96	.87

the replication sample: on the happiness scale, the original sample yielded a .74 reliability versus a .76 for the replication sample, and on the social affiliation scale, the original sample produced an .81 reliability versus an .84 for the replication sample. The reliability of the anger scale decreased from .85 (original sample) to .77 (replication sample).

Combined Sample

After the reliability and homogeneity of the scales had been established in two different samples of infants, the data from these samples were combined to create a larger sample of infants for statistical analyses. The reliabilities of the domain scales calculated for the combined sample, based on the items of the revised scales, were .80 or better with the exception of the happiness scale, for which coefficient alpha was .73 (see Table 23).

Internal Consistency by Age

Because it is important to examine the psychometric properties of the scales from a developmental perspective, the combined sample was divided into three age groups: (1) infants younger than 12 months (n = 22); (2) infants 13–18 months old (n = 18); and (3) infants 19 months and older (n = 26).

Age could have been divided at any number of points, such as 3–9 months versus 9 months and older or 3–12 months versus 12 months and older. The particular age groups selected were based on several considerations. First, an attempt was made to equalize the number of subjects in each group in order that the correlational differences would be less likely to be a function of the number of subjects in a group. Second, the ages were chosen to correspond to meaningful developmental milestones. With more subjects, it might have been possible to investigate smaller age categories. The age divisions chosen, however, are not unreasonable, since others have found strong age changes to occur at the end of the first year, at the end of the first half of the second year, and at the end of the second year. A further division of subjects within the first year of life, looking at children prior to 8 months of age versus infants older than 8 months, would have been valuable, but the small sample size precluded this division.

In general, the domain scales seemed to be reliable for each age group, and the reliabilities compared favorably with those calculated for the combined sample of infants of all ages (see Table 24). All coef-

Table 24. Internal Consistency of the Revised Scales by Age Group

Domain scale	Age group			
	≤12 Months	13–18 Months	≥19 Months	All ages
Fear	.81	.96	.89	.88
Anger	.86	.85	.64	.80
Happiness	.76	.70	.73	.73
Affiliation	.84	.85	.74	.82
Competence	.60	1.00	.88	.87

ficients for the age groups were above .70, and most were above .80, with the exceptions of competence in the youngest group (.60) and anger in the oldest group (.64). Thus, the groups of items selected for the five domain scales seemed to be valid measures of emotions for children between the ages of 3 months and 30 months.

Through the use of coefficient alpha and the elimination of items, a psychometrically sound measurement instrument has been developed. The items that were dropped from the scales because of their failure to correlate with other items constitute unique situations in which children's behaviors do not appear to be reliably related to other events.

Independence of the Domain Scales

Once we had established the reliabilities of the domain scales, the next question to be addressed was whether the scales were measuring different and distinct emotions or a single dimension such as arousal. In the measurement of emotional development, it is particularly important that one be able to tap differences among various emotions. Although much of the past work on the physiological correlates of emotional behavior has demonstrated differences in arousal levels, it has not demonstrated much differentiation among various emotions. If an attempt to construct measures of emotional development and to study specific emotions is to be profitable, it is desirable to demonstrate such differences with the system of measurement.

This measurement issue is related to the fundamental question of whether individuals who express intense levels of emotional behavior in one emotional domain are the same individuals who express intense levels of behavior in other domains. That is, in addition to the measurement issue, there is also an issue about whether or not specific emotions are differentially expressed by individuals. It may be the case that no matter how accurate a measurement system is, individuals who show high levels of one particular emotion are likely to be high emotional expressors in another.

The present analyses are designed to determine whether the domain scales are independent of each other and thus are measuring five different emotions or whether they measure a common emotional dimension such as arousal. This issue was addressed in three different ways: (1) through correlational analyses based on the total domain scores; (2) through intraclass correlational analyses of the consistency of the subjects' scores across the five socioemotional domains; and (3) through correlational analyses based on the item scores for situations that were included in more than one domain scale.

Domain Correlations

Product–moment correlations were computed between the domains using the total affect scores from the revised scales. Since the aim of these analyses was not to examine the specific relationships between pairs of emotions but to determine whether the domain scales were tapping a common arousal dimension or measuring independent and distinct emotions, zero-order correlation coefficients were computed instead of partial correlation coefficients. The relationships among emotions, investigated by partial correlations, will be discussed later in this chapter. Large positive correlations between domains would suggest that children who were rated high on one emotional expression were rated high on another and that the domain scales might be tapping a general arousal dimension. Small positive or negative correlations, on the other hand, would indicate that the domain scales were probably independent and measuring different and distinct emotional states.

In the following analyses, average correlations were obtained by transforming the values of r to z_r, calculating the mean of the z_r values, and converting this value back to an r value. Missing data were dropped from the computations, and the total affect scores for each subject were based only on the situations of the revised scales that were observed.

The domain correlations for Sample 1 ranged from $-.31$ to $.42$, with an average correlation between the domains of $.10$ (see Table 25). Only the correlation between fear and social affiliation was statistically significant ($r = .42$, $p < .05$).

The replicability of these findings was tested on the second sample of infants. Product–moment correlations between the domains ranged

Table 25. Domain Correlations (Original Sample)

	Anger	Happiness	Affiliation	Competence
Fear	.24	−.09	.42[a]	.18
Anger		.30	.18	.19
Happiness			−.06	−.04
Affiliation				−.31

[a] $p < .05$.

from −.48 to .36, with an average correlation of .08 (see Table 26). One positive correlation, between anger and social affiliation, was statistically significant ($r = .36, p < .05$), and one negative correlation, between fear and competence, was significant ($r = −.48, p < .01$).

Since the ranges and average correlations of the two samples were not dissimilar, the data of the two samples were combined, and product–moment correlations between the domains were computed on the larger sample of infants. The average correlation for the combined sample was .09, with correlations ranging from −.23 to .29 (see Table 27). The correlations between anger and social affiliation ($r = .27, p < .05$) and between fear and social affiliation ($r = .29, p < .05$) were statistically significant. These data suggest that the scales are probably not tapping some general emotional dimension but, in fact, measure distinct emotional states.

Subject Consistency

The issue of whether the domain scales measure different and distinct emotions or general arousal was investigated further by examining the consistency of a subject's total affect scores across the five domains. If the domain scales were not measuring different emotions

Table 26. Domain Correlations (Replication Sample)

	Anger	Happiness	Affiliation	Competence
Fear	.10	.19	.19	−.48[b]
Anger		−.03	.36[a]	.09
Happiness			.06	.05
Affiliation				.27

[a] $p < .05$.
[b] $p < .01$.

Table 27. Domain Correlations (Combined Sample)

	Anger	Happiness	Affiliation	Competence
Fear	.17	.06	.29[a]	− .23
Anger		.15	.27[a]	.13
Happiness			.01	− .02
Affiliation				.03

[a] $p < .05$.

but instead were measuring general arousal, a subject's affect scores should be similar on all the domains. That is, a subject's rank vis-à-vis the other subjects should remain constant across the domains. Infants who scored high on fear should also have high scores on the other four emotions if arousal was the common denominator of emotional state. If arousal was not a primary factor, the infants' affect scores should be random (i.e., not consistent) across the five emotional domains. Consequently, individual consistency in the total affect scores across the domains would implicate general arousal as a significant factor in the emotional state of infants, whereas a lack of consistency would confirm the independence of the domain scales.

The consistency of the subjects' affect scores across the five domains was assessed by an intraclass correlation coefficient according to the formula (Winer, 1971):

$$r = 1 - \frac{MS_{w.S}}{MS_{bet.\ S}}$$

If the variance within subjects is small (i.e., the subjects are consistent) compared to the variance between subjects (as it would be if the scores or ranks of a subject vis-à-vis the other subjects were similar across the five domains), this equation will produce a large correlation, reflecting high intrasubject consistency. On the other hand, if the subjects are not consistent in the intensity of their emotional responses across the five domains, the variance within subjects would be similar to the variance between subjects and the resulting correlation will be small. Because intraclass correlations are descriptive measures, not unlike measures of the reliability of observers or judges, no tests of the statistical significance of the correlations were conducted.

Intraclass correlations were computed for the original sample, the replication sample, and the combined sample. Only subjects with total scores for all five domains could be included in these analyses.* The intraclass correlation for Sample 1 subjects, calculated on the data from the revised form of the scales, was .17. The intraclass correlation for Sample 2 was .28, and for the combined sample, .21. These correlations are quite low for reliability measures and account for little of the variance. In general, the findings support the notion of domain independence and provide little support for the notion that the scales are measuring general arousal.

Shared Situations

The independence of the domain scales was investigated finally through a series of correlational analyses based on the item scores of situations that were included in more than one domain scale. Recall that some situations were found to elicit more than one emotion and were therefore included in more than one domain scale. For example, the situation "toy breaks" could elicit fear, anger, or competence behaviors. Therefore, "toy breaks" appeared as an item in three domain scales, with different sets of behaviors, depending on which emotion was elicited. If the dominant factor in emotional state is general arousal, the scores based on the same situation should be similar, and large positive correlations would result. In contrast, if the domain scales measure different emotions, the item scores would not necessarily be similar but would differ as a function of the particular emotion elicited by the situation, and small positive or negative correlations would be produced.

In the final version of the scales, seven situations were included in more than one domain: "toy breaks" (fear, anger, competence); "peer attacks" (fear, anger); "unfamiliar room" (fear, competence); "stranger" (fear, social affiliation); "peer gets attention" (anger, social affiliation); "teased" (anger, happiness); and "mother puts child down" (social affiliation, competence). Most of the domain scales, then, shared at least one situation with another domain scale, and some domain scales had situations in common with two other scales.

Product–moment correlations were computed between the item scores on each situation shared by two domains. In cases where two

---

* After the scales were revised and some items were discarded, four subjects from Sample 2 were missing a total affect score on at least one domain scale. Therefore, in analyses requiring total scores for all five domains, $n = 28$ in Sample 2 and $n = 62$ in the combined sample.

domains shared more than two situations, average correlations were computed by transforming the r values to z values, calculating the mean z value, and converting the mean z value back to an r value.

The domain correlations based on the shared situations ranged from −.46 to .86, with an average correlation of .22. With two exceptions, all the correlations were either quite small or negative. Although statistically significant, the large negative correlation between anger and happiness ($r = -.46$, $p < .01$) does not support a general arousal theory of emotional expression; instead it indicates that different intensities of two separate emotions (anger and happiness) were elicited in an inverse relationship by the same situation ("teased"). That is, teasing a child tended to elicit either high intensities of happiness or high intensities of anger. It did not evoke similar levels of these emotions, as would be expected if the critical factor of emotional expression was general arousal.

On the other hand, these analyses produced two large positive correlations, which might support an arousal theory. The correlation between fear and anger ($r = .86$, $p < .01$) represents an average correlation based on two situations: "peer attacks" ($r = .44$, $p < .01$) and "toy breaks" ($r = .97$, $p < .01$). The other large positive correlation is based on one situation ("peer gets attention"), which could elicit anger and/or social affiliation ($r = .74$, $p < .01$).

The results of the shared-situations analyses were not as clear-cut as those based on the domain correlations and the subject consistency analyses in confirming the independence of the domain scales. The majority of the evidence, however, argues against the notion that the domain scales assess a single arousal dimension and for the notion that they measure different and distinct emotions. Such a finding provides support for the study of different enduring emotions and encourages the study of individual differences.

That the data for subjects in different age groups are similar does not necessarily mean that individual differences in domain consistency and arousal are not to be found. Indeed, it may be the case that for certain children, perhaps as a function of gender, certain emotions may form a more coherent dimension for which arousal might be the appropriate explanation. As was suggested in Chapter 5, one of the strong developmental changes may be from a relatively undifferentiated emotional state to a variety of highly differentiated states. If this is the case, one might expect to find that the emotional domains tapped by the scales are less differentiated at earlier ages (i.e., more consistent) and become more differentiated (i.e., less consistent) with age.

This consistency issue is addressed in the following analyses in terms of both age and gender. The general hypothesis was that there would be less differentiation (i.e., more general arousal) in younger infants than in older infants and no differences in degree of differentiation between boys and girls.

Age and Gender Differences

Age and gender differences were studied both through the domain correlations and through the subject consistency methods previously described for the sample as a whole. For the study of age and gender differences, Sample 1 and Sample 2 were combined to increase the number of subjects in the analyses.

Age Differences

For the age analysis, the combined sample was divided into three age groups as before: (1) 12 months and younger (n = 22); (2) 13–18 months (n = 18); and (3) 19 months and older (n = 26). Age correlations between domains were computed for each age group (see Table 28). In the youngest age group, the average domain correlation was .13, which, although not significant, was the highest average correlation of the three age groups. The correlations ranged from −.22 to .52, and two of the correlations were statistically significant: anger and social affiliation (r

Table 28. Domain Correlations by Age Group

	Anger	Happiness	Affiliation	Competence
≤ 12 months old				
Fear	.06	.09	.41	−.22
Anger		.12	.44[a]	.52[a]
Happiness			−.15	−.10
Affiliation				.05
13–18 months old				
Fear	.12	.40	.24	−.36
Anger		.07	.26	−.18
Happiness			−.13	.16
Affiliation				−.13
≥ 19 months old				
Fear	.33	−.07	.09	−.23
Anger		.15	.13	.00
Happiness			.38	−.05
Affiliation				.10

[a] p < .05.

= .44, $p < .05$) and anger and competence ($r = .52$, $p < .05$). As predicted, this was the only age group in which there were significant domain correlations.

The average domain correlation for the middle age group was .05. Correlations ranged from $-.36$ to .40, and none were statistically significant. The average domain correlation for the oldest infants was .09, and the correlations ranged from $-.23$ to .38. Again, none were statistically significant. It should be noted that in the youngest age group, three correlations were equal to or greater than .40. Only one correlation in the 13- to 18-month-old group was greater than .40, and none in the oldest age group reached this level.

The differences in the average domain correlations across the age groups (between .13 for the youngest infants, .05 for the middle age group, and .08 for the oldest infants) provide minimal support for the notion that domain independence varies as a function of age and that arousal, as a general factor in emotional expression, changes with age. The differences among the correlations for the three age groups were not statistically significant, according to an analysis of variance based on Fisher z-transformations of the r values. Even so, there were three correlations .40 or better for the youngest age group, one for the middle age group, and none for the oldest age group.

Age differences were also investigated by calculating subject consistency. Recall that subject consistency is the degree to which the variation within subjects is greater than the variation between subjects. Again, by dividing the combined sample into three age groups as before, the results showed the intraclass correlations calculated separately for each age group to be .41 for the youngest infants, .04 for the middle age group, and $-.11$ for the oldest infants. These data suggest the possibility of age differences in domain consistency.

Both sets of consistency data indicate that infants under 12 months of age show greater emotional consistency than infants over 12 months. There appears to be little difference in emotional consistency between the middle and oldest age groups. Taken together, the two sets of data provide stronger support for the notion of emotional differentiation as a function of age.

Although domain consistency may be age related to some extent, the relatively low level of this consistency reflected by the correlations indicates that the scales are still valid measures of separate emotions across the first three years of life. Thus, the age data confirm the data for the combined sample by indicating relatively low domain consistency and therefore providing relatively little evidence of a general emotional state, such as arousal. At the same time, the age data support the belief that emotional development may proceed from undifferentiated to differentiated emotional states.

Gender Differences

Age differences having been examined, the effects of gender differences on domain independence were tested. The independence of the domain scales was examined separately for the boys (n = 38) and the girls (n = 28) of the combined sample. It was possible that arousal might play a larger and more significant role in the expressions of emotion for one gender than the other.

The average correlation for the boys was .10, with correlations ranging from − .23 to .43 (see Table 29). The correlation between fear and social affiliation was statistically significant for the boys (r = .43, p < .01), as was the correlation between anger and social affiliation (r = .34, p < .05). In contrast, an average correlation of .06 was obtained for the girls, with correlations ranging from − .10 to .22. None of these correlations were statistically significant. Although the average domain correlation for the boys was larger than that for the girls (.10 compared to .06), the difference between the domain correlations was not statistically significant, according to an analysis of variance based on Fisher z-transformations of the r values.

Subject consistency, as compared with domain consistency, was also examined as a function of gender. An intraclass correlation of .13 for the boys (n = 37) was only slightly smaller than a correlation of .19 for the girls (n = 25). Both correlations are low and suggest that

Table 29. Domain Correlations by Gender

	Anger	Happiness	Affiliation	Competence
Boys				
Fear	.16	− .09	.43[b]	− .23
Anger		.23	.34[a]	.21
Happiness			− .05	.01
Affiliation				− .08
Girls				
Fear	.22	.01	.20	− .10
Anger		.11	.01	.00
Happiness			.19	− .02
Affiliation				.01

[a] p < .05.
[b] p < .01.

general arousal is not the critical factor in the emotional expression of either boys or girls.

The data from both analyses indicate no gender effects on the independence of emotions as measured by the scales. The independence of emotions as measured by the scales indicates that the scales are not measuring only a general arousal dimension. In other words, the emotional domains do not seem to be highly related. Such a finding supports the contention that the scales are useful in the measurement of enduring emotional states and measure distinct emotions rather than general arousal. Of some interest is the possibility of age differences in the consistency of emotional expressions. This result could be viewed as reflecting a weakness in the scales. However, since there is strong support for the notion of emotional differentiation as a function of age, we suspect that rather than a measurement flaw, the finding reflects the reality of age differences.

≈≈≈≈≈≈≈≈≈≈≈≈≈

The need to examine empirically the development of enduring emotional states led to the construction of scales in which five emotions were measured. Predicated on a situation-by-behavioral analysis, a measurement instrument was constructed and administered to two samples of infants in order to answer a variety of questions. Of particular importance were the issues of (1) observer reliability (i.e., the ability of different observers to obtain the same information on the same subject through the use of the scales), (2) subject reliability (i.e., the ability of the instrument to measure subject consistency across the various items of a particular domain); and (3) emotional independence (i.e., whether the scales measured independent emotions or whether they measured a general state such as arousal).

Observer Reliability

Given the complexity of the scales, that is, the requirement that the scales measure particular behaviors in particular situations that represent the various scale items, the task for observers is difficult. Indeed, one concern in the development of the instrument was whether an observer could successfully carry out the task and whether high observer reliability was possible. The finding that observer reliability was high is encouraging, since one goal was to create an instrument that could be used by trained observers in the field. The use of a behavioral scheme that incorporates facial, vocal, and bodily activities in determining the intensity of a particular emotional response is a complex task. The results indicate that, although the observational system may be difficult, with the proper training and the careful definition of behaviors and situations, observer agreement is possible.

Subject Reliability

Another measurement issue confronted in constructing the scales was test reliability. This is the problem of determining the consistency of behavior or the extent to which a single observation provides a sufficient and reliable measure of how a person behaves. Two methods of determining consistency were undertaken: the first used the conventional method of determining retest reliability by observing a child twice within a short period of time under the same conditions. This method was used for a small group of infants. Although the range of reliability coefficients was variable, the reliability coefficients themselves agreed with results reported by others studying emotional behavior.

The retest method is less than satisfactory, since the ability to observe a child twice in order to obtain test reliability is subject to (1) the same situation's occurring twice and (2) the child's changing between retest times. Thus, for example, if the time interval is long enough, developmental factors may alter a child's response, not as a function of the reliability of the instrument but as a function of changes in the child's state. The ability to observe the same state in the same situation is also a problem, since the repetition of a situation can represent a different situation. Although the retest reliability of the scales was relatively high, other methods of determining the consistency of a child's behavior had to be used.

The second method used to assess test reliability was to collect many observations of infants' behaviors across a variety of situations, each believed to be related to the same emotional state. Thus, for example, from a study of the literature and from observations of infants in day-care settings, it was determined that the mother's leaving, the approach of a stranger, and a jack-in-the-box are related to fear. If it could be shown that individual differences in the behavioral manifestations of fear remained consistent across a variety of situations, then a reliable estimate of the consistency of an emotion within and between individuals could be made by judging the extent to which the expressions of the emotions were consistent not across time but across situations.

Coefficient alphas were calculated to obtain estimates of such reliability. In the scale construction, the use of the alpha coefficient also allowed the exclusion of items that did not contribute to consistency. Thus, this method was useful not only in demonstrating that the subjects did behave consistently but also in enabling us to eliminate situations that were not elicitors of particular emotions. Item elimination appeared to follow three principles: (1) some items occurred infrequently; (2) some items did not produce individual differences; and (3) some items did not elicit emotional behavior. The analysis of the situations thought *a priori* to elicit particular emotions suggests that in day-care centers, certain situations may not be particularly reliable in eliciting particular emotions. Nevertheless, these situations have been thought to be effective elicitors, and their failure to measure emotions in the scales may have important implications for individual differences and for unique situational analyses.

The elimination of some scale items was necessary to construct a scale with the property of subject consistency. The construction of the scales through the inclusion of items found to be empirically related in Sample 1 produced the high consistency that we sought to establish. The replication of the findings on a second sample confirms our belief that these items measure consistent emotional behaviors and individual differences. The data do not in themselves necessarily answer the question of whether a child who showed, for example, a high degree of happiness would show that behavior consistently under conditions usually thought of as eliciting happiness. Only a test–retest procedure could establish that result. The results of the test–retest analysis indicated a relatively high consistency in subjects' emotional expressions over time. Thus, individual differences in enduring emotional states may exist, and these differences may be observed and measured both across time and across situations.

Domain Independence

In the construction of an assessment instrument purporting to measure distinct attributes, it is important to make certain that the instrument contains the property of attribute independence. One of the advantages in the construction of scales measuring a variety of emotions is the possibility of testing whether the instrument measures different emotions or a single state, such as general arousal. In measuring a single emotion, one cannot logically determine whether one is, in fact, measuring a particular emotion or general arousal. Thus, for example, a system that assesses only fear might find individual differences and differences that are consistent across time and situations. However, investigators would not know from such results whether they were measuring differences in fear per se or differences in a general state such as arousal. The logic of measurement necessitates the measurement of more than one emotion at a time in order to conclude whether one is measuring a particular emotion or a general state. This measurement concern is implicitly addressed in debates on the topic of arousal versus particular emotions. Nevertheless, few investigators have paid attention to the logical measurement constraints that such a question involves.

In the construction of the measurement scales, our intention was to measure five specific, enduring emotional states and to generate individual profiles reflecting the configuration of these states. It was desirable from the point of view of both scale construction and scale usage that discrete states be measured rather than general arousal. The results of our inquiry using three different procedures concur in finding that there appears to be no homogeneous entity consisting of items that all measure general arousal. Rather, the five domain scales seem to be measuring different and distinct emotional states. The demonstration of this psychometric property suggests the existence of multiple emotional states in young children. Of particular interest in the measurement of distinct emotional states is the suggestion that these states become increasingly differentiated after 12 months of age. This result supports theories of emotional development built on a differentiation hypothesis (see Chapter 5).

The findings reported in this chapter lend support to the belief that it is possible to measure the enduring emotions of young children in naturalistic settings. The properties of the scales include high observer reliability, high individual consistency, and emotional differentiation. The demonstration of these properties and the procedures used in obtaining individual data allow us to examine research issues further through the use of the scales. In Chapter 11, issues of individual differences are considered.

11

Individual Differences in Emotional States

In the previous chapters, the issues of enduring emotional states, their developmental changes, and specific response measures were discussed. Scale construction and the internal properties of the scales were described. In this chapter, the results from the administration of the scales are discussed. Of particular interest are the individual differences in emotions observed when administering the scales.

Earlier we stated that emotional states are private acts of the individual and that one of the effects of socialization is to modify emotional expressions and states. Nevertheless, we believe that the best way to measure emotional states in infants and young children is through an expression-by-situation analysis. While recognizing the limitations inherent in any measurement system that purports to measure emotional states, we view our data as reflecting emotional states. Consequently, when we refer to emotions in our discussion, we are referring to emotional states as measured in an expression-by-situation analysis.

Three major issues pertain to the data gathered. The first concerns individual differences in specific emotional expressions and their relationship to age, gender, and social milieu. From a naive psychological point of view, it is believed that boys express more anger than girls, although both are probably equally happy. Children express more anger with age, as well as more competence. Fear and happiness are apparent from the early periods. Furthermore, children who have been in day care for long periods of time are likely to show more affiliation, and possibly more competence, than children newly enrolled in a day-care program. Statements such as these address individual differences in the expression of specific emotions as a function of age, gender, and social milieu.

Information about individual differences *per se* may also serve to validate the scales by confirming results reported by other investigators. That is, do the results generated by the scales show any correspondence to findings generated by laboratory experiments using different procedures? The body of literature existing on children's fear and sociability and the available data on happiness, anger, and competence can be used to help validate the scales.

The second issue concerns the relationships among different emotional expressions. That is, are there naturally covarying aspects of emotional behavior among individuals, aspects that vary as a function of age or gender? Are angry children also fearful children? In everyday experience, certain emotions are often thought of as somehow going together: angry people are not likely to be happy, and competent people are generally not afraid. The analyses reported in this chapter are designed in part to examine whether there are natural groupings of emotions.

The third issue in the analysis of individual differences again focuses on the relationships among the five emotions. The specific question concerns the configurations of emotions and their relationship to personality. The relationship between enduring emotions and personality was discussed in Chapter 2. There, a case was made that configurations of enduring emotions may be similar to "personality structures." Through the use of multivariate techniques, different patterns of emotions were generated from the data collected on the scales. These profiles of enduring emotions provide information about possible personality types (i.e., possible configurations of enduring emotions) as well as about the individuals that fit such types. If the measurement instrument is successful in measuring individual differences, this success must depend not only on its ability to assess an individual child on the expression of specific emotions but, more important, on its ability to classify individual children in terms of profiles of emotional expressions. The clinical application of the scales is further discussed in Chapter 12. These profiles are of particular importance inasmuch as they allow one to look at more than individual differences in the expressions of single emotions and to examine the broader issue of differences in patterns of emotions. This chapter, then, is a discussion of the empirical study of individual differences in emotional expressions through the use of the Scales of Socioemotional Development to measure emotional states.

Age and Gender Differences

Analyses of individual differences in the degree to which emotions are expressed are important for several reasons. Such analyses provide specific information on individual differences in the expression of particular emotions. Such analyses also allow the comparison of results obtained by means of these scales with results obtained in more standardized laboratory procedures. There is a relatively large literature on individual differences in fear and affiliation, and some information is available on happiness and anger. Relatively little information exists on competence.

The subjects of the combined sample were divided into six groups according to their gender and age at the time the scales were administered. The number of subjects in each group is reported in Table 30.

The data were analyzed in a two-way (age $\times$ gender) multivariate analysis of variance (MANOVA), based on all five dependent variables (total affect scores). To clarify and extend the results of the MANOVA, five two-way (age $\times$ gender) univariate ANOVAs were computed, one for each dependent variable. Because the number of subjects in the cells of the two-way ANOVAs varied considerably and was quite small in some instances, the effects of age and gender were tested separately in one-way ANOVAs as well as together in two-way ANOVAs. Since similar results were obtained from both designs, only the findings from the two-way ANOVAs are reported. These analyses produced the following results.

The first question addressed was whether age or gender differences existed in emotional expression. Figure 13 shows the mean affect scores by age. Age of infant proved to be a highly significant effect in the MANOVA ($F[10,108] = 2.93$, $p < .003$). Individual analyses of specific emotions were conducted to examine particular age effects, since the

Table 30. Number of Subjects by Age and Gender

Age group	Gender		
	Male	Female	Total
≤12 months (young)	17	4	21
13–18 months (middle)	9	7	16
≥19 months (old)	11	14	25
Total	37	25	62

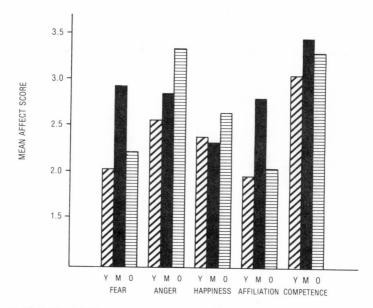

Figure 13. Individual differences in emotions as a function of the child's age: young (3 to 12 months), middle (13 to 18 months), and old (19 to 30 months).

data in Figure 13 reveal several different trends. For example, expressions of fear and social affiliation show an inverted U function, while expressions of anger show a linear increase. Expressions of happiness follow a U-shaped function.

Gender differences were found for specific emotions, but the overall MANOVA did not reveal a significant gender difference. Gender differences, when they appear, will be discussed by emotional domain.

Fear

The research literature on the development of fear reveals a general increase in the number of infants expressing fear over the first 12 or 18 months of life. After this time, depending on the particular fear elicitor, there appears to be either a decrease or a slight increase in fear over the last half of the second year.

The data of the present study are generally in agreement with these results. Specifically, the mean fear scores were 2.03 for the youngest age group, 2.91 for the middle age group, and 2.21 for the oldest age group. These differences were significant according to a univariate ANOVA ($F[2,56] = 3.41$, $p < .04$). The middle age group showed significantly more intense expressions of fear than either the youngest or the oldest age groups, according to a .05-level Newman-Keuls test on the means (Winer, 1971). The difference between the youngest and the oldest age groups was not significant.

Although few infants younger than 7 months of age show stranger fear (Emde et al., 1976; Morgan, 1973; Morgan & Ricciuti, 1969; Scarr & Salapatek, 1970; Schaffer, 1966; Tennes & Lampl, 1964; Waters et al., 1975), between 20% and 40% may exhibit fear of masks, startle toys, and the visual cliff (Scarr & Salapatek, 1970). During the last half of the first year, fear of strangers emerges, and expressions of fear in general increase steadily. The number of infants showing stranger fear may decline slightly in the beginning of the second year but rises once again between 18 and 24 months (Scarr & Salapatek, 1970). The largest number of infants showing fear of startle toys occurs somewhat earlier than for stranger fear, peaking between 13 and 18 months, then declining over the last half of the second year. Virtually all infants throughout the second year of life display signs of fear on the visual cliff (Scarr & Salapatek, 1970). Studies of separation anxiety report a similar developmental trend. Fear emerges around 8–9 months of age, reaches a peak at the beginning of the second year, then gradually disappears toward the end of the second year (Maccoby & Feldman, 1972; Marvin, 1977; Serafica, 1978; Weinraub & Lewis, 1977).

According to the research literature, then, incidences of fear are not widely observed in the first months of life, except in response to certain events, such as masks. Fear expressions tend to peak at the end of the first year and during the second half of the second year. For some events, the number of infants exhibiting fear remains high (e.g., the visual cliff), whereas for others it falls off (e.g., startle toys) but may peak again at the end of the second year, as is the case with fear of strangers.

As well as normative trends, gender differences in fear expressions have also been reported in the research literature. For example, with few exceptions, girls react negatively to strangers somewhat earlier (Robson, Pedersen, & Moss, 1969; Schaffer, 1966), more intensely (Morgan & Ricciuti, 1969; Tennes & Lampl, 1964), and more frequently (Goulet, 1974). Girls are also more variable in their fear response (Bronson, 1972; Shaffran & Décarie, 1973) than boys, although these differences are not always statistically significant. While Skarin (1977) found that at 6 months of age, girls tended to be more fearful than boys, at 11 months this trend was reversed, with boys exhibiting more fear than girls. Maccoby and Jacklin (1973) found boys to be more immobilized by a fear stimulus (a loud, angry male voice) than girls. Other findings, however, suggest girls show more fear behaviors to male strangers than do boys (Lewis & Brooks, 1974), and that they are more interested in female strangers (Bronson, 1971; Maccoby & Feldman, 1972). The results from our study also indicated a significant gender difference in fear expressions. Girls showed a mean fear score of 2.71 and boys a mean score of 2.07. This difference was statistically significant ($F[1,56] = 5.44$, $p < .03$).

Attempts to assess the influence of other individual differences on expressions of fear consistently show significant differences between firstborn and later-born children. In general, firstborn infants have been shown to develop fear of strangers earlier (Schaffer, 1966) and to express it more frequently (Collard, 1968; Weinraub & Putney, 1978) than later-born children. Data also suggest that temperament and heredity may influence the infant's fear responses to strangers. Among the temperament variables that have been related to stranger fear are negative quality of mood, low response thresholds, poor adaptability, and low rhythmicity (Scarr & Salapatek, 1970); distress reactions to startling stimuli (Bronson, 1972); and distress responses to new objects and situations (Paradise & Curcio, 1974). Feinman and Lewis (1981) have also shown that temperament differences affect infants' responses to strangers insofar as differences in temperament are related to the child's ability to use information provided by the mother about the stranger.

Anger

Relatively little research exists on the emotion of anger. This fact is somewhat surprising, since mothers believe that infants show anger in the earliest months of life (Pannabecker et al., 1980). Head turning to being fed and rage at being restrained are responses used to infer anger. Watson (1919) claimed that anger is the infant's natural response to frustration and thus is one of three innate emotions. More recently, angry faces have been observed in young infants and children, and the associated facial musculature has been described in some detail (Izard, 1979b).

There are few studies of anger in the contemporary literature, however. The Ainsworth–Wittig (1969) strange-situation paradigm, in which the infant experiences the appearance and disappearance of the mother and a stranger in a set sequence of episodes, is thought to elicit anger in some children, this anger being expressed during the reunion of the child with the mother. Observations of mothers and infants interacting naturally in their own homes show expressions of anger to increase in frequency over the first year of life. In 10 hours of observation during each quarter of the first year of the infant's life, an average of only three episodes of angry behavior was found during each of the first two quarters. In contrast, an average of 12 episodes occurred during the fourth quarter (Main, 1981). An increased frequency in the occasions of anger between 6 and 12 months of life was reported in an early study by Goodenough (1931, 1934).

Feiring and Lewis (1979) examined age differences in children's responses to a frustration caused by a barrier. The major response to this frustration was primarily negative at both 1 and 2 years of age. However, a general decrease was observed from 1 to 2 years of age in the amount of time spent crying, fretting, and pushing the barrier concurrent with an increase in "competence" behaviors associated with solving the barrier problem (e.g., climbing the barrier and manipulating the latch). These findings suggest that expressions of anger as a consequence of frustration may decline over the second year of life as infants develop an ability to use more instrumental responses in attempting to overcome a frustrating obstacle.

On the other hand, one might expect to find an increase in the occasions of anger during the second year of life continuing the trend reported by Goodenough (1931) in the first year. This increase may be the result of the maturation of the infant's sense of self, which generates stronger and more defined desires. One consequence of this development of autonomy may be the increased likelihood of interference with or thwarting of the infant's intended actions. For example, consider the phenomenon of the "terrible twos," characterized by increased amounts of negativism, anger, and temper tantrums. These behaviors are a function of children's emerging sense of self and their first attempts at negotiation. These negotiations are essentially children's attempts to assert their own will. Sullivan (1953) has noted that relationships are not possible unless there are two negotiating selves. Although these 2-year-old negotiations are often negative in tone and filled with anger, they probably represent an important developmental milestone characterized by the emergence of the self (see Chapter 5). The child's frequent comments, such as "I don't want to," "I hate you," or "no," reflect this underlying sense of self. This period is marked by expressions of negativism and anger because the emerging self focuses on and is defined by a change from what is to what is to become.

Given both the increased ability of children and the opportunities for greater commerce with the social environment and children's increased self-awareness and desire to act in their own way, one might hypothesize that expressions of frustration and anger should increase with age during infancy and early childhood. Further support for this hypothesis comes from the increased motoric ability and the limited degree of socialization and moral constraints during this age period. Thus, both the research literature and theory would predict an increase in the amount of anger expressed during the first two years of life.

The data presented in Figure 13 show a significant increase in expressions of anger over the first two years of life. The mean anger scores were 2.56, 2.82, and 3.32 for the youngest, middle, and oldest age groups, respectively ($F[2,56] = 3.77$, $p < .03$). The more intense expressions of anger by the oldest infants were significantly different from the intensities of anger expressions for either the youngest or the middle groups ($p < .05$, Neuman-Keuls). The difference between the youngest and middle age groups was not significant.

Other research on individual differences in expressions of anger suggest possible gender differences, although the pattern of these differences is not clear. The results of the present research indicate that girls tended to show more anger than boys, although the difference was not statistically significant.

The reports of gender differences in the research literature are ambiguous. At approximately 1 year of age, girls stay longer at the center of a barrier separating them from their mothers and cry more than do boys. Boys spend more time at the ends of the barrier (Goldberg & Lewis, 1969), especially if the subjects are initially placed near their mothers (Jacklin et al., 1973). After the age of 18 months, however, this trend is reversed, and boys tend to show more negative emotion in frustrating situations than do girls (Goodenough, 1931; Landreth, 1941; Maccoby & Feldman, 1972; Van Lieshout, 1975). More recently, Feiring and Lewis (1979) reported longitudinal data showing that although at 1 year of age girls cry more than boys in the barrier situation, at 2 years the same girls spend less time fretting and more time manipulating the latch and vocalizing than do the boys. Thus, the frequency of negative reactions to frustration seems to decline faster in girls than in boys (Feiring & Lewis, 1979; Maccoby & Jacklin, 1973), whereas the use of instrumental responses to the barrier increases more for girls than for boys (Feiring & Lewis, 1979).

No gender differences have been reported in infants' angry reactions to separations from and reunions with the mother (Ainsworth et al., 1978; Blanchard & Main, 1979). However, we recently looked at how mothers label their infants' behavior in response to separation and reunion (Lewis & Michalson, 1982c; see also Chapter 7). While relatively few mothers labeled their children's emotional behavior in this situation (26%), anger was one of the four emotions mentioned. Furthermore, the label *angry* was applied more frequently to boys than to girls. It should be noted that maternal labeling showed a high correspondence to the infants' behavior. This fact suggests not only that mothers were more likely to label boys' behavior as angry but also that boys' behavior probably reflects more anger than the behavior of girls.

The nature of the infant's prior social experiences may be another source of individual differences in expressions of anger. Main (1981) reported finding a "tremendous range" of individual differences in the number of angry responses by infants toward their mothers in the first year of life. During 40 hours of observation, one infant exhibited no angry behavior, while another exhibited as many as 111 episodes. Infants who displayed the most anger in interactions with their mothers during the second six months of life had mothers who showed a strong aversion to physical contact with their infants; who were emotionally inexpressive, rigid, and compulsive; and who failed to respond to episodes of angry behavior during the first three months of the infants' life (Ainsworth et al., 1978; Main, Tomasini, & Tolan, 1979). Early child abuse has also been related to anger toward the mother during reunion (Lewis & Schaeffer, 1979), as well as to the frequency with which children assault both verbally and nonverbally their peers and harass caregivers in a day-care center (George & Main, 1979).

Happiness

Happiness is the expression of positive emotion and includes pleasure, joy, and delight. Happiness is most often associated with, and characterized by, smiling. Smiling behavior has a clear developmental course; the endogenous smiling appears at birth or shortly thereafter. Whether the early smiling corresponds to the construct called *happiness* is uncertain, especially in the case of the newborn or very young infant. Nevertheless, the smile of the infant serves as a powerful signal to the caregiver inasmuch as it represents the first positive emotional expression. It is often used by parents to infer an underlying state of happiness, contentment, or even affection. The child's smile to the parent represents "He loves me" or "She likes what I'm doing." That infant smiles can be elicited by almost any facial-like configuration during the first months of life does not affect the caregiver's interpretation of the behavior. In fact, caregivers often respond to such behavior as an example of "She like you, too" when the infant smiles at a stranger or a neighbor.

The relationship of these reflex-like smiles to an underlying emotional state such as happiness must be questioned. Nevertheless, the social environment appears ready to use this indiscriminate response for that purpose. As was pointed out previously, whether or not early infant behavior represents a manifestation of a particular state, the caregiver's interpretation of the behavior surely facilitates the connection between expression and state if one does not already exist (see Chapters 5, 6, and 7). After smiling becomes a more discriminating response, it seems more appropriate to use it as an index of general pleasure and positive emotional tone.

The literature on happiness is essentially a literature on the developmental course of smiling as well as on individual and cultural differences in smiling. Studies of developmental changes in smiling indicate that the endogenous smiles of the neonate, which involve simply turning up the corners of the mouth during sleep, decrease in frequency over the first three months of life (Spitz et al., 1970). The first elicited smiles can be observed in 1-week-old infants during sleep and drowsiness (Wolff, 1963). These smiles, like the spontaneous endogenous smiles, are low-intensity responses involving only the corners of the mouth (Sroufe & Waters, 1976). During the second week of life, the first smiles readily elicited when the infant is awake occur (Wolff, 1963). Now the smiling response is of a larger magnitude, being neither the "grimace" of the first week nor the overt smile of the fourth week (Sroufe & Waters, 1976).

By the third week of life, the first alert smiles occur (Wolff, 1963). At this time, the infant smiles more actively and with shorter latencies. This alert smile involves a wide grin as the corners of the mouth are retracted and is accompanied by brightening and twinkling of the eyes. Since human stimuli elicit smiling more than any other stimulus configurations at this age, this smile has been labeled the *social smile*. The results of several studies concur that the smiling response can be evoked by the human face at or before 4 weeks of age (Bühler, 1933; Gesell & Thompson, 1934; Jones, 1926; Shirley, 1933; Wolff, 1963). This progression of shorter latencies to smile and more active smiling continues into the fourth week. "Cooing" begins to accompany smiling some time during the fifth to the eighth week of life. The human face does not consistently elicit smiling, however, until the eighth or tenth week of life (Ambrose, 1961; Gewirtz, 1965; Spitz et al., 1970; Wolff, 1963), when endogenous smiling declines (Spitz et al., 1970).

As the infant becomes more responsive to the environment, elicited smiles no longer depend entirely on external stimulation per se, but on the infant's effort to assimilate the content of the stimulus (Sroufe & Waters, 1976). At this stage, between 3 and 6 months of age, smiling becomes more selective. There is a general decline in the rate of smiling to faces (Ambrose, 1961; Gewirtz, 1965; Kagan, 1967; Lewis, 1969; Spitz *et al.*, 1970; Takahashi, 1973) and to repeatedly presented stimuli, although smiling may reappear if a novel aspect is introduced into the stimulus configuration (Kagan, 1971; Shultz & Zigler, 1970; Sroufe & Wunsch, 1972; Zelazo, 1972; Zelazo & Komer, 1971). Furthermore, older infants smile sooner than younger infants at the same novel stimulus situations (Zelazo, 1972). At the same time that smiling becomes more discriminating, the number of stimuli capable of eliciting it increases as a function of the increasing cognitive awareness of the infant. Thus, there may actually be an increase in the frequency of smiling over the first year (Washburn, 1929) or even the first two years of life.

Laughter may represent another measure of positive affect. Unlike smiling, laughter is not observed during the early weeks of life and usually follows smiling by at least one month (Rothbart, 1973). In some instances, laughter has been observed in infants as young as 5–9 weeks old (Church, 1966; Darwin, 1872; Wolff, 1963). On the other hand, laboratory observations of infants in a strange situation typically find that the first laugh does not occur until the infants are 12–16 weeks of age (Escalona, 1968; Sroufe & Wunsch, 1972; Washburn, 1929), and for some infants, the first laugh may not be exhibited until 52 weeks of age (Washburn, 1929). Although developmental trends have been reported in the nature of items likely to elicit laughter, the frequency of laughter appears to remain constant, at least over the first 12 months of life (Washburn, 1929).

Observations of the expression of happiness in the present study indicate that infants older than 19 months showed the most happiness, with a mean score of 2.65, compared to a mean score of 2.38 for the youngest infants, and 2.33 for the middle age group (see Figure 13). Although the oldest infants showed the most intense expressions of happiness, the age differences were not significant. Thus, the data do not show any developmental trend in expressions of happiness. If one adopts the view that emotions develop from a single bipolar hedonic state, one would not expect to find a developmental trend related to the general positive emotional state labeled *happiness*.

This view does not preclude the possibility that individual differences might appear in the expression of happiness. When data on smiling or laughter are examined in terms of gender, the results suggest that although boys look longer than girls at static images of the human face, girls exhibit more smiling and vocalizing as well as more differential expressions to pictures of the face (Kagan, Henker, Hen-Tov, Levine, & Lewis, 1966; Lewis, 1969). Gender differences in positive affect expressions have been demonstrated in several samples of infants with various types of visual and auditory stimuli (Kagan & Lewis, 1965; Lewis *et* al., 1966); tactile stimuli (Bell & Costello, 1964); and play behavior (Goldberg & Lewis, 1969). Although the analysis on gender differences in the present study failed to detect any significant effects, the girls tended to show more intense expressions of happiness than the boys.

Social Affiliation

The measure of social affiliation in the scales attempts to assess the child's social contacts with other people, including the mother, the caregiver, peers, other mothers, and even strangers. The items selected are a combination of situations that measure the mother–child relationship as well as situations that measure the child's peer contact and responses to caregivers. Consequently, the social affiliation scale is designed to assess individual differences in children's contact with others.

The notion of social affiliation is similar to what Lamb (1982) referred to as "sociability." There is some support for the belief that sociability may be influenced by temperament characteristics (Goldsmith & Campos, 1982). A temperament variable is implicated insofar as physical proximity (e.g., touching and cuddliness) is considered to be a dimension of temperament (Thomas et al., 1963). In order to understand individual differences in social affiliation or sociability, one must look at the literature on children's relationships with both caregivers and peers.

Longitudinal studies of the infant–mother relationship concur that after a very early period of nondifferentiated social behavior, infants begin to exhibit a strong preference for a particular person (usually the mother) at about 6 months of age (Ainsworth, 1963, 1967; Schaffer & Emerson, 1964). The infant cries when this person leaves, seeks this person when afraid, and clings to this person when being held (Stayton, Ainsworth, & Main, 1973). Attachment to the primary caregiver intensifies during the third quarter of the first year. Following behaviors and crying on separation appear in the third and fourth quarters (Ainsworth, 1973). There is some evidence that this relationship may intensify through 18 months of age. Connell (1976), for instance, noted that 18-month-olds show somewhat stronger reactions in a strange situation than do 12-month-olds (Ainsworth et al., 1978). Studies of infants' responses to separation also find separation protest peaks during the second year of life (Weinraub & Lewis, 1977).

Developmental changes in the behaviors used to measure this primary relationship have also been documented. In particular, proximal behaviors (such as touching and staying close to the caregiver) tend to decrease from 1 to 2 years of age, while distal behaviors, such as looking and vocalizing, increase with age (Lewis & Ban, 1971; Lewis et al., 1972; Lewis & Weinraub, 1974; Rheingold & Eckerman, 1969). Maccoby and Feldman (1972) reported continued decreases in proximal behaviors and increases in distal behaviors (e.g., smiling, showing toys, and vocalizing) in the third year.

The nature of the situations eliciting social affiliation may also change over time. Schaffer and Emerson (1964) have reported that protest behaviors when mothers put their infants down after having held them decline over age, whereas being left with someone other than the primary caregiver or being left alone outdoors increases in effectiveness as an elicitor of protest up to 18 months of age.

A review of the research literature also portrays a rather consistent picture regarding the development of peer relationships (Mueller & Vandell, 1979). The majority of recent studies document a progression of peer-directed behaviors in the first two years of life that is quite similar to findings reported during the 1930s (Bridges, 1933; Maudry & Nekula, 1939). Social skills are generally found to be closely related to other developing motor and vocal skills. Specifically, looking at and touching peers can be observed in the first months of life. Around 6 months of age, more "social" behaviors appear, such as smiling (Vincze, 1971). Not long afterwards infants begin to approach, follow, and reach for peers (Durfee & Lee, 1973; Vincze, 1971). During the last quarter of the first year, infants begin to play games with each other (Vincze, 1971), and at 13–14 months of age, infants may begin to imitate one another (Eckerman, Whatley, & Kutz, 1975; Lewis et al., 1975). Conversational patterns of speech are observed during this period (Mueller & Vandell, 1979).

Between 12 and 24 months of age, an overall increase in the frequency of social behaviors occurs (Mueller & Vandell, 1979), particularly in the imitation of a peer's activity (Eckerman et al., 1975); in the incidence of personal versus impersonal encounters (Maudry & Nekula, 1939); and in negative episodes such as struggling over toys, hair-pulling, and biting (Maudry & Nekula, 1939). In addition to an increase in the frequency of social behaviors during the second year, the complexity of social behavior may increase as infants become more capable of combining discrete behaviors into coordinated social patterns (Mueller & Brenner, 1977; Mueller & Rich, 1976).

The data of the present study indicate expressions of social affiliation follow an inverted-U function (see Figure 13). Such expressions were most intense in the middle age group, with a mean score of 2.80, compared with mean scores of 1.95 and 2.05 for the youngest and oldest age groups. These differences were significant ($F[2,56] = 4.78$, $p < .01$). The differences between the middle age group and each of the other two groups were also significant ($p < .01$, Newman-Keuls), although the difference between the youngest and the oldest age groups was not.

These findings suggest that social affiliation increases across the first 18 months of life and declines thereafter. A similar pattern was shown for fear expressions. Thus, there is some reason to believe that social affiliation may be related to fear in young children: perhaps some of their affiliative behavior is a response to fear situations. If this is the case, then social affiliation should increase in those periods when fear is the greatest. This relationship may have inflated the social affiliation scores somewhat.

Social affiliation toward peers and people other than the primary caregiver should increase over age. Indeed, the short-term developmental pattern indicates that contact behaviors decrease toward the mother and the father (Lewis & Weinraub, 1974), while peer contacts increase (Mueller & Vandell, 1979). Long-term trends and longitudinal research clearly demonstrate a decrease in contact behavior (either direct proximal contact or interaction) toward the parents and an increase toward peers. Thus by 6 or 7 years of age, peers are the primary agents of sociability.

The present results, showing an increase and then a decline in social affiliation that parallels the age trend in expressions of fear, suggest that the scales are tapping social affiliation vis-à-vis the child's relationship toward adult caregivers (either the mother or the caregiver at the day-care center) rather than peers. These results concur with the findings of the attachment literature.

While the research literature contains no evidence of gender differences in infant's behaviors toward the mother or the father in the strange situation (Ainsworth, 1963; Ainsworth & Bell, 1970; Ainsworth et al., 1978), the literature suggests that gender differences may be observed in less stressful settings as well as when discrete affiliative and social behaviors are measured (Brooks & Lewis, 1974a). When gender differences are found, girls are usually observed to be more social than boys. For instance, newborn girls have been observed to be more responsive than boys to another baby's cry (Hoffman & Levine, 1976; Sagi & Hoffman, 1976). Moreover, during the first year, girls may show significantly more proximal behaviors than boys toward their mothers in free-play situations (Brooks & Lewis, 1974a; Goldberg & Lewis, 1969; Messer & Lewis, 1972).

These gender differences are confirmed in some studies (Bronson, 1971a; Klein & Durfee, 1978; Maccoby & Jacklin, 1973) but not in others

(Rheingold & Eckerman, 1969, 1970). Gender differences in sociability toward the mother have been observed to increase with age (Clarke-Stewart, 1973). Data show that boys are more likely than girls to be upset when the mother leaves the room, crying, following, and staying close to her on her return (Brooks & Lewis, 1974a; Maccoby & Jacklin, 1973; Weinraub & Lewis, 1977). Our findings also indicated a gender difference in expressions of social affiliation. The mean score for girls was 2.48 and for boys 2.03, which approached significance ($F[1,56] = 3.41$, $p < .07$). These results support the existence of early gender differences in expressions of affiliation.

It is obvious that from the moment of birth, male and female infants are perceived and treated differently by their parents and that parents continue to interact differently with them throughout the life cycle (Lewis, 1972; Lewis & Weinraub, 1979; Rubin, Provenzano, & Luria, 1974; Serbin, O'Leary, Kent, & Tonick, 1973). In the first months of life, boys receive more proximal stimulation, such as rocking and handling, while girls receive more distal stimulation, such as talking and looking (Lewis, 1972; Moss, 1967). Moreover, people other than the parents interact with infants differently according to the infant's gender (Fagot, 1973; Seavey, Katz, & Zalk, 1975). By 6 months of age, proximal stimulation to boys has decreased (Goldberg & Lewis, 1969). Although all children are socialized to move from proximal to distal modes of relating to others, this socialization appears to occur earlier and more vigorously for boys than for girls (Lewis & Weinraub, 1974).

Birth-order differences in affiliative expressions are also reported in the literature. Firstborn infants tend to show more affiliative behaviors, smiling or laughing and looking at the mother more often than later-born infants (Lewis & Kreitzberg, 1979). Firstborn infants also display more distress reactions on separation from and reunion with the mother than do later-born infants (Fox, 1977). Furthermore, firstborn neonates receive more attention and have a more intense relationship with their mothers than later-born infants (Thoman, Leiderman, & Olson, 1972). This birth-order effect continues into the third month of life (Jacobs & Moss, 1976), when it is observed for fathers and siblings as well as for mothers (Lewis & Kreitzberg, 1979). While firstborns showed more affiliative behavior toward parents and adults in general, there is evidence that later-borns show more affiliative behaviors toward peers (Forer & Still, 1976; Sutton-Smith & Rosenberg, 1970).

Individual differences as a function of the object of affiliation once again point out the difficulties in studying affiliation per se. As was pointed out earlier, affiliation may be difficult to study since a person may show high social affiliation with some people but not with others.

Summing across groups, then, may equalize the amount of affiliative behavior for two children who show dissimilar patterns in terms of the objects of affiliation. Worse yet, any assessment system that measures affiliation with respect to only one social group is likely to produce individual differences that may distort the actual case. Measuring affiliation toward adults may present a different picture from measuring affiliation toward peers.

The social affiliation scale used in the present study measured social affiliation toward diverse groups. Thus, this scale may be better able to tap individual differences in social affiliation and developmental trends. Developmental trends, as we have seen, are likely to be complex, since the decline in affiliation toward one group may be accompanied by an increase in affiliation toward another. The effect would be to cancel out age differences. The finding of significant age differences probably reflects the unique aspect of the first two years of life, when affiliation and fear appear to be highly related. Basically, the scales are more sensitive to expressions of social affiliation toward adults, since social affiliation toward peers shows its greatest developmental change toward the end of the age period that the scales were designed to measure.

Competence

The issue of competence is complex, and even the definition of competence is in question. For example, *competence* has been defined as a set of universal adaptive functions without specific content (Sroufe, 1979a). It has also been defined as a more limited set of tasks and skills (Scarr, 1981; Zigler & Trickett, 1978). Regardless of the nature of the theoretical construct, however, the measurement of competence requires that something be measured. To the degree that a genotype has a phenotypic expression, the choice of measures limits as well as defines the concept. For the purpose of our scale construction, *competence* was defined as the ability to participate in a set of age-related tasks, which is accompanied by a positive feeling. Competence, in other words, concerns children's feelings about themselves and their ability to obtain the goals that they seek in their environment. The nature of these goals is both culturally determined and self-determined and may include actions as well as feelings. Feelings of competence have also been studied as "efficacy" (Lewis & Goldberg, 1969b) and its reciprocal, "learned helplessness" (Seligman, 1975).

Feelings of efficacy are acquired early in life and are visible in the first three months after birth (Lewis, 1971; Lewis & Coates, 1980; Lewis

& Goldberg, 1969b). Unfortunately, the developmental course of competence is relatively uncharted. Wenar (1976) reported data indicating that the infant's status at 12 months, whether high competence or low competence, is a more potent variable affecting the subsequent development of competence than are maternal child-rearing techniques. An overall increase in the intensity of competence responses was also discovered in infants between 12 and 20 months of age, whereas the frequency of competence responses declined. Wenar speculated that this decline reflects more an increase in interpersonal interactions and a decline in physical-motor encounters with the environment than a decline in competence per se.

Infants at this age still prefer exploring the physical environment over initiating social interactions with the mother, however. Interestingly, there appears to be no relationship between expressions of competence in the physical environment and expressions of competence in the social realm (Wenar, 1978). Infants apparently combine physical and social orientations to varying degrees and do not prefer one mode of competence expression over another.

Although competence is usually studied in infants about 18 months old and has been marked by some as a critical point in development (White, 1975), there is considerable evidence suggesting that competence has its roots in earlier ages. Research with 10-week-old infants indicates that they were able to learn to effect a particular outcome when the outcome was turning on a slide through an armpull (see Chapter 6). Learning this task was accompanied by changes in state; infants showed changes in positive affect and were able to stay awake longer (Lewis et al., 1983). These changes in state associated with learning to control an aspect of the environment confirm other results indicating that a more responsive environment leads to improved scores on attention distribution and on infant mental-development tests (Coates & Lewis, 1981; Lewis & Coates, 1980; Lewis & Goldberg, 1969b).

The variable hypothesized to mediate between the responsive environment and the child's subsequent more alert state and happier emotional tone is generalized expectancy or competence (Lewis & Goldberg, 1969b). Whether this competence is anything more than a short-term transient event rather than an enduring state is unknown. The data do suggest that at least by 3 months of age, infants manifest competence within a task. This competence ability may generalize across tasks (Finkelstein & Ramey, 1977) and across responses (Brinker & Lewis, 1982). Whether this competence is an enduring disposition, however, is open to debate.

Whatever the time of emergence, it is clear from the literature on learned helplessness that feelings of competence are not easily altered once they emerge. In one study with rats, it was shown that the development of efficacy protects the rat from subsequent failures. Early feelings of helplessness were shown not to be easily altered by subsequent experience (Seligman & Maier, 1967). Thus, once established, any changes in competence may more likely be changes in task choice associated with increased cognitive ability than in the feeling state underlying the behavior (Lewis, 1978). Again, the issue is raised about the difference between competence as a trait-like structure and competence as a measure of specific age-related behaviors. The problem remains how to measure an underlying capacity without depending on specific behaviors that are often age-related and culturally defined.

The data on competence collected on our scales reveal no significant age changes across the first three years of life (see Figure 13). Individual differences as a function of gender also were not significant. Other research on infants' exploratory activities has also demonstrated that male and female infants are quite similar in their willingness to explore a novel environment (Rheingold & Eckerman, 1969; Ross, Rheingold, & Eckerman, 1972; Rubenstein, 1967).

In contrast, social class differences in competence have been documented (White, 1975). Such differences may be a function of social class differences in the nature of contingency experiences in infant–mother interactions. For example, although middle-class mothers do not do more for their infants than lower-class mothers, they employ a different style of responding (Lewis & Wilson, 1972). Tulkin and Kagan (1972) have also reported social class differences in maternal behaviors to a 10-month-old infant. Social class differences, then, may be more related to differences in patterns of infant–mother interaction that create different contingency experiences for infants than to a static group variable such as social class.

External Validity

Confirmation of the external validity of the scales comes from the ability of the scales to detect individual differences in infants' emotional expressions that have been reported elsewhere in the literature. Specifically, expressions of both fear and social affiliation were found to be most intense during 12–18 months of age and to decline in intensity thereafter. These findings confirm the research literature, reviewed above, that also shows that expressions of fear peak during the middle of the second year. The research literature on the infant–mother relationship also indicates that expressions of this relationship intensify through 18 months of age. Separation protest also increases most rapidly between 12 and 18 months. Furthermore, an increase in "social initiatives" directed toward the mother has been observed in infants between 12 and 20 months of age. There is even some evidence of an increase in affiliative behaviors directed toward peers during this age period.

The scales also detected individual differences in expressions of anger, with the oldest infants exhibiting the highest levels of anger. Although there is relatively little research on anger in infants, the increase in expressions of anger across age is not inconsistent with results reported by others.

Happiness and competence expressions were not found to change significantly over age. Izard (1977) has stated that joy is a primary emotion and emerges early. The failure to detect age changes in the happiness scale is taken as support for that view. Unfortunately, there is too little information in the research literature to support or refute the results obtained on the competence scale.

Significant gender differences in infants' expressions of emotion were found only on the domain scale for fear. The finding that girls showed more intense expressions of fear than boys is consistent with the reports of other investigators described above. In the current study, girls also tended to show more intense expressions of social affiliation, anger, and happiness than boys, although the differences between girls and boys were not statistically significant. While reports of gender differences in expressions of anger are difficult to interpret (Feiring & Lewis, 1979), other data confirm the observation that girls generally tend to be more affable (expressed in measures of happiness and attachment) than boys.

Social Milieu Differences

The context in which children develop, the availability of different people, and the social functions of these people for the children have been cited as important factors in sociability and possibly emotional development. The need to consider the social environment as a milieu larger than the parent–child relationship has been emphasized (Bronfenbrenner, 1979; Harlow & Harlow, 1965; Hartup, 1979; Lewis, 1982b; Lewis, et al., 1982). Several research studies have looked at emotional development in relationship to children's social environment. Most of this research focuses on expressions of fear; for example, attempts have been made to relate stranger fear to the number of different people encountered in the daily activity of the child. While Schaffer (1966) showed that infants with more exposure to strangers show a later onset of stranger fear, later studies failed to confirm this relationship (Morgan & Ricciuti, 1969; Harmon, Morgan, & Klein, 1977). The number of different adults caring for the infant has been related to stranger fear in some studies (Blehar, 1974; Collard, 1968) but not in others (Schaffer, 1966; Ricciuti, 1974). The number of siblings may be related to later ages of onset of stranger fear (Collard, 1968), but the number of adults in the family appears not to be related (Bronson, 1972). Anecdotal evidence suggests that children raised by students living in graduate student housing show less fear than children not raised in such an environment and that day-care infants show less fear than home-reared infants (Kagan, Kearsley, & Zelazo, 1978).

There is also some evidence regarding the effects of the social milieu on expressions of anger and happiness. Studies of day-care infants show that during the first few months that the infant is enrolled in a day-care program, the infant exhibits more avoidance of the mother during reunion than home-reared infants (Blehar, 1974). However, infants who have spent more time in day care are less likely to avoid the mother (i.e., to show anger) on reunion and do not differ significantly from home-reared infants (Blanchard & Main, 1979). This finding suggests that the length of time an infant has participated in day care may affect emotional expressions. Finally, the environment may be a source of individual differences in positive emotional expressions. The results of several studies show that institutionalized infants exhibit a somewhat delayed development of smiling compared with home-reared infants and infants raised in a kibbutz (Ambrose, 1961; Gewirtz, 1965; Spitz & Wolf, 1946).

Since the Scales of Socioemotional Development were administered in day-care settings, the effects of day-care variables on the development of emotional expressions and individual differences could be analyzed. A preliminary MANOVA was computed to determine whether the mean intensity of emotional expression differed as a function of the day-care center that an infant was enrolled in. No significant differences were found. Therefore, the combined sample was divided into eight groups according to the age of the infants at the time they entered a day-care program ("age at entry") and the length of time they had participated in a day-care program at the time the scales were administered ("time in program"). The number of subjects in each group is reported in Table 31. An eight-cell grouping of subjects was chosen since this grouping came the closest to equalizing the number of subjects in each cell when both effects—age at entry and time in program—

Table 31. Number of Subjects by Age at Entry into
Day Care and Length of Time in Program

Age at entry	Time in program		Total
	≤3 months (short term)	>3 months (long term)	
≤6 months	8	8	16
7–12 months	9	10	19
13–18 months	7	7	14
≥19 months	9	3	12
Total	33	28	61[a]

[a] The number of subjects totals 61 instead of 62 because the date
of entry was not available for one infant.

were considered. It is recognized that a different division, or a finer
division in terms of time in program, might have produced different
results.

The data were subjected to a two-way (age at entry × time in
program) MANOVA, based on all five dependent variables. In addition,
five two-way (age at entry × time in program) univariate ANOVAs were
computed, one for each of the dependent variables. Since the cell sizes
of the two-way analyses were small, the effects of age at entry and time
in program were tested separately in one-way ANOVAs as well as concurrently in two-way ANOVAs. Both designs yielded similar results.
Since the factorial design provided somewhat more information, only
the results of the two-way analyses are reported in the text.

Because the infant's age is related to the independent variables,
age at entry and time in program, and because the infant's age was
found to be a significant factor in emotional expression, differences
between the groups were further examined after statistical adjustments
had been made for the effects of the infant's age on the affect scores.
This was accomplished through a series of analyses of covariance (AN-
COVAs), using the infant's age as the covariate. Because a two-way
design provided too few subjects per cell for computing the regression
lines necessary to the ANCOVA, only single-factor ANCOVAs—one for
age at entry and one for time in program—were computed on each of
the dependent variables.

The assumption underlying the analysis of covariance regarding
the homogeneity of the within-cell regressions was tested by an F ratio
(Winer, 1971) and confirmed in all but one instance. A significant difference between the within-cell regression line slopes was found on

the dependent variable, social affiliation, in the ANCOVA testing the effect of age at entry. Consequently, the results of the ANCOVAs can be used to supplement those of the ANOVAs in all of the analyses but one.

Age at Entry

The main effect of the infant's age at entry into day care on emotional expression was not significant, according to the MANOVA. This finding was confirmed by the nonsignificant results of the individual univariate ANOVAs. The finding suggests that it may not be possible to detect an age-at-entry effect without first removing the effect of the infant's age on emotional expression. That is, the age of the infants at the time the observation was made (referred to as the *age of the infant*) is different from the age of the infants when they entered day care (referred to as the *age of entry*). For example, an infant could have entered day care at 3 months of age and been tested on the scales at 10 months of age. Both of these age-related variables might contribute to the infants' emotional expression. Thus it was necessary to make some correction for the age of the infant when the data were gathered. Such adjustments were made in the ANCOVAs.

After statistical adjustments were made for the effect of the infant's age in an ANCOVA, age at entry emerged as a significant factor in the expression of anger ($F[3,53] = 3.21, p < .03$). An examination of the adjusted mean anger scores showed an increase in anger when infants entered day care at older ages: 1.45 (6 months or younger at entry); 1.49 (7–12 months old at entry); 1.71 (13–18 months old at entry); and 3.13 (19 months and older at entry). Multiple tests between the means using the average effective error (Winer, 1971) revealed that the infants entering day care at older ages exhibited significantly more anger expressions than infants entering day care at (1) 6 months of age or younger ($F[1,53] = 30.24, p < .01$); (2) 7–12 months ($F[1,53] = 28.82, p < .01$); and (3) 13–18 months ($F[1,53] = 21.60, p < .01$). The differences among the other groups were not statistically significant.

In other words, infants who entered day care at younger ages were less likely to express anger than infants who entered when they were older. Whether day care per se and separation from the mother that is associated with day care are causes of that difference is undetermined. It may well be that older infants express separation and loss of the familiar in terms of anger rather than sadness or fear. Alternatively, it may be that as children get older and become more angry, they are more likely to be placed in day care, since they are less pleasant to have at home. Such an explanation is unlikely to apply to the present findings, however. In this study, day care was used as a place for children to be taken care of when their mothers went to work.

The ANCOVAs computed on the other affect measures confirmed the results of the ANOVAs in not detecting any significant age-at-entry differences in the expressions of fear, happiness, or competence. Recall that an ANCOVA on the social affiliation scores could not be performed because the within-cell regressions were not homogeneous.

These findings indicate that age at entry appears to affect only expression of anger. That it is unrelated to fear or happiness suggests that there may, in fact, be a relationship between age of entry into day care and anger, so that older children are angrier than younger children about being placed in day care.

Time in Program

Unlike the effect of age at entry, the main effect of time in program on emotional expressions was highly significant in the MANOVA ($F[5,52] = 4.84$, $p < .001$). How long a child has been in day care seems to affect the child's emotional expressions. The effects of time in the day-care program on individual emotions were examined first without controlling for the age of the child. To discover which emotional expressions were significantly affected by time in program, individual univariate ANOVAs were computed for each emotional state. Figure 14 presents differences in emotional expressions as a function of length of time in day care. The length of time in day care varied between 1 and over 20 months. Because an eight-cell grouping was desirable if both time in program and age at entry were to be considered, only two age groups for time in program (three months or less versus more than three months) were used. However, a different division or a finer division might be more desirable and might produce different results.

The mean fear scores were 2.38 for infants enrolled in day care for three months or less ("short-term" infants) and 2.25 for infants enrolled for more than three months ("long-term" infants). This difference was not significant and indicates that length of time in day care did not affect the children's expressions of fear.

The mean anger scores were 3.36 and 2.56 for long-term and short-term infants, respectively. These scores were significantly different ($F[1,53] = 16.45$, $p < .001$). Thus, expressions of anger were affected both by age at entry and by time in program.

Long-term infants also showed more intense expressions of happiness than did the short-term infants, with a mean score of 2.68 for the long-term group and a mean score of 2.30 for the short-term group.

352   CHAPTER 11

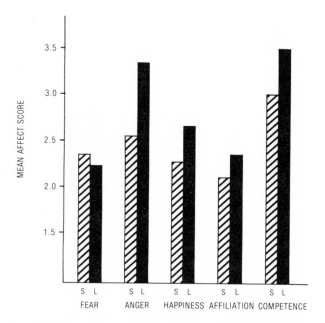

Figure 14. Individual differences in emotions as a function of length of time in day care: short-term (3 months or less) and long-term (more than 3 months).

This difference approached statistical significance ($F[1,53] = 2.92$, $p < .09$). If such a finding is reliable, it indicates that infants who have spent a longer time in day care are happier than infants who have spent less time in day care. It is possible that infants recently enrolled in day care are at first less happy as they try to cope with the new situation. Their expressions of happiness under these circumstances may be temporarily depressed.

The mean social affiliation scores of 2.35 for the long-term infants and 2.12 for the short-term infants did not differ significantly. However, long-term infants showed significantly more intense expressions of competence, with a mean score of 3.44 compared with the short-term infants' mean score of 3.02 ($F[1,53] = 4.17$, $p < .05$). Thus, infants participating in day care for over three months seem to show more competence as well as more happiness, social affiliation, and anger. They also exhibit a slight decrease in fear expressions compared with infants who have been in day care for less than three months.

The validity of these results tends to be confirmed in the results generated by the ANCOVAs. After statistical adjustments were made for the age of the infant, the overall effect of the variable, time in program, was not statistically significant in expressions of fear. However, time in program was highly significant in anger expressions ($F[1,57]$ = 10.36, $p < .002$). Again, long-term infants expressed anger more intensely than did short-term infants, with adjusted mean anger scores of 2.87 and 1.87, respectively. While differences in expressions of happiness and social affiliation were not statistically significant, according to the ANCOVAs, differences in expressions of competence approached a level of statistical significance ($F[1,57]$ = 3.44, $p < .07$). The long-term infants, with an adjusted mean competence score of 3.37, showed more intense expressions of competence than did the short-term infants, with an adjusted mean of 2.96.

The most conservative conclusion after adjusting for age of infant on the effects of time in program is that an increased time in the program produces more anger. There is some indication that time in program also increases children's expressions of competence and, to some extent, happiness. If such results were to be replicated in a larger study, the effects of day care on enduring emotional states might be of some concern, if gains in competence are offset by the increases in anger. Caution should be used in interpreting the meaning of the increase in anger as a function of the length of time in the program, however. Too often, anger is viewed as an inappropriate negative emotion. While this may be the case at times, the situations used to elicit anger in the current study may be appropriate ones for the expression of anger. Consequently, increases in anger may not be the result of an aversive environment. Indeed, the expression of emotion in appropriate situations is an important socialization task (see Chapter 6). Therefore, one could argue that the ability to express emotions, even negative emotions, as a function of length of time in the program demonstrates positive effects of successful child-rearing.

Age at Entry by Time in Program

Since emotions are affected by both age at entry and time in program, the interaction of these two variables was examined as it influenced emotional expressions. First, the interaction of age at entry × time in program was analyzed by a MANOVA. The results indicated that across all five emotional states, there was no significant emotional effect. However, an individual univariate ANOVA indicated a significant effect in the expression of social affiliation ($F[3,53]$ = 3.05, $p < .04$).

A trend in affiliative expressions across age at entry was observed for infants who had participated in day care for three months or less (see Table 32). Intensity of affiliative expressions steadily increased across the first three age groups, peaking with infants who entered day care between the ages of 13–18 months. The intensity of affiliative expressions declined in infants who entered day care at 19 months of age or older. Individual comparisons between cell means (Winer, 1971) showed statistically significant differences in mean affiliation scores between short-term infants with an entry age of 13–18 months and short-term infants with entry ages of (1) 6 months or younger ($F[1,53] = 9.03$, $p < .01$) and (2) 19 months or older ($F[1,53] = 5.27$, $p < .05$). No trend in social affiliative expressions across entry age was observed for infants who had been in a day-care program for more than three months (see Table 32). Moreover, individual comparisons among the cell means showed no statistically significant differences between the mean social affiliation scores of the long-term infants.

Finally, two statistically significant differences were found between the short-term and long-term infants. Of the infants who entered day care between 13 and 18 months of age, the short-term infants showed significantly more intense expressions of social affiliation than did the long-term infants ($F[1,53] = 4.16$, $p < .05$). Significant differences in social affiliation were also observed between long-term infants who entered day care between the ages 7 and 12 months and short-term infants who entered day care at 6 months of age or younger ($F[1,53] = 5.37$, $p < .05$).

The finding of an age-at-entry × time-in-program effect on expressions of social affiliation suggests that affiliative expressions increase in intensity for infants who have participated in day care for three months or less. No such trend is evident for infants who have been in day care longer. Short-term infants, thus, show the more typical trend

Table 32. Mean Social Affiliation Scores for an Age-at-Entry × Time-in-Program Effect

Age at entry	Time in program	
	≤3 months (short term)	>3 months (long term)
≤6 months	1.50	2.42
7–12 months	2.37	2.58
13–18 months	2.90	1.95
≥19 months	1.83	2.32

in affiliative behavior, with peak expressions occurring between 13 and 18 months of age.

When the data are examined in terms of the chronological ages of the long-term infants at the time the scales were administered, they reveal that although affiliative expressions peak for infants who entered day care between 7 and 12 months of age, at the time the affiliative expressions were measured, the majority of these infants were between 13 and 18 months old. This is the age group in which one would expect to observe the most intense expressions of affiliation. In contrast, infants who entered day care between the ages 13 and 18 months and who had participated in the program for longer than three months were usually older than 19 months at the time the affiliative expressions were observed. Thus, one would not expect to observe high affiliation scores in this group. It would appear that the decline in affiliation for long-term infants is not necessarily related to the length of time they have been in a day-care program but may be more related to their chronological age. There is no reason to believe that a long-term day-care experience affects children's affiliative behaviors. The emerging literature on day care indicates that day care or communal child-rearing does not have an adverse effect on children's development (Belsky & Steinberg, 1978; Lewis & Schaeffer, 1979).

External Validity

The social milieu differences detected by the scales compare favorably with what has been reported elsewhere in the literature (Belsky & Steinberg, 1978). For example, the age at which the infant enters a day-care program was found to influence expressions of anger. In particular, infants who entered day care after 19 months of age showed more intense anger than infants who entered before they were 19 months old. Yet, age at entry did not affect other emotional states. The failure to detect effects of age at entry on social affiliation agrees with the findings from other studies that age of entry into day care has no systematic effect on children's attachment to their mothers (e.g., Portnoy & Simmons, 1978).

The scales also detected individual differences in emotional states resulting from the length of time the infant was enrolled in a day-care program. Specifically, infants participating in programs for longer than three months exhibited higher levels of anger than did infants enrolled for shorter periods of time. Long-term infants also tended to show more competence than did short-term infants. Research on the effects of this variable on emotional development is scarce. Somewhat relevant is a finding that the amount of prior exposure to group experiences in nursery schools is related to negative interactions with first-grade teachers (Raph, Thomas, Chess, & Korn, 1964). Moreover, one would expect to observe an increase in competence as a function of the amount of time spent in day care, since one of the goals of most day-care programs is to foster children's abilities to interact effectively with their environment.

What effects day care in general might have had on the results generated by the scales is not known. However, at least two pieces of information suggest that the findings are probably not restricted to day-care populations. First, the results obtained by the scales regarding both normative trends and individual differences in emotional states confirm findings obtained by other investigators testing home-reared infants. Second, studies examining the effects of day care have found few differences between day-care infants and their home-reared counterparts (Belsky & Steinberg, 1978; Kagan et al., 1978). For the most part, the mother–infant attachment relationship has been the primary focus of those interested in the influence of day care on emotional development. Very little research exists on the effects of day care on other emotional variables. With regard to attachment, the bulk of the evidence indicates that day care does not disrupt children's relationships to their mothers even when it is initiated in the first year of life (e.g., Brookhart & Hock, 1976; Caldwell, Wright, Honig, & Tannenbaum, 1970; Doyle, 1975; Kagan et al., 1978; Portnoy & Simmons, 1978; Roopnarine & Lamb, 1978). Other data indicate that day-care children may interact more with peers in both positive and negative ways than home-reared children (e.g., Kagan et al., 1978; Ricciuti, 1974). Finally, there is some evidence showing that children enrolled in day care for extended periods of time show increased aggression toward peers and adults and decreased cooperation with adults once the children enter first grade (Schwarz, Strickland, & Krolick, 1974). However, Belsky and Steinberg (1978) suggested that this consequence may be more a function of particular socialization values than of day care in general.

That the scales are capable of detecting individual differences in day-care experiences suggests that they might be used to assess day-care experiences in addition to or instead of cognitive measures. The overall picture provided by cognitive assessment shows that day-care experience has neither beneficial nor adverse effects on the intellectual development of most children (as measured by standardized tests). At best, day care may attenuate the declines in test scores of economically disadvantaged children after 18 months of age (Belsky & Steinberg, 1978).

On the other hand, the differential effects of day-care experiences on emotional development may be more pronounced. For example, in this study, the competence scores were found to be somewhat higher for children in one day-care center, while the levels of affiliation were greater for children in another center. Investigations of differences in the day-care programs uncovered philosophical curricular differences: one center was primarily interested in fostering independence and competence in infants, whereas the other center was more concerned with nurturing social relationships. Although the evidence is not overwhelming, the fact that the scales were sensitive to program differences calls for a systematic study of the feasibility of using these scales to evaluate differences in intervention programs.

Relationships among Emotional States

The demonstration that some emotions have different developmental courses while others share similarities suggests that there may be relationships among some emotions. Moreover, common sense suggests that some emotions are more likely to be related than others. A child who is fearful is not likely to be happy, nor is a child who is happy likely to be angry. On the other hand, fearful children may be more affiliative and happy children more competent. The notion of a natural confluence of certain enduring emotional states has a lot in common with what is called *personality structure*. To study this problem we investigated similarities and differences in relationships among emotions not only for the entire sample but also for different age groups. The questions addressed in a series of intercorrelation analyses do not bear on the more general issue of arousal or the relative independence of the domain scales. These issues were discussed in the preceding chapter. The intercorrelation patterns of concern here are predicated on the belief that some emotions are more related than others.

If one is to explore the specific relationship between any two emotions, the extraneous effects of the other emotions must be removed from the correlation coefficient. We accomplished this statistically through partial correlation analyses. The partial correlation analyses were based on the total affect scores. Only subjects with total scores for all five domains were included in these analyses. In order to eliminate the spurious correlations that can occur in a small sample of subjects, we combined Samples 1 and 2 to produce a larger sample of infants. Combining the samples of infants also allowed for the investigation of age and gender differences in the relationships among various emotions.

Table 33 presents the partial correlations between pairs of domain

Table 33. Partial Correlations between the Domains

	Anger	Happiness	Affiliation	Competence
Fear	.18	−.07	.33[a]	−.21
Anger		.21	.18	.18
Happiness			.04	−.05
Affiliation				−.02

[a] p < .01.

scores. The only significant correlation was between fear and social affiliation ($r = .33$, $p < .01$). The finding is consistent with the group data on age trends in which the same developmental function was found for fear and social affiliation.

The result suggests that infants and young children who exhibit high levels of fear also show high levels of social affiliation. Although the correlation is significant, the amount of variability accounted for between the domain scores is low (about 10%). The relationship between fear and social affiliation during this period of time is thus rather weak. Nevertheless, most displays of social affiliation appear to be attempts to reduce fear rather than to seek pleasure in social contacts.

Although the correlation is not significant, fear and competence are negatively related, as one might expect ($r = -.21$, n.s.). Children who showed fear did not show competence. Most surprising are the positive correlations between anger and the other emotions, especially happiness, social affiliation, and competence. One would have expected anger to be negatively related to each of these emotions. That this is not the case again underscores the belief that anger does not reflect a maladaptive and inappropriate state. Anger may be an appropriate response in certain situations.

Age Differences

The relationships among emotions as a function of developmental level need to be carefully considered. While many studies have looked at age changes in transient emotions and a few have looked at age changes in more enduring ones, virtually no studies have examined age changes in the relationships among emotions. The present analysis affords a unique opportunity to investigate developmental changes in the relationships of emotions. One would expect that the relationships should undergo developmental change. The findings of the current study on age differences in the expression of different emotions suggest that certain emotions are more likely to be associated at particular age levels. For example, fear and social affiliation are likely to be most related in very young children. As we previously suggested, however, social affiliation may be related to other emotions (e.g., competence) as the children grow older. Likewise, anger, as a reflection of a negative state, might be related to fear.

In order to examine the developmental trends in emotional relationships, we divided the combined sample into three age groups: (1) 12 months and younger ($n = 21$); (2) 13–18 months ($n = 16$); and (3) 19 months and older ($n = 25$). Partial correlations between pairs of domain scores were computed for each age group (see Table 34). These data can be examined in two ways: first, by looking at correlational differences between age groups, and second, by plotting correlational changes between any two emotions as a function of age (see Figure 15). Looking at Table 34, the reader can see that two statistically significant relationships emerged from the correlational analysis for the youngest age group: anger was positively related to competence ($r = .57$, $p < .01$) and to social affiliation ($r = .48$, $p < .05$). In the middle age group only one relationship was statistically significant: social affiliation was negatively related to competence ($r = -.65$, $p < .01$). Finally, in the

Table 34. Partial Correlations between the Domains by Age Group

	Anger	Happiness	Affiliation	Competence
≤12 months old				
Fear	−.04	.13	.40	−.18
Anger		.31	.48[a]	.57[b]
Happiness			−.26	−.21
Affiliation				−.18
13–18 months old				
Fear	.28	.12	.27	−.18
Anger		.30	.11	−.01
Happiness			−.10	.12
Affiliation				−.65[b]
≥19 months old				
Fear	.33	−.18	.13	−.26
Anger		.12	.11	.07
Happiness			.42[a]	.14
Affiliation				.16

[a] $p < .05$.
[b] $p < .01$.

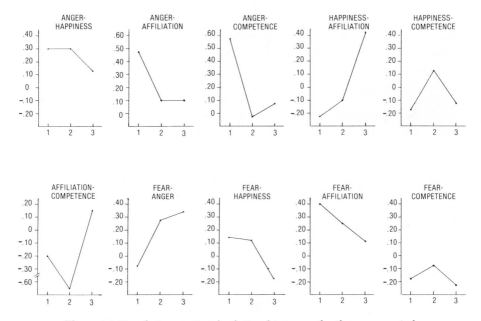

Figure 15. Trends in emotional relationships over the three age periods.

oldest age group, a significant positive relationship was found between happiness and social affiliation ($r = .42$, $p < .05$).

Although relatively few significant correlations were detected in these data, the patterning between emotions is made more obvious in Figure 15. An examination of the relationship between fear and each of the other emotions indicates that the relationship between fear and (1) happiness, (2) social affiliation, and (3) competence decreases with age, while the relationship between fear and anger increases. This result suggests that fear and social affiliation are most likely to be related early in life and that social affiliation is more related to fear than to other emotions. The strengthening of the relationship between fear and anger across age suggests that with increasing age, anger may become a less appropriate emotion and more related to fear. Thus, in a sense, anger may become more related to maladaptive feelings. The fear and competence relationship remains unchanged over time. Fear and happiness show a declining relationship, a finding that again indicates that fear may be a less adaptive behavior and, as one would expect, that fearful children show less happiness.

Although it was suggested earlier that anger may be an appropriate response to certain situations, the data on age changes indicate that anger may become maladaptive with age. Children who show more anger, show more fear as they grow older. In addition, as they get older, children who show more anger show less happiness, less affiliation, and less competence. Indeed, the argument that the expressions of anger change over age is supported by changes in the relationships of the emotions that anger is associated with. At the earliest ages, anger is positively associated with competence, happiness, and affiliation, and negatively related to fear. This relationship reverses as children grow older.

Happiness follows the expected age trend for the most part. With increasing age, happiness becomes less related to fear and anger and more related to social affiliation. The only correlation that does not fit the intuitive view of happiness is with competence. Although the correlation between happiness and competence changes from negative to positive between the first and second age periods, the correlation does not continue to increase for the oldest age group. The most parsimonious explanation is that no relationship exists between happiness and competence. One would expect the relationship between happiness and competence to increase across age periods, as the happiness–social affiliation relationship does. The fact that it does not is surprising. However, when the scales were constructed, happiness and competence items that overlapped were usually included only in the competence scale. The competence scale tended to contain more complex items (e.g., "completes task") and the happiness scale less complex items (e.g., "gets snack"). Thus, any relationship that might naturally exist between happiness and competence may have been masked.

Social affiliation also undergoes interesting age changes. Social affiliation is initially most related to fear and anger, suggesting that angry and fearful children may more likely seek the company of others. Over age, however, fear and anger become less related to social affiliation, and affiliation becomes more related to happiness and competence. This finding corroborates the idea expressed earlier that in early infancy, social affiliation is in the service of fear reduction more than in the service of pleasure; only later does affiliation become an independent competence and thus show a relationship to competence and happiness scores.

The domain least related to the other emotions is competence. Competence does show, however, a declining relationship with anger and an increasing one with social affiliation. Its lack of relationship to happiness and fear makes age changes in competence relationships difficult to interpret.

Although of considerable interest, these results need further explication. Unfortunately, almost no data exist on the relationships among emotions, especially as a function of age. The data presented are based on a limited number of subjects, and as a result, some caution is necessary in their interpretation. The findings on the relationships among emotions as a function of age suggest that the meaning of emotions must be considered within the context both of other emotions and of the developmental level of the child. From this perspective, displays of anger, for example, may reflect instrumentality and competence in young infants. Later on, displays of anger may be related to maladaptive behavior in fearful and less competent children. Likewise, the meaning of social affiliation may also change over time. At first, affiliation may be associated with children's attempts to cope with other emotions, such as fear. Only later may affiliation emerge as an independent and important competence representing a desire for and a need to engage in social commerce.

The developmental psychologist once again is forced to face the issue of the meaning of behavior (see Chapter 8). The Oriental metaphysics can be applied to the emotional domain: the meaning of behavior (in this case, the underlying state) can be known only in context (Lewis, 1967). This principle not only influenced the scale construction but also must guide the interpretation of the results.

Patterns of Emotional States

Throughout the chapter, individual differences and relationships among emotions have been the focal topics. Both the mean data and the intercorrelation matrices underscored the importance of observing emotions in the context of other emotions. For example, information about the relationship between anger and competence or between fear and social affiliation enriches our understanding of the meaning of socialization in the early years of life.

A study of the relationships among emotions is of further importance to an examination of the relationship between personality and patterns of enduring emotional states. The connection between personality and enduring emotional states has seldom been addressed from a developmental perspective. In Chapter 2, an enduring emotional state, or mood, was discussed as the disposition to act in a certain way, given particular classes of events, the likelihood of maintaining a certain level of response intensity, and the likelihood of perceiving particular classes of events in certain ways. Thus, a person having an enduring emotional state of anger would be a person (1) in whom many stimuli would evoke anger; (2) who would be more angry and angry for a longer time;

and (3) who would perceive anger more readily. Such people are re-garded as having an angry or hostile personality. Likewise, one might categorize people as having a sociable personality, a sad or depressed personality, a fearful personality, a happy personality, or a competent personality. (Often, *competence* may not be used; instead, adjectives such as *curious, bold, adventurous,* or *assertive* are used.) As we made clear in Chapter 2, personality and enduring states have much in com-mon and indeed may be indistinguishable.

Izard and Buechler (1980) have regarded personality traits as a mixture of primary affects. For example, hostility (a personality trait) is viewed as a pattern of anger, disgust, and contempt. The distinction between a personality trait as a mixture of primary emotions and a personality trait as a single emotion is a taxonomical issue open to debate. Of importance to the present discussion is the similarity be-tween enduring emotions and what has been called *personality.* One's personality (if such a term is meaningful) may consist of a configuration of enduring emotional states. Personality as a pattern of characteristics or enduring emotional states has been considered by others (e.g., Izard, 1977; Plutchik, 1981a).

One goal of the present research was to examine aspects of chil-dren's personality by studying the relationships among the five emo-tional domains. Is it possible to look at the patterning of children's enduring emotional states and to make statements about children's personalities? The construction of individual profiles based on the pat-terning of children's enduring emotional states not only provides in-formation about children's separate emotional states but also places these states in a context of other emotional states. For example, two children may exhibit equally high degrees of affiliation. However, the child who shows high affiliation and little fear may be very different from the child who shows high affiliation and high fear. In the first case, the child's affiliation may be predicated on fear reduction, while in the second, the child's affiliation may occur for its own sake.

To construct profiles of enduring emotional states, the affect scores of the combined sample first were transformed to standardized scores and an emotional profile based on the five affect scores was generated for each subject. Next, a D^2 matrix of dissimilarities was produced between the subjects' profiles and was analyzed according to Ward's clustering procedures (Ward & Hook, 1963). Ward's method entails a hierarchical approach to cluster analysis in which individual clusters are combined at various levels according to their degree of similarity until one cluster encompassing the entire sample is formed. The op-timal number of clusters was identified by examining discontinuities in the objective function (which reflects within-group variation) for each successive level of the combining process. Only subjects with total affect scores for all five domains were included in the cluster analysis.

Five clusters were identified from the data of the combined sample (see Figure 16). These clusters ranged in size from 7 to 22 infants and were shown to be significantly different from each other by means of univariate and multivariate analyses of variance. In the univariate AN-OVAs, significant F values were obtained between the clusters for each emotional state (fear: $F[4,57] = 11.95$, $p < .001$; anger: $F[4,57] = 17.06$, $p < .001$; happiness: $F[4.57] = 12.56$, $p < .001$; social affiliation: $F[4,57] = 8.37$, $p < .001$; competence: $F[4,57] = 8.41$, $p < .001$). The statistical values produced by the multivariate analysis were also highly significant ($p < .001$).

Figure 16 illustrates the five clusters. Each cluster will be characterized in the discussion that follows. Recall that the ordinate presents standardized scores that enable us to look at relationships among emotions both within particular clusters and across clusters.

Cluster 1 was made up of 22 children whose most outstanding feature was a high happiness score that was almost one standard score

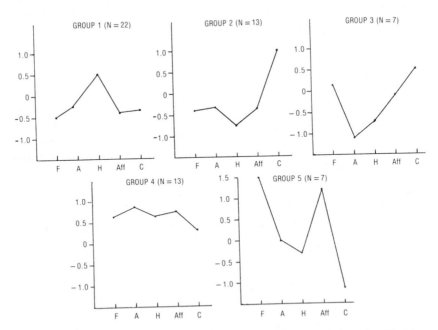

Figure 16. Profiles of enduring emotional states: F = Fear; A = Anger; H = Happiness; Aff = Social Affiliation; C = Competence.

greater than the other scores. The scores on the other four domains were similar and considerably lower than the happiness score. These children may be best characterized as having "happy" personalities.

Cluster 2 was comprised of a group of 13 children whose highest score was competence. This score was quite high in relationship to the other scores, which were low and showed little variability. In fact, the competence score was over 1.5 standard scores greater than the other scores. The second group of children may best be characterized as having "competent" or "achieving" personalities.

Cluster 3 consisted of 7 children who had rather low affect scores in general. They had low affect scores for anger, happiness, and social affiliation, and their fear scores were lower than their competence scores. These children may be characterized as having "depressed" personalities. They were children who were quiet, and unassuming and did not demand attention. It may be because they did not demand attention that their competence scores were moderately high. It is often assumed that children at this age who do not ask for help or attention are competent.

Cluster 4 included 13 infants who exhibited extremely high levels of all emotions. Their standard scores varied little across domains. While their scores on each domain were not necessarily the highest of all the clusters, the overall and undifferentiated high scores on happiness, anger, and fear reflected a generally aroused and perhaps hyperactive group of infants. This group contrasted with Cluster 3, who from their scores appeared to be depressed. Cluster 4 reflected an "excitable" personality.

The fifth cluster was a group of 7 infants who appeared to be fearful and dependent. They obtained the highest fear and affiliation scores and the lowest competence score. The profile of these children reflected a "dependent" personality. It also confirmed the relationship between fear and social affiliation.

These five different clusters may represent five distinctive personalities that can be characterized as happy, competent, depressed, excitable, and dependent. These profiles would seem to correspond well with the intrinsic features of personality commonly observed in young children. Moreover, these clusters appear to support the results of the correlation analyses, in particular the fear–affiliation relationship (Cluster 5) and the competence–anger relationship (Cluster 2).

Figures 17, 18, and 19 present the five clusters for each of the three age groups: children 12 months and younger, 13–18 months, and 19 months and older. The cluster analyses by age must be interpreted cautiously since the breakdown of the sample into three age groups resulted in a small number of subjects in each analysis. Nevertheless, the results can be used to support the findings for the sample as a whole in determining whether the clusters are age-related.

The clusters depicted in Figures 17-19, support the belief that the clusters obtained for the sample as a whole represent important personality differences. The clusters for the children 12 months and younger portray a pattern similar to that found for the sample as a whole (see Figure 17). Cluster 3 represents the happy personality, Cluster 4 the competent personality (which includes a slight elevation of anger), Cluster 1 the excitable personality, Cluster 2 the dependent personality, and Cluster 5 the depressed personality. Interestingly, the fear score in this group of depressed, quiet children was elevated.

The profiles generated for the middle age group also support the general findings, although some differences are apparent (see Figure 18). Cluster 1 represents the happy personality. Unlike the happy personality cluster for the entire sample, the competence scores were elevated in this cluster. The group was marked by a high happiness score. Cluster 4 was most similar to the competent personality marked by high

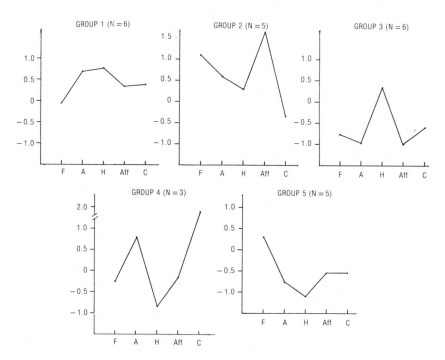

Figure 17. Profiles for children 3 to 12 months of age. (For abbreviations see Figure 16.)

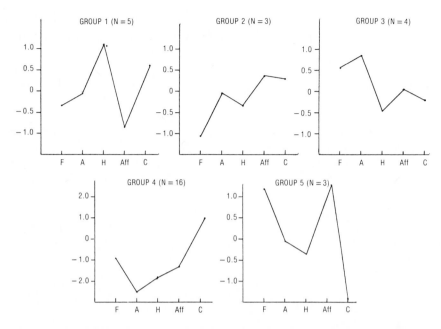

Figure 18. Profiles for children 13 to 18 months of age. (For abbreviations see Figure 16.)

scores on competence and achievement. Cluster 5 represented the dependent personality, with high scores on fear and social affiliation. These three clusters correspond to the clusters found for the youngest age group and for the group as a whole.

Clusters 2 and 3 differed somewhat from the clusters reported previously. Clusters 2 and 3 showed no clear interpretable pattern. Cluster 2 showed the lowest score for fear, whereas Cluster 3 showed the highest scores for fear and anger. Both clusters showed low scores for happiness. Cluster 3 might be characterized as an angry personality type, and Cluster 2 characterized as nonfearful or courageous. The small number of subjects in each group makes the results difficult to interpret; nevertheless, they are, for the most part, consistent with the other results.

Children 19 months and older were considered next (see Figure 19). Cluster 1 was characteristic of the dependent personality; Cluster 2 appeared to be the happy personality; and Cluster 3 excitable. In Cluster 3, the activity level, which reflected their general excitability, seems to have been independent of competence insofar as their competence score was the lowest of all the groups. Cluster 4 represents the competent group with the highest score in competence and the lowest

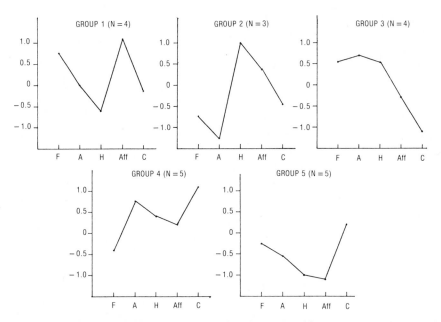

Figure 19. Profiles for children 19 to 30 months of age. (For abbreviations see Figure 16.)

score in fear and affiliation. Some elevation is evident in the anger score. Finally, Cluster 5 is reminiscent of the depressed personality with low scores on happiness and affiliation and the highest scores on fear and competence. Once again, this finding may indicate that isolated or uninvolved children are perceived as competent.

In short, the data for each of the three age groups generated similar clusters. The personality types that characterized the sample as a whole appear to have been constant across ages. Such information testifies to the validity of the scales as providing a reasonable measurement of children's enduring emotions across this age range. Although some of the differences that appeared may represent age differences, the small sample size prevents one from making too much of these findings.

Cluster analyses by gender produced similar results. A gender-by-age analysis would have been of particular interest, since gender differences in personality types might appear at different ages. Unfortunately, the sample was too small to allow such an analysis.

The robustness of the clusters obtained across age and gender groups gained additional support in one final analysis. One way to observe whether age and gender influenced the composition of the clusters was to examine whether any age or gender group was more represented in a particular cluster. An overall test on the distribution of frequencies (chi-square analysis) was not appropriate because the expected value in some of the cells was too small. Therefore, the formula for the sampling distribution of the binomial was used to test for significant age and gender differences in each cluster (Siegel, 1956). Since one of the requirements for the binomial test is that the "scores" be in two classes, two age groups were established by dividing the combined sample into infants 15 months and younger ($n = 30$) and infants older than 15 months ($n = 32$). The two-class breakdown by gender produced 37 boys and 25 girls. The two-tailed binomial tests did not detect any statistically significant age or gender differences in any of the clusters.

In summary, the cluster analyses provided some interesting findings. These analyses generated clusters or "personality types" that were unrelated to age or gender. The cluster analyses also confirmed results reported earlier on the distribution of mean values as well as the correlational relationships among emotions.

＊＊＊＊＊＊＊＊＊＊＊

The results of these investigations of individual differences and patterns of emotions confirmed what naive psychology suggests is true as well as the empirical results reported in the research literature. The Scales of Socioemotional Development, which measure emotions in naturally occurring situations, generate findings similar to those obtained in more controlled laboratory settings. The similarity of the results attests to the vigor of the phenomena and to the usefulness of our measurement system. These results establish the validity of the instrument and indirectly support the theory underlying it. The final test of the usefulness of the scales is a demonstration of their applicability on a set of individual case histories. This endeavor is described in the following chapter.

12

Profiles of Enduring Emotional States (Moods)

The usefulness of the scales depends on their ability to differentiate individual children on the basis of past experience and current behavior as well as to evaluate groups of children or programs. We have chosen to look at five emotions, the ones that we feel have been studied the most and that are the most important in children's lives. We recognize, however, that the number of emotions studied could be larger and that a truly representative sample would include more than five. Although our measurement system is still imperfect, the statistical procedures used to generate measures of five distinct emotions provide strong support for its use in a natural setting by observers with minimal training.

The availability of such an instrument should enhance our ability to characterize children. Furthermore, it should enable us to evaluate groups of children and programs in terms of outcomes other than the traditional cognitive ones frequently used as the sole criteria of excellence or fiscal worth. Our interest, though, goes beyond the measurement of single emotions to the measurement of the patterns of emotional states and changes in these patterns as a function of both normal and deviant development.

In previous chapters, we presented the data collected from the measurement scales in order to demonstrate the construct validity of the scales. The data on individual differences in emotional expressions confirm, for the most part, findings derived from laboratory-based research. Moreover, we showed through a series of cluster analyses that the data generate reasonable patterns of enduring emotional states that resemble personality types.

In the present chapter, we turn to the application of the scales at the level of the individual child. Data on children's previous, concurrent, and subsequent behavior (emotional and social, as well as cognitive) would be useful to an examination of this application. For example, if we could show that teachers' ratings of individual children correspond to results obtained on our scales, the validity of these scales would be further enhanced. Unfortunately, such data are unavailable for the entire sample. One major problem we faced in trying to collect such data was teaching the caregivers how to think in terms of these emotional dimensions. Our discussions with the caregivers indicated that prior to this work, they had been unable to observe or differentiate children on these dimensions. They tended to see almost all of their children as happy, and they saw little or no evidence of any fear or anger. Thus, we might add parenthetically that the scales are useful not only for assessing children but also for educating teachers and parents about these important dimensions of children's behavior. Also of value to an individual assessment would be a demonstration that happy and competent children score better on standardized cognitive tests. As we discussed in Chapter 1, there are some data suggesting that happy children are likely to score better on a variety of cognitive and achievement-oriented tasks.

Our desire in presenting the measurement scales is to generate enough enthusiasm to create a large data set on these variables, as well as on other subject characteristics, including cognitive, social, and familial variables. From such a data set, it might be possible to relate emotional dimensions to other variables historically as well as concurrently and predictively. Our task is not unlike that of researchers who have, on the basis of theory and research, generated systems that others have later validated and perfected. Thus, for example, the Uzgiris–Hunt scales (Uzgiris & Hunt, 1975) were constructed by testing a small sample of children. Currently, these scales are being widely used to judge children's cognitive ability in terms of genetic epistemological principles in the first two years of life. Likewise, the usefulness of the Brazelton Neonatal Behavioral Assessment Scale (Brazelton, 1973) was established only after further research beyond the scope of single laboratories (Sameroff, 1978).

Thus far, the application of our measurement scales in several daycare settings has confirmed their usefulness in assessing children and programs and in sensitizing teachers and parents to new dimensions of children's behavior. In this chapter, the ability of the scales to characterize individual children is considered. First, we describe the steps necessary for generating emotional profiles for individual subjects. Then, we present sample profiles of four children and show through case histories how the individual profiles generated from our scales match other characteristics of these children.

Constructing Individual Profiles

Gathering the Data

In Chapter 10, the procedures for gathering data using the scales were described in detail. Briefly, one observer watches one child each day, arriving at the day-care center before the child and staying until the child leaves. The observer checks off on the scales which behaviors the child expresses as each item described in the scales occurs. (A list of situations, behaviors, and their definitions is contained in Chapter 9; the scales are located in the Appendixes.) If an item does not occur and if the observer cannot "arrange" for its occurrence, the observer also notes this on the scales. If an item occurs and the child makes no response, this, too, is recorded on the scales. It is also possible for a situation to occur and for the child not to notice; the observer would note this next to the item. Thus, each item of the scales is filled in with (1) checkmarks for the particular behaviors observed; (2) "situation did not occur"; (3) "child made no response"; or (4) "child didn't notice."

By way of illustration, Figure 20 presents four items from the revised version of the scales, one for happiness and three for fear. Notice that the item for happiness (#16), "peek-a-boo," was arranged by the observer; this is noted on the item, and the behaviors of the child are checked off. On the first fear item (#9), in this figure, "peer cries," the child made no response; this observation has been checked off at the bottom of the item. The next fear item (#35), "stranger approaches," occurred naturally, and the behaviors that the child exhibited are checked off accordingly. Finally, the fourth item (#36), "strange child," did not occur naturally and could not be arranged by the observer. This fact is recorded on the item.

Coding the Data

The data from the scales are transferred to coding sheets for the purpose of "scoring" the child's emotional responses. As can be seen from the sample coding form for the fear domain, presented in Figure 21, the coding sheet is laid out in the form of a situation-by-behavior matrix. On this sample coding sheet, all of the situations used to mea-

9. When another child (peer) cries, does the child

    ☐ stare at (P)   ☐ suck thumb
                                ☐ decrease activity
    ☐ look and avoid   ☐ hesitate
    ☐ sober   ☐ tense
    ☐ tongue   ☐ tremble
    ☐ pucker   ☐ freeze
    ☐ frown
                                ☐ refuse to look/not look
    ☐ whimper   ☐ turn away
    ☐ fret/cry   ☐ move away
    ☐ scream   ☐ grasp/cling

    ☐ Other _____
    ☑ No response
    ☐ Child didn't notice

16. When the caregiver plays peek-a-boo or hide-and-seek, does the child

    ☐ eyes glow   ☐ relax
    ☐ slight smile   ☐ bounce
    ☑ broad smile   ☐ flail
                                ☐ clap hands
    ☐ vocalize   ☐ act silly
    ☐ chatter
    ☐ laugh/giggle   ☐ play actively
    ☑ squeal

    ☑ Other _Situation arranged_
    ☐ No response

Figure 20. Sample scale items.

35. When the stranger approaches (smiles at, talks to, moves toward) the child, does the child

☐ stare/watch intently (S)   ☐ suck thumb
                                    ☐ decrease activity
☐ look and avoid   ☐ hesitate
☐ refuse to look/not look   ☐ tense

☐ sober   ☐ tremble
☐ tongue   ☐ freeze
☐ pucker   ☑ grasp/cling (C)
☐ frown
                                    ☐ lean away
☐ whimper   ☑ turn away
☐ fret/cry   ☐ move away
☑ scream

☐ Other _____
☐ No response
☐ Child didn't notice

36. When the child notices an unfamiliar child (peer) in the room, does the child

☐ stare (P)   ☐ suck thumb
                                    ☐ decrease activity
☐ look and avoid   ☐ hesitate
☐ refuse to look/not look   ☐ tense

☐ sober   ☐ tremble
☐ tongue   ☐ freeze
☐ pucker   ☐ grasp/cling (C)
☐ frown
                                    ☐ lean away
☐ whimper   ☐ turn away
☐ fret/cry   ☐ move away
☐ scream

☐ Other _Situation didn't occur_
☐ No response

Figure 20. (Continued)

Fear

Situations	Sober	Decrease activity	Tongue	Hesitate	Stare	Look and avoid	Lean away	Suck thumb	Pucker	Frown	Turn away	Tense	Not look	Move away	Whimper	Tremble	Grasp/cling	Freeze	Fret/cry	Scream	Observer Comments	
P cries (9)	✓																				no response	0
P attacks (11)								✓						✓	✓							4
C yells (20)																✓			✓			5
Toys breaks (26)																					no fear response	0
Unfamiliar room (29)															✓		✓				didn't notice	5
Stranger (34)																						X
S approaches (35)											✓						✓			✓	didn't occur	5
Strange child (36)																						X
Behavior rank	1				2				3				4				5					

Mean score: 3.2

Figure 21. Sample coding form.

sure fear on the revised version of the scales are listed in a column down the left side of the form. The numbers of the items on the scales to which the situations correspond appear in parentheses. For example, the fear situation, "peer cries," appears as item #9 on the scales. Across the top of the coding form is a list of all of the behaviors used on the scales to measure fear. The behaviors are arranged from left to right in order of increasing intensity as judged by a group of psychologists. Recall that the behaviors of each domain were assigned ranks (see Chapter 9). These categories are illustrated on the coding sheets by bold lines drawn between the boundary behaviors; the ranks are printed across the bottom of the page. On the sample coding sheet, the reader can see that the first four fear behaviors are all ranked 1, the next four are ranked 2, and so forth.

There is a separate coding form for each of the five emotional domains, with one exception: the social affiliation domain requires two sheets, one for high-stress situations and another for low-stress situations. Two different sheets are used because the two kinds of situations elicit different sets of behaviors. Thus, for each subject there should be six summary sheets. (A complete set is presented in the Appendixes.)

The data from the scales are transferred onto the coding sheets item by item. For each of the coding sheets, the observer locates the items on the scales that correspond to the situations listed on the coding form. As each item is located on the scales, the observer checks off on the coding sheet all of the behaviors relevant to that particular emotional domain that were recorded on the scales. If the child did not express any emotional behaviors (as was the case in the example above, in response to "peer cries"), or if the child expressed only behaviors that reflect an emotional state other than the one being coded, "no response" should be written in the right margin of the form. The latter would be the case if, for example, on the scale item "toy breaks," the child attempted to fix it. Since this behavior is not considered a fear response, it does not appear as a fear behavior on the fear coding sheet. Although "toy breaks" does appear on the coding sheet as a fear item, in the right margin of the fear coding sheet the observer would note "no fear response" across from this item (see Figure 21). Since this item is also on the competence scale, the child's coping response would eventually appear on the competence coding form. Finally, if a situation did not occur at any time during the observation period, the observer should note in the right margin across from that situation "didn't occur." For example, the fear situation "strange child" did not occur and is so marked (see Figure 21).

Scoring the Data

Every item on each coding sheet should be marked either in terms of (1) the behaviors the child exhibited; (2) "no response"; (3) "didn't occur"; or (4) "child didn't notice." These notations form the basis of the scoring system. As was described in Chapter 9, each item is scored according to the rank of the most intense behavior elicited by the situation described in the item. For example, in the "unfamiliar room" situation in the fear domain, three behaviors were checked off on the fear coding sheet: "sober," "whimper," and "grasp/cling." On the coding sheet, "sober" is assigned a rank of 1, whereas "whimper" has a rank of 4, and "grasp/cling" a rank of 5 (see Figure 21). Since, according to the ranks, "grasp/cling" is a more intense behavior than the other two, the fear item "unfamiliar room" is scored 5, the rank of the most intense behavior. This score is written in the right margin of the coding form.

Items that are coded "didn't occur" or "child didn't notice" are not scored. Items on which the child made no response receive a score of 0. In Figure 21, the reader can see that this subject scored 4, 5, and 5 on three other fear items: "peer attacks," "caregiver yells," and "unfamiliar room."

The item scores appear in a column along the right margin of each coding form. By summing these scores and dividing by the number of items scored, the observer can calculate a mean affect score for each child for each emotional state. In the present example, the mean affect score is 3.2. Each child will have five mean affect scores, one for each emotional state. Although there are two coding sheets for the affiliation domain, once the scores are assigned to the individual items, affiliation is treated as a single domain: the scores from both coding sheets are summed together and this total is divided by the number of items scored on both forms.

Converting Raw Scores to Standard Scores

In order to make meaningful any comparison of the child's emotional responses across the five domains, one must convert the child's raw affect scores into standard scores. This conversion can be accomplished in one of two ways. First, we can use the present data as the basis for the normative sample. For each domain, Table 35 converts the raw scores into standard scores based on the data generated from the two samples of children ($n = 62$). Alternatively, if enough data are gathered, investigators may wish to generate their own standard scores

Table 35. Standard Scores for All Children (3–30 Months Old)

Raw score	Fear	Anger	Happiness	Affiliation	Competence
			Emotional state		
0.0	−2.2	−3.3	−2.6	−2.4	−3.7
0.1	−2.1	−3.2	−2.5	−2.3	−3.6
0.2	−2.0	−3.0	−2.4	−2.2	−3.5
0.3	−1.9	−2.9	−2.3	−2.1	−3.4
0.4	−1.8	−2.8	−2.2	−2.0	−3.3
0.5	−1.7	−2.7	−2.1	−1.8	−3.3
0.6	−1.6	−2.6	−2.0	−1.7	−3.0
0.7	−1.5	−2.5	−1.9	−1.6	−2.9
0.8	−1.4	−2.4	−1.8	−1.5	−2.8
0.9	−1.3	−2.3	−1.7	−1.4	−2.7
1.0	−1.2	−2.2	−1.6	−1.3	−2.6
1.1	−1.1	−2.0	−1.5	−1.2	−2.5
1.2	−1.1	−1.9	−1.3	−1.1	−2.3
1.3	−1.0	−1.8	−1.2	−1.0	−2.2
1.4	−0.9	−1.7	−1.1	−0.9	−2.1
1.5	−0.8	−1.6	−1.0	−0.8	−2.0
1.6	−0.7	−1.5	−0.9	−0.7	−1.9
1.7	−0.6	−1.4	−0.8	−0.6	−1.8
1.8	−0.5	−1.3	−0.7	−0.4	−1.7
1.9	−0.4	−1.2	−0.6	−0.3	−1.5
2.0	−0.3	−1.0	−0.5	−0.2	−1.4
2.1	−0.2	−0.9	−0.4	−0.1	−1.3
2.2	−0.1	−0.8	−0.3	0	−1.2
2.3	0	−0.7	−0.2	0.1	−1.1
2.4	0.1	−0.6	−0.1	0.2	−1.0
2.5	0.1	−0.5	0	0.3	−0.9
2.6	0.2	−0.4	0.1	0.4	−0.7
2.7	0.3	−0.3	0.2	0.5	−0.6
2.8	0.4	−0.2	0.3	0.6	−0.5
2.9	0.5	0	0.4	0.7	−0.4
3.0	0.6	0.1	0.5	0.9	−0.3
3.1	0.7	0.2	0.7	1.0	−0.2
3.2	0.8	0.3	0.8	1.1	0
3.3	0.9	0.4	0.9	1.2	0.1
3.4	1.0	0.5	1.0	1.3	0.2
3.5	1.1	0.6	1.1	1.4	0.3
3.6	1.2	0.7	1.2	1.5	0.4
3.7	1.2	0.8	1.3	1.6	0.5
3.8	1.3	1.0	1.4	1.7	0.6
3.9	1.4	1.1	1.5	1.8	0.8

(Continued)

Table 35 (Continued)

	Emotional state				
Raw score	Fear	Anger	Happiness	Affiliation	Competence
4.0	1.5	1.2	1.6	1.9	0.9
4.1	1.6	1.3	1.7	2.0	1.0
4.2	1.7	1.4	1.8	2.1	1.1
4.3	1.8	1.5	1.9	2.3	1.2
4.4	1.9	1.6	2.0	2.4	1.3
4.5	2.0	1.7	2.1	2.5	1.4
4.6	2.1	1.8	2.2	2.6	1.6
4.7	2.2	2.0	2.3	2.7	1.7
4.8	2.3	2.1	2.4	2.8	1.8
4.9	2.4	2.2	2.6	2.9	1.9
5.0	2.4	2.3	2.7	3.0	2.0

to compare children within and across programs. This comparison is accomplished by first calculating a mean affect score and standard deviation for each emotional domain for all of the subjects tested. Standard scores for individual subjects for each domain can then be computed by subtracting the population mean of an emotional domain from the subject's raw affect score for that same domain and dividing by the standard deviation of the population.

It should be noted that it is possible, and at times may be desirable, to examine an individual subject's emotional response vis-à-vis some subpopulation of children. Thus, for example, we might want to look at Molly's responses in the context of a subpopulation of girls, upper-middle-class children, or even infants born prematurely rather than in the context of the population of all children 3–30 months of age. In this case, one would calculate the mean affect scores and standard deviations for the subpopulation of interest (e.g., girls), subtract this mean affect score from Molly's raw affect score, and divide by the standard deviation, for each individual domain.

Table 35 should be useful for those interested in our normative data as the basis for generating standard scores. Because this sample contains subjects varying in age and gender, we have also broken down the data by gender and age groups (see Table 36). These breakdowns are based on small samples of infants and should be used cautiously, however.

Table 36. Standard Scores by Gender and Age

Raw score	Emotional state				
	Fear	Anger	Happiness	Affiliation	Competence
			Boys		
0.0	−2.2	−2.8	−2.4	−2.3	−3.9
0.1	−2.1	−2.7	−2.3	−2.2	−3.8
0.2	−2.0	−2.6	−2.2	−2.1	−3.7
0.3	−1.9	−2.5	−2.1	−1.9	−3.6
0.4	−1.7	−2.4	−2.0	−1.8	−3.4
0.5	−1.6	−2.3	−1.9	−1.7	−3.3
0.6	−1.5	−2.2	−1.8	−1.6	−3.2
0.7	−1.4	−2.1	−1.7	−1.5	−3.1
0.8	−1.3	−2.0	−1.6	−1.4	−3.0
0.9	−1.2	−1.9	−1.5	−1.3	−2.8
1.0	−1.1	−1.8	−1.4	−1.2	−2.7
1.1	−1.0	−1.7	−1.3	−1.0	−2.6
1.2	−0.9	−1.6	−1.2	−0.9	−2.5
1.3	−0.8	−1.5	−1.1	−0.8	−2.4
1.4	−0.7	−1.4	−1.0	−0.7	−2.3
1.5	−0.6	−1.3	−0.9	−0.6	−2.1
1.6	−0.5	−1.2	−0.8	−0.5	−2.0
1.7	−0.4	−1.1	−0.7	−0.4	−1.9
1.8	−0.3	−1.0	−0.6	−0.3	−1.8
1.9	−0.2	−0.9	−0.5	−0.1	−1.7
2.0	−0.1	−0.8	−0.4	0	−1.5
2.1	0	−0.7	−0.3	0.1	−1.4
2.2	0.1	−0.6	−0.2	0.2	−1.3
2.3	0.2	−0.5	−0.1	0.3	−1.2
2.4	0.3	−0.4	0	0.4	−1.1
2.5	0.5	−0.3	0.1	0.5	−1.0
2.6	0.6	−0.2	0.2	0.6	−0.8
2.7	0.7	−0.1	0.3	0.8	−0.7
2.8	0.8	0	0.4	0.9	−0.6
2.9	0.9	0.1	0.5	1.0	−0.5
3.0	1.0	0.2	0.6	1.1	−0.4
3.1	1.1	0.3	0.7	1.2	−0.2
3.2	1.2	0.4	0.8	1.3	−0.1
3.3	1.3	0.5	0.9	1.4	0
3.4	1.4	0.6	1.0	1.5	0.1
3.5	1.5	0.7	1.1	1.7	0.2
3.6	1.6	0.8	1.2	1.8	0.3
3.7	1.7	0.9	1.3	1.9	0.5
3.8	1.8	1.0	1.4	2.0	0.6
3.9	1.9	1.1	1.5	2.1	0.7

(Continued)

Table 36 (Continued)

Raw score	Emotional state				
	Fear	Anger	Happiness	Affiliation	Competence
			Boys (continued)		
4.0	2.0	1.2	1.6	2.2	0.8
4.1	2.1	1.3	1.7	2.3	0.9
4.2	2.2	1.4	1.8	2.4	1.0
4.3	2.3	1.5	1.9	2.5	1.2
4.4	2.4	1.6	2.0	2.7	1.3
4.5	2.5	1.7	2.1	2.8	1.4
4.6	2.7	1.8	2.2	2.9	1.5
4.7	2.8	1.9	2.3	3.0	1.6
4.8	2.9	2.0	2.4	3.1	1.8
4.9	3.0	2.1	2.5	3.2	1.9
5.0		2.2	2.6	3.3	2.0
			Girls		
0.0	−2.4	−4.3	−3.0	−2.6	−3.4
0.1	−2.3	−4.2	−2.9	−2.5	−3.3
0.2	−2.2	−4.1	−2.8	−2.4	−3.2
0.3	−2.1	−3.9	−2.7	−2.3	−3.1
0.4	−2.0	−3.8	−2.6	−2.2	−3.0
0.5	−2.0	−3.6	−2.4	−2.1	−2.9
0.6	−1.9	−3.5	−2.3	−2.0	−2.8
0.7	−1.8	−3.4	−2.2	−1.9	−2.7
0.8	−1.7	−3.2	−2.1	−1.8	−2.6
0.9	−1.6	−3.1	−2.0	−1.7	−2.5
1.0	−1.5	−2.9	−1.9	−1.6	−2.4
1.1	−1.4	−2.8	−1.8	−1.5	−2.2
1.2	−1.3	−2.7	−1.6	−1.4	−2.1
1.3	−1.3	−2.5	−1.5	−1.3	−2.0
1.4	−1.2	−2.4	−1.4	−1.2	−1.9
1.5	−1.1	−2.2	−1.3	−1.0	−1.8
1.6	−1.0	−2.1	−1.2	−0.9	−1.7
1.7	−0.9	−2.0	−1.1	−0.8	−1.6
1.8	−0.8	−1.8	−1.0	−0.7	−1.5
1.9	−0.7	−1.7	−0.8	−0.6	−1.4
2.0	−0.7	−1.6	−0.7	−0.5	−1.3
2.1	−0.6	−1.4	−0.6	−0.4	−1.1
2.2	−0.5	−1.3	−0.5	−0.3	−1.0
2.3	−0.4	−1.1	−0.4	−0.2	−0.9
2.4	−0.3	−1.0	−0.3	−0.1	−0.8
2.5	−0.2	−0.9	−0.2	0	−0.7

(Continued)

Table 36 (Continued)

| Raw score | Emotional state | | | | |
	Fear	Anger	Happiness	Affiliation	Competence
Girls (continued)					
2.6	−0.1	−0.7	0	0.1	−0.6
2.7	0	−0.6	0.1	0.2	−0.5
2.8	0	−0.4	0.2	0.3	−0.4
2.9	0.1	−0.3	0.3	0.5	−0.3
3.0	0.2	−0.2	0.4	0.6	−0.2
3.1	0.3	0	0.5	0.7	0
3.2	0.4	0.1	0.6	0.8	0.1
3.3	0.5	0.3	0.8	0.9	0.2
3.4	0.6	0.4	0.9	1.0	0.3
3.5	0.6	0.5	1.0	1.1	0.4
3.6	0.7	0.7	1.1	1.2	0.5
3.7	0.8	0.8	1.2	1.3	0.6
3.8	0.9	0.9	1.3	1.4	0.7
3.9	1.0	1.1	1.5	1.5	0.8
4.0	1.1	1.2	1.6	1.6	0.9
4.1	1.2	1.4	1.7	1.7	1.1
4.2	1.3	1.5	1.8	1.8	1.2
4.3	1.3	1.6	1.9	2.0	1.3
4.4	1.4	1.8	2.0	2.1	1.4
4.5	1.5	1.9	2.1	2.2	1.5
4.6	1.6	2.1	2.3	2.3	1.6
4.7	1.7	2.2	2.4	2.4	1.7
4.8	1.8	2.3	2.5	2.5	1.8
4.9	1.9	2.5	2.6	2.6	1.9
5.0	1.9	2.6	2.7	2.7	2.0
Children 3–12 months old					
0.0	−2.3	−2.6	−2.3	−2.2	−5.0
0.1	−2.2	−2.5	−2.2	−2.1	−5.0
0.2	−2.1	−2.4	−2.1	−1.9	−4.8
0.3	−2.0	−2.3	−2.0	−1.8	−4.6
0.4	−1.9	−2.2	−1.9	−1.7	−4.5
0.5	−1.8	−2.1	−1.8	−1.6	−4.3
0.6	−1.7	−2.0	−1.7	−1.5	−4.1
0.7	−1.5	−1.9	−1.6	−1.4	−4.0
0.8	−1.4	−1.8	−1.5	−1.3	−3.8
0.9	−1.3	−1.7	−1.4	−1.2	−3.6
1.0	−1.2	−1.6	−1.3	−1.1	−3.5
1.1	−1.1	−1.5	−1.2	−0.9	−3.3

(Continued)

Table 36 (Continued)

Raw score	Emotional state				
	Fear	Anger	Happiness	Affiliation	Competence
Children 3–12 months old (continued)					
1.2	−1.0	−1.4	−1.2	−0.8	−3.1
1.3	−0.8	−1.3	−1.1	−0.7	−2.9
1.4	−0.7	−1.2	−1.0	−0.6	−2.8
1.5	−0.6	−1.1	−0.9	−0.5	−2.6
1.6	−0.5	−1.0	−0.8	−0.4	−2.4
1.7	−0.4	−0.9	−0.7	−0.3	−2.3
1.8	−0.3	−0.8	−0.6	−0.2	−2.1
1.9	−0.1	−0.7	−0.5	−0.1	−1.9
2.0	0	−0.6	−0.4	0.1	−1.8
2.1	0.1	−0.5	−0.3	0.2	−1.6
2.2	0.2	−0.4	−0.2	0.3	−1.4
2.3	0.3	−0.3	−0.1	0.4	−1.3
2.4	0.4	−0.2	0	0.5	−1.1
2.5	0.6	−0.1	0.1	0.6	−0.9
2.6	0.7	0	0.2	0.7	−0.7
2.7	0.8	0.1	0.3	0.8	−0.6
2.8	0.9	0.2	0.4	0.9	−0.4
2.9	1.0	0.3	0.5	1.0	−0.2
3.0	1.1	0.4	0.6	1.2	−0.1
3.1	1.2	0.5	0.7	1.3	0.1
3.2	1.4	0.6	0.8	1.4	0.3
3.3	1.5	0.7	0.9	1.5	0.4
3.4	1.6	0.8	1.0	1.6	0.6
3.5	1.7	0.9	1.1	1.7	0.8
3.6	1.8	1.0	1.2	1.8	0.9
3.7	1.9	1.1	1.3	1.9	1.1
3.8	2.1	1.2	1.4	2.0	1.3
3.9	2.2	1.3	1.5	2.2	1.5
4.0	2.3	1.4	1.6	2.3	1.6
4.1	2.4	1.5	1.7	2.4	1.8
4.2	2.5	1.6	1.8	2.5	2.0
4.3	2.6	1.7	1.9	2.6	2.1
4.4	2.8	1.8	2.0	2.7	2.3
4.5	2.9	1.9	2.1	2.8	2.5
4.6	3.0	2.0	2.2	2.9	2.6
4.7	3.1	2.1	2.3	3.0	2.8
4.8	3.2	2.2	2.4	3.2	3.0
4.9	3.3	2.3	2.5	3.3	3.1
5.0	3.5	2.4	2.5	3.4	3.3

(Continued)

Table 36 (Continued)

Raw score	Emotional state				
	Fear	Anger	Happiness	Affiliation	Competence
	Children 13–18 months old				
0.0	−2.9	−3.3	−3.2	−3.1	−4.1
0.1	−2.8	−3.2	−3.1	−3.0	−4.0
0.2	−2.7	−3.1	−2.9	−2.9	−3.9
0.3	−2.6	−2.9	−2.8	−2.7	−3.8
0.4	−2.5	−2.8	−2.7	−2.6	−3.7
0.5	−2.4	−2.7	−2.5	−2.5	−3.5
0.6	−2.3	−2.6	−2.4	−2.4	−3.4
0.7	−2.2	−2.5	−2.2	−2.3	−3.3
0.8	−2.1	−2.4	−2.1	−2.2	−3.2
0.9	−2.0	−2.2	−2.0	−2.1	−3.1
1.0	−1.9	−2.1	−1.8	−2.0	−2.9
1.1	−1.8	−2.0	−1.7	−1.9	−2.8
1.2	−1.7	−1.9	−1.6	−1.8	−2.7
1.3	−1.6	−1.8	−1.4	−1.6	−2.6
1.4	−1.5	−1.7	−1.3	−1.5	−2.5
1.5	−1.4	−1.5	−1.1	−1.4	−2.3
1.6	−1.3	−1.4	−1.0	−1.3	−2.2
1.7	−1.2	−1.3	−0.9	−1.2	−2.1
1.8	−1.1	−1.2	−0.7	−1.1	−2.0
1.9	−1.0	−1.1	−0.6	−1.0	−1.9
2.0	−0.9	−1.0	−0.5	−0.9	−1.7
2.1	−0.8	−0.8	−0.3	−0.8	−1.6
2.2	−0.7	−0.7	−0.2	−0.7	−1.5
2.3	−0.6	−0.6	0	−0.5	−1.4
2.4	−0.5	−0.5	0.1	−0.4	−1.2
2.5	−0.4	−0.4	0.2	−0.3	−1.1
2.6	−0.3	−0.3	0.4	−0.2	−1.0
2.7	−0.2	−0.1	0.5	−0.1	−0.9
2.8	−0.1	0	0.6	0	−0.8
2.9	0	0.1	0.8	0.1	−0.6
3.0	0.1	0.2	0.9	0.2	−0.5
3.1	0.2	0.3	1.1	0.3	−0.4
3.2	0.3	0.4	1.2	0.4	−0.3
3.3	0.4	0.6	1.3	0.6	−0.2
3.4	0.5	0.7	1.5	0.7	0
3.5	0.6	0.8	1.6	0.8	0.1
3.6	0.7	0.9	1.7	0.9	0.2
3.7	0.8	1.0	1.9	1.0	0.3
3.8	0.9	1.1	2.0	1.1	0.4
3.9	1.0	1.3	2.2	1.2	0.6

(Continued)

Table 36 (Continued)

Raw score	Emotional state				
	Fear	Anger	Happiness	Affiliation	Competence
Children 13–18 months old (continued)					
4.0	1.1	1.4	2.3	1.3	0.7
4.1	1.2	1.5	2.4	1.4	0.8
4.2	1.3	1.6	2.6	1.5	0.9
4.3	1.4	1.7	2.7	1.7	1.0
4.4	1.5	1.8	2.8	1.8	1.2
4.5	1.6	2.0	3.0	1.9	1.3
4.6	1.7	2.1	3.1	2.0	1.4
4.7	1.8	2.2	3.3	2.1	1.5
4.8	1.9	2.3	3.4	2.2	1.6
4.9	2.0	2.4	3.5	2.3	1.8
5.0	2.1	2.4	3.7	2.4	1.9
Children 19–30 months old					
0.0	− 1.9	− 4.8	− 2.6	− 2.5	− 3.1
0.1	− 1.8	− 4.7	− 2.5	− 2.4	− 3.0
0.2	− 1.7	− 4.5	− 2.4	− 2.3	− 2.9
0.3	− 1.6	− 4.4	− 2.3	− 2.1	− 2.8
0.4	− 1.6	− 4.3	− 2.2	− 2.0	− 2.7
0.5	− 1.5	− 4.1	− 2.1	− 1.9	− 2.6
0.6	− 1.4	− 4.0	− 2.0	− 1.8	− 2.5
0.7	− 1.3	− 3.8	− 1.9	− 1.6	− 2.4
0.8	− 1.2	− 3.7	− 1.8	− 1.5	− 2.3
0.9	− 1.1	− 3.5	− 1.7	− 1.4	− 2.2
1.0	− 1.1	− 3.4	− 1.6	− 1.3	− 2.1
1.1	− 1.0	− 3.2	− 1.5	− 1.2	− 2.0
1.2	− 0.9	− 3.1	− 1.4	− 1.0	− 2.0
1.3	− 0.8	− 2.9	− 1.3	− 0.9	− 1.9
1.4	− 0.7	− 2.8	− 1.2	− 0.8	− 1.8
1.5	− 0.6	− 2.7	− 1.1	− 0.7	− 1.7
1.6	− 0.5	− 2.5	− 1.0	− 0.5	− 1.6
1.7	− 0.5	− 2.4	− 0.9	− 0.4	− 1.5
1.8	− 0.4	− 2.2	− 0.8	− 0.3	− 1.4
1.9	− 0.3	− 2.1	− 0.7	− 0.2	− 1.3
2.0	− 0.2	− 1.9	− 0.6	− 0.1	− 1.2
2.1	− 0.1	− 1.8	− 0.5	0.1	− 1.1
2.2	0	− 1.6	− 0.4	0.2	− 1.0
2.3	0	− 1.5	− 0.3	0.3	− 0.9
2.4	0.1	− 1.3	− 0.3	0.4	− 0.8
2.5	0.2	− 1.2	− 0.2	0.5	− 0.7

(Continued)

	Emotional state				
Raw score	Fear	Anger	Happiness	Affiliation	Competence
Children 19–30 months old (continued)					
2.6	0.3	−1.1	−0.1	0.7	−0.6
2.7	0.4	−0.9	0	0.8	−0.5
2.8	0.5	−0.8	0.1	0.9	−0.5
2.9	0.5	−0.6	0.2	1.0	−0.4
3.0	0.6	−0.5	0.3	1.2	−0.3
3.1	0.7	−0.3	0.4	1.3	−0.2
3.2	0.8	−0.2	0.5	1.4	−0.1
3.3	0.9	0	0.6	1.5	0
3.4	1.0	0.1	0.7	1.6	0.1
3.5	1.0	0.3	0.8	1.8	0.2
3.6	1.1	0.4	0.9	1.9	0.3
3.7	1.2	0.5	1.0	2.0	0.4
3.8	1.3	0.7	1.1	2.1	0.5
3.9	1.4	0.8	1.2	2.2	0.6
4.0	1.5	1.0	1.3	2.4	0.7
4.1	1.5	1.1	1.4	2.5	0.8
4.2	1.6	1.3	1.5	2.6	0.9
4.3	1.7	1.4	1.6	2.7	1.0
4.4	1.8	1.6	1.7	2.8	1.0
4.5	1.9	1.7	1.8	3.0	1.1
4.6	2.0	1.8	1.9	3.1	1.2
4.7	2.1	2.0	2.0	3.2	1.3
4.8	2.1	2.1	2.1	3.3	1.4
4.9	2.2	2.3	2.2	3.5	1.5
5.0	2.3	2.4	2.3	3.6	1.6

Constructing Profiles of Emotional States

Standard scores are the basis for constructing a profile of enduring emotional states for individual children. Standard scores rather than raw data are used in order to compare the child's scores across the five different emotions. In this way, a profile (i.e., differences in the five emotions) can be studied. A sample profile form is presented in Figure 22. Along the abscissa are listed the five socioemotional domains, and along the left ordinate, the standard scores of this population are listed, with a mean equal to 0 and a standard deviation equal to 1. For the total sample of children, the total range of standard scores varies between −3.5 and 3.0. Also presented in this figure are the corresponding

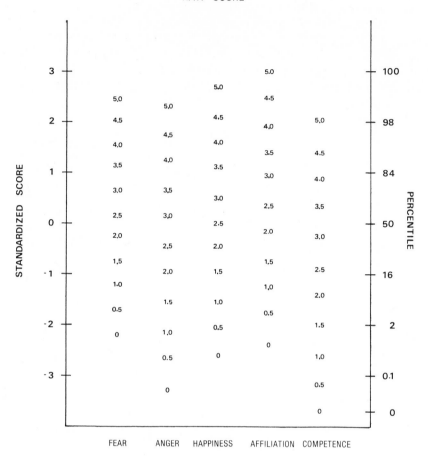

Figure 22. Profile form for children 3 to 30 months of age.

percentiles for the population (along the right ordinate). The interior space in this profile sheet contains the raw scores, which range between 0 and 5.

By plotting the child's raw scores on this graph, it is possible to depict visually the patterning of an individual child's emotional expression in the form of an emotional profile. Each subject's score is in this way compared with those of the entire sample of children who participated in this study. For example, if a subject had a raw score of 3.5 on happiness, one would plot this at 3.5 on the interior grid of the happiness scale. This raw score would corrrespond to a standard score of approximately 1.0 and would indicate that this subject had a happiness score 85% higher than the rest of the sample.

Figures 23 and 24 present the same data for male and female subjects, respectively. These data could be used if one were interested in seeing how a male child, for example, compared with a group of male infants. Notice that a fear score of 5 for boys places them 3 standard deviations above the mean, whereas for girls a score of 5 is only 1.9 standard deviations from the mean. This difference reflects the fact that boys in general show less fear than girls. The anger scale, in contrast,

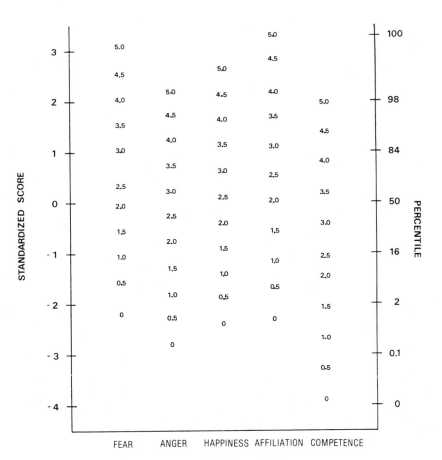

Figure 23. Profile form for boys.

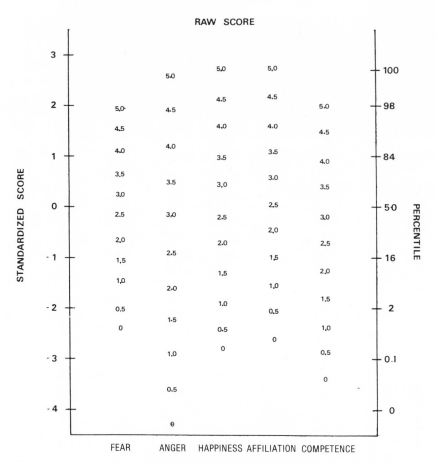

Figure 24. Profile form for girls.

reflects the fact that it is more usual for girls *not* to show anger, although there are no overall gender differences in anger scores (see Chapter 11).

Case Studies

The following case studies are an attempt to relate a narrative record kept by an observer to the emotional profiles generated by the scales. These four case studies are presented in order to demonstrate the validity of the instrument vis-à-vis the behaviors of children. In each discussion, the patterning of the enduring emotional states is what

seems to be of particular importance. The names, of course, are fictitious.

Case Study 1: Sanya

Sanya is a 16-month-old girl who has been in the day-care program for two
months. She was enrolled in the program after it came to the court's attention
that she had been neglected and left alone much of the day. Sanya is the only
child of an 18-year-old high-school dropout. Figure 25 presents her profile. An
observation of the profile shows a child relatively low in happiness and affil-

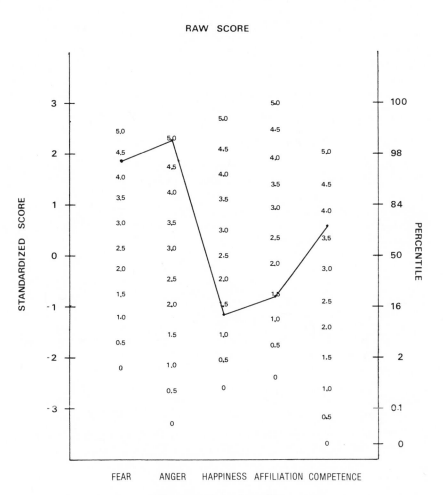

Figure 25. Sanya's profile.

iation with high scores on fear and anger. She often plays by herself for relatively long periods of time, showing some interest in toys in the playroom.

This profile supports the general information that we have about this child's early experiences of being neglected. While we might have anticipated high affiliative needs as a result of the deprivation, it is also likely that low affiliation is a consequence of that experience. The observer wrote, "When left alone to play, Sanya initiates her own activity. She persists in her play, and when she tries to reach something too high for her she stands on a box or moves a chair (in imitation of another child) to reach it." Such behavior suggests some competence in object play, which is reflected in Sanya's moderate competence score. A score of 112 on the Bayley Scales of Mental Development shows this child to be performing at an above-average level of cognitive capacity.

In talking about Sanya's behavior toward caregivers, mother, and peers, the observer wrote, "She has fear of strangers and hesitates or freezes when she sees a stranger looking at her, attempting to pick her up, or directing any attention to her, as in starting a conversation. . . . She does not appear to be attached to the caregivers, and while accepting what they give her, she is likely to move away from them soon." Her behavior toward peers appears to be distant, cold, and aggressive: "She often plays by herself and vocalizes very little to other children. When they approach her or when she engages them in play, she is often physically aggressive. It is necessary to separate her from her peers on many occasions. She seems easily frustrated and is easily angered." Her lack of happiness is reflected in such comments as "She often plays alone, she cries or frets easily and seldom goes to a caregiver for help." This observer's comments generally confirm the data from the scales.

Sanya shows many of the more traditional signs of neglect. One way in which the scores might be used for this child would be to assess the effects of day-care intervention on the child's emotional functioning by making ratings on the scales before and after the day-care experience. In a study of maltreated and normal children in day care, Lewis and Schaeffer (1979) argued that although the child's relationship to the mother might not show marked improvement, the availability of the day-care situation and the daily interactions with other more positive social figures should go a long way toward alleviating many of the dysfunctional social-affective consequences of poor parenting. Such a view is predicated on the belief that social relationships with peers and other adults are not necessarily causally related to, although they are influenced by, poor maternal experiences (Lewis, 1982b; Lewis & Rosenblum, 1979). That the child has spent less than two months in day care may indicate that a relatively longer time is needed before the effects of dysfunctional parenting can be overcome. The high cognitive score corresponds to the child's competence score and suggests that with the proper intervention, Sanya has the capacity to function at an above-normal level.

Case Study 2: Michelle

Michelle is a 20-month-old child of a working family. She has spent the last 13 months in a day-care program and was placed in the program so that her mother could return to work. She is one of the few children in the program with a father living in the family. Both parents work, and both parents have a high-school education.

Michelle's profile is one in which happiness and competence are the two dominant emotions (see Figure 26). However, compared with the group, she shows moderate amounts of the other emotional states: she shows affiliative behavior as well as some fear and anger. She does not exhibit a flat or depressed emotional profile.

The observer reported the following in terms of her competence: "Michelle is quite mature compared with the other children. She is beginning to talk, knows the other children's names and uses them, and knows the names of

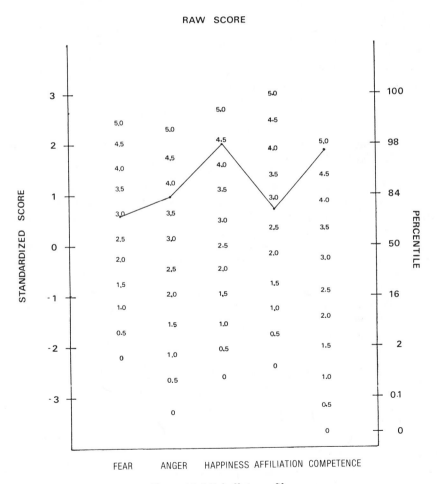

Figure 26. Michelle's profile.

many objects. She can describe from memory what is happening in the storybook as the caregiver turns the pages." Her Bayley score was the highest of the group (MDI = 120), which conforms both to the observer's observations and to Michelle's competence score on the scales. The combination of happiness and competence suggests that Michelle's interactions with objects and people are predicated on enjoyment rather than withdrawal, as was the case with Sanya: "She is very cheerful and competent; she can initiate her own activity."

Her social behavior toward peers, caregivers, and strangers seems appropriate for a child of this age: "She is willing to relinquish her parent when she is brought in in the morning. When her father comes to pick her up, she breaks into a broad smile and runs to him. Occasionally, she has been observed to run away from him, but it is not clear whether this is a game or reflects her desire to stay at the nursery."

Her behavior toward other adults is open but not dependent. For example, the observer wrote, "She is fairly affectionate and likes to be picked up, but not for too long a period of time. After a while, she begs or struggles to be put down. She has little fear of strangers but is wary and watches carefully if a stranger is in the room." Her peer interactions receive minimal comment, except for the following: "When another child interferes with her, she is generally able to extricate herself from the situation or she may fight back to obtain a toy." Such comments reflect a social competence and at the same time a moderate amount of anger.

Her high degree of happiness is probably reflected most in such comments as "She doesn't cry often, even when hurt." In addition to her being affectionate and cheerful, this child is characterized by a competence seeming to reflect an almost idealized development. Her happiness and competence scores seem to characterize the earlier finding of a happiness–competence relationship, especially found in older children.

The total picture that emerges from Michelle's profile is that of a child who is both active and extroverted; who has relatively high fear, anger, and affiliation scores; and who is at the same time cheerful and competent. When confronted by challenges, her competent and happy personality should generate active attempts at problem solving, and when necessary, she will involve other people, including adults.

Case Study 3: Lizette

Lizette just turned 17 months old and has spent all but her first five months in the day-care center. Her mother is a single working parent. Lizette is the middle child of the family and has an older sister and younger brother. The older sister is also in a day-care center, and her baby brother, 2 months old, is scheduled to enter the program shortly. The profile of Lizette (see Figure 27) shows relatively little fear and competence and much happiness and affiliation. Such a profile seems to reflect a "sociable" and relatively fearless personality. Competence, when exhibited, is directed toward social exchanges. Like Mich-

RAW SCORE

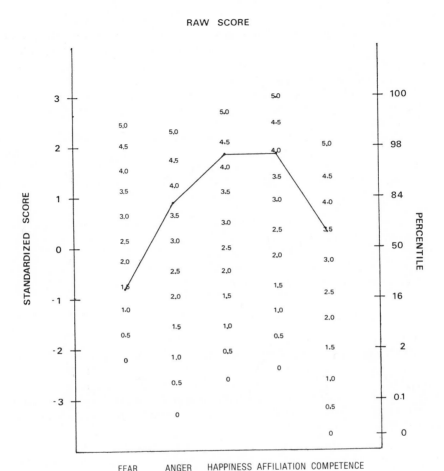

Figure 27. Lizette's profile.

elle (Case Study 2), Lizette appears to be person-oriented; she is also happy. This profile shares some commonality with the descriptions offered by the observer. Her sociability extends to other children, adults, strangers, and caregivers: "Lizette is a very affectionate child. She goes to strangers and raises her arms to be picked up. She is very trusting. When her mother leaves, she is not overly concerned, and when her mother returns, she runs to her and smiles. She is willing and often goes to the caregiver for help and for affection, although she does not cling."

Her peer relationships also appear to reflect a general sociability: "She knows and uses the other children's names. She often leads the children in a new 'game' she's made up." The observer also commented on her lack of fear: "She is very trusting. She doesn't seem to have much fear of anything, and she likes to climb and obtain objects in remote places." This type of behavior probably also reflects her competence and agrees with the normal Bayley score that she obtained (MDI = 103).

Lizette's sociability, her lack of fear, her happiness, and her free engagement with others may be a consequence of her long and early group upbringing in the day-care center. It has been noted by others (Kagan et al., 1978) that children raised from an early age in a communal setting, such as graduate-student housing or day care, are not likely to have fear of strangers and are socially oriented. Such behavior is reflected in the observer's descriptions as well as in Lizette's emotional profile.

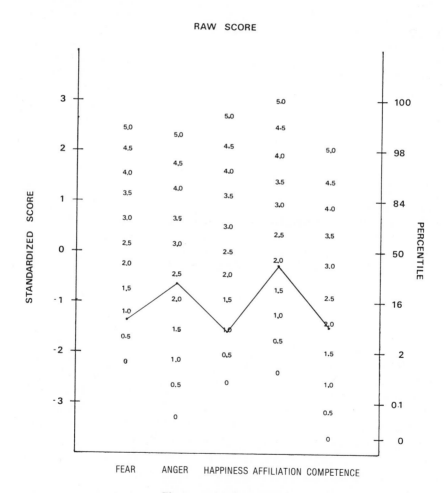

Figure 28. Mark's profile.

Case Study 4: Mark

Mark has spent the last four of his eleven months in a day-care setting. Mark's mother is a single parent. She was thrown out of her home for becoming pregnant, her parents being leaders in a local church. Mark's mother is quite punitive and harsh, although in no way does she appear abusing or neglectful. On the contrary, she is highly demanding, and Mark comes to day care well dressed and clean. The demands that Mark's mother places on him appear excessive for his developmental level. Mark's profile is indicative of a depressed personality, showing, relative to the other children, low emotional states across almost all domains (see Figure 28). In particular, his lowest score is on happiness and this low score, as well as his low scores on fear and anger, suggests that the child is depressed and may be overwhelmed by parental demands and regulations.

Mark's affiliation score (the highest of his scores) indicates that he may have unfulfilled needs in this area. Specifically, he seems particularly attached to one caregiver, Pauline, who has been his caregiver all along. The observer noted, "Mark seems to be having problems with caregivers. He usually refuses to go with anyone but Pauline. He often needs affection and one-to-one attention from Pauline." His depression may be manifested by sleeping difficulties: "He usually has trouble taking a nap and needs to be rocked and held before falling asleep." The observer noted that Mark infrequently engages peers and needs assistance in playing with objects because of his short attention span. His relatively low affiliation score probably reflects his inability to engage adults other than the single caregiver and his mother, as well as his low peer interaction. His low happiness score and the flat nature of the profile suggest a general depression, which may also be reflected in his low anger score. The observer noted, "When Mark is attacked by other children, he rarely fights back and usually allows them to take the toy he is playing with."

Mark appears to be a child seriously affected by harsh and punitive child-rearing practices. His response to such experiences is low and relatively flat affect. Mark may be a prime example of a depressed infant.

❧❧❧❧❧❧❧❧❧❧❧

These four case studies do not offer empirical support for the relationship of these scales to children's general, ongoing behaviors. Nevertheless, they suggest a strong concordance between the observations of an observer and the results obtained by our measurement system. The children differ not only in the degree of specific emotions expressed but, more important, in the profiles of their emotional states. Moreover, the limited cognitive data available seem to support the measurement of competence made on three of the children. Clearly, much more information is necessary before one would be satisfied that the profiles generated from the scales show a high correspondence to the patterns of enduring emotions that these children exhibit. Nevertheless, the narratives are encouraging.

The day-care centers in which we developed the instrument emphasize (as do most day-care centers) the cognitive and social achievements of these children. The "educational programs" focus on improving these children's cognitive capacities and scores on tasks reflecting intellectual ability. The need for programs that will improve the likelihood that poor, inner-city children will do well in school-related tasks is great, and such programs as these may do much to foster children's intellectual development.

The evidence that the achievements of these children may decline within a year or two after these programs end brings disappointment, however. Yet, there is some indication that much of the positive effect of early day care, although initially disappearing, may influence later school performance (Lazar & Darlington, 1982; Zigler & Valentine, 1979). Not answered is the question of whether the primary effects of these early programs are on the development and maintenance of cognitive structures that have a subsequent effect on later cognitive ability or whether the effects are on affective-motivational structures that influence later cognitive achievement. The demonstration that children in day-care programs are less likely to fall behind their grade level and to drop out of high school may be taken as evidence of either position, namely, that day-care experience has its major impact on cognitive structures or on affective-motivational ones.

Day-care programs that deliver manifest curricula designed around principles of cognitive development also contain curricula, which may be hidden, pertaining to children's social-emotional behavior. These day-care programs, almost by their very nature, attend to children's emotional needs, responding to their distress and attending to their happiness. However, it is still to be determined whether the effect of these programs is due to their manifest cognitive curricula or to their hidden curricula, the care and comfort of young children.

The Scales of Socioemotional Development, by assessing children's emotional states and by documenting changes in these states over time, can be used to address this issue. For example, Sanya (Case Study 1), who has just entered the program, appears to be fearful, angry, and unhappy. Will Sanya, after many more months in the program, be less fearful and more happy? Will Sanya's change or lack of change on these dimensions affect her concurrent and/or subsequent cognitive ability? Mark (Case Study 4) appears depressed. His cognitive ability, at least as measured by his competence score, is below average. Is it the manifest or the hidden curriculum that will affect Mark's behavior and, as a consequence, alter his subsequent cognitive achievement?

Without a measurement system, one that looks at the socioemotional states of children, questions about the effects of early day-care experiences on children's cognitive achievement cannot be answered. Perhaps even more to the point, we may have missed our mark entirely by assuming that one of the primary tasks of society is to raise the intellectual status of disadvantaged children, or children in general. It may instead be that nurturing the socioemotional development of children is the task before us. While it may be that children who are happier, less fearful, and less angry are also more competent and cognitively achieving, without a measurement system to assess these dimensions the questions remain unanswered and the task is left undone.

Concluding Remarks

Our success in measuring individual differences in patterns of enduring emotional states (i.e., moods) lends support to our theory of emotional development, which we have described. Our theory was predicated on a need in studying emotion for a more articulated understanding of the nature of emotional processes. This need is obvious, yet few have attempted to meet it. Without specifying the various components of cognition (such as memory, attention, perception, and learning), cognitive science would not have progressed as far as it has. Likewise, a failure to consider the components of emotion has been an obstacle to the study of emotional development. To this end we attempted to specify and define five components that comprise emotion: elicitors, receptors, states, expressions, and experiences. We discussed not only the general issues pertaining to each separate component and to the connections among components but also their developmental features.

The particular need to consider emotional expressions as distinct from emotional states led us to focus on the developmental relationship between expressions and internal states. We argued that only by considering this problem can one hope to devise measures that correspond to some extent with the internal states of the subject. This belief derives from the simple observation that emotions are private acts. Both everyday experience and empirical inquiry inform us that expressions per se are not sufficient evidence for inferring the feelings of another individual. As we have stressed throughout the volume, emotional expressions are subject to intense socialization pressures; any one-to-one correspondence that might exist between expressions and internal states as the result of evolutionary forces or the organism's biological disposition is vulnerable to strong adaptive pressures. For instance, observing a happy face in a particular context does not tell us much, if anything, about the subject's underlying state. In Western cultures, smiling is a polite mannerism and consequently it does not necessarily reflect the subject's genuine emotional state(s).

What is needed, at least in order to measure an individual's level of emotion, is to measure expressions (and we do not restrict expressions to the face alone) in a *class* of situations that are related to that emotion. The matrix formed between expressions and situations provides us with the best estimate of children's feeling states, independent of their verbal report. By observing the expressions of particular emotions across multiple situations, we are in a better position to assess a subject's emotional states apart from the socialization effects that may alter an expression in any single situation.

This type of measurement system, derived from our theory of emotional development, allowed us to study emotional states as enduring as well as transient. Enduring emotional states provide the context for transient events which exist only in the context of other emotions. The notion that even within the experimental laboratory one can easily elicit a "pure" emotional response, independent of the subject's enduring emotional state, or mood, and independent of preceding transient emotional events has an intrinsic appeal to investigators, yet its likelihood is low.

Our efforts to integrate theory and measurement have given us the opportunity to examine emotional development both from an abstract and from a practical point of view. We do not pretend to offer a complete theory of emotional development; it is unlikely that such a theory will ever exist. Nevertheless, by outlining the broad dimensions of a developmental theory and by collecting data from within the perspective of this theory, we have begun the task. Ultimately, any developmental theory must be prepared to consider both evolutionary forces and the organism's biological disposition in the expressions of emotional states, as well as the socialization influences on the creation and elaboration of the feeling rules that govern emotional expressions, states, and experiences.

References

Abelson, R. Script processing in attitude formation and decision making. In J. S. Carroll & J. Payne (Eds.), *Cognition and social behavior*. Hillsdale, N.J.: Erlbaum, 1976.

Adler, A. *The practice and theory of individual psychology*. New York: Harcourt, 1927.

Ainsworth, M. D. S. The development of infant-mother interaction among the Ganda. In B. M. Foss (Ed.), *Determinants of infant behavior* (Vol. 2). New York: Wiley, 1963.

Ainsworth, M. D. S. *Infancy in Uganda: Infant care and the growth of love*. Baltimore: Johns Hopkins University Press, 1967.

Ainsworth, M. D. S. The development of infant-mother attachment. In B. M. Caldwell & H. N. Ricciuti (Eds.), *Review of child development research* (Vol. 3). Chicago: University of Chicago Press, 1973.

Ainsworth, M. D. S. Infant-mother attachment. *American Psychologist*, 1979, *34*, 932–937.

Ainsworth, M. D. S., & Bell, S. M. Attachment, exploration, and separation illustrated by the behavior of one-year-olds in a strange situation. *Child Development*, 1970, *41*, 49–67.

Ainsworth, M. D. S., & Bell, S. M. Mother-infant interaction and development of competence. In K. J. Connolly & J. Bruner (Eds.), *The growth of competence*. New York: Academic Press, 1974.

Ainsworth, M. D. S., & Wittig, B. A. Attachment and exploratory behavior of one-year-olds in a strange situation. In B. M. Foss (Ed.), *Determinants of infant behavior* (Vol. 4). New York: Wiley, 1969.

Ainsworth, M. D. S., Blehar, M., Waters, E., & Wall, S. *Patterns of attachment: A psychological study of the strange situation*. Hillsdale, N.J.: Erlbaum, 1978.

Akert, K. Diencephalon. In D. E. Sheer (Ed.), *Electrical stimulation of the brain*. Austin: University of Texas Press, 1961.

Als, H. *The human newborn and his mother: An ethological study of their interaction*. Ph.D. dissertation, University of Pennsylvania, 1975.

Als, H., Tronick, E., Lester, B. M., & Brazelton, T. B. Specific neonatal measures: The Brazelton Neonatal Behavior Assessment Scale. In J. D. Osofsky (Ed.), *Handbook of infant development*. New York: Wiley, 1979.

Ambrose, A. The development of the smiling response in early infancy. In B. Foss (Ed.), *Determinants of infant behavior* (Vol. 1). New York: Wiley, 1961.

Amen, E. Individual differences in apperceptive reaction: A study of the responses of preschool children to pictures. *Genetic Psychology Monographs*, 1941, *23*, 319–385.

Amsterdam, B. K. Mirror self-image reactions before age two. *Developmental Psychology*, 1972, *5*, 297–305.

Anderson, S., & Messick, S. Social competency in young children. *Developmental Psychology*, 1974, *10*, 282–293.

Arend, R., Gove, F. L., & Sroufe, L. A. Continuity of individual adaptation from infancy to kindergarten: A predictive study of ego resiliency and curiosity in preschoolers. *Child Development*, 1979, *50*, 950–959.

Argyle, M. *Bodily communication*. New York: International Universities Press, 1975.

Arnold, M. B. An excitatory theory of emotion. In M. L. Reymert (Ed.), *Feelings and emotions*. New York: McGraw-Hill, 1950.

Arnold, M. B. *Emotion and personality* (2 vols.). New York: Columbia University Press, 1960.

Arnold, M. B. Brain function in emotion: A phenomenological analysis. In P. Black (Ed.), *Physiological correlates of emotion*. New York: Academic Press, 1970.

Asch, S. E. Studies of independence and conformity: I. A minority of one against a unanimous majority. *Psychological Monographs*, 1956, *70*, No. 9 (Whole No. 416).

Averill, J. R. On the paucity of positive emotions. In K. R. Blankstein, P. Pliner, & J. Polivy (Eds.), *Assessment and modification of emotional behavior*. New York: Plenum, 1980.

Ax, A. F. The physiological differentiation of fear and anger in humans. *Psychosomatic Medicine*, 1953, *15*, 433–442.

Ban, P. L., & Lewis, M. Mothers and fathers, girls and boys: Attachment behaviors in the one-year-old. *Merrill-Palmer Quarterly*, 1974, *20*, 195–204.

Bandura, A. *Social learning theory*. Englewood Cliffs, N.J.: Prentice-Hall, 1977.

Bard, P. A diencephalic mechanism for the expression of rage with special reference to the sympathetic nervous system. *American Journal of Physiology*, 1928, *84*, 490–515.

Barker, R. G. Explorations in ecological psychology. *American Psychologist*, 1965, *20*, 1–4.

Bayley, N. A study of fear by means of the psychogalvanic technique. *Psychological Monographs*, 1928, *176*.

Beck, A. T. Cognition, affect and psychopathology. *Archives of General Psychiatry*, 1971, *24*, 495–500.

Beck, A. T. *Cognitive therapy and emotional disorders*. New York: International Universities Press, 1976.

Beilin, H. Developmental stages and developmental processes. In D. R. Green, M. P. Ford, & G. B. Flamer (Eds.), *Measurement and Piaget*. New York: McGraw-Hill, 1971.

Bell, R. Q., & Costello, N. S. Three tests for sex differences in tactile sensitivity in the newborn. *Biologia Neonatorum*, 1964, *7*, 335–347.

Bell, R. Q., Weller, G. M., & Waldrop, M. F. Newborn and preschooler: Organization of behavior and relations between periods. *Monographs of the Society for Research in Child Development*, 1971, *36* (1-2, Serial No. 142).

Bell, S. M., & Ainsworth, M. D. S. Infant crying and maternal responsiveness. *Child Development*, 1972, *43*, 1171–1190.

Belsky, J. Early human experience: A family perspective. *Developmental Psychology*, 1981, *17*, 3–23.

Belsky, J., & Steinberg, L. D. The effects of day care: A critical review. *Child Development*, 1978, *49*, 929–949.

Benedict, R. Anthropology and the abnormal. *Journal of Genetic Psychology*, 1934, *10*, 59–82.

Benjamin, J. S. Some developmental observations relating to the theory of anxiety. *Journal of the American Psychoanalytic Association*, 1961, *9*, 652–668.

Benson, H. *The relaxation response*. New York: Morrow, 1975.

Berg, I. *Education and jobs: The great training robbery*. New York: Praeger, 1970.

Berlyne, D. E. *Conflict, arousal and curiosity*. New York: McGraw-Hill, 1960.

Berlyne, D. E. Children's reasoning and thinking. In P. H. Mussen (Ed.), *Carmichael's manual of child psychology* (Vol. 1). New York: Wiley, 1970.

Bernstein, B. Social class and linguistic development: A theory of social learning. In A. Halsey, V. Floyd, & A. Anderson (Eds.), *Society, economy, and education*. Glencoe, Ill.: Free Press, 1961.

Bertenthal, B. I., & Fischer, K. W. Development of self-recognition in the infant. *Developmental Psychology*, 1978, *14*, 44–50.

Bindra, D. A neuropsychological interpretation of the effects of drive and incentive-motivation on general activity and instrumental behavior. *Psychological Review*, 1968, *75*, 1–22.

Bindra, D. A unified interpretation of emotion and motivation. *Annals of the New York Academy of Science*, 1969, *159*, 1071–1083.

Birdwhistell, R. L. *Kinesics and context*. Philadelphia: University of Pennsylvania Press, 1970.

Birns, B., & Golden, M. Prediction of intellectual performance at 3 years from infant tests and personality measures. *Merrill-Palmer Quarterly*, 1972, *18*, 53–58.

Bischof, N. A systems approach towards the functional connection of fear and attachment. *Child Development*, 1975, *46*, 801–817.

Black, P. (Ed.), *Physiological correlates of emotion*. New York: Academic Press, 1970.

Blanchard, M., & Main, M. Avoidance of the attachment figure and social-emotional development in day care infants. *Developmental Psychology*, 1979, *15*, 445–446.

Blatz, W. E., & Millichamp, D. A. The development of emotion in the infant. *University of Toronto Studies, Child Development Series*, 1935,4.

Blehar, M. C. Anxious attachment and defensive reactions associated with day care. *Child Development*, 1974, *45*, 683–692.

Blurton-Jones, N. G. Criteria for use in describing facial expressions of children. *Human Biology*, 1971, *43*, 365–413.

Borke, H. Interpersonal perception of young children: Egocentrism or empathy. *Developmental Psychology*, 1971, *5*, 263–269.

Borke, H. The development of empathy in Chinese and American children between three and six years of age: A cross-cultural study. *Developmental Psychology*, 1973, *9*, 102–108.

Bower, G. H. Mood and memory. *American Psychologist*, 1981, *36*, 129–148.

Bowers, K. S. Situationism in psychology: An analysis and a critique. *Psychological Review*, 1973, *80*, 307–336.

Bowlby, J. A symposium on the contribution of current theories to an understanding of child development: I. An ethological approach to research in child development. *British Journal of Medical Psychology*, 1957, *30*, 230–240.

Bowlby, J. The nature of a child's tie to his mother. *International Journal of Psychoanalysis*, 1958, *39*, 350–373.

Bowlby, J. *Attachment and loss, Vol. 1: Attachment*. New York: Basic Books, 1969.

Bowlby, J. *Attachment and loss, Vol. 2: Separation*. London: Hogarth, 1973.

Brady, J. V., & Nauta, W. J. H. Subcortical mechanisms in emotional behaviour: Affective changes following septal forebrain lesions in the albino rat. *Journal of Comparative Physiological Psychology*, 1953, *46*, 339–346.

Brazelton, T. B. *Infants and mothers: Differences in development.* New York: Delacorte, 1969.

Brazelton, T. B. *Neonatal Behavioral Assessment Scale.* Clinics in Developmental Medicine, No. 50. Philadelphia: Lippincott, 1973.

Brazelton, T. B., Robey, J. S., & Collier, G. A. Infant development in the Zinacanteco Indians of southern Mexico. *Pediatrics,* 1969, *44,* 274–290.

Brazelton, T. B., Koslowski, B., & Main, M. The origins of reciprocity: The early mother-infant interaction. In M. Lewis & L. A. Rosenblum (Eds.), *The effect of the infant on its caregiver.* New York: Wiley, 1974.

Brenner, C. On the nature and development of affects: A unified theory. *Psychoanalytic Quarterly,* 1974, *43,* 532–556.

Bretherton, I. Making friends with one-year-olds: An experimental study of infant- stranger interaction. *Merrill-Palmer Quarterly,* 1978, *24,* 29–51.

Bretherton, I., & Ainsworth, M. Responses of one-year-olds to a stranger in a strange situation. In M. Lewis & L. A. Rosenblum (Eds.), *The origins of fear.* New York: Wiley, 1974.

Bridges, K. M. B. A genetic theory of the emotions. *Journal of Genetic Psychology,* 1930, *37,* 514–527.

Bridges, K. M. B. Emotional development in early infancy. *Child Development,* 1932, *3,* 324–334.

Bridges, K. M. B. A study of social development in early infancy. *Child Development,* 1933, *4,* 36–49.

Brinker, R., & Lewis, M. Contingency intervention in infancy. In J. Anderson (Ed.), *Curriculum materials for high risk and handicapped infants.* Chapel Hill, N.C.: Technical Assistance and Development System, 1982.

Bronfenbrenner, U. Developmental research, public policy and the ecology of childhood. *Child Development,* 1974, *45,* 1–5.

Bronfenbrenner, U. Toward an experimental ecology of human development. *American Psychologist,* 1977, *32,* 513–531.

Bronfenbrenner, U. *The ecology of human development: Experiments by nature and design.* Cambridge, Mass.: Harvard University Press, 1979.

Bronson, G. W. Fear of the unfamiliar in human infants. In H. R. Schaffer (Ed.), *The origins of human social relations.* London: Academic Press, 1971.

Bronson, G. W. Infants' reactions to unfamiliar persons and novel objects. *Monographs of the Society for Research in Child Development,* 1972, *37,* 148.

Bronson, W. C. *Exploratory behavior of 15-month-old infants in a novel situation.* Paper presented at the biennial meeting of the Society for Research in Child Development, Minneapolis, 1971. (a)

Bronson, W. C. The growth of competence: Issues of conceptualization and measurement. In H. R. Schaffer (Ed.), *The origins of human social relations.* New York: Academic Press, 1971. (b).

Bronson, W. C. Mother-toddler interaction: A perspective on studying the development of competence. *Merrill-Palmer Quarterly,* 1974, *20,* 275–300.

Bronson, W. C. *Toddlers' behaviors with age mates: Issues of interaction, cognition, and affect.* Norwood, N.J.: Ablex, 1981.

Brookhart, J., & Hock, E. The effects of experimental context and experiential background on infants' behavior toward their mothers and a stranger. *Child Development,* 1976, *47,* 333–340.

Brooks, J., & Lewis, M. Attachment behavior in thirteen-month-old, opposite sex twins. *Child Development,* 1974, *45,* 243–247. (a)

Brooks, J., & Lewis, M. The effects of time on attachment as measured in a free-play situation. *Child Development*, 1974, *45*, 311–316. (b)

Brooks, J., & Lewis, M. Infants' responses to strangers: Midget, adult, and child. *Child Development*, 1976, *47*, 323–332.

Brooks-Gunn, J., & Lewis, M. Affective exchanges between normal and handicapped infants and their mothers. In T. Field & A. Fogel (Eds.), *Emotion and early interaction*. Hillsdale, N.J.: Erlbaum, 1982.

Buck, R. W. Nonverbal communication of affect in children. *Journal of Personality and Social Psychology*, 1975, *31*, 644–653.

Buck, R. W. *Human motivation and emotion*. New York: Wiley, 1976.

Buck, R. W. Nonverbal behavior and the theory of emotion: The facial feedback hypothesis. *Journal of Personality and Social Psychology*, 1980, *38*, 811–824.

Buck, R. W. The evolution and development of emotional expression and communication. In S. S. Brehm, S. M. Kassin, & F. X. Gibbons (Eds.), *Developmental social psychology*. New York: Oxford University Press, 1981.

Buck, R. W. *Nonverbal behavior and emotion communication*. New York: Guilford, 1982.

Buck, R. W., Savin, V. J., Miller, R. E., & Caul, W. F. Communication of affect through facial expressions in humans. *Journal of Personality and Social Psychology*, 1972, *23*, 362–371.

Buck, R. W., Miller, R. E., & Caul, W. F. Sex, personality, and physiological variables in the communication of affect via facial expression. *Journal of Personality and Social Psychology*, 1974, *30*, 587–596.

Bühler, C. The social behaviour of children. In C. A. Murchison (Ed.), *Handbook of child psychology* (2nd ed., revised). Worcester, Mass.: Clark University Press, 1933.

Bull, N. The attitude theory of emotion. *Nervous and Mental Disease Monograph*, 1951, No. 81.

Burns, N., & Cavey, L. Age differences in empathic ability among children. *Canadian Journal of Psychology*, 1957, *11*, 227–230.

Buss, A. H., & Plomin, R. *A temperament theory of personality development*. New York: Wiley, 1975.

Cain, W. S. To know with the nose: Keys to odor identification. *Science*, 1979, *203*, 467–470.

Cairns, R. B. (Ed.). *The analysis of social interactions: Methods, issues, and illustrations*. Hillsdale, N.J.: Erlbaum, 1979.

Caldwell, B. M., Wright, C. M., Honig, A. S., & Tannenbaum, J. Infant care and attachment. *American Journal of Orthopsychiatry*, 1970, *40*, 397–412.

Campos, J. J., & Johnson, H. J. The effect of verbalization instructions and visual attention on heart rate and skin conductance. *Psychophysiology*, 1966, *2*, 305–310.

Campos, J., & Stenberg, C. Perception, appraisal, and emotion: The onset of social referencing. In M. E. Lamb & L. R. Sherrod (Eds.), *Infant social cognition: Empirical and theoretical considerations*. Hillsdale, N.J.: Erlbaum, 1981.

Campos, J. J., Langer, A., & Krowitz, A. Cardiac responses on the visual cliff in prelocomotor human infants. *Science*, 1970, *170*, 196–197.

Campos, J. J., Emde, R. N., Gaensbauer, T., & Sorce, J. Cardiac and behavioral responses of human infants to strangers: Effects of mother's absence and of experimental sequence. *Developmental Psychology*, 1973, *11*, 589.

Campos, J. J., Emde, R., Gaensbauer, T., & Henderson, C. Cardiac and behavioral interrelationships in the reactions of infants to strangers. *Developmental Psychology*, 1975, *11*, 589–601.

Cannon, W. B. The James-Lange theory of emotion: A critical examination and an alternative theory. *American Journal of Psychology*, 1927, *39*, 106–124.

Cannon, W. B. Neural organization for emotional expression. In M. L. Reymert (Ed.), *Feelings and emotions: The Wittenberg Symposium*. Worcester, Mass.: Clark University Press, 1928.

Cannon, W. B. *Bodily changes in pain, hunger, fear, and rage*. New York: Appleton, 1929.

Cannon, W. B. Again the James-Lange and the thalamic theories of emotions. *Psychological Review*, 1931, *38*, 281–295.

Carmichael, L. (Ed.). *Manual of child psychology*. New York: Wiley, 1946.

Carmichael, L. (Ed.). *Manual of child psychology* (2nd ed.). New York: Wiley, 1954.

Caron, R. F., Caron, A. J., & Myers, R. S. Abstraction of invariant face expressions in infancy. *Child Development*, 1982, *53*, 1008–1015.

Carr, H. A. *Psychology, a study of mental activity*. New York: McKay, 1929.

Castell, R. Effect of familiar and unfamiliar environments in proximity behavior of young children. *Journal of Experimental Child Psychology*, 1970, *9*, 342–347.

Cattell, R. B. *The description and measurement of personality*. New York: Harcourt Brace Jovanovich, 1946.

Cattell, R. B. *The scientific analysis of personality*. Baltimore, Md.: Penguin, 1965.

Cattell, R. B. Anxiety and motivation: Theory and crucial experiments. In C. D. Spielberger (Ed.), *Anxiety and behavior*. New York: Academic Press, 1966.

Cattell, R. B. *Personality and mood by questionnaire*. San Francisco: Jossey-Bass, 1973.

Caudill, W., & Weinstein, H. Maternal care and infant behavior in Japan and America. *Psychiatry*, 1969, *32*, 12–43.

Charlesworth, W. R. The role of surprise in cognitive development. In D. Elkind & J. H. Flavell (Eds.), *Studies in cognitive development: Essays in honor of Jean Piaget*. London: Oxford University Press, 1969.

Charlesworth, W. R., & Kreutzer, M. A. Facial expressions of infants and children. In P. Ekman (Ed.), *Darwin and facial expression: A century of research in review*. New York: Academic Press, 1973.

Cherry, L. *Sex differences in child speech: McCarthy revisited* (ETS RB-75-3). Princeton, N.J.: Educational Testing Service, 1975.

Cherry, L. How the mind affects our health. *The New York Times Magazine*, Nov. 23, 1980, p. 94.

Cherry, L., & Lewis, M. Differential socialization of girls and boys: Implications for sex differences in language development. In N. Waterson & C. Snow (Eds.), *The development of communication: Social and pragmatic factors in language acquisition*. London: Wiley, 1978.

Chevalier-Skolnikoff, S. Facial expression of emotion in nonhuman primates. In P. Ekman (Ed.), *Darwin and facial expression*. New York: Academic Press, 1973.

Church, J. (Ed.). *Three babies: Biographies of cognitive development*. New York: Random House, 1966.

Cicchetti, D., & Sroufe, L. A. An organizational view of affect: Illustration from the study of Down's syndrome infants. In M. Lewis & L. A. Rosenblum (Eds.), *The development of affect*. New York: Plenum, 1978.

Clark, R. W. *Einstein: The life and times*. New York: Avon, 1972.

Clarke-Stewart, K. A. Interactions between mothers and their young children: Characteristics and consequences. *Monographs of the Society for Research in Child Development*, 1973, *38*(5, Serial No. 153).

Coates, D., & Lewis, M. *Early mother-infant interaction and infant cognitive status as predictors of school performance and cognitive behavior in 6-year-olds.* Unpublished manuscript, 1981.

Coates, B., Anderson, E. P., & Hartup, W. W. Interrelations in the attachment behavior of human infants. *Developmental Psychology,* 1972, *6,* 218–230. (a)

Coates, B., Anderson, E. P., & Hartup, W. W. The stability of attachment behaviors in the human infant. *Developmental Psychology,* 1972, *6,* 231–237. (b)

Cohen, L. J., & Campos, J. J. Father, mother and stranger as elicitors of attachment behavior in infancy. *Developmental Psychology,* 1974, *10,* 146–154.

Collard, R. Social and play responses of first born and later born infants in an unfamiliar situation. *Child Development,* 1968, *39,* 324–334.

Connell, D. B. Individual differences in infant attachment: An investigation into stability, implications, and relationships to structure of early language development. Unpublished doctoral dissertation, Syracuse University, 1976.

Cousins, N. *Anatomy of an illness as perceived by the patient: Reflections in healing and regeneration.* New York: Norton, 1979.

Darwin, C. R. *The expression of the emotions in man and animals.* London: John Murray, 1872.

Davitz, J. R. *The language of emotion.* New York: Academic Press, 1969.

Davitz, J. R., & Davitz, L. J. The communication of feelings by content-free speech. *Journal of Communication,* 1959, *9,* 6–13.

Décarie, T. G. (Ed.). *The infant's reaction to strangers.* New York: International Universities Press, 1974.

Delgado, J. M. R. Emotional behavior in animals and humans. *Psychiatric Research Report,* 1960, *12,* 259–271.

Delgado, J. M. R. Free behavior and brain stimulation. *International Review of Neurobiology,* 1964, *6,* 349–449.

Delgado, J. M. R. *Emotions.* Dubuque, Ia.: Brown, 1966.

Demos, E. V. Facial expressions of infants and toddlers: A descriptive analysis. In T. Field & A. Fogel (Eds.), *Emotion and early interaction.* Hillsdale, N.J.: Erlbaum, 1982.

Dennis, W. A bibliography of baby biographies. *Child Development,* 1936, *7,* 71–73.

DePaulo, B. M., & Rosenthal, R. Ambivalence, discrepancy, and deception in nonverbal communication. In R. Rosenthal (Ed.), *Skill in nonverbal communication.* Cambridge, Mass.: Oelgeschlager, Gunn, & Hain, 1979. (a)

DePaulo, B. M., & Rosenthal, R. Telling lies. *Journal of Personality and Social Psychology,* 1979, *37,* 1713–1722. (b)

DeRivera, J. *A structural theory of the emotions.* New York: International Universities Press, 1977.

Diamond, S. *The roots of psychology.* New York: Basic Books, 1974.

Doyle, A. Infant development in day care. *Developmental Psychology,* 1975, *11,* 655–656.

Doyle, A., Connolly, J., & Rivest, L. The effect of playmate familiarity on the social interaction of young children. *Child Development,* 1980, *51,* 217–223.

Duffy, E. Emotion: An example of the need for reorientation in psychology. *Psychological Review,* 1934, *41,* 184–198.

Duffy, E. An explanation of "emotional" phenomena without the use of the concept "emotion." *Journal of General Psychology,* 1941, *25,* 283–293.

Duffy, E. *Activation and behaviour.* New York: Wiley, 1962.

Duncan, O. D., Featherman, D. L., & Duncan, B. *Socioeconomic background and achievement.* New York: Seminar Press, 1972.

Durfee, J. T., & Lee, L. C. *Infant-infant interaction in a day care setting.* Paper presented at the meetings of the American Psychological Association, Montreal, 1973.

Dweck, C. S., & Repucci, N. D. Learned helplessness and reinforcement responsibility in children. *Journal of Personality and Social Psychology*, 1973, *25*, 109–116.

Eaves, L. J., & Eysenck, H. J. The nature of extroversion: A genetical analysis. *Journal of Personality and Social Psychology*, 1975, *32*, 102–112.

Eckerman, C. O., Whatley, J., & Kutz, S. Growth of social play with peers during the second year of life. *Developmental Psychology*, 1975, *11*, 42–49.

Edwards, C. P., & Lewis, M. Young children's concepts of social relations: Social functions and social objects. In M. Lewis & L. A. Rosenblum (Eds.), *The child and its family*. New York: Plenum, 1979.

Eibl-Eibesfeldt, I. *Ethology: The biology of behavior*. New York: Holt, Rinehart & Winston, 1970.

Eibl-Eibesfeldt, I. The expressive behavior of the deaf- and blind-born. In M. von Cranach & I. Vine (Eds.), *Social communication and movement*. New York: Academic Press, 1973.

Ekman, P. Universal and cultural differences in facial expression of emotion. In J. R. Cole (Ed.), *Nebraska Symposium on Motivation*, 1971. Lincoln: University of Nebraska Press, 1972.

Ekman, P. Cross-cultural studies of facial expression. In P. Ekman (Ed.), *Darwin and facial expression*. New York: Academic Press, 1973. (a)

Ekman, P. (Ed.). *Darwin and facial expression: A century of research in review*. New York: Academic Press, 1973. (b)

Ekman, P. Biological and cultural contributions to body and facial movement. In J. Blacking (Ed.), *Anthropology of the body*. New York: Academic Press, 1977.

Ekman, P., & Friesen, W. V. The repertoire of nonverbal behavior: Categories, origins, usage, and coding. *Semiotica*, 1969, *1*, 49–98.

Ekman, P., & Friesen, W. V. Detecting deception from the body or face. *Journal of Personality and Social Psychology*, 1974, *29*, 288–298.

Ekman, P., & Friesen, W. V. *Unmasking the face*. Englewood Cliffs, N.J.: Prentice-Hall, 1975.

Ekman, P., & Friesen, W. V. *The Facial Action Coding System (FACS)*. Palo Alto, Cal.: Consulting Psychologists Press, 1978.

Ekman, P., & Oster, H. Facial expressions of emotion. *Annual Review of Psychology*, 1979, *30*, 527–554.

Ekman, P., Malmstron, E. J., & Friesen, W. V. *Heart rate changes with facial displays of surprise and disgust*. Unpublished manuscript, 1971.

Ekman, P., Friesen, W. V., & Ellsworth, P. *Emotion in the human face: Guidelines for research and an integration of findings*. New York: Pergamon, 1972.

Ekman, P., Friesen, W. V., & Scherer, K. R. Body movement and voice pitch in deceptive interaction. *Semiotica*, 1976, *16*, 23–27.

Emde, R. N., & Koenig, K. L. Neonatal smiling and rapid eye movement states. *American Academy of Child Psychiatry*, 1969, *8*, 57–67.

Emde, R. N., Gaensbauer, T., & Harmon, R. Emotional expression in infancy: A biobehavioral study. *Psychological Issues*, 1976, *10* (1, Whole No. 37).

Emde, R. N., Campos, J., Reich, J., & Gaensbauer, T. J. Infant smiling at five and nine months: Analysis of heart rate and movement. *Infant Behavior and Development*, 1978, *1*, 26–35.

Emmerich, W. Continuity and stability in early social development: II. Teacher ratings. *Child Development*, 1966, *37*, 17–27.

Endler, N. S., & Magnusson, D. Interactionism, trait psychology, and situationism. *Reports from the Psychological Laboratories*, University of Stockholm, 1974.

Erikson, E. H. *Childhood and society*. New York: Norton, 1950.

Escalona, S. *The roots of individuality*. Chicago: Aldine, 1968.

Fagot, B. I. Sex-related stereotyping of toddlers' behaviors. *Developmental Psychology*, 1973, *9*, 429.

Farran, D. C., & Ramey, C. T. Infant day care and attachment behavior toward mother and teachers. *Child Development*, 1977, *48*, 1112–1116.

Fehr, F. S., & Stern, J. A. Peripheral physiological variables and emotion: The James-Lange theory revisited. *Psychological Bulletin*, 1970, *74*, 411–424.

Feinman, S. Infant response to race, size, proximity, and movement of strangers. *Infant Behavior and Development*, 1980, *3*, 187–204.

Feinman, S., & Lewis, M. Social referencing and second order effects in ten-month-old infants. *Child Development*, in press.

Feinman, S., Roberts, D., & Grumbles, D. *Grandmothers, aunts, and friends of the family: Infants' social relationships beyond the nuclear family*. In preparation, 1982.

Feiring, C., & Lewis, M. Sex and age differences in young children's reactions to frustration: A further look at the Goldberg and Lewis subjects. *Child Development*, 1979, *50*, 848–853.

Feiring, C., Lewis, M., & Starr, M. *Indirect and direct effects on children's reactions to unfamiliar adults*. Submitted for publication, 1982.

Feldman, S. S., & Ingham, M. E. Attachment behavior: A validation study in two age groups. *Child Development*, 1975, *46*, 319–330.

Fenichel, O. *The psychoanalytic theory of neurosis*. Boston: Routledge and Kegan Paul, 1946.

Feshbach, N. The effects of violence in childhood. *Journal of Clinical Child Psychology*, 1973, *2*, 28–31.

Feshbach, N., & Roe, K. Empathy in six- and seven-year-olds. *Child Development*, 1968, *39*, 133–145.

Feshbach, S. Aggression. In P. H. Mussen (Ed.), *Carmichael's manual of child psychology* (Vol. 2). New York: Wiley, 1970.

Festinger, L. A theory of social comparison processes. *Human Relations*, 1954, *7*, 17–40.

Field, T. M., Woodson, R., Greenberg, R., & Cohen, D. Discrimination and imitation of facial expressions by neonates. *Science*, 1982, *218*, 179–181.

Finkelstein, N. W., & Ramey, C. T. Learning to control the environment in infancy. *Child Development*, 1977, *48*, 806–819.

Flavell, J. H. The development of inferences about others. In T. Mischel (Ed.), *Understanding other persons*. Oxford: Blackwell, Basil & Mott, 1974.

Flavell, J. H., Botkin, P. T., Fry, C. L., Wright, J. W., & Jarvis, P. E. *The development of role-taking and communication skills in children*. New York: Wiley, 1968.

Fleener, D. E. Experimental production of infant-maternal attachment behaviors. *Proceedings of the 81st Annual Convention of the American Psychological Association*, 1973, *8*, 57–58.

Fogel, A. Temporal organization in mother-infant, face-to-face interaction. In H. R. Schaffer (Ed.), *Studies in mother-infant interaction*. London: Academic Press, 1977.

Fogel, A. Affect dynamics in early infancy. In T. Field & A. Fogel (Eds.), *Emotion and early interaction*. Hillsdale, N.J.: Erlbaum, 1982. (a)

Fogel, A. Early adult-infant interaction: Expectable sequences of behavior. *Journal of Pediatric Psychology*, 1982, *7*, 1–22. (b)

Ford, M. E. The construct validity of egocentrism. *Psychological Bulletin*, 1979, *86*, 1169–1188.

Forer, L. K., & Still, H. *The birth order factor*. New York: McKay, 1976.

Fox, N. Attachment of kibbutz infants to mother and metapelet. *Child Development*, 1977, *48*, 1228–1239.

Fredericksen, N. Toward a taxonomy of situations. *American Psychologist*, 1972, *27*, 114–123.

Freedman, D. G. *Human infancy: An evolutionary perspective*. Hillsdale, N.J.: Erlbaum, 1974.

Freedman, D. G. Ethnic differences in babies. *Human Nature*, 1979, 36–43. (a)

Freedman, D. G. *Human sociobiology*. New York: Free Press, 1979. (b)

Freud, S. *Selected papers on hysteria and other psychoneuroses* (A. A. Brill, trans.) (3rd enl. ed.). New York: Nervous and Mental Disease, 1920.

Freud, S. *Repression*. In S. Freud, *Collected Papers* (Vol. 3). London: Hogarth, 1949. (Originally published in 1915.)

Freud, S. *The psychopathology of everyday life* (A. Tyson, trans.). New York: Norton, 1960.

Friedman, M., & Rosenman, R. H. *Type A behavior and your heart*. New York: Knopf, 1974.

Frodi, A. M., Lamb, M. E., Leavitt, L. A., & Donovan, W. L. Fathers' and mothers' responses to infant smiles and cries. *Infant Behavior and Development*, 1978, *1*, 187–198.

Gaensbauer, T. J., Mrazek, D., & Emde, R. N. Patterning of emotional response in a playroom laboratory situation. *Infant Behavior and Development*, 1979, *2*, 163–178.

Gallup, G. G., Jr. Self-recognition in chimpanzees and man: A developmental and comparative perspective. In M. Lewis & L. A. Rosenblum (Eds.), *The child and its family*. New York: Plenum, 1979.

Gardiner, H. N., Gardiner, R. C. M., & Beebe-Center, J. G. *Feeling and emotion: A history of theories*. Westport, Conn.: Greenwood, 1970.

Geertz, C. *The interpretation of cultures*. New York: Basic, 1973.

Geertz, H. The vocabulary of emotion. *Psychiatry*, 1959, *22*, 225–237.

Gellhorn, E. *Biological foundations of emotion*. Glenview, Ill.: Scott, Foresman, 1968.

George, C., & Main, M. Social interaction of young abused children: Approach, avoidance, and aggression. *Child Development*, 1979, *50*, 306–318.

Gesell, G., & Thompson, H. *Infant behavior: Its genesis and growth*. New York: McGraw Hill, 1934.

Gewirtz, J. L. The course of infant smiling in four child-rearing environments in Israel. In B. M. Foss (Ed.), *Determinants of infant behavior* (Vol. 3). New York: Wiley, 1965.

Gewirtz, J. L., & Boyd, E. F. Does maternal responding imply reduced infant crying? A critique of the 1972 Bell and Ainsworth report. *Child Development*, 1977, *48*, 1200–1207. (a)

Gewirtz, J. L., & Boyd, E. F. In reply to the rejoinder to our critique of the 1972 Bell and Ainsworth report. *Child Development*, 1977, *48*, 1217–1218. (b)

Ghiselli, E. E. *The validity of occupational aptitude tests*. New York: Wiley, 1966.

Gibson, E. J., & Walk, R. D. The "visual cliff." *Scientific American*, 1960, *202*, 64–71.

Gibson, J. J. The concept of the stimulus in psychology. *American Psychologist*, 1960, *15*, 694–703.

Glass, D. C. *Behavior patterns, stress, and coronary disease*. New York: Erlbaum, 1977.

Goffman, E. *The presentation of self in everyday life*. New York: Doubleday Anchor, 1959.

Goffman, E. *Behavior in public places*. Glencoe, Ill.: Free Press, 1963.

Goldberg, S., & Lewis, M. Play behavior in the year-old infant: Early sex differences. *Child Development*, 1969, *40*, 21–31.

Goldsmith, H., & Campos, J. J. Toward a theory of infant temperament. In R. Emde & R. Harmon (Eds.), *Attachment and affiliative systems*. New York: Plenum Press, 1982.

Goodenough, F. L. *Anger in young children*. Minneapolis: University of Minnesota Press, 1931.

Goodenough, F. L. *Developmental psychology: An introduction to the study of human behavior* (2nd ed.). New York: Appleton-Century, 1934.

Gould, S. J. *Ever since Darwin: Reflections in natural history.* Toronto: George J. McLeod, 1977.

Goulet, J. The infant's conception of causality and his reactions to strangers. In T. Décarie (Ed.), *The infant's reaction to strangers.* New York: International Universities Press, 1974.

Graham, F. K., & Clifton, R. K. Heart-rate change as a component of the orienting response. *Psychological Bulletin,* 1966, *65,* 305–320.

Graham, F. K., & Jackson, J. Arousal systems and infant heart rate responses. In H. W. Reese & L. P. Lipsitt (Eds.), *Advances in child development and behavior* (Vol. 5). New York: Academic Press, 1970.

Grant, E. C. Human facial expression. *Man,* 1969, *4,* 525–536.

Greenberg, D. J., Hillman, D., & Grice, D. Infant and stranger variables related to stranger anxiety in the first year of life. *Developmental Psychology,* 1973, *9,* 207–212.

Greenspan, S. Is social competence synonymous with school performance? *American Psychologist,* 1980, *35,* 938–939.

Greif, E. B., Alvarez, M., & Ulman, K. *Recognizing emotions in other people: Sex differences in socialization.* Paper presented at the biennial meetings of the Society for Research in Child Development, Boston, April 1981.

Grings, W. W., & Dawson, M. E. *Emotions and bodily responses: A psychophysiological approach.* New York: Academic Press, 1978.

Gross, C. J., Rocha-Miranda, C. E., & Bender, D. B. Visual properties of neurons in inferotemporal cortex of the macaque. *Journal of Neurophysiology,* 1972, *35,* 96–111.

Grossman, S. P. The biology of motivation. *Annual Review of Psychology,* 1979, *30,* 209–242.

Gunnar, M. R. Control, warning signals and distress in infancy. *Developmental Psychology,* 1980, *16,* 281–289.

Gunnar-Vongnechten, M. R. Changing a frightening toy into a pleasant toy by allowing the infant to control its actions. *Developmental Psychology,* 1978, *14,* 157–162.

Haith, M. M. The forgotten message of the infant smile. *Merrill-Palmer Quarterly,* 1972, *18,* 321–322.

Haith, M. M. Visual competence in early infancy. In R. Held, H. Liebowitz, & H. L. Teuber (Eds.), *Handbook of sensory psychology* (Vol. 3). Berlin: Springer-Verlag, 1976.

Hall, E. T. Proxemics. *Current Anthropology,* 1968, *9,* 83–95.

Hamburg, D. A., Hamburg, B. A., & Barchas, J. D. Anger and depression in perspective of behavioral biology. In L. Levi (Ed.), *Emotions: Their parameters and measurement.* New York: Raven, 1975.

Hamlyn, D. W. *Sensation and perception.* London: Routledge & Kegan Paul, 1961.

Harlow, H. F., & Harlow, M. K. The affectional systems. In A. M. Schrier, H. F. Harlow, & F. Stollnitz (Eds.), *Behavior of nonhuman primates* (Vol. 2). New York: Academic Press, 1965.

Harlow, H. F., & Harlow, M. K. Effects of various mother-infant relationships on rhesus monkey behaviors. In B. M. Foss (Ed.), *Determinants of infant behavior* (Vol. 4). London: Methuen, 1969.

Harmon, R. J., Morgan, G. A., & Klein, R. P. Determinants of normal variation in infants' negative reactions to unfamiliar adults. *Journal of the American Academy of Child Psychiatry,* 1977, *16,* 670–683.

Harter, S. Effectance motivation reconsidered: Toward a developmental model. *Human Development,* 1978, *1,* 34–64.

Hartmann, H. Ego psychology and the problem of adaptation (D. Rapaport, trans.). *Journal of the American Psychoanalytic Association*, Monograph #1. New York: International Universities Press, 1958. (Originally published in 1939).

Hartup, W. W. Social learning, social interaction and social development. In P. J. Elich (Ed.), *Social learning*. New York: Western Washington Press, 1973.

Hartup, W. W. The social worlds of childhood. *American Psychologist*, 1979, *34*, 944–950.

Haviland, J. Looking smart: The relationship between affect and intelligence in infancy. In M. Lewis (Ed.), *Origins of intelligence*. New York: Plenum, 1976.

Haviland, J., & Lewis, M. *Infants' greeting patterns to strangers*. Paper presented at the Human Ethology session of the Animal Behavior Society meeting, Wilmington, N.C., May 1975.

Hayes, L. A., & Watson, J. S. Neonatal imitation: Fact or artifact. *Developmental Psychology*, 1981, *17*, 655–660.

Hebb, D. O. On the nature of fear. *Psychological Review*, 1946, *53*, 259–276.

Hebb, D. O. *The organization of behaviour*. New York: Wiley, 1949.

Hebb, D. O. The motivating effects of exteroceptive stimulation. *American Psychologist*, 1958, *13*, 109–113.

Heinicke, C., & Westheimer, I. *Brief separations*. New York: International Universities Press, 1966.

Hellmuth, J. (Ed.). *Disadvantaged child: Head start and early intervention*. New York: Brunner/Mazel, 1968.

Helson, H. *Adaptation-level theory*. New York: Harper & Row, 1964.

Hess, W. R. *Diencephalon: Autonomic and extrapyramidal functions*. New York: Grune & Stratton, 1954.

Hess, W. R. *The functional organization of the diencephalon*. New York: Grune & Stratton, 1957.

Hess, E. H. Attitude and pupil size. *Scientific American*, 1965, *212*, 46–54.

Hess, E. H. Ethology. In A. M. Freedman & H. I. Kaplan (Eds.), *Comprehensive textbook of psychiatry*. Baltimore, Md.: Williams and Wilkins, 1967.

Hess, E. H. Ethology and developmental psychology. In P. H. Mussen (Ed.), *Carmichael's manual of child psychology*. New York: Wiley, 1970.

Hess, R., & Shipman, V. Early experiences and the socialization of cognitive modes in children. *Child Development*, 1965, *36*, 869–886.

Hewes, G. W. World distribution of certain postural habits. *American Anthropologist*, 1955, *57*, 231–244.

Hochschild, A. R. Emotion work, feeling rules, and social structure. *American Journal of Sociology*, 1979, *85*, 551–575.

Hoffman, M. L. Empathy, its development and prosocial implications. In H. E. Howe, Jr. & C. B. Keasey (Eds.), *Nebraska Symposium on Motivation* (Vol. 25). Lincoln: University of Nebraska Press, 1978.

Hoffman, M. L., & Levine, L. E. Early sex differences in empathy. *Developmental Psychology*, 1976, *12*, 557–558.

Hofstadter, D. *Gödel, Escher, Bach: An eternal golden braid*. New York: Random House, 1980.

Hubel, D. H., & Weisel, T. N. Receptive fields, binocular interaction, and functional architecture in the cat's visual cortex. *Journal of Physiology*, 1962, *160*, 106–154.

Hubel, D. H., & Wiesel, T. N. Receptive fields and functional architecture of monkey striate cortex. *Journal of Physiology*, 1968, *195*, 215–243.

Hull, C. L. *Principles of behavior*. New York: Appleton-Century, 1943.

Hume, D. *A treatise of human nature* (L. A. Selby-Bigge, Ed.). Oxford: Clarendon, 1888. (Originally published in 1739.)

Hunt, J. McV. *Intelligence and experience.* New York: Ronald, 1961.

Hunt, J. McV. Intrinsic motivation and its role in psychological development. In D. Levine (Ed.), *Nebraska Symposium on Motivation,* (Vol. 13). Lincoln: University of Nebraska Press, 1965.

Izard, C. E. *The face of emotion.* New York: Appleton, 1971.

Izard, C. E. *Patterns of emotion: A new analysis of anxiety and depression.* New York: Academic Press, 1972.

Izard, C. E. *Human emotions.* New York: Plenum, 1977.

Izard, C. E. Emotions and emotion-cognition relationships. In M. Lewis & L. A. Rosenblum (Eds.), *The development of affect.* New York: Plenum, 1978.

Izard, C. E. Emotions as motivators: An evolutionary-developmental perspective. In R. Dienstbier (Ed.), *Nebraska Symposium on Motivation.* Lincoln: University of Nebraska Press, 1979. (a)

Izard, C. E. *The Maximally Discriminative Facial Movement Coding System (MAX).* Newark, Del.: Instructional Resources Center, University of Delaware, 1979. (b)

Izard, C. E., & Buechler, S. Emotion expressions and personality integration in infancy. In C. E. Izard (Ed.), *Emotions in personality and psychopathology.* New York: Plenum, 1979.

Izard, C. E., & Buechler, S. Aspects of consciousness and personality in terms of differential emotions theory. In R. Plutchik & H. Kellerman (Eds.), *Emotion: Theory, research, and experience* (Vol. 1): *Theories of emotion.* New York: Academic Press, 1980.

Izard, C. E., & Dougherty, L. M. Two complementary systems for measuring facial expressions in infants and children. In C. E. Izard (Ed.), *Measuring emotions in infants and children.* New York: Cambridge University Press, 1982.

Izard, C. E., Huebner, R. R., Risser, D., McGinnes, G. C., & Dougherty, L. M. The young infant's ability to produce discrete emotion expressions. *Developmental Psychology,* 1980, *16,* 132–140.

Jacklin, C. N., Maccoby, E. E., & Dick, A. E. Barrier behavior and toy preference: Sex differences (and their absence) in the year-old child. *Child Development,* 1973, 44, 196–200.

Jacobs, B. S., & Moss, H. A. Birth order and sex of sibling as determinants of mother-infant interaction. *Child Development,* 1976, 47, 315–322.

James, W. What is emotion? *Mind,* 1884, 19, 188–205.

James, W. *The principles of psychology.* New York: Holt, 1890.

Jaynes, J. *The origins of consciousness in the breakdown of the bicameral mind.* Boston: Houghton Mifflin, 1977.

Jencks, C. *Inequality: A reassessment of the effect of family and schooling in America.* New York: Basic Books, 1972.

Jensen, A. R. The heritability of intelligence. *Saturday Evening Post,* 1972, 244(2), 9.

Jersild, A. T. *Child psychology.* New York: Prentice-Hall, 1933.

Jones, H. E. The study of patterns of emotional expression. In M. Reynart (Ed.), *Feelings and emotions.* New York: McGraw-Hill, 1950.

Jones, H. E. The longitudinal method in the study of personality. In I. Iscoe & H. W. Stevenson (Eds.), *Personality development in children.* Austin: University of Texas Press, 1960.

Jones, H. E., & Wechsler, D. Galvanometric technique in studies of association. *American Journal of Psychology,* 1928, 40, 607–612.

Jones, M. C. The development of early behavior patterns in young children. *Journal of Genetic Psychology*, 1926, *33*, 537–585.

Kagan, J. On the need for relativism. *American Psychologist*, 1967, *22*, 131–142.

Kagan, J. *Change and continuity in the first two years.* New York: Wiley, 1971.

Kagan, J. Discrepancy, temperament, and infant distress. In M. Lewis & L. A. Rosenblum (Eds.), *The origins of fear.* New York: Wiley, 1974.

Kagan, J. On emotion and its development: A working paper. In M. Lewis & L. A. Rosenblum (Eds.), *The development of affect.* New York: Plenum, 1978.

Kagan, J. *The second year: The emergence of self-awareness.* Cambridge, Mass.: Harvard University Press, 1981.

Kagan, J., & Lewis, M. Studies of attention in the human infant. *Merrill-Palmer Quarterly*, 1965, *11*, 95–127.

Kagan, J., Henker, B. A., Hen-Tov, A., Levine, J., & Lewis, M. Infants' differential reactions to familiar and distorted faces. *Child Development*, 1966, *37*, 519–532.

Kagan, J., Kearsley, R. B., & Zelazo, P. R. The emergence of an initial apprehension to unfamiliar peers. In M. Lewis & L. A. Rosenblum (Eds.), *Friendship and peer relationships.* New York: Wiley, 1975.

Kagan, J., Kearsley, R. B., & Zelazo, P. R. *Infancy: Its place in human development.* Cambridge, Mass.: Harvard University Press, 1978.

Kamin, L. J. *The science and politics of I.Q.* Potomac, Md.: Erlbaum, 1974.

Kant, I. *Critique of pure reason* (N. Kemp Smith, trans.). New York: Macmillan, 1958.

Kaye, K. *The mental and social life of babies: How parents create persons.* Chicago: University of Chicago Press, 1982.

Kaye, K., & Fogel, A. The temporal structure of face-to-face communication between the mothers and infants. *Developmental Psychology*, 1980, *16*, 454–464.

Klein, R. P., & Durfee, J. T. Effects of sex and birth order on infant social behavior. *Infant Behavior and Development*, 1978, *1*, 106–117.

Klinnert, M. D., Campos, J. J., Sorce, J. F., Emde, R. N., & Svejda, M. Emotions as behavior regulators: Social referencing in infancy. In R. Plutchik & H. Kellerman (Eds.), *Emotions in early development.* New York: Academic Press, 1982.

Kohlberg, L., LaCrosse, J., & Ricks, D. The predictability of adult mental health from childhood behavior. In B. Wolman (Ed.), *Handbook of child psychopathology.* New York: McGraw-Hill, 1970.

Kotelchuck, M. The infant's relationship to the father: Experimental evidence. In M. E. Lamb (Ed.), *The role of the father in child development.* New York: Wiley, 1976.

Kuhn, T. S. *The structure of scientific revolutions* (2nd ed.). Chicago: University of Chicago Press, 1970.

LaBarbera, J. D., Izard, C. E., Vietze, P., & Parisi, S. A. Four- and six-month-old infants' visual responses to joy, anger, and neutral expressions. *Child Development*, 1976, *47*, 535–538.

Lacey, J. I., & Lacey, B. C. Verification and extension of the principle of autonomic response stereotype. *American Journal of Psychology*, 1958, *71*, 50–73.

Lacey, J. I., & Lacey, B. C. Some autonomic-central nervous system interrelationships. In P. Black (Ed.), *Physiological correlates of emotion.* New York: Academic Press, 1970.

Lacey, J. I., Bateman, D. E., & Van Lehn, R. Autonomic response specificity. *Psychosomatic Medicine*, 1953, *15*, 8–21.

Lacey, J. I., Kagan, J., Lacey, B. C., & Moss, H. A. The visceral level: Situational determinants and behavioural correlates of autonomic response patterns. In P. H. Knapp (Ed.), *Expressions of the emotions in man.* New York: International Universities Press, 1963.

Laird, J. D. Self-attribution of emotion: The effects of expressive behavior on the quality of emotional experience. *Journal of Personality and Social Psychology,* 1974, *29,* 475–486.

Lamb, M. E. Effects of stress and cohort on mother- and father-infant interaction. *Developmental Psychology,* 1976, *12,* 435–443.

Lamb, M. E. Father-infant and mother-infant interaction in the first year of life. *Child Development,* 1977, *48,* 167–181. (a)

Lamb, M. E. A reexamination of the infant social world. *Human Development,* 1977, *20,* 65–85. (b)

Lamb, M. E. The father's role in the infant's social world. In J. H. Stevens & M. Mathews (Eds.), *Mother/child, father/child relationships.* Washington, D.C.: National Association for the Education of Young Children, 1978.

Lamb, M. E. Paternal influences and the father's role. *American Psychologist,* 1979, *34,* 938–943.

Lamb, M. E. (Ed.), *The role of the father in child development* (2nd ed.). New York: Wiley, 1981.

Lamb, M. E. Individual differences in infant sociability: Their origins and implications for cognitive development. In H. W. Reese & L. P. Lipsitt (Eds.), *Advances in child development and behavior* (Vol. 16). New York: Academic Press, 1982.

Lamb, M. E., & Sutton-Smith, B. (Eds.). *Sibling relationships: Their nature and significance across the lifespan.* Hillsdale, N.J.: Erlbaum, 1982.

Landis, C. Studies of emotional reactions: II. General behaviors and facial expression. *Journal of Comparative Psychology,* 1924, *4,* 447–509.

Landreth, C. Factors associated with crying in young children in the nursery school and the home. *Child Development,* 1941, *12,* 81–97.

Lange, C. G. *The emotions.* Baltimore: Williams & Wilkins, 1922. (Originally published in 1885.)

Laurendeau, M., & Pinard, A. *Development of the concept of space in the child.* New York: International Universities Press, 1970.

Lazar, I., & Darlington, R. B. Lasting effects of early education. *Monographs of the Society for Research in Child Development,* 1982, *47,* Serial No. 195(nos. 2–3).

Lazarus, R. S. *Psychological stress and the coping response.* New York: McGraw-Hill, 1966.

Lazarus, R. S. Emotions and adaptation: Conceptual and empirical relations. In W. J. Arnold (Ed.), *Nebraska Symposium on Motivation.* Lincoln: University of Nebraska Press, 1968.

Lazarus, R. S. A cognitively oriented psychologist looks at feedback. *American Psychologist,* 1975, *30,* 553–561.

Lazarus, R. S. Thoughts on the relations between emotion and cognition. *American Psychologist,* 1982, *37,* 1019–1024.

Lazarus, R. S., Averill, J. R., & Opton, E. M., Jr. Towards a cognitive theory of emotion. In M. B. Arnold (Ed.), *Feelings and emotions.* New York: Academic Press, 1970.

Lazarus, R. S., Kanner, A. D., & Folkman, S. Emotions: A cognitive-phenomenological analysis. In R. Plutchik & H. Kellerman (Eds.), *Emotion: Theory, research, and experience.* New York: Academic Press, 1980.

Lazarus, R. S., Coyne, J. C., & Folkman, S. Cognition, emotion, and motivation: The doctoring of Humpty-Dumpty. In R. W. J. Neufeld (Ed.), *Psychological stress and psychopathology.* New York: McGraw-Hill, 1982.

Leeper, R. W. A motivational theory of emotion to replace "emotion as disorganized response." *Psychological Review,* 1948, *55,* 5–21.

Leeper, R. W. Feelings and emotions. In M. D. Arnold (Ed.), *Feelings and emotions.* New York: Academic Press, 1970.

Leiblum, S. R., & Pervin, L. A. *Principles and practice of sex therapy.* New York: Guilford, 1980.

LeShan, L. *You can fight for your life: Emotional factors in the causation of cancer.* New York: Evans, 1977.

LeShan, L. *You can fight for your life: Emotional factors in the treatment of cancer.* New York: Evans, 1980.

Lester, B. M. The organization of crying in the neonate. *Journal of Pediatric Psychology,* 1978, *3,* 122–130.

Lester, B. M., Kotelchuck, M., Spelke, E., Sellers, M. J., & Klein, R. P. Separation protest in Guatemalan infants: Cross-cultural and cognitive findings. *Developmental Psychology,* 1974, *10,* 79–85.

Levi, L. *Emotions: Their parameters and measurement.* New York: Raven, 1975.

Levine, J. Humor and psychopathology. In C. E. Izard (Ed.), *Emotions in personality and psychopathology.* New York: Plenum, 1979.

Lewis, M. The meaning of a response or why researchers in infant behavior should be Oriental metaphysicians. *Merrill-Palmer Quarterly,* 1967, *13,* 7–18.

Lewis, M. Infants' responses to facial stimuli during the first year of life. *Developmental Psychology,* 1969, *1,* 75–86.

Lewis, M. *Learning to learn in infancy: The development of competence motivation.* Paper prepared for the Select Education Subcommittee of the Education and Labor Committee of the House of Representatives, 1971.

Lewis, M. State as an infant-environment interaction: An analysis of mother-infant interaction as a function of sex. *Merrill-Palmer Quarterly,* 1972, *18,* 95–121.

Lewis, M. The cardiac response during infancy. In R. F. Thompson & M. M. Patterson (Eds.), *Methods in physiological psychology: I. Bioelectric recording techniques, Part C, Receptor and effector processes.* New York: Academic Press, 1974.

Lewis, M. The development of attention and perception in the infant and young child. In W. M. Cruickshank & D. P. Hallahan (Eds.), *Perceptual and learning disabilities in children* (Vol. 2). Syracuse, N.Y.: Syracuse University Press, 1975.

Lewis, M. (Ed.) *Origins of intelligence: Infancy and early childhood.* New York: Plenum, 1976.

Lewis, M. The infant and its caregiver: The role of contingency. *Allied Health and Behavioral Sciences,* 1978, *1,* 469–492.

Lewis, M. Situational analysis and the study of behavioral development. In L. Pervin & M. Lewis (Eds.), *Perspectives in interactional psychology.* New York: Plenum, 1978.

Lewis, M. *Issues in the study of imitation.* Paper presented at a Symposium on Imitiation in Infancy: What, When and How? at the meetings of the Society for Research in Child Development, San Francisco, March 1979.

Lewis, M. Developmental theories. In I. L. Kutash, L. B. Schlesinger, *et al.* (Eds.), *Handbook on stress and anxiety.* San Francisco: Jossey-Bass, 1980.

Lewis, M. Newton, Einstein, Piaget and the concept of self: The role of the self in the process of knowing. In L. S. Liben (Ed.), *Piaget and the foundation of knowledge.* Hillsdale, N.J.: Erlbaum, 1982. (a)

Lewis, M. The social network systems model: Toward a theory of social development. In T. Field (Ed.), *Review in human development.* New York: Wiley, 1982. (b)

Lewis, M., & Ban, P. *Stability of attachment behavior: A transformational analysis.* Paper presented at the meetings of the Society for Research in Child Development, Minneapolis, 1971.

Lewis, M., & Brooks, J. Self, other, and fear: Infants' reactions to people. In M. Lewis & L. A. Rosenblum (Eds.), *The origins of fear.* New York: Wiley, 1974.

Lewis, M., & Brooks, J. Infants' social perception: A constructivist view. In L. Cohen & P. Salapatek (Eds.), *Infant perception: From sensation to cognition* (Vol. 2). New York: Academic Press, 1975.

Lewis, M., & Brooks, J. Self-knowledge and emotional development. In M. Lewis & L. A. Rosenblum (Eds.), *The development of affect.* New York: Plenum, 1978.

Lewis, M., & Brooks-Gunn, J. *Social cognition and the acquisition of self.* New York: Plenum, 1979.

Lewis, M., & Cherry, L. Social behavior and language acquisition. In M. Lewis & L. A. Rosenblum (Eds.), *Interaction, conversation and the development of language.* New York: Wiley, 1977.

Lewis, M., & Coates, D. L. Mother-infant interaction and cognitive development in 12-week-old infants. *Infant Behavior and Development,* 1980, *3,* 95–105.

Lewis, M., & Feiring, C. The child's social network: Social object, social functions, and their relationship. In M. Lewis & L. A. Rosenblum (Eds.), *The child and its family.* New York: Plenum, 1979.

Lewis, M., & Feiring, C. Direct and indirect interactions in social relationships. In L. Lipsett (Ed.), *Advances in infancy research* (Vol. 1). New York: Ablex, 1981.

Lewis, M., & Fox, N. Predicting cognitive development from assessments in infancy. In B. Camp (Ed.), *Advances in behavioral pediatrics* (Vol. 1). Greenwich, Conn.: JAI Press, 1980.

Lewis, M., & Freedle, R. Mother-infant dyad: The cradle of meaning. In P. Pliner, L. Krames, & T. Alloway (Eds.), *Communication and affect: Language and thought.* New York: Academic Press, 1973.

Lewis, M., & Freedle, R. The mother and infant communication system: The effects of poverty. In H. McGurk (Ed.), *Ecological factors in human development.* Amsterdam: North-Holland, 1977.

Lewis, M., & Goldberg, S. The acquisition and violation of expectancy: An experimental paradigm. *Journal of Experimental Child Psychology,* 1969, *7,* 70–80. (a)

Lewis, M., & Goldberg, S. Perceptual-cognitive development in infancy: A generalized expectancy model as a function of the mother-infant interaction. *Merrill-Palmer Quarterly,* 1969, *15,* 81–100. (b)

Lewis, M., & Kreitzberg, V. S. Effects of birth order and spacing on mother-infant interactions. *Developmental Psychology,* 1979, *15,* 617–625.

Lewis, M., & Lee-Painter, S. An interactional approach to the mother-infant dyad. In M. Lewis & L. A. Rosenblum (Eds.), *The effect of the infant on its caregiver.* New York: Wiley, 1974.

Lewis, M., & Michalson, L. From emotional state to emotional expression. Paper presented at the Symposium on Human Development from the Perspective of Person and Environment Interactions, University of Stockholm, Stockholm, Sweden, June 1982. (a)

Lewis, M., & Michalson, L. The measurement of emotional state. In C. E. Izard (Ed.), *Measuring emotions in infants and children.* New York: Cambridge University Press, 1982. (b)

Lewis, M., & Michalson, L. The socialization of emotions. In T. Field & A. Fogel (Eds.), *Emotion and early interaction.* Hillsdale, N.J.: Erlbaum, 1982. (c)

Lewis, M., & Rosenblum, L. A. (Eds.). *The effect of the infant on its caregiver.* New York: Wiley, 1974. (a)

Lewis, M., & Rosenblum, L. A. (Eds.). *The origins of fear.* New York: Wiley, 1974. (b)

Lewis, M., & Rosenblum, L. A. (Eds.). *Friendship and peer relations: The origins of behavior* (Vol. 4). New York: Wiley, 1975.

Lewis, M., & Rosenblum, L. A. *Interaction, conversation, and the development of language.* New York: Wiley, 1977.

Lewis, M., & Rosenblum, L. A. (Eds.). *The development of affect.* New York: Plenum, 1978. (a)

Lewis, M., & Rosenblum, L. A. Introduction: Issues in affect development. In M. Lewis & L. A. Rosenblum (Eds.), *The development of affect.* New York: Plenum, 1978. (b)

Lewis, M., & Rosenblum, L. A. (Eds.). *The child and its family.* New York: Plenum, 1979.

Lewis, M., & Saarni, C. (Eds.). *The socialization of emotion.* New York: Plenum, in press.

Lewis, M., & Schaeffer, S. Peer behavior and mother-infant interaction in maltreated children. In M. Lewis & L. A. Rosenblum (Eds.), *The uncommon child.* New York: Plenum, 1979.

Lewis, M., & Starr, M. D. Developmental continuity. In J. D. Osofsky (Ed.), *Handbook of infant development.* New York: Wiley, 1979.

Lewis, M., & Sullivan, M. W. *Imitation in the first six months of life: Phenomenon in the eye of the beholder.* Submitted for publication, 1982.

Lewis, M., & Weinraub, M. Sex of parent × sex of child: Socioemotional development. In R. C. Friedman, R. M. Richart, & R. L. Vande Wiele (Eds.), *Sex differences in behavior.* Huntington, N.Y.: Krieger, 1974.

Lewis, M., & Weinraub, M. The father's role in the infant's social network. In M. Lamb (Ed.), *The role of the father in child development* (Vol. 1). New York: Wiley, 1976.

Lewis, M., & Weinraub, M. Origins of early sex-role development. *Sex Roles,* 1979, *5,* 135–153.

Lewis, M., & Wilson, C. D. Infant development in lower class American families. *Human Development,* 1972, *15,* 112–127.

Lewis, M., Kagan, J., Kalafat, J., & Campbell, H. The cardiac response as a correlate of attention in infants. *Child Development,* 1966, *37,* 63–71.

Lewis, M., Dodd, C., & Harwitz, M. Cardiac responsivity to tactile stimulation in waking and sleeping infants. *Perceptual and Motor Skills,* 1969, *29,* 259–269.

Lewis, M., Wilson C. D., Ban, P., & Baumel, M. H. An exploratory study of resting cardiac rate and variability from the last trimester of prenatal life through the first year of postnatal life. *Child Development,* 1970, *41,* 800–811.

Lewis, M., Weinraub, M., & Ban, P. Mothers and fathers, girls and boys: *Attachment behavior in the first two years of life.* Research Bulletin 72-60. Princeton, N.J.: Educational Testing Service, 1972.

Lewis, M., Young, G., Brooks, J., & Michalson, L. The beginning of friendship. In M. Lewis & L. A. Rosenblum (Eds.), *Friendship and peer relations.* New York: Wiley, 1975.

Lewis, M., Brooks, J., & Haviland, J. Hearts and faces: A study in the measurement of emotion. In M. Lewis & L. A. Rosenblum (Eds.), *The development of affect.* New York: Plenum, 1978.

Lewis, M., Feiring, C., & Weinraub, M. The father as a member of the child's social network. In M. Lamb (Ed.), *The role of the father in child development* (2nd ed.). New York: Wiley, 1981.

Lewis, M., Feiring, C., & Kotsonis, M. *The social network of the young child.* In M. Lewis (Ed.), *Beyond the dyad.* New York: Plenum, in press.

Lewis, M., Sullivan, M. W., & Brooks-Gunn, J. *The affective consequences of contingent stimulation in early infancy.* Unpublished manuscript, 1983.

Lewis, M., Sullivan, M., & Michalson, L. The cognitive-emotional fugue. In C. E. Izard, J. Kagan, & R. Zajonc (Eds.), *Emotions, cognition, and behavior.* New York: Cambridge University Press, in press.

Lewis, W. C., Wolman, R. N., & King, M. The development of the language of emotions: II. Intentionality in the experience of affect. *Journal of Genetic Psychology,* 1972, *120,* 303–316. (a)

Lewis, W. C., Wolman, R. N., & King, M. The development of the language of emotions: III. Type of anxiety in the experience of affect. *Journal of Genetic Psychology,* 1972, *120,* 325–342. (b)

Lindsley, D. B. Emotions and the electroencephalogram. In M. L. Reymert (Ed.), *Feelings and emotions: The Moosehart Symposium.* New York: McGraw-Hill, 1950.

Lindsley, D. B. Emotion. In S. S. Stevens (Ed.), *Handbook of experimental psychology.* New York: Wiley, 1951.

Lindsley, D. B. Psychophysiology and motivation. In M. R. Jones (Ed.), *Nebraska Symposium on Motivation.* Lincoln: University of Nebraska Press, 1957.

Lindsley, D. B. The role of nonspecific reticulo-thalamocortical systems in emotion. In P. Black (Ed.), *Physiological correlates of emotion.* New York: Academic Press, 1970.

Loftus, E. F. *Eyewitness testimony.* Cambridge, Mass.: Harvard University Press, 1979.

Lorenz, K. Z. *Evolution and modification of behavior.* Chicago: University of Chicago Press, 1965.

Lowenthal, D. Research in environmental perception and behavior: Perspectives on current problems. *Environment and Behavior,* 1972, *4,* 333–342.

Lutz, C. Situation based emotion frames and the cultural construction of emotions. In *Proceedings of the Third Annual Conference of the Cognitive Science Society.* Berkeley, California, 1981.

Maccoby, E. E., & Feldman, S. S. Mother-attachment and stranger-reactions in the third year of life. *Monographs of the Society for Research in Child Development,* 1972 (37, Serial No. 146).

Maccoby, E. E., & Jacklin, C. N. Stress, activity, and proximity seeking: Sex differences in the year-old child. *Child Development,* 1973, *44,* 34–42.

MacLean, P. D. Psychosomatic disease and the "visceral brain." *Psychosomatic Medicine,* 1949, *3,* 338–353.

MacLean, P. D. The limbic system and its hippocampal formation: Studies in animals and their possible application to man. *Journal of Neurosurgery,* 1954, *2,* 29–44.

MacLean, P. D. Phylogenesis. In P. H. Knapp (Ed.), *Expression of the emotions in man.* New York: International Universities Press, 1963.

MacLean, P. D. The limbic brain in relation to the psychoses. In P. D. Black (Ed.), *Physiological correlates of emotion.* New York: Academic Press, 1970.

Mahler, M. S., Pine, F., & Gerbman, A. *The psychological birth of the infant.* New York: Basic, 1975.

Main, M. Analysis of a peculiar form of reunion behavior seen in some day care children: Its history and sequelae in children who are home reared. In R. Webb (Ed.), *Social development in day care.* Baltimore: Johns Hopkins University Press, 1977.

Main, M. Abusive and rejecting infants. In N. Frude (Ed.), *Psychological approaches to child abuse.* Totowa, N.J.: Roman & Littlefield, 1981.

Main, M., & Weston, D. R. The independence of infant-mother and infant-father attachment relationships: Security of attachment characterizes relationships, not infants. Unpublished manuscript, 1979.

Main, M., Tomasini, L., & Tolan, W. Differences among mothers of infants judged to differ in security. *Developmental Psychology,* 1979, *15,* 472–473.

Malatesta, C. Z. Infant emotion and the vocal affect lexicon. *Motivation and Emotion,* 1981, *5*(1).

Malatesta, C. Z., & Haviland, J. M. *Age- and sex-related changes in infant affect expression.* Paper presented at the Society for Research in Child Development meetings, Boston, 1981.

Mandler, G. *Mind and emotion.* New York: Wiley, 1975.

Mandler, G. The generation of emotion: A psychological theory. In R. Plutchik & H. Kellerman (Eds.), *Emotion: Theory, research, and experience.* New York: Academic Press, 1980.

Marler, P. Sensory templates, vocal perception, and development: A comparative view. In M. Lewis & L. A. Rosenblum (Eds.), *Interaction, conversation, and the development of language.* New York: Wiley, 1977.

Marvin, R. S. An ethological-cognitive model for the attenuation of mother-child attachment behavior. In T. M. Alloway, L. Krames, & P. Pliner (Eds.), *Advances in the study of communication and affect* (Vol. 3): *The development of social attachments.* New York: Plenum, 1977.

Masangkay, Z. S., McCluskey, K. A., McIntyre, C. W., Sims-Knight, J., Vaughn, B. E., & Flavell, J. H. The early development of inferences about the visual percepts of others. *Child Development,* 1974, *45,* 357–366.

Masters, J. C., & Wellman, H. M. The study of human infant attachment: A procedural critique. *Psychological Bulletin,* 1974, *81,* 218–237.

Maudry, M., & Nekula, M. Social relations between children of the same age during the first two years of life. *Journal of Genetic Psychology,* 1939, *54,* 193–215.

McCall, R. B. Smiling and vocalization in infants as indicies of perceptual-cognitive processes. *Merrill-Palmer Quarterly,* 1972, *18,* 341–347.

McClelland, D. C. Testing for competence rather than for "intelligence." *American Psychologist,* 1973, *28,* 1–14.

McDougall, W. *An introduction to social psychology.* Boston: Luce, 1921.

Mead, G. H. *Mind, self, and society: From the standpoint of a social behaviorist.* Chicago: University of Chicago Press, 1934.

Mehrabian, A. Relationship of attitude to seated posture, orientation and distance. *Journal of Personality and Social Psychology,* 1968, *10,* 26–30.

Mehrabian, A. Significance of posture and position in the communication of attitude and status relationships. *Psychological Bulletin,* 1969, *71,* 359–372.

Mehrabian, A. *Nonverbal communication.* Chicago: Aldine, 1972.

Meltzoff, A. N., & Moore, M. K. Imitation of facial expressions and manual gestures by human neonates. *Science,* 1977, *198,* 75–78.

Messer, S. B., & Lewis, M. Social class and sex differences in the attachment and play behavior of the one-year-old infant. *Merrill-Palmer Quarterly,* 1972, *18,* 295–306.

Millenson, J. R. *Principles of behavioral analysis.* New York: Macmillan, 1967.

Mischel, W. Toward a cognitive social learning reconceptualization of personality. *Psychological Review,* 1973, *80,* 252–283.

Mischel, W. Processes in delay of gratification. In L. Berkowitz (Ed.), *Advances in experimental social psychology* (Vol. 7). New York: Academic Press, 1974.

Mischel, W. The interaction of person and situation. In D. Magnusson & N. S. Endler (Eds.), *Personality at the crossroads: Current issues in interactional psychology.* Hillsdale, N.J.: Erlbaum, 1977.

Mood, D., Johnson, J., & Shantz, C. U. *Affective and cognitive components of empathy in young children.* Paper presented at the southeast regional meeting of the Society for Research in Child Development, Chapel Hill, North Carolina, 1974.

Moore, B. Emotion, self, and others. In C. E. Izard, J. Kagan, & R. B. Zajonc (Eds.), *Emotion, cognition, and behavior*. New York: Cambridge University Press, in press.

Morgan, G. A. *Determinants of infants' reactions to strangers*. Revised version of a paper presented at the meetings of the Society for Research in Child Development, Philadelphia, April 1973.

Morgan, G. A., & Ricciuti, H. N. Infants' responses to strangers during the first year. In B. M. Foss (Ed.), *Determinants of infant behavior* (Vol. 4). New York: Wiley, 1969.

Moss, H. Sex, age, and state as determinants of mother-infant interaction. *Merrill-Palmer Quarterly*, 1967, *13*, 19–35.

Mueller, E., & Brenner, J. The growth of social interaction in a toddler playgroup: The role of peer experience. *Child Development*, 1977, *48*, 854–861.

Mueller, E., & Rich, A. Clustering and socially-directed behaviors in a playgroup of one-year-old boys. *Journal of Child Psychology and Psychiatry*, 1976, *17*, 315–322.

Mueller, E., & Vandell, D. Infant-infant interaction. In J. D. Osofsky (Ed.), *Handbook of infant development*. New York: Wiley, 1979.

Müller, E., Hollien, H., & Murry, T. Perceptual responses to infant crying: Identification of cry types. *Journal of Child Language*, 1974, *1*, 89–95.

Murchison, C. (Ed.), *A handbook of child psychology* (2nd ed., rev.) Worcester, Mass.: Clark University Press, 1933.

Murray, H. A. *Explorations in personality*. New York: Oxford University Press, 1938.

Mussen, P. H. (Ed.). *Carmichael's manual of child psychology* (3rd ed., 2 vols.). New York: Wiley, 1970.

Mussen, P. H., Conger, J. J., & Kagan, J. *Child development and personality* (5th ed.). New York: Harper & Row, 1979.

Neisser, U. *Cognitive psychology*. New York: Appleton-Century-Crofts, 1967.

Newman, E. B., Perkins, F. T., & Wheeler, R. H. Cannon's theory of emotion: A critique. *Psychological Review*, 1930, *37*, 305–326.

Norman, D. A., & Rumelhart, D. F. *Explorations in cognition*. San Francisco: Freeman, 1975.

Nowlis, V. Research with the mood adjective checklist. In S. S. Tomkins & C. E. Izard (Eds.), *Affect, cognition, and personality*. New York: Springer, 1965.

Nowlis, V. Mood: Behavior and experience. In M. B. Arnold (Ed.), *Feelings and emotions*. New York: Academic Press, 1970.

Nunnally, J. C. *Psychometric theory*. New York: McGraw-Hill, 1967.

Nuttall, R. L., & Fozard, T. A. Age, socioeconomic status and human abilities. *Aging and Human Development*, 1970, *1*, 161–169.

Obrist, P. A., Webb, R. A., Stutter, J. R., & Howard, J. L. Cardiac deceleration and reaction time: An evaluation of two hypotheses. *Psychophysiology*, 1970, *6*, 695–706.

Olds, J. Physiological mechanisms of reward. In M. R. Jones (Ed.), *Nebraska Symposium on Motivation*. Lincoln: University of Nebraska Press, 1955.

Olds, J. Hypothalamic substrates of reward. *Physiological Review*, 1962, *42*, 554–604.

Olds, M. E., & Fobes, J. L. The central basis of motivation: Intracranial self-stimulation studies. *Annual Review of Psychology*, 1981, *32*, 523–576.

Orne, M. T. Communication by the total experimental situation: Why it is important, how it is evaluated, and its significance for the ecological validity of findings. In P. Pliner, L. Krames, & T. Alloway (Eds.), *Communication and affect: Language and thought*. New York: Academic Press, 1973.

Osofsky, J. D. *Handbook of infant development*. New York: Wiley, 1979.

Oster, H. Facial expression and affect development. In M. Lewis & L. A. Rosenblum (Eds.), *The development of affect*. New York: Plenum, 1978.

Oster, H. "Recognition" of emotional expression in infancy? In M. E. Lamb & L. R. Sherrod (Eds.), *Infant social cognition: Empirical and theoretical considerations.* Hillsdale, N.J.: Erlbaum, 1981.

Oster, H., & Ekman, P. Facial behavior in child development. In A. Collins (Ed.), *Minnesota symposia on child psychology* (Vol. 11). Hillsdale, N.J.: Erlbaum, 1978.

Pannabecker, B. J., Emde, R. N., Johnson, W., Stenberg, C., & Davis, M. *Maternal perceptions of infant emotions from birth to 18 months: A preliminary report.* Paper presented at the International Conference of Infant Studies, New Haven, Conn., April 1980.

Papez, J. W. A proposed mechanism of emotion. *Archives of Neurological Psychiatry,* 1937, *38,* 725–743.

Papoušek, H., & Papoušek, M. Mirror-images and self-recognition in young human infants: I. A new method of experimental analysis. *Developmental Psychobiology,* 1974, *7,* 149–157.

Paradise, E. B., & Curcio, F. Relationship of cognitive and affective behaviors to fear of strangers in male infants. *Developmental Psychology,* 1974, *10,* 476–483.

Parke, R. D. Social cues, social control and ecological validity. *Merrill-Palmer Quarterly,* 1976, *22,* 111–118.

Parke, R. D. Interactional designs. In R. B. Cairns (Ed.), *The analysis of social interactions: Methods, issues, and illustrations.* Hillsdale, N.J.: Erlbaum, 1979. (a)

Parke, R. D. Perspectives on father-infant interaction. In J. D. Osofsky (Ed.), *Handbook of infant development.* New York: Wiley, 1979. (b)

Parke, R. D., & O'Leary, S. E. Father-mother-infant interaction in the newborn period: Some findings, some observations, and some unresolved issues. In K. Riegel & J. Meachem (Eds.), *The developing individual in a changing world, Vol. 2: Social and environmental issues.* The Hague: Mouton, 1976.

Patterson, E. A. A qualitative and quantitative study of the emotion of surprise. *Psychological Monographs,* 1930, *181,* 85–108.

Pedersen, F. A., & Bell, R. Q. Sex differences in preschool children without histories of complications of pregnancy and delivery. *Developmental Psychology,* 1970, *3,* 10–15.

Pedersen, F. A., & Robson, K. S. Father participation in infancy. *American Journal of Orthopsychiatry,* 1969, *39,* 466–472.

Pervin, L. A. Performance and satisfaction as a function of individual-environment fit. *Psychological Bulletin,* 1968, *69,* 56–68.

Pervin, L. A. Definitions, measurements, and classifications of stimuli, situations, and environments. *Research Bulletin 75-23.* Princeton, N.J.: Educational Testing Service, 1975.

Pervin, L. A. *Personality: Theory, assessment, and research* (3rd ed.). New York, Wiley, 1980.

Piaget, J. *Play, dreams and imitation in childhood.* New York: Norton, 1951.

Piaget, J. *The construction of reality in the child.* New York: Basic Books, 1954.

Piaget, J., & Inhelder, B. *The child's conception of space.* London: Routledge & Kegan Paul, 1956.

Plutchik, R. *The emotions: Facts, theories and a new model.* New York: Random House, 1962.

Plutchik, R. Emotions, evolution and adaptive processes. In M. Arnold (Ed.), *Feelings and emotions.* New York: Academic Press, 1970.

Plutchik, R. *Emotion: A psychoevolutionary synthesis.* New York: Harper & Row, 1980. (a)

Plutchik, R. A general psychoevolutionary theory of emotion. In R. Plutchik & H. Kellerman (Eds.), *Emotion: Theory, research, and experience*. New York: Academic Press, 1980. (b)

Plutchik, R., & Kellerman, H. (Eds.). *Emotion: Theory, research, and experience* Vol. 1: *Theories of emotion*. New York: Academic Press, 1980.

Portnoy, F., & Simmons, C. Day care and attachment. *Child Development*, 1978, 49, 239–242.

Pribram, K. H. Emotion: Steps toward a neuropsychological theory. In D. C. Glass (Ed.), *Neurophysiology and emotions*. New York: Rockefeller University Press, 1967. (a)

Pribram, K. H. The new neurology and the biology of emotion: A structural approach. *American Psychologist*, 1967, 22, 830–838. (b)

Pribram, K. H. Feelings as monitors. In M. B. Arnold (Ed.), *Feelings and emotions*. New York: Academic Press, 1970.

Pribram, K. H. *Language of the brain: Experimental paradoxes and principles in neuropsychology*. Englewood Cliffs, N.J.: Prentice-Hall, 1971.

Pribram, K. H. Peptides and protocritic processes. In L. H. Miller, C. A. Sandman, & A. J. Kastin (Eds.), *Neuropeptide influences on the brain and behavior*. New York: Raven, 1977.

Pribram, K. H. The biology of emotions and other feelings. In R. Plutchik & H. Kellerman (Eds.), *Emotion: Theory, research and experience*. New York: Academic Press, 1980.

Prideaux, E. The psychogalvanic reflex: A review. *Brain*, 1920, 43, 50–73.

Rado, S. *Adaptational psychodynamics: Motivation and control*. New York: Science House, 1969.

Rapaport, D. On the psychoanalytic theory of affects. *International Journal of Psychoanalysis*, 1953, 34, 177–198.

Rapaport, D. On the psychoanalytic theory of motivation. In M. K. Jones (Ed.), *Nebraska symposium on motivation*. Lincoln: University of Nebraska Press, 1960.

Raph, J. B., Thomas, A., Chess, S., & Korn, S. J. The influence of nursery school on social interactions. *American Journal of Orthopsychiatry*, 1964, 38, 144–152.

Ramsay, D. S., & Campos, J. J. The onset of representation and entry into stage 6 of object permanence development. *Developmental Psychology*, 1978, 14, 79–86.

Rebelsky, F., & Hanks, C. Fathers' verbal interaction with infants in the first three months of life. *Child Development*, 1971, 42, 63–68.

Reeves, J. W. *Body and mind in Western thought*. Harmondsworth: Penguin, 1958.

Reich, W. *Character analysis* (3rd ed.). New York: Noonday, 1949.

Rheingold, H. L., & Eckerman, C. O. The infants' free entry into a new environment. *Journal of Experimental Child Psychology*, 1969, 8, 271–283.

Rheingold, H. L., & Eckerman, C. O. The infant separates himself from his mother. *Science*, 1970, 168, 78–83.

Rheingold, H. L., & Eckerman, C. J. Fear of the stranger: A critical review. In H. W. Reese (Ed.), *Advances in child development and behavior* (Vol. 8). New York: Academic Press, 1973.

Ricciuti, H. N. Fear and the development of social attachments in the first year of life. In M. Lewis & L. A. Rosenblum (Eds.), *The origins of fear*. New York: Wiley, 1974.

Ricciuti, H. N., & Poresky, R. H. Emotional behavior and development in the first year of life: An analysis of arousal, approach-withdrawal, and affective responses. In A. D. Pick (Ed.), *Minnesota Symposium on Child Psychology* (Vol. 6). Minneapolis: University of Minnesota Press, 1972.

Riegel, K., & Meacham, J. (Eds.). *The developing individual in a changing world, Vol. 2: Social and environmental issues*. The Hague: Mouton, 1976.

Robson, K. S., Pedersen, F. A., & Moss, H. A. Developmental observations of diadic gazing in relation to the fear of strangers and social approach behavior. *Child Development*, 1969, *40*, 619–627.

Roopnarine, J. L., & Lamb, M. E. The effect of day care on attachment and exploratory behavior in a strange situation. *Merrill-Palmer Quarterly*, 1978, *24*, 85–95.

Rosenthal, R. Covert communication in the psychological experiment. *Psychological Bulletin*, 1967, *67*, 356–367.

Rosenthal, M. K. Attachment and mother-infant interaction: Some research impasse and a suggested change in orientation. *Journal of Child Psychology and Psychiatry*, 1973, *14*, 201–207.

Ross, H. S. The influence of novelty and complexity on exploratory behavior in 12-month-old infants. *Journal of Experimental Child Psychology*, 1974, *17*, 436–451.

Ross, H. S. The effects of increasing familiarity on infants' reactions to adult strangers. *Journal of Experimental Child Psychology*, 1975, *20*, 226–239.

Ross, H. S., & Goldman, B. D. Infants' sociability toward strangers. *Child Development*, 1977, *48*, 638–642.

Ross, H. S., Rheingold, H. L., & Eckerman, C. O. Approach and exploration of a novel alternative by 12-month-old infants. *Journal of Experimental Child Psychology*, 1972, *13*, 85–93.

Rothbart, M. K. Laughter in young children. *Psychological Bulletin*, 1973, *80*, 247–256.

Rotter, J. B. The role of the psychological situation in determining the direction of human behavior. In M. R. Jones (Ed.), *Nebraska symposium on motivation*. Lincoln: University of Nebraska Press, 1955.

Rotter, J. B. Generalized expectancies for internal versus external control of reinforcement. *Psychological Monographs*, 1966, *80*, No. 1 (Whole No. 609).

Royce, J. R., & Diamond, S. R. A multifactor-system dynamics theory of emotion: Cognitive-affective interaction. *Motivation and Emotion*, 1980, *4*, 263–298.

Rubenstein, J. Maternal attentiveness and subsequent exploratory behavior. *Child Development*, 1967, *38*, 1089–1100.

Rubin, J. Z., Provenzano, F. J., & Luria, Z. The eye of the beholder: Parents' views on sex of newborns. *American Journal of Orthopsychiatry*, 1974, *44*, 512–519.

Ryan, T. J., & Watson, P. Frustrative nonreward theory applied to children's behavior. *Psychological Bulletin*, 1968, *69*, 111–125.

Saarni, C. Cognitive and communicative features of emotional experience, or do you show what you think you feel? In M. Lewis & L. A. Rosenblum (Eds.), *The development of affect*. New York: Plenum, 1978.

Saarni, C. Children's understanding of display rules for expressive behavior. *Developmental Psychology*, 1979, *15*, 424–429. (a)

Saarni, C. When not to show what you think you feel: Children's understanding of relations between emotional experience and expressive behavior. Paper presented at the meetings of the Society for Research in Child Development, San Francisco, March 1979. (b)

Saarni, C. Observing children's use of display rules: Age and sex differences. Paper presented at the meetings of the American Psychological Association, Montreal, September 1980.

Saarni, C. Emotional experience and regulation of expressive behavior. Paper presented at the meetings of the Society for Research in Child Development, Boston, April 1981.

Saarni, C. Social and affective functions of nonverbal behavior: Developmental concerns. In R. Feldman (Ed.), *Development of nonverbal behavior*. New York: Springer Verlag, 1982.

Sackett, G. P. The lag sequential analysis of contingency and cyclicity in behavioral interaction research. In J. D. Osofsky (Ed.), *Handbook of infant development*. New York: Wiley, 1979.

Sagi, A., & Hoffman, M. L. Empathic distress in newborns. *Developmental Psychology*, 1976, *12*, 175–176.

Salapatek, P. *The visual investigation of geometric patterns by the one- and two-month-old infant*. Paper presented at the meetings of the American Association for the Advancement of Science, Boston, December 1969.

Salzen, E. A. Visual stimuli eliciting the smiling response in the human infant. *Journal of Genetic Psychology*, 1963, *102*, 51–54.

Sameroff, A. J. (Ed.). Organization and stability of newborn behavior: A commentary on the Brazelton Neonatal Behavior Assessment Scale. *Monographs of the Society for Research in Child Development*, 1978, *43* (Whole nos. 5-6).

Sander, L. W. Infant and caretaking environment: Investigation and conceptualization of adaptive behavior in a system of increasing complexity. In E. J. Anthony (Ed.), *The child psychiatrist as investigator*. New York: Plenum, 1977.

Sarason, I. G. *Test anxiety: Theory, research, and applications*. Hillsdale, N.J.: Erlbaum, 1980.

Scarr, S. Testing for children: Assessment and the many determinants of intellectual competence. *American Psychologist*, 1981, *36*, 1159–1166.

Scarr, S., & Salapatek, P. Patterns of fear development during infancy. *Merrill-Palmer Quarterly*, 1970, *16*, 53–90.

Schachter, S. *The psychology of affiliation*. Stanford, Calif.: Stanford University Press, 1959.

Schachter, S. The interaction of cognitive and physiological determinants of emotional state. In L. Berkowitz (Ed.), *Advances in experimental social psychology* (Vol. 1). New York: Academic Press, 1964.

Schachter, S., & Singer, J. E. Cognitive, social, and physiological determinants of emotional state. *Psychological Review*, 1962, *69*, 379–399.

Schaffer, H. R. The onset of fear of strangers and the incongruity hypothesis. *Journal of Child Psychology and Psychiatry*, 1966, *7*, 95–106.

Schaffer, H. R. Cognitive components of the infant's response to strangers. In M. Lewis & L. A. Rosenblum (Eds.), *The origins of fear*. New York: Wiley, 1974.

Schaffer, H. R., & Emerson, P. E. The development of social attachments in infancy. *Monographs of the Society for Research in Child Development*, 1964 (29, Serial No. 94).

Schaffer, H. R., Greenwood, A., & Parry, M. H. The onset of wariness. *Child Development*, 1972, *43*, 165–175.

Scheflen, A. E. The significance of posture in communication systems. *Psychiatry*, 1964, *27*, 316–321.

Scheflen, A. E. *Body language and the social order*. Englewood Cliffs, N.J.: Prentice-Hall, 1972.

Scheflen, A. E. *Human territories*. Englewood Cliffs, N.J.: Prentice-Hall, 1975.

Scherer, K. R. Nonlinguistic vocal indicators of emotion and psychopathology. In C. E. Izard (Ed.), *Emotions in personality and psychopathology*. New York: Plenum, 1979.

Scherer, K. R. The assessment of vocal expression in infants and children. In C. E. Izard (Ed.), *Measuring emotions in infants and children*. New York: Cambridge University Press, 1982.

Scherer, K. R., Koivumaki, J., & Rosenthal, R. Minimal cues in the vocal communication of affect: Judging emotions from content-masked speech. *Journal of Psycholinguistic Research*, 1972, *1*, 269–285.

Schlosberg, H. The description of facial expression in terms of two dimensions. *Journal of Experimental Psychology*, 1952, *44*, 229–237.

Schlosberg, H. Three dimensions of emotion. *Psychological Review*, 1954, *61*, 81–88.

Schneirla, T. C. An evolutionary and developmental theory of biphasic processes underlying approach and withdrawal. In M. R. Jones (Ed.), *Nebraska symposium on motivation*. Lincoln: University of Nebraska Press, 1959.

Schwartz, A., Campos, J., & Baisel, E. The visual cliff: Cardiac and behavioral correlates on the deep and shallow sides at five and nine months of age. *Journal of Experimental Child Psychology*, 1973, *15*, 86–99.

Schwartz, G. E. Biofeedback, self-regulation, and the patterning of physiological processes. *American Scientist*, 1975, *63*, 314–324.

Schwartz, G. E. Psychophysiological patterning and emotion revisited: A systems perspective. In C. E. Izard (Ed.), *Measuring emotions in infants and children*. New York: Cambridge University Press, 1982.

Schwartz, G. E., & Weinberger, D. A. Patterns of emotional responses to affective situations: Relations among happiness, sadness, anger, fear, depression, and anxiety. *Motivation and Emotion*, 1980, *4*, 175–191.

Schwartz, G. E., Fair, P. L., Greenberg, P. G., Friedman, J. J., & Klerman, G. L. Facial electromyography in the assessment of emotion. *Psychophysiology*, 1974, *11*, 237.

Schwartz, G. E., Fair, P. L., Salt, P., Mandel, M. R., & Klerman, G. L. Facial muscle patterning to affective imagery in depressed and nondepressed subjects. *Science*, 1976, *192*, 489–491. (a)

Schwartz, G. E., Fair, P. L., Salt, P., Mandel, M. R., & Klerman, G. L. Facial expression: An electromyographic study. *Psychosomatic Medicine*, 1976, *38*, 337–347. (b)

Schwartz, G. E., Ahern, G. L., & Brown, S. L. Lateralized facial muscle response to positive and negative emotional stimuli. *Psychophysiology*, 1979, *16*, 561–571.

Schwartz, G. E., Brown, S. L., & Ahern, G. L. Facial muscle patterning and subjective experience during affective imagery: Sex differences. *Psychophysiology*, 1980, *17*, 75–82.

Schwarz, J. C., Strickland, R. G., & Krolick, G. Infant day care: Behavioral effects at preschool age. *Developmental Psychology*, 1974, *10*, 502–506.

Scott, J. P. The process of primary socialization in canine and human infants. *Monographs of the Society for Research in Child Development*, 1963, *28*(1, Serial No. 85).

Seavey, C. A., Katz, P. A., & Zalk, S. R. Baby X: The effect of gender label on adult responses to infants. *Sex Roles*, 1975, *2*, 103–109.

Seligman, M. E. P. *Helplessness: On depression, development, and death*. San Francisco: Freeman, 1975.

Seligman, M. E. P., & Maier, S. F. Failure to escape traumatic shock. *Journal of Experimental Psychology*, 1967, *74*, 1–9.

Sells, S. B. (Ed.). *Stimulus determinants of behavior*. New York: Ronald, 1963.

Serafica, F. C. The development of attachment behaviors: An organismic-developmental perspective. *Human Development*, 1978, *21*, 119–140.

Serbin, L. A., O'Leary, K. D., Kent, R. N., & Tonick, L. J. A comparison of teacher response to the pre-academic and problem behavior of boys and girls. *Child Development*, 1973, *44*, 796–804.

Seward, J. P., & Seward, G. H. The effect of repetition on reaction to electric shock. *New York Archives of Psychology*, 1934, *168*, 103.

Shaffran, R., & Décarie, T. Short-term stability of infants' responses to strangers. Paper presented at the meetings of the Society for Research in Child Development, Philadelphia, March 1973.

Shantz, C. U. The development of social cognition. In E. M. Hetherington (Ed.), *Review of child development research*. Chicago: University of Chicago Press, 1975.

Sherif, M. Group influences upon the formation of norms and attitudes. In E. M. Maccoby, T. Newcomb, & E. Hartley (Eds.), *Readings in social psychology*. New York: Holt, Rinehart & Winston, 1958.

Sherman, M. The ability of observers to judge the emotional characteristics of the crying of infants, and of the voice of an adult. *Journal of Comparative Psychology*, 1927, 7, 335–351. (a)

Sherman, M. The differentiation of emotional responses in infants: I. Judgments of emotional responses from motion picture views and from actual observation. *Journal of Comparative Psychology*, 1927, 7, 265–285. (b)

Shirley, M. M. *The first two years: A study of twenty-five babies, Vol. 2: Intellectual development*. Minneapolis: University of Minnesota Press, 1933.

Shock, N. W., & Coombs, C. H. Changes in skin resistance and affective tone. *American Journal of Psychology*, 1937, 49, 611–620.

Shott, S. Emotion and social life. *American Journal of Sociology*, 1979, 84, 1317–1334.

Shultz, T. R., & Zigler, E. Emotional concomitants of visual mastery in infants: The effects of stimulus movement on smiling and vocalizing. *Journal of Experimental Child Psychology*, 1970, 10, 390–402.

Siegel, S. *Nonparametric statistics for the behavioral sciences*. New York: McGraw-Hill, 1956.

Siminov, P. V. Studies of emotional behavior of humans and animals by Soviet physiologists. *Annals of the New York Academy of Sciences*, 1969, 159, 3.

Siminov, P. V. The information theory of emotion. In M. B. Arnold (Ed.), *Feelings and emotions*. New York: Academic Press, 1970.

Simms, T. M. Pupillary response of male and female subjects to pupillary difference in male and female pictures. *Perception and Psychophysics*, 1967, 2, 553–555.

Skarin, K. Cognitive and contextual determinants of stranger fear in six-and eleven-month-old infants. *Child Development*, 1977, 48, 537–544.

Skinner, B. F. *The behavior of organisms*. New York: Appleton-Century-Crofts, 1938.

Skinner, B. F. *Science and human behavior*. New York: Macmillan, 1953.

Solomon, R. L., & Corbitt, J. D. An opponent-process theory of motivation: I. Temporal dynamics of affect. *Psychological Review*, 1974, 81, 119–146.

Spelke, E., Zelazo, P. R., Kagan, J., & Kotelchuck, M. Father interaction and separation protest. *Developmental Psychology*, 1973, 9, 89–90.

Spitz, R. A. *The first year of life*. New York: International Universities Press, 1965.

Spitz, R. A., & Wolf, K. M. The smiling response: A contribution to the ontogenesis of social relations. *Genetic Psychology Monographs*, 1946, 34, 57–125.

Spitz, R. A., Emde, R. N., & Metcalf, D. R. Further prototypes of ego formation: A working paper from a research project on early development. *The Psychoanalytic Study of the Child*, 1970, 25, 417–441.

Sroufe, L. A. The developmental significance of the infant's wariness of strangers. *Child Development*, 1977, 48, 731–746.

Sroufe, L. A. The coherence of individual development: Early care, attachment and subsequent developmental issues. *American Psychologist*, 1979, 34, 834–841. (a)

Sroufe, L. A. Socioemotional development. In J. D. Osofsky (Ed.), *Handbook of infant development*. New York: Wiley, 1979. (b)

Sroufe, L. A., & Ward, M. J. Seductive behavior of mothers of toddlers: Occurrence, correlates, and family origins. *Child Development*, 1980, 51, 1222–1229.

Sroufe, L. A., & Waters, E. The ontogenesis of smiling and laughter: A perspective on the organization of development in infancy. *Psychological Review*, 1976, *83*, 173–189.

Sroufe, L. A., & Waters, E. Heart rate as a convergent measure in clinical and developmental research. *Merrill-Palmer Quarterly*, 1977, *23*, 3–25.

Sroufe, L. A., & Wunsch, J. P. The development of laughter in the first year of life. *Child Development*, 1972, *43*, 1326–1344.

Sroufe, L. A., Waters, E., & Matas, L. Contextual determinants of infant affective response. In M. Lewis & L. A. Rosenblum (Eds.), *The origins of fear*. New York: Wiley, 1974.

Stass, J. W., & Willis, F. N. Eye contact, pupil dilation, and personal preference. *Psychonomic Science*, 1967, *7*, 375–376.

Stayton, D. J., Ainsworth, M. D. S., & Main, M. B. The development of separation behavior in the first year of life: Protest, following, and greeting. *Developmental Psychology*, 1973, *9*, 213–225.

Steele, W., & Lewis, M. A longitudinal study of the cardiac response during a problem-solving task and its relationship to general cognitive function. *Psychonomic Science*, 1968, *11*, 275–276.

Stein, L. Reward transmitters: Catecholamines and opiod peptides. In M. A. Lipton, A. DiMascio, & K. R. Killan (Eds.), *Psychopharmacology: A generation of progress*. New York: Raven, 1978.

Sternbach, R. A. *Principles of psychophysiology*. New York: Academic Press, 1966.

Strongman, K. T. *The psychology of emotion* (2nd ed.). New York: Wiley, 1978.

Sullivan, H. S. *The interpersonal theory of psychiatry*. New York: Norton, 1953.

Sutton-Smith, B., & Rosenberg, B. G. *The sibling*. New York: Holt, Rinehart & Winston, 1970.

Tagiuri, R. Person perception. In G. Lindzey & E. Aronson (Eds.), *The handbook of social psychology*. Reading, Mass.: Addison-Wesley, 1969.

Takahashi, M. Smiling responses in newborn infants: Relations to arousal level, spontaneous movements, and the tactile stimulus. *Japanese Journal of Psychology*, 1973, *44*, 46–50.

Tautermannová, M. Smiling in infants. *Child Development*, 1973, *44*, 701–704.

Taylor, C., Smith, W. R., & Ghiselin, B. The creative and other contributions of one sample of research scientists. In C. W. Taylor & F. Barron (Eds.), *Scientific creativity: Its recognition and development*. New York: Wiley, 1963.

Tennes, K. H., & Lampl, E. E. Stranger and separation anxiety in infancy. *Journal of Nervous and Mental Diseases*, 1964, *139*, 247–254.

Terman, L. M., & Oden, M. H. *The gifted child grows up*. Stanford, Calif.: Stanford University Press, 1947.

Thoman, E. B., Leiderman, P. H., & Olson, J. P. Neonate-mother interaction during breast-feeding. *Developmental Psychology*, 1972, *6*, 110–118.

Thomas, A., & Chess, S. *Temperament and development*. New York: Bruner/Mazel, 1977.

Thomas, A., Chess, S., Birch, H. G., Hertzig, M., & Korn, S. *Behavioral individuality in early childhood*. New York: New York University Press, 1963.

Thomas, A., Chess, S., & Birch, H. G. *Temperament and behavior disorders in children*. New York: New York University, 1968.

Thomas, A., Chess, S., & Birch, H. G. The origin of personality. *Scientific American*, 1970, *223*, 102–109.

Thompson, J. Development of facial expression in blind and seeing children. *Archives of Psychology*, 1941, *264*, 1–47.

Thorndike, R. L., & Hagen, E. *10,000 careers*. New York: Wiley, 1959.

Thurman, S. K. A review of contingency in infancy: Avenues for the handicapped infant. Unpublished manuscript, Institute for the Study of Exceptional Children, Princeton, N.J., 1978.

Tomkins, S. S. Affect, imagery, consciousness, Vol. 1: The positive affects. New York: Springer, 1962.

Tomkins, S. S. Affect, imagery, consciousness, Vol. 2: The negative affects. New York: Springer, 1963.

Tomkins, S. S. Affect as the primary motivational system. In M. Arnold (Ed.), Feelings and emotions. New York: Academic Press, 1970.

Tomkins, S. S. Affect as amplification: Some modifications in theory. In R. Plutchik & H. Kellerman (Eds.), Emotion: Theory, research, and experience. New York: Academic Press, 1980.

Tomkins, S. S. The quest for primary motives: Biography and autobiography of an idea. Journal of Personality and Social Psychology, 1981, 41, 306–329.

Trause, M. A. Stranger responses: Effects of familiarity, stranger's approach, and sex of infant. Child Development, 1977, 48, 1657–1661.

Tulkin, S. R., & Kagan, J. Mother-infant interaction in the first year of life. Child Development, 1972, 43, 31–41.

Tversky, A., & Kahneman, D. Causal schemes in judgement under uncertainty. Science, 1974, 184, 1124–1131.

Uzgiris, I. C., & Hunt, J. McV. Toward ordinal scales of psychological development in infancy. Urbana, Ill.: University of Illinois Press, 1975.

Vaillant, G. Adaptation to life. Boston: Little, Brown, 1977.

Valentine, C. W. The innate bases of fear. Journal of Genetic Psychology, 1930, 37, 394–420.

Van Lieshout, C. F. M. Young children's reactions to barriers placed by their mothers. Child Development, 1975, 46, 879–886.

Vincze, M. The social contacts of infants and young children reared together. Early Child Development and Care, 1971, 1, 99–109.

Waite, L. H., & Lewis, M. Early imitation with several models: An example of socio-affective development. Paper presented at the biennial meeting of the Society for Research in Child Development, San Francisco, March 1979.

Ward, J. H., Jr. & Hook, M. E. Application of an hierarchical grouping procedure to a problem of grouping profiles. Educational and Psychological Measurement, 1963, 23, 69–81.

Washburn, R. W. A study of the smiling and laughing of infants in the first year of life. Genetic Psychology Monographs, 1929, 6, 396–537.

Waters, E. The reliability and stability of individual differences in infant-mother attachment. Child Development, 1978, 49, 483–494.

Waters, E., Matas, L., & Sroufe, L. A. Infants' reactions to an approaching stranger: Description, validation and functional significance of wariness. Child Development, 1975, 46, 348–356.

Waters, E., Wippman, J., & Sroufe, L. A. Attachment, positive affect, and competence in the peer group: Two studies in construct validation. Child Development, 1979, 50, 821–829.

Watson, J. B. Psychology from the standpoint of a behaviorist. Philadelphia: Lippincott, 1919 (1st ed.), 1924 (2nd ed.), 1929 (3rd ed.).

Watson, J. B., & Rayner, R. Conditioned emotional reactions. Journal of Experimental Psychology, 1920, 3, 1–14.

Watson, J. S. Cognitive-perceptual development in infancy: Settings for the seventies. *Merrill-Palmer Quarterly*, 1971, *17*, 139–152.

Weinraub, M., & Lewis, M. The determinants of children's responses to separation. *Monographs of the Society for Research in Child Development*, 1977, *42*(4, Serial No. 172).

Weinraub, M., & Putney, E. The effects of height on infants' social responses to unfamiliar persons. *Child Development*, 1978, *49*, 598–603.

Weinraub, M., Brooks, J., & Lewis, M. The social network: A reconsideration of the concept of attachment. *Human Development*, 1977, *20*, 31–47.

Weitz, S. *Nonverbal communication: Readings with commentary*. New York: Oxford University Press, 1974.

Weitz, S. *Nonverbal communication: Readings with commentary* (2nd ed.). New York: Oxford University Press, 1979.

Wenar, C. Competence at one. *Merrill-Palmer Quarterly*, 1964, *10*, 329–342.

Wenar, C. Executive competence and spontaneous social behavior in one-year-olds. *Child Development*, 1972, *43*, 256–260.

Wenar, C. Executive competence in toddlers: A prospective, observational study. *Genetic Psychology Monographs*, 1976, *93*, 189–285.

Wenar, C. Social initiative in toddlers. *Journal of Genetic Psychology*, 1978, *132*, 213–246.

Wenger, M. A. Emotion as visceral action: An extension of Lange's theory. *Feelings and emotions: The Moosehart Symposium*. New York: McGraw-Hill, 1950.

Wenger, M. A., Jones, F. N., & Jones, M. H. *Physiological psychology*. New York: Holt, 1956.

Wessman, A. E. Moods: Their personal dynamics and significance. In C. E. Izard (Ed.), *Emotions in personality and psychopathology*. New York: Plenum, 1979.

Wessman, A. E., & Ricks, D. F. *Mood and personality*. New York: Holt, Rinehart & Winston, 1966.

Wheatley, M. D. The hypothalamus and effective behavior in cats: A study of the effects of experimental lesions, with anatomic correlations. *Archives of Neurological Psychiatry*, 1944, *52*, 296–316.

White, B. L. Critical influences in the origins of competence. *Merrill-Palmer Quarterly*, 1975, *21*, 243–266.

White, B. L. *Experience and environment—Major influences on the development of young children* (Vol. 2). Englewood Cliffs, N.J.: Prentice-Hall, 1978.

White, B. L., & Watts, J. C. *Experience and environment: Major influences on the development of the young child* (Vol. 1). Englewood Cliffs, N.J.: Prentice-Hall, 1973.

White, R. W. Motivation reconsidered: The concept of competence. *Psychological Review*, 1959, *66*, 297–333.

Willemsen, E., Flaherty, D., Heaton, C., & Ritchey, G. Attachment behavior of one-year-olds as a function of mother versus father, sex of child, session and toys. *Genetic Psychology Monographs*, 1974, *90*, 305–324.

Wilson, E. O. *Sociobiology*. Cambridge, Mass.: Belknap Press, Harvard University Press, 1975.

Winer, B. J. *Statistical principles in experimental design* (2nd ed.). New York: McGraw-Hill, 1971.

Wolf, S., & Wolff, H. G. *Human gastric function*. New York: Oxford University Press, 1947.

Wolff, P. H. Observations on the early development of smiling. In B. M. Foss (Ed.), *Determinants of infant behavior* (Vol. 2). New York: Wiley, 1963.

Wolff, P. H. The natural history of crying and other vocalizations in early infancy. In B. M. Foss (Ed.), *Determinants of infant behavior* (Vol. 4). New York: Wiley, 1969.

Wolff, P. H. Biological variations and cultural diversity: An exploratory study. In P. H. Leiderman, S. R. Tulkin, & A. Rosenfeld (Eds.), *Culture and infancy: Variations in the human experience.* New York: Academic Press, 1977.

Wolman, R. N., Lewis, W. C., & King, M. The development of the language of emotions: Conditions of emotional arousal. *Child Development,* 1971, *42,* 1288–1293.

Wolman, R. N., Lewis, W. C., & King, M. The development of the language of emotions: I. Theoretical and methodological introduction. *Journal of Genetic Psychology,* 1972, *120,* 167–176. (a)

Wolman, R. N., Lewis, W. C., & King, M. The development of the language of emotions: IV. Bodily referents and the experience of affect. *Journal of Genetic Psychology,* 1972, *121,* 65–81. (b)

Wundt, W. *Outlines of psychology.* New York: Stechert, 1897.

Yarrow, L. J. Maternal deprivation: Toward an empirical and conceptual re-evaluation. *Psychological Bulletin,* 1961, *58,* 459–490.

Yarrow, L. J. The development of focused relationships during infancy. In J. Hellmuth (Ed.), *Exceptional infant* (Vol. 1). Seattle, Wash.: Special Child Publications, 1967.

Yarrow, L. J. Emotional development. *American Psychologist,* 1979, *34,* 951–957.

Yarrow, L. J., & Messer, S. B. Motivation and cognition in infancy. In M. Lewis (Ed.), *Origins of intelligence* (2nd ed.). New York: Plenum, in press.

Yarrow, L. J., & Pedersen, F. A. The interplay between cognition and motivation in infancy. In M. Lewis (Ed.), *Origins of intelligence.* New York: Plenum, 1976.

Yarrow, L. J., Rubenstein, J. L., & Pedersen, F. A. *Infant and environment: Early cognitive and motivational development.* New York: Wiley, 1975.

Yarrow, L. J., Rubenstein, J. L., Pedersen, F. A., & Jankowski, J. J. Dimensions of early stimulation and their different effects on infant development. *Merrill-Palmer Quarterly,* 1972, *18,* 205–218.

Young, G., & Lewis, M. Effects of familiarity and maternal attention on infant peer relations. *Merrill-Palmer Quarterly,* 1979, *24,* 105–119.

Young, G., & Décarie, T. G. An ethology-based catalogue of facial/vocal behaviors in infancy. *Animal Behavior,* 1977, *25,* 95–107.

Young, P. T. *Motivation and emotion.* New York: Wiley, 1961.

Young, P. T. *Emotions in man and animals.* New York: Wiley, 1943; 2nd rev. ed., 1973.

Young-Browne, G., Rosenfeld, H. M., & Horowitz, F. Infant discrimination of facial expressions. *Child Development,* 1977, *48,* 555–562.

Zahn-Waxler, C., Radke-Yarrow, M., & King, R. Child rearing and children's prosocial initiations towards victims of distress. *Child Development,* 1979, *50,* 319–330.

Zajonc, R. B. Feeling and thinking: Preferences need no inferences. *American Psychologist,* 1980, *35,* 151–175.

Zaporozhets, A. V. The development of perception in the preschool child. In P. H. Mussen (Ed.), *European research in cognitive development. Monographs of the Society for Research in Child Development,* 1965, *30* (2, Whole No. 100).

Zelazo, P. R. Smiling and vocalizing: A cognitive emphasis. *Merrill-Palmer Quarterly,* 1972, *18,* 350–365.

Zelazo, P. R., & Komer, M. J. Infant smiling to nonsocial stimuli and the recognition hypothesis. *Child Development,* 1971, *42,* 1327–1339.

Zeskind, P. S., & Lester, B. M. Acoustic features and auditory perceptions of the cries of newborns with prenatal and perinatal complications. *Child Development,* 1978, *49,* 580–589.

Zigler, E. Project Head Start: Success or failure? In E. Zigler & J. Valentine (Eds.), *Project Head Start*. New York: Fress Press, 1979.

Zigler, E., & Child, I. L. Socialization. In G. Lindzey & E. Aronson (Eds.), *Handbook of social psychology* (Vol. 3). Reading, Mass.: Addison-Wesley, 1969.

Zigler, E., & Trickett, P. K. IQ, social competence, and evaluation of early childhood intervention programs. *American Psychologist,* 1978, *33,* 789–798.

Zigler, E., & Valentine, J. (Eds.). *Project head start.* New York: Free Press, 1979.

Zivin, G. (Ed.). *The development of self-regulation through private speech.* New York: Wiley, 1979.

Scales of Socioemotional Development

REVISED VERSION

Child's Name _____

Date _____ Observer _____

Arrival

Item 1 Parent puts down
2 Caregiver greets
3 Parent leaves
4 Another parent arrives

Free Play

5 Free play

Group

6 Group

Peer

7 Wants—peer has
8 Peer gets attention
9 Peer cries
10 Peer grabs toy
11 Peer attacks

Caregiver

Item 12 Interaction with
caregiver
13 Demonstration
14 Wants—caregiver has
15 Praise
16 Peek-a-boo
17 Caregiver teases
18 Caregiver acts silly
19 Hidden object

20 Caregiver yells
21 Caregiver scolds

22 Caregiver leaves
23 Caregiver returns
24 Caregiver puts down

Interaction with Inanimates

25 Surprise toy
26 Toy breaks
27 Wants—unreachable
28 Obstacle
29 Unfamiliar room
30 Mirror–self
31 Mirror–other
32 Music
33 Snack

Stranger

34 Stranger
35 Stranger approaches
36 Strange child

Departure

37 Parent returns

Code

M = Mother, parent, parent substitute; C = Caregiver; P = Peer, another child; S = Stranger.
Note: Responses are grouped in similar classes of behavior. Behaviors that are unlikely to occur in a particular situation are not listed in the item, but should be noted in "other" if they do occur. Refer to Dictionaries of Situations and Behaviors for definitions.

1. When the parent puts the child down, does the child

☐ look/glance at (M)
☐ look around alertly
☐ watch intently (M)

☐ eyes glow
☐ slight smile
☐ broad smile

☐ sober
☐ frown
☐ pout/pucker
☐ hold back tears

☐ vocalize
☐ chatter
☐ call to
☐ squeal
☐ call attention to self

☐ whimper
☐ fret/cry
☐ yell/scream

☐ relax
☐ bounce
☐ skip/strut
☐ flail
☐ clap hands

☐ lean toward (M)
☐ touch (M)
☐ raise arms (M)
☐ grasp/cling (M)
☐ follow (M)
☐ show toy (M)

☐ mouth objects
☐ join group
☐ reach for toys
☐ manipulate/examine
☐ initiate activity
☐ create activity
☐ play actively

☐ suck thumb
☐ tense
☐ tremble

☐ Other _____
☐ No response

2. When the caregiver greets the child, does the child

☐ look/glance at (C)
☐ watch intently (C)

☐ slight smile (C)
☐ broad smile (C)

☐ vocalize to (C)
☐ chatter
☐ laugh/giggle

☐ lean toward (C)
☐ move toward (C)
☐ reach toward (C)
☐ touch (C)
☐ raise arms (C)
☐ hug/kiss (C)
☐ show/share toy (C)

☐ Other _____
☐ No response

3. When the parent leaves, does the child

☐ look/glance at (M)   ☐ lean toward (M)
☐ watch intently   ☐ move toward (M)
                                        ☐ reach toward (M)
☐ sober   ☐ touch (M)
☐ frown   ☐ raise arms (M)
☐ pout/pucker   ☐ grasp/cling (M)
☐ hold back tears   ☐ follow (M)
                                        ☐ search for (M)
☐ call to (M)

☐ whimper   ☐ suck thumb
☐ fret/cry   ☐ tense
☐ yell/scream   ☐ tremble

☐ Other _____
☐ No response
☐ Child didn't notice

4. When *another* parent and child (peer) arrive at the day-care
    center, does the child

☐ look/glance at (other M/P)   ☐ whimper
☐ watch intently (other M/P)   ☐ fret/cry
☐ search for own mother   ☐ yell/scream

☐ slight smile   ☐ lean toward (other M/P)
☐ broad smile   ☐ move toward (other M/P)
                                        ☐ reach toward (other M/P)
☐ sober   ☐ touch (other M/P)
☐ frown   ☐ raise arms (other M/P)
☐ pout/pucker   ☐ hug/kiss (other M/P)
☐ hold back tears   ☐ follow (other M/P)
                                        ☐ show/share toy (other M/P)
☐ vocalize to (other M/P)
☐ chatter   ☐ suck thumb
☐ call to (other M/P)   ☐ tense
☐ call for own parent   ☐ tremble

☐ Other _____
☐ No response
☐ Child didn't notice

5. During free play, does the child

□ look/glance
□ look around alertly
□ watch intently

□ eyes glow
□ slight smile
□ broad smile

□ vocalize
□ chatter
□ squeal
□ call attention to self

□ relax
□ bounce
□ flail
□ skip/strut
□ clap hands

□ mouth objects
□ reach for toys
□ manipulate/examine
□ play actively
□ join group
□ show/share toys
□ imitate
□ rehearse activities
□ initiate activities
□ create activities

□ Other _____
□ No response

6. When the child sees a group of children and caregivers playing together, does the child

□ look/glance at (C/P)
□ watch intently

□ eyes glow
□ slight smile at (C/P)
□ broad smile at (C/P)

□ vocalize to (C/P)
□ chatter
□ call to (C/P)
□ call attention to self
□ laugh/giggle
□ squeal

□ bounce
□ flail
□ clap hands

□ lean toward (C/P)
□ move toward (C/P)
□ reach toward (C/P)
□ touch (C/P)
□ raise arms (C)
□ hug/kiss (C/P)

□ join group
□ show/share toy
□ play actively
□ imitate
□ initiate own activity
□ create activity

□ Other _____
□ No response
□ Child didn't notice

7. When the child wants something another child (peer) has, does
    the child

☐ look hard at (P)   ☐ lean toward (P)

☐ look away   ☐ move toward (P)
☐ shut eyes   ☐ reach toward
                                      ☐ refuse to be distracted
☐ sober   ☐ struggle, grab toy
☐ frown
☐ pout/pucker   ☐ suck thumb
☐ grimace   ☐ tense
☐ hold back tears   ☐ clench fists
                                      ☐ tremble
☐ whimper   ☐ bang/pound
☐ fret/cry   ☐ stomp
☐ yell   ☐ throw objects
☐ scream   ☐ attack

☐ Other _____   ☐ turn away
☐ No response   ☐ move away

8. When another child (peer) receives special attention from a
    caregiver, does the child

☐ look/glance at (C/P)   ☐ follow
☐ watch intently/look hard   ☐ reach toward (C/P)
   at (C/P)   ☐ lean toward (C/P)
                                      ☐ move toward (C/P)
☐ look away   ☐ touch (C/P)
☐ shut eyes tightly   ☐ raise arms (C)
                                      ☐ grasp/cling (C)
☐ sober
☐ frown   ☐ suck thumb
☐ pout/pucker   ☐ increase activity
☐ grimace   ☐ tense
☐ hold back tears   ☐ tremble

☐ call to   ☐ flail
☐ whimper   ☐ clench fists
☐ fret/cry   ☐ struggle
☐ yell   ☐ bang/pound
☐ scream   ☐ stomp
                                      ☐ throw objects
                                      ☐ attack
☐ Other _____
☐ No response   ☐ turn away
☐ Child didn't notice   ☐ move away

9. When another child (peer) cries, does the child

☐ stare at (P)

☐ look and avoid

☐ sober
☐ tongue
☐ pucker
☐ frown

☐ whimper
☐ fret/cry
☐ scream

☐ suck thumb
☐ decrease activity
☐ hesitate
☐ tense
☐ tremble
☐ freeze

☐ refuse to look/not look
☐ turn away
☐ move away
☐ grasp/cling

☐ Other _____
☐ No response
☐ Child didn't notice

10. When another child (peer) grabs the child's toy, does the child

☐ look hard at (P)

☐ look away
☐ shut eyes tightly

☐ sober
☐ frown
☐ pout/pucker
☐ grimace
☐ hold back tears

☐ whimper
☐ fret/cry
☐ yell
☐ scream

☐ reach toward
☐ move toward

☐ suck thumb
☐ increase activity
☐ tense
☐ tremble

☐ clench fists
☐ flail
☐ struggle
☐ bang/pound
☐ stomp
☐ throw objects
☐ attack

☐ turn away
☐ move away

☐ Other _____
☐ No response

11. When another child (peer) attacks the child, does the child

☐ look hard at/stare (P)   ☐ suck thumb
                                   ☐ decrease activity
☐ look away   ☐ hesitate
☐ refuse to look/not look   ☐ increase activity
☐ shut eyes tightly   ☐ tense

☐ sober   ☐ tremble
☐ tongue   ☐ freeze
☐ grimace   ☐ grasp/cling (P)
☐ pout/pucker
☐ frown   ☐ flail
☐ hold back tears   ☐ clench fists
                                   ☐ struggle
☐ whimper   ☐ bang/pound
☐ fret/cry   ☐ stomp
☐ yell   ☐ throw objects
☐ scream   ☐ attack

☐ reach toward (P)   ☐ lean away
☐ move toward (P)   ☐ turn away
                                   ☐ move away
☐ Other _____
☐ No response

12. When the caregiver gives special attention to (interacts with) the child, does the child

☐ eyes glow   ☐ relax
☐ slight smile   ☐ clap hands
☐ broad smile   ☐ bounce
                                   ☐ flail
☐ vocalize   ☐ act silly
☐ chatter   ☐ play actively
☐ laugh/giggle
☐ squeal

☐ Other _____
☐ No response

13. When the caregiver shows the child (demonstrates) how to do something, does the child

☐ look/glance at
☐ watch intently

☐ eyes glow
☐ slight smile
☐ broad smile

☐ vocalize
☐ chatter
☐ squeal
☐ call attention to self

☐ bounce
☐ flail
☐ clap hands

☐ mouth object
☐ reach for
☐ manipulate/examine
☐ play actively
☐ persist
☐ show/share toy
☐ seek help
☐ refuse help
☐ imitate
☐ rehearse activity
☐ select alternate activity

☐ Other _____
☐ No response

14. When the child wants something a caregiver has, does the child

☐ look/glance at (C)
☐ watch intently

☐ slight smile (C)
☐ broad smile (C)

☐ vocalize to (C)
☐ chatter
☐ call attention to self
☐ squeal

☐ bounce
☐ flail

☐ imitate
☐ reach for (toy)
☐ initiate own activity
☐ create activity
☐ persist
☐ show/share toy
☐ select alternate activity

☐ Other _____
☐ No response

15. When the caregiver praises the child, does the child

☐ eyes glow
☐ slight smile
☐ broad smile

☐ vocalize
☐ chatter
☐ laugh/giggle
☐ squeal

☐ relax
☐ bounce
☐ flail
☐ clap hands
☐ act silly

☐ play actively

☐ Other _____
☐ No response

16. When the caregiver plays peek-a-boo or hide-and-seek, does the child

☐ eyes glow
☐ slight smile
☐ broad smile

☐ vocalize
☐ chatter
☐ laugh/giggle
☐ squeal

☐ relax
☐ bounce
☐ flail
☐ clap hands
☐ act silly

☐ play actively

☐ Other _____
☐ No response

17. When the caregiver teases the child, does the child

☐ look hard at (C)

☐ eyes glow
☐ slight smile
☐ broad smile

☐ look away
☐ shut eyes tightly

☐ sober
☐ frown
☐ pout/pucker
☐ grimace
☐ hold back tears

☐ vocalize
☐ chatter
☐ laugh/giggle
☐ squeal

☐ whimper
☐ fret/cry
☐ yell
☐ scream

☐ Other _____
☐ No response

☐ relax
☐ bounce
☐ clap hands
☐ increase activity
☐ flail

☐ reach toward
☐ move toward
☐ play actively
☐ act silly

☐ suck thumb
☐ tense
☐ tremble
☐ clench fists
☐ struggle
☐ bang/pound
☐ stomp
☐ throw objects
☐ attack

☐ turn away
☐ move away

18.   When the caregiver acts silly, does the child

☐ eyes glow   ☐ relax
☐ slight smile   ☐ bounce
☐ broad smile   ☐ skip/strut
                          ☐ flail
☐ vocalize   ☐ clap hands
☐ chatter   ☐ act silly
☐ laugh/giggle
☐ squeal   ☐ play actively

☐ Other _____
☐ No response
☐ Child didn't notice

19.   While the child watches, the caregiver hides a toy; does the child

☐ look hard at   ☐ increase activity
                          ☐ flail
☐ look away
☐ shut eyes tightly   ☐ suck thumb
                          ☐ tense
☐ sober   ☐ tremble
☐ frown   ☐ clench fists
☐ pout/pucker   ☐ refuse to (participate)
☐ grimace   ☐ bang/pound
☐ hold back tears   ☐ struggle
                          ☐ throw object
☐ whimper   ☐ attack
☐ fret/cry
☐ yell   ☐ turn away
☐ scream   ☐ move away

☐ Other _____
☐ No response

20. When the caregiver yells, does the child

☐ stare   ☐ suck thumb
                           ☐ decrease activity
☐ look and avoid   ☐ hesitate
☐ refuse to look/not look ☐ tense
☐ sober   ☐ tremble
☐ tongue   ☐ freeze
☐ pucker   ☐ grasp/cling
☐ frown
                           ☐ lean away
☐ whimper   ☐ turn away
☐ fret/cry   ☐ move away
☐ scream

☐ Other _____
☐ No response
☐ Child didn't notice

21. When the caregiver scolds the child, does the child

☐ look hard at (C)   ☐ suck thumb
                           ☐ tense
☐ look away   ☐ tremble
☐ shut eyes tightly
                           ☐ clench fists
☐ sober   ☐ refuse to obey
☐ frown   ☐ flail
☐ pout/pucker   ☐ bang/pound
☐ grimace   ☐ stomp
☐ hold back tears   ☐ throw objects
                           ☐ attack
☐ whimper
☐ fret/cry   ☐ reach toward
☐ yell   ☐ move toward
☐ scream
                           ☐ turn away (from C)
                           ☐ move away (from C)

☐ Other _____
☐ No response

22. When the caregiver leaves, does the child

- ☐ look/glance at (C)
- ☐ watch intently
- ☐ sober
- ☐ frown
- ☐ pout/pucker
- ☐ hold back tears
- ☐ call to (C)
- ☐ whimper
- ☐ fret/cry
- ☐ yell/scream
- ☐ lean toward (C)
- ☐ move toward (C)
- ☐ reach toward (C)
- ☐ touch (C)
- ☐ raise arms (C)
- ☐ grasp/cling (C)
- ☐ follow (C)
- ☐ search for (C)
- ☐ suck thumb
- ☐ tense
- ☐ tremble
- ☐ Other _____
- ☐ No response
- ☐ Child didn't notice

23. When the caregiver returns, does the child

- ☐ look/glance at (C)
- ☐ watch intently
- ☐ slight smile at (C)
- ☐ broad smile at (C)
- ☐ vocalize to
- ☐ chatter
- ☐ call to (C)
- ☐ laugh/giggle
- ☐ lean toward (C)
- ☐ move toward (C)
- ☐ reach toward (C)
- ☐ touch (C)
- ☐ raise arms (C)
- ☐ hug/kiss (C)
- ☐ show/share toy
- ☐ follow (C)
- ☐ Other _____
- ☐ No response
- ☐ Child didn't notice

24. When the caregiver puts the child down, does the child

- ☐ look/glance at (C)
- ☐ watch intently (C)

- ☐ sober
- ☐ frown
- ☐ pout/pucker
- ☐ hold back tears

- ☐ call to
- ☐ whimper
- ☐ fret/cry
- ☐ yell/scream

- ☐ Other _____
- ☐ No response

- ☐ lean toward (C)
- ☐ touch (C)
- ☐ raise arms (C)
- ☐ grasp/cling (C)
- ☐ follow (C)

- ☐ suck thumb
- ☐ tense
- ☐ tremble

25. When the child is given or shown a surprise toy, does the child

- ☐ eyes glow
- ☐ slight smile
- ☐ broad smile

- ☐ vocalize
- ☐ chatter
- ☐ laugh/giggle
- ☐ squeal

- ☐ Other _____
- ☐ No response

- ☐ clap hands
- ☐ flail
- ☐ bounce

- ☐ play actively
- ☐ act silly

26. When the child breaks a toy, does the child

☐ look/glance
☐ watch intently/stare/look hard at

☐ eyes glow
☐ slight smile
☐ broad smile

☐ look and avoid
☐ look away
☐ refuse to look/not look
☐ shut eyes tightly

☐ sober
☐ tongue
☐ frown
☐ pout/pucker
☐ grimace
☐ hold back tears

☐ vocalize
☐ chatter
☐ call attention to self
☐ squeal

☐ whimper
☐ fret/cry
☐ yell
☐ scream

☐ Other _____
☐ No response
☐ Child didn't notice

☐ flail
☐ bounce
☐ clap hands

☐ mouth object
☐ manipulate/examine
☐ seek help
☐ refuse help
☐ show/share toy
☐ try to fix
☐ select alternate activity
☐ initiate activity
☐ create activity

☐ suck thumb
☐ decrease activity
☐ hesitate
☐ increase activity
☐ tense
☐ tremble
☐ clench fists
☐ freeze
☐ grasp/cling
☐ bang/pound
☐ stomp
☐ throw object

☐ lean away
☐ turn away
☐ move away

27. When the child wants something that is out of easy reach
    (unreachable), does the child

☐ look/glance at (object)   ☐ bounce
☐ watch intently   ☐ flail
                               ☐ reach for (object)
☐ vocalize   ☐ initiate own activity
☐ chatter   ☐ create activity
☐ squeal   ☐ persist
☐ call attention to self
                               ☐ seek help
☐ Other _____   ☐ select alternate activity
☐ No response   ☐ refuse help
                               ☐ test alternatives

28. When there is an obstacle between the child and her or his goal,
    does the child

☐ look/glance at (C)   ☐ bounce
☐ watch intently   ☐ flail
☐ look around alertly   ☐ reach toward
                               ☐ manipulate/examine
☐ vocalize   ☐ persist/struggle
☐ chatter   ☐ seek help
☐ call attention to self   ☐ refuse help
☐ squeal   ☐ select alternate activity
                               ☐ initiate activity
                               ☐ create activity
                               ☐ test alternatives

☐ Other _____
☐ No response

29. When the child is taken to an unfamiliar place, does the child

- ☐ look/glance at
- ☐ look around alertly
- ☐ watch intently/stare

- ☐ eyes glow
- ☐ slight smile
- ☐ broad smile

- ☐ look and avoid
- ☐ refuse to look/not look

- ☐ sober
- ☐ pucker
- ☐ frown

- ☐ vocalize
- ☐ chatter
- ☐ laugh/giggle
- ☐ squeal

- ☐ whimper
- ☐ fret/cry
- ☐ scream

- ☐ relax
- ☐ bounce
- ☐ skip/strut
- ☐ flail

- ☐ mouth object
- ☐ reach for toys
- ☐ manipulate/examine (explore)
- ☐ play actively
- ☐ show/share toy
- ☐ join group
- ☐ initiate activity
- ☐ create activity

- ☐ tongue
- ☐ suck thumb
- ☐ decrease activity
- ☐ hesitate
- ☐ tense
- ☐ tremble
- ☐ freeze
- ☐ grasp/cling

- ☐ turn away
- ☐ move away (to exit)

- ☐ Other _____
- ☐ No response

30. When the child sees himself or herself in a mirror, does the child

- ☐ eyes glow
- ☐ slight smile
- ☐ broad smile

- ☐ vocalize
- ☐ chatter
- ☐ laugh/giggle
- ☐ squeal

- ☐ Other _____
- ☐ No response

- ☐ relax
- ☐ bounce
- ☐ flail
- ☐ clap hands
- ☐ skip/strut
- ☐ act silly

31. When the child sees the reflection of another person in a mirror, does the child

☐ eyes glow   ☐ relax
☐ slight smile   ☐ bounce
☐ broad smile   ☐ flail
                               ☐ clap hands
☐ vocalize
☐ chatter   ☐ act silly
☐ laugh/giggle
☐ squeal

☐ Other _____
☐ No response

32. When music is played or the caregiver sings, does the child

☐ eyes glow   ☐ relax
☐ slight smile   ☐ bounce (dance)
☐ broad smile   ☐ flail
                               ☐ clap hands
☐ vocalize   ☐ skip/strut
☐ chatter (sing)   ☐ play actively
☐ laugh/giggle   ☐ act silly
☐ squeal

☐ Other _____
☐ No response

33. When the caregiver offers a snack to the child, does the child

☐ eyes glow   ☐ relax
☐ slight smile   ☐ bounce
☐ broad smile   ☐ flail
                               ☐ clap hands
☐ vocalize   ☐ skip/strut
☐ chatter   ☐ act silly
☐ laugh/giggle
☐ squeal

☐ Other _____
☐ No response

34. When the child notices a stranger in the room, does the child

☐ look/glance at (S)
☐ stare/watch intently (S)

☐ slight smile (S)
☐ broad smile (S)

☐ look and avoid
☐ refuse to look/not look

☐ sober
☐ tongue
☐ pucker
☐ frown

☐ vocalize to
☐ chatter
☐ call to (S)

☐ whimper
☐ fret/cry
☐ scream

☐ Other _____
☐ No response

☐ lean toward (S)
☐ move toward (S)
☐ reach toward (S)
☐ touch (S)
☐ raise arms (S)
☐ hug/kiss (S)
☐ show/share toy (S)
☐ follow (S)

☐ suck thumb
☐ decrease activity
☐ hesitate
☐ tense
☐ tremble
☐ freeze
☐ grasp/cling (C)

☐ lean away
☐ turn away
☐ move away

35. When the stranger approaches (smiles at, talks to, moves toward) the child, does the child

☐ stare/watch intently (S)

☐ look and avoid
☐ refuse to look/not look

☐ sober
☐ tongue
☐ pucker
☐ frown

☐ whimper
☐ fret/cry
☐ scream

☐ Other _____
☐ No response
☐ Child didn't notice

☐ suck thumb
☐ decrease activity
☐ hesitate
☐ tense
☐ tremble
☐ freeze
☐ grasp/cling (C)

☐ lean away
☐ turn away
☐ move away

36. When the child notices an unfamiliar child (peer) in the room, does the child

☐ stare (P)

☐ look and avoid
☐ refuse to look/not look

☐ sober
☐ tongue
☐ pucker
☐ frown

☐ whimper
☐ fret/cry
☐ scream

☐ suck thumb
☐ decrease activity
☐ hesitate
☐ tense
☐ tremble
☐ freeze
☐ grasp/cling (C)

☐ lean away
☐ turn away
☐ move away

☐ Other _____
☐ No response

37. When the parent returns, does the child

☐ look/glance at (M)
☐ watch intently (M)

☐ slight smile (M)
☐ broad smile (M)

☐ vocalize to (M)
☐ chatter (M)
☐ call to (M)
☐ laugh/giggle

☐ Other _____
☐ No response

☐ lean toward (M)
☐ move toward (M)
☐ reach toward (M)
☐ touch (M)
☐ raise arms (M)
☐ hug/kiss (M)
☐ show/share toy (M)
☐ follow (M)

Comments:

Coding Forms for the Scales of Socioemotional Development

Fear

	Sober	Decrease activity	Tongue	Hesitate	Stare	Look and avoid	Lean away	Suck thumb	Pucker	Frown	Turn away	Tense	Not look	Move away	Whimper	Tremble	Grasp/cling	Freeze	Fret/cry	Scream	Observer Comments
P cries (9)																					
P attacks (11)																					
C yells (20)																					
Toy breaks (26)																					
Unfamiliar room (29)																					
Stranger (34)																					
S approach (35)																					
Strange child (36)																					
Behavior rank	1				2				3				4				5				

Anger

	Sober	Look away	Suck thumb	Frown	Look hard at	Pout/pucker	Increase activity	Grimace	Tense	Hold back tears	Turn away	Move away	Whimper	Reach toward	Shut eyes	Flail	Clench fists	Refuse to	Fret/cry	Tremble	Move toward	Struggle	Bang/pound	Stomp	Yell	Throw object	Scream	Attack	Observer Comments
Wants from P (7)																													
P gets attention (8)																													
P grabs toy (10)																													
P attacks (11)																													
C teases (17)																													
Hidden object (19)																													
C scolds (21)																													
Toy breaks (26)																													
Behavior rank	1					2						3						4						5					

455

Happiness

	Relax	Slight smile	Vocalize	Eyes glow	Chatter	Clap hands	Play actively	Broad smile	Flail	Skip/strut	Bounce	Laugh/giggle	Act silly	Squeal	Observer Comments
C interaction (12)															
C praises (15)															
C peek-a-boo (16)															
C teases (17)															
C acts silly (18)															
Surprise toy (25)															
Mirror—self (30)															
Mirror—other (31)															
Music (32)															
Snack (33)															
Behavior rank	1		2			3			4			5			

Affiliation (Low-Stress)

	Look/glance at	Lean toward	Slight smile at	Vocalize to	Watch	Chatter	Move toward	Reach toward	Touch	Broad smile at	Imitate	Show/share toy	Laugh/giggle	Raise arms	Call to	Follow	Search for	Hug/kiss	Observer Comments
C greets (2)																			
Another M arrives (4)																			
Group (6)																			
C returns (23)																			
Stranger (34)																			
M returns (37)																			
Behavior rank	1			2			3					4				5			

457

Affiliation (High-Stress)

	Sober	Look/glance at	Suck thumb	Lean toward	Frown	Pout/pucker	Tense	Hold back tears	Watch	Touch	Move toward	Reach toward	Whimper	Tremble	Raise arms	Follow	Call to/for	Fret/cry	Search for	Grasp/cling	Yell/scream	Observer Comments
M puts down (1)																						
M leaves (3)																						
Another M arrives (4)																						
P gets attention (8)																						
C leaves (22)																						
C puts down (24)																						
Behavior rank	1				2				3					4				5				

Competence

Situation	Look/glance	Look around alertly	Vocalize	Relax	Mouth object	Slight smile	Chatter	Eyes glow	Reach for	Watch intently	Broad smile	Imitate	Bounce	Flail	Skip/strut	Manipulate/examine	Clap hands	Play actively	Persist	Squeal	Call attention to self	Join group	Show/share toy	Select alternate activity	Refuse help	Rehearse/repeat act	Initiate activity	Create activity	Test alternatives	Observer Comments
M puts down (1)																														
Free play (5)																														
Group (6)																														
Demonstration (13)																														(3) seek help__ [a]
Wants—C has (14)																														
Toy breaks (26)																														(3) seek help__ [a] (5) try to fix__ [a]
Wants—unreachable (27)																														(3) seek help__ [a]
Obstacle (28)																														(3) seek help__ [a]
Unfamiliar room (29)																														
Behavior rank	1							2						3						4					5					

[a] Special behavior likely to occur in a restricted situation. (Number indicates behavior's rank).

Author Index

Italic numbers indicate pages where complete reference citations are given.

Subject Index

Affect, 31–32
Affiliation, See Social affiliation
Anger
  coding form, 455
  definition of, 269
  development of, 334–336
  individual differences in, 336–337
  response measures, 270–272
  situations, 270
Appraisal theories, 67–69, 83
Arousal, 60–64, 76–77, 315–324
Attachment, 15–16. See also Social
      affiliation
Attribution, 235–236

Behavior, Emotional
  components of, 241–247, 249–250
  individual differences, 238–239
  meaning of, 236–255
  measurement methods, 247–251
  response intensity, 239–241
Behaviors
  definitions of, 294–297
Biological model
  in emotional development, 134–137
  in psychopathology, 224–225
  in the socialization of emotion, 158

Central theories, 55–59
Cluster analysis, 363–369
Cognition
  versus emotion, 7–18
Cognitive-emotional fugue, 87–93
Cognitive theories, 65–78

Competence
  coding form, 459
  definition of, 264, 281–282
  development of, 344–346
  individual differences in, 346
  as predictor of success, 16
  response measures, 283–284
  situations, 282–283
  See also Social competence
Context
  meaning of, 255–261

Day care, 285–286
  effects on emotional expression,
      350–357, 398–399
Derived emotions, 32–35
Differentiation hypothesis, 108–109,
      139–145
Discrepancy theories, 69–72
Discrete systems theory, 109–111, 140
Display rules, 160–166

Efficacy
  feelings of. See Competence
Emotion
  biological model, 134–137, 158,
      224–225
  versus cognition, 7–18
  cognitive mechanisms, 65–78
  components of, 30–31, 95–126,
      128–139
  definition of, 21–26, 30–31, 95–126
  derived, 32–35